Artificial Intelligence in Engineering Design

VOLUME I

DESIGN REPRESENTATION AND
MODELS OF ROUTINE DESIGN

Artificial Intelligence in Engineering Design

VOLUME I

DESIGN REPRESENTATION AND
MODELS OF ROUTINE DESIGN

EDITED BY

CHRISTOPHER TONG
DEPARTMENT OF COMPUTER SCIENCE
RUTGERS UNIVERSITY
NEW BRUNSWICK, NEW JERSEY

DUVVURU SRIRAM
INTELLIGENT ENGINEERING SYSTEMS LABORATORY
MASSACHUSETTS INSTITUTE OF TECHNOLOGY
CAMBRIDGE, MASSACHUSETTS

ACADEMIC PRESS, INC.

Harcourt Brace Jovanovich, Publishers

Boston   San Diego   New York
London   Sydney   Tokyo   Toronto

ACADEMIC PRESS, INC.
1250 Sixth Avenue
San Diego, CA 92101-4311

United Kingdom Edition published by
ACADEMIC PRESS LIMITED
24–28 Oval Road, London NW1 7DX

ISBN 0-12-660561-0

Printed in the United States of America

92 93 94 95 BB 9 8 7 6 5 4 3 2 1

C. TONG DEDICATES THIS EDITORIAL WORK TO
HEART-MASTER SRI DA AVABHASA,
WITH LOVE AND GRATITUDE

D. SRIRAM DEDICATES THIS EDITORIAL WORK TO
SUCHI, NAGI, AND RAVI,
WITH FOND MEMORIES OF CHILDHOOD

Contents

Contents of Volume II

Contents of Volume III

Contributors

Numbers in parentheses refer to the pages on which the authors' contributions begin.

ARAYA, AGUSTIN (273), Expert Systems Group Metaphor Computer Systems, 1965 Charleston Road, Mountain View, California 94043.

BAYKAN, CAN A. (395), Robotics Institute, Carnegie Mellon University, 5000 Forbes Avenue, Pittsburgh, Pennsylvania 15213.

BOETTNER, DAISIE (135), 21 Willis Avenue, Cornwall-on-Hudson, New York 15250.

BREWER, FORREST D. (357), Department of Electrical and Computer Engineering, University of California at Santa Barbara, Santa Barbara, California 93106.

BROWN, DAVID C. (221), Department of Computer Science, Worcester Polytechnic Institute, 100 Institute Road, Worcester, Massachusetts 01609.

CHANDRASEKARAN, B. (221), Laboratory for Artificial Intelligence Research, Department of Computer and Information Sciences, Ohio State University, 2036 Neil Avenue, Columbus, Ohio 43210-1277.

DYER, MICHAEL (193), Artificial Intelligence Laboratory, 3531 Boelter Hall, University of California at Los Angeles, Los Angeles, California 90024.

FLOWERS, MARGOT (193), Artificial Intelligence Laboratory, 3531 Boelter Hall, University of California at Los Angeles, Los Angeles, California 90024.

FOX, MARK S. (395), Robotics Institute, Carnegie Mellon University, 5000 Forbes Avenue, Pittsburgh, Pennsylvania 15213.

GAJSKI, DANIEL D. (357), Department of Computer Science, University of California at Irvine, Irvine, California 92717.

GOSSARD, DAVID (71), Computer Aided Design Laboratory, Department of Mechanical Engineering, Massachusetts Institute of Technology, Cambridge, Massachusetts 02139.

HODGES, JACK (193), Department of Computer Science, San Francisco State University, 1600 Holloway Street, San Francisco, California 94312.

LIN, JIANG (117), Department of Computer Science, Wayne State University, Detroit, Michigan 48202.

MARCUS, SANDRA (317), Computing Management Organization, Boeing Commercial Airplanes, P.O. Box 3707, Seattle, Washington 98124.

MCDERMOTT, JOHN (317), Artificial Intelligence Research Center, Digital Equipment Corporation, 290 Donald Lynch Boulevard, Marlborough, Massachusetts 01752.

MITTAL, SANJAY (273), Expert Systems Group Metaphor Computer Systems, 1965 Charleston Road, Mountain View, California 94043.

NADEL, BERNARD A. (117), Department of Computer Science, Wayne State University, Detroit, Michigan 48202.

SERRANO, DAVID (71), Department of Mechanical Engineering, University of Puerto Rico at Mayaguez, Mayaguez, Puerto Rico 00708.

SILETTI, CHARLES A. (295), Mobil Research and Development Corporation, Engineering Department, P.O. Box 1026, Princeton, New Jersey 08540.

SRIRAM, DUVVURU (1), Intelligent Engineering Systems Laboratory, Department of Civil Engineering, Massachusetts Institute of Technology, Cambridge, Massachusetts 02139.

STEINBERG, LOUIS I. (251), Department of Computer Science, Rutgers University, New Brunswick, New Jersey 08903.

STEPHANOPOULOS, GEORGE (295), Department of Chemical Engineering, Massachusetts Institute of Technology, Cambridge, Massachusetts 02139.

STOUT, JEFFREY (317), Advanced Technology Center, Boeing Computer Services, P.O. Box 24346, Seattle, Washington 98124.

SUBRAHMANYAM, P.A. (57), AT&T/Bell Laboratories, 101 Crawfords Corner Road, Holmdel, New Jersey 07733.

TONG, CHRISTOPHER (1), Department of Computer Science, Rutgers University, New Brunswick, New Jersey 08903.

WARD, AL (135), Department of Mechanical Engineering, University of Michigan, Ann Arbor, Michigan 48109.

WEITZMAN, LOUIS (433), Media Laboratory, Massachusetts Institute of Technology, 20 Ames Street, Cambridge, Massachusetts 02139.

Preface

The three-volume collection, "Artificial Intelligence in Engineering Design", has been put together incrementally over the course of the last six years. Most of the research efforts described herein are ongoing and thus chapters originally written early on in the enterprise are still representative of the state of the field. Some of these chapters additionally include updates that indicate the current status of the work.

For a variety of reasons, the order of the editors' names was chosen at random and fixed to be the same for each of the three volumes. However, both editors contributed equally to the making of all three volumes.

The editors would like to gratefully acknowledge the support and computational resources provided by the Computer Science Department of Rutgers University and the Intelligent Engineering Systems Laboratory at MIT, during the making of this collection.

Chapter 1
INTRODUCTION

Chris Tong and Duvvuru Sriram

1.1. WHAT THIS BOOK IS ABOUT

What is *design*? Design is the process of constructing a description of an artifact that satisfies a (possibly informal) functional specification, meets certain performance criteria and resource limitations, is realizable in a given target technology, and satisfies criteria such as simplicity, testability, manufacturability, reusability, etc.; the design process itself may also be subject to certain restrictions such as time, human power, cost, etc.

Design problems arise everywhere, and come in many varieties. Some are born spontaneously amidst the circumstances of ordinary human lives: design a dish for dinner that uses last night's leftovers; design some kind of hook-like artifact that will enable me to retrieve a small object that fell down a crack; design a "nice-looking" arrangement of the flowers in a vase. Other design problems are small but commercial in nature: design a paper clip-like device that doesn't leave a mark on the paper; design a lamp whose light can be turned to aim in any particular direction; design an artifact for storing up to twenty pens and pencils, in an easily accessible fashion. Still other design problems are formidable, and their solutions can require the efforts and coordination of hundreds of people: design a space shuttle; design a marketable electric car; design an international trade agreement; etc.

Because design is so ubiquitous, anything generic we can say about the *design process* -- the activities involved in actually solving a design problem -- can have great impact. Even better would be to provide active help to designers.

This book is all about how ideas and methods from Artificial Intelligence can help engineering designers. By "engineering design", we primarily mean the design of *physical artifacts* or *physical processes* of various kinds. In this book, we will see the design of a wide variety of artifacts exemplified, including: circuits and chips (Volume I, Chapters 2, 8, 12 and Volume II, 2, 8, 9, 10), swinging doors (Volume I, Chapter 6), copying machines (Volume I, Chapter 9 and Volume III, Chapter 6), cantilever beams (Volume I, Chapter 3), space telescopes (Volume II, Chapter 5), air cylinders (Volume I, Chapter 7), protein purifaction processes (Volume I, Chapter 10), fluid-mechanical devices (Volume II, Chapters 4 and 6), new alloys (Volume II, Chapter 7), graphics interfaces (Volume I, Chapter 14), automobile transmissions (Volume I, Chapter 4), spatial layouts (Volume I, Chapter 13), elevators (Volume I, Chapter 11), light-weight load-bearing structures (Volume II, Chapter 11), mechanical linkages (Volume II, Chapter 12), buildings (Volume III, Chapter 12), etc.

What you will not find in this book is anything on AI-assisted software design. On this point, our motivation is twofold: no book can (or should try to) cover everything; and AI and software engineering has already been treated in a number of edited collections (including [15, 30]).

This book is an edited collection of key papers from the field of AI and design. We have aimed at providing a state of the art description of the field that has coverage and depth. Thus, this book should be of use to engineering designers, design tool builders and marketeers, and researchers in AI and design. While a small number of other books have surveyed research on AI and design at a particular institution (e.g., [12, 31]), this book fills a hole in the existing literature because of its breadth.

The book is divided into three volumes, and a number of parts. This first chapter provides a conceptual framework that integrates a number of themes that run through all of the papers. It appears at the beginning of each of the three volumes. Volume I contains Parts I and II, Volume II contains Parts III, IV, and V, and Volume III contains Parts VI through IX.

Part I discusses issues arising in *representing* designs and design information. Parts II and III discuss a variety of models of the design process; Part II discusses models of routine design, while Part III discusses innovative design models. We felt that creative design models, such as they are in 1991, are still at too preliminary a stage to be included here. However, [11] contains an interesting collection of workshop papers on this subject. Parts IV and V talk about the formalization of common sense knowledge (in engineering) that is useful in many design tasks, and the reasoning techniques that accompany this knowledge; Part IV discusses knowledge about physical systems, while Part V gives several examples of formalized geometry knowledge. Part VI discusses techniques for acquiring knowledge to extend or improve a knowledge-based system. Part VII touches on the issue of building a knowledge-based design system; in particular, it presents a number of commercially available tools that may serve as modules within a larger knowledge-based system. Part VIII contains several articles on integrating design with the larger engineering process of which it is a part; in particular, some articles focus on designing for manufacturability. Finally, Part IX contains a report on a workshop in which leaders of the field discussed the state of the art in AI and Design.

1.2. WHAT DOES AI HAVE TO OFFER TO ENGINEERING DESIGN?

In order to answer this question, we will first examine the nature of engineering design a little more formally. Then we will briefly summarize some of the major results in AI by viewing AI as a software engineering methodology. Next we will look at what non-AI computer assistance is currently available, and thus what gaps are left that represent opportunities for AI technology. Finally, we outline how the AI software engineering methodology can be applied to the construction of knowledge-based design tools.

1.2.1. Engineering Design: Product and Process

Engineering design involves mapping a specified *function* onto a (description of a) realizable physical *structure* -- the designed artifact. The desired function of the artifact is what it is supposed to do. The artifact's physical structure is the actual physical parts out of which it is made, and the part-whole relationships among them. In order to be realizable, the described physical structure must be capable of being assembled or fabricated. Due to restrictions on the available assembly or fabrication process, the physical structure of the artifact is often required to be expressed in some *target technology*, which delimits the kinds of parts from which it is built. A *correct design* is one whose physical structure correctly implements the specified function.

Why is design usually not a classification task [6], that is, a matter of simply looking up the right structure for a given function in (say) a parts catalog? The main reason is that the mapping between function and structure is not simple. For one thing, the connection between the function and the structure of an artifact may be an indirect one, that involves determining specified behavior (from the specified function), determining actual behavior (of the physical structure), and ensuring that these match. For another, specified functions are often very complex and must be realized using complex organizations of a large number of physical parts; these organizations often are not hierarchical, for the sake of design quality. Finally, additional non-functional constraints or criteria further complicate matters. We will now elaborate on these complications.

Some kinds of artifacts -- for example, napkin holders, coat hangers, and bookcases -- are relatively "inactive" in the sense that nothing is "moving" inside them. In contrast, the design of a *physical system* involves additionally reasoning about the artifact's *behavior*, both external and internal. The external behavior of a system is what it does from the viewpoint of an outside observer. Thus, an (analog) clock has hands that turn regularly. The internal behavior is based on observing what the *parts* of the system do. Thus, in a clock, we may see gears turning. Behavior need not be so visible: electrical flow, heat transmission, or force transfer are also forms of behavior.

In a physical system, behavior *mediates* function and structure. The *function* is achieved by the *structure behaving* in a certain way. If we just possessed the physical structure of a clock, but had no idea of how it (or its parts) behaved, we would have no way of telling that it achieves the function of telling time.

Not only in a physical system but also in *designing* a physical system, behavior tends to act as intermediary between function and structure. Associated with a specified function is a *specified behavior*; we would be able to tell time if the angle of some physical structure changed in such a way that it was a function of the time. Associated with a physical structure is its *producible behavior*; for example, a gear will *turn*, provided that some rotational force is applied to it. In rough terms then, designing a physical system involves selecting (or refining) a physical structure (or description thereof) in such a way that its producible behavior matches the specified behavior, and thus achieves the desired function. Thus, we could successfully refine the "physical structure whose angle is a function of the hour" as either the hand on an electromechanical clock, or as the shadow cast by a sundial.

Complex functions often require complex implementations. For example, a jet aircraft consists of thousands of physical parts. Parts may *interact* in various ways. Thus the problems of *designing* the parts also interact, which complicates the design process. Such interactions (among physical parts or among the problems of designing those parts) can be classified according to their strength.

For instance, many parts of the aircraft (the wings, the engine, the body, etc.) must, together, behave in such a way that the plane stays airborne; thus the subproblems of designing these parts can be said to *strongly interact* with respect to this specification of global behavior. Non-functional requirements such as global resource limitations or optimization criteria are another source of strong interactions. For example, the total cost of the airplane may have to meet some budget. Or the specification may call for the rate of fuel consumption of the plane to be "fairly low". Not all ways of implementing some function may be equally "good" with respect to some global criterion. The design process must have some means for picking the best (or at least a relatively good) implementation alternative. Good implementations often involve *structure-sharing*, i.e., the mapping of several functions onto the same structure. For example, the part of the phone which we pick up serves multiple functions: we speak to the other person through it; we hear the other person through it; and it breaks the phone connection when placed in the cradle. Important resources such as "total amount of space or area" and "total cost" tend to used more economically through such structure-sharing. On the other side of the coin, allowing structure-sharing complicates both the representation of designs and the process of design.

That neighboring parts must fit together -- both structurally and behaviorally

-- exemplifies a kind of *weak* or *local interaction*. Thus the wings of the plane must be attachable to the body; the required rate of fuel into the engine on the left wing had better match the outgoing rate of fuel from the pump; and so forth. The *design process* must be capable of ensuring that such constraints are met.

1.2.2. Artificial Intelligence as a Software Engineering Methodology

Now that we've briefly examined engineering design, we will equally briefly examine (the most relevant aspects of) Artificial Intelligence (AI).

Problem-solving as search. The late 1950s and the 1960s saw the development of the *search paradigm* within the field of Artificial Intelligence. Books such as "Computers and Thought" [10], which appeared in 1963, were full of descriptions of various weak methods whose power lay in being able to view the solving of a particular kind of problem as search of a space. In the late 1960s, the notion of heuristic search was developed, to account for the need to search large spaces effectively.

Knowledge as power. Nonetheless, most of the problems considered in those early days were what are now commonly called "toy problems". As the 1970s began, many practitioners in the field were concerned that the weak methods, though *general*, would never be *powerful* enough to solve real problems (e.g., medical diagnosis or computer configuration) effectively; the search spaces would just be too large. Their main criticisms of the earlier work were that solving the toy examples required relatively little knowledge about the domain, and that the weak methods required knowledge to be used in very restrictive and often very weak ways. (For example, in state space search, if knowledge about the domain is to be used, it must be expressed as either operators or evaluation functions, or else in the choice of the state space representation.) Solving real problems requires extensive knowledge. The "weak method" critics took an engineering approach, being primarily concerned with *acquiring* all the relevant knowledge and *engineering* it into some usable form. Less emphasis was placed on conforming the final program to fit some general problem-solving schema (e.g., heuristic search); more concern was placed on just getting a system that worked, and moreover, that would produce (measurably) "expert level" results. Thus was born the "expert systems" paradigm.

Evolution of new programming paradigms. Several list-processing languages were developed in the late 1950s and early 1960s, most notably, LISP. The simple correspondence between searching a space for an acceptable solution and picking an appropriate item in a list made the marriage of AI (as it was at that time) and list-processing languages a natural one. Various dialects of LISP evolved, and the developers of the main dialects began evolving programming environments whose features made LISP programming more user-friendly (e.g., procedural enrichments of a language that was originally purely functional; debuggers; file packages; windows, menus, and list structure editors).

At the same time as the "expert systems" paradigm was developing, a new wave of programming languages (often referred to as "AI languages") was arriving. Like the evolution of expert systems, this development phase seemed to be motivated by the need for less general (but more powerful) languages than LISP. Many of these languages were (part of) Ph.D. theses (e.g., MICROPLANNER [42, 47] and Guy Steele's constraint language [35]). Often these languages were built on top of the LISP language, a possibility greatly facilitated because of the way LISP uniformally represents both data and process as lists. Often these languages were never used in anything but the Ph.D. dissertation for which they were developed, because they were overly specialized or they were not portable.

Exploring tradeoffs in generality and power. During the 1970s, at the same time as many researchers were swinging to the "power" end of the "generality-power" tradeoff curve in their explorations, others were striking a middle ground. Some researchers, realizing the limitations of the weak methods, began enriching the set of general building blocks out of which search algorithms could be configured. New component types included: constraint reasoning subsystems, belief revision subsystems, libraries or knowledge bases of various kinds; a variety of strategies for controlling problem-solving, etc. Other programming language designers than those mentioned previously developed new, specialized (but not overly specialized), and portable programming paradigms, including logic programming languages, frame-based and object-oriented languages, and rule-based languages. Rule-based languages such as OPS5 arrived on the scene at an opportune moment. In many cases, their marriage to "expert systems" seemed to work well, because the knowledge acquired from observing the behavior of domain experts often took the simple associational (stimulus-response) form: "IF the problem is of type P, then the solution is of type S."

Synthesis, consolidation and formalization. AI researchers of the late 1950s and the 1960s posed the *thesis*, "Generality is sufficient for problem-solving." 1970s researchers criticized this thesis, claiming the resulting methods were insufficient for solving real problems, and responded with the *antithesis*, "Power is sufficient." However, that antithesis has been critiqued in turn: "Expert systems are too brittle"; "special languages only work for the application for which they were originally developed"; etc.

Since the early 1980s, AI seems to be in a period of *synthesis*. One useful tool for illustrating the kind of synthetic framework that seems to be emerging out of the last few decades of research is depicted in Figure 1-1. Rather than pitting generality against power, or the "search paradigm" against the "expert systems" or "knowledge-based paradigm", the framework unifies by providing three different levels of abstraction for viewing the same "knowledge-based system": the knowledge level; the algorithm level; and the program level.

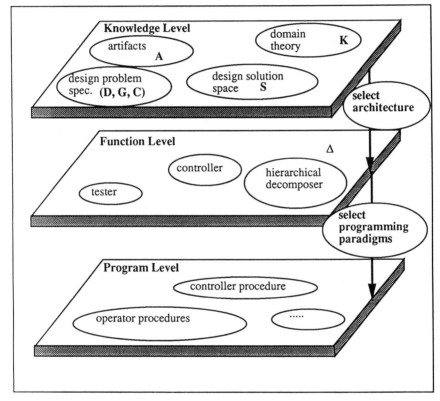

Figure 1-1: Rationally Reconstructed Knowledge-Based System Development

These three levels directly reflect the history of AI as we have just rationally reconstructed it. The "knowledge level" view of a knowledge-based system describes the knowledge that is used by and embedded in that system. The "algorithm level" view describes the system as a search algorithm, configured out of standard component types (e.g., generators, testers, patchers, constraint propagators, belief revisers, etc.). Finally the "program level" view expresses the system in terms of the elements of existing programming paradigms (rules, objects, procedures, etc.). Within the "algorithm level", a spectrum of search algorithms -- ranging from weak to strong methods -- can be created depending on the choice of component configuration, and the choice of how knowledge (at the knowledge level) is mapped into the search algorithm components. A similar set of choices exists relative to the mapping of the "algorithm level" search algorithms into "program level" knowledge-based systems.

Many of the ideas and insights of this period of synthesis can be viewed as either: stressing the importance of distinguishing these levels (e.g., [6]); introducing criteria for evaluating systems at the different levels (e.g., epistemological adequacy [17] at the knowledge level; (qualitative) heuristic adequacy [17] at the algorithm level; and (quantitative) heuristic adequacy at the program level); fleshing out the primitives at each level (e.g., ATMSs [7] or constraint propagators [36] at the algorithm level); understanding and validating established correspondences between entities at different levels (e.g., between search algorithms and list-processing languages; or expert knowledge and rule-based languages), or on discovering new correspondences.

AI as a software engineering methodology. Viewed as a software engineering methodology, AI works best for developing those knowledge-based systems whose construction is usefully aided by creating explicit knowledge level and function level abstractions. More specifically, the AI methodology works well when:

- the problems addressed by the desired knowledge-based system are ill-structured, and involve large or diverse types of knowledge (when expressed at the knowledge level);

- that knowledge can be incorporated into an *efficient* search algorithm, that can be viewed as a configuration of standard building blocks for search algorithms;

- that search algorithm, in turn, can be implemented as an *efficient* program, using currently available programming paradigms.

1.2.3. Computer-aided Design

1.2.3.1. Opportunities for AI in computer-aided design

In many design areas (e.g., VLSI design or mechanical design), progress in automating the design process passes through a sequence (or partial ordering) of somewhat predictable stages (see Table 1-1). As we see it, design tool developers proceed through the following stages: permitting design capture; automating specific expert tasks; constructing unifying representations and system architectures; modeling and automating the complete design process; automatically controlling the design process; automatically re-using design experience; automatically improving tool performance. The central intuition is that, with the passage of time, design tools play an increasingly more *active* role in the design process. Note that the sequence is not meant to imply that the user is (or should ever be) removed from the design process; instead, the user receives increasingly greater assistance (and a more cooperative and powerful design environment) with time. Table 1-2 lists some particular technological contributions that have been made to design automation by academia and by industry.

Permitting design capture. In the beginning, graphical editors are created that allow the user to enter, visualize, modify, and store new designs, as well as retrieve old designs, in a simple manner. This is such a universal starting point for design automation in any new area that "CAD/CAM" (Computer-Aided Design/Computer-Aided Manufacturing) tends to be used as a synonym for fancy graphical, object-oriented interfaces. The development of these tools is largely aided by techniques drawn from graphics and database management (including such AI-related areas as deductive or object-oriented databases).

Automating the execution of expert tasks. As time passes, tool users become less satisfied with a purely passive use of CAD. CAD tool builders identify specific *analysis* and *synthesis* tasks which have been carefully delimited so as to be automatically executable (e.g., placement, routing, simulation). AI research can make a contribution at this stage; the software engineering methodology mentioned in Section 1.2.2 can facilitate the incremental creation, testing, and development of knowledge-based systems which carry out the more ill-structured analysis and synthesis tasks. (Well-structured tasks are carried out by algorithms.)

Constructing unifying representations and system architectures. A problem of integration arises; the set of available CAD tools is growing increasingly richer, but the tools are diverse, as are the design representation languages they

Table 1-1: Stages in the Evolution of Design Automation

DESIGN AUTOMATION GOAL	PROBLEM	AI ISSUE
Permit design capture	What functions does the user interface provide?	Deductive or object-oriented databases
Build tools for specific tasks	How to automate specialized types of reasoning?	Inference; Expert systems
Integrate tools	How to communicate between tools?	Representation; Architectures
Manage versions	Which task, tool, parameters?	Search space
Model design process	Which model is right for the task?	Taxonomy of tasks and corresponding methods
Find good design fast	How to guide choices?	Control
Improve design system	Where and how to improve?	Machine learning
Reuse design knowledge	How to acquire? How to re-use?	Machine learning, Case-based reasoning

utilize. AI can enter again to contribute ideas about unifying representation languages (e.g., object-oriented languages) that enable the creation of "design toolboxes", and unifying system architectures (e.g., blackboard architectures).

Modeling the design process. Having a single unified environment is good but not sufficient. How can we guarantee that we are making the most of our available tools? AI contributes the notion of the design process as a search through a space of alternative designs; the synthesis tools are used to help generate new points in this space; the analysis tools are used to evaluate the consistency, correctness, and quality of these points; the idea of search is used to guarantee that *systematic progress* is made in the use and re-use of the tools to generate new designs or design versions.

Table 1-2: Increasingly More Sophisticated Technological Contributions
From Industry and Academia

Technology	University	Industry	Design Automation Goal
Interactive graphics	Sketchpad (MIT, 1963)	DAC-1 (GM, early 60s)	design capture
Drafting (2D)		Autocad^{TM} ADE^{TM}	design capture
Solid modelers (3D) (CSG, BREP)	BUILD (UK) PADL (Rochester) (see [29])	I-IDEAS^{TM} ACIS^{TM} MicroStation^{TM}	design capture + specific tools etc.
Solid modelers (super-quadrics, nonmanifold)	ThingWorld [28] Noodles (CMU)		design capture
Physical modelers (spatial + physics)	ThingWorld		design capture + specific tools
Parametric modelers (variational geometry + constraint management)	Work at MIT-CAD Lab PADL-2 (U. Rochester)	DesignView^{TM} (2D) ICONEX^{TM} (2D) PRO/ENGINEER^{TM} (3D) Vellum^{TM}	design capture + specific tools
Semantic modeling + geometry (mostly wire frame) + constraint management + layout		ICAD^{TM} WISDOM^{TM} DESIGN++^{TM}	design capture + specific tools
Logic synthesis (ECAD) [18, 27]		Logic Synthesizer^{TM}	design process model (algorithmic)
Concept generators (routine design)	VEXED DSPL CONGEN	PRIDE (in-house)	design process model
Concept generators (innovative design)	BOGART CADET EDISON KRITIK ALADIN DONTE etc.	ARGO (in-house)	design process model + control
Integrated frameworks (cooperative product development [33])	DICE (MIT, WVU) PACT (Stanford) IBDE (CMU)	PACT (HP, EIT, Lockheed) Falcon^{TM}	integrate tools, version management

Controlling the design process. The priced paid for search is efficiency, as the search space is generally quite large. Exhaustive search of the space is usually intractable; however, a search which focuses its attention on restricted but promising *subspaces* of the complete design space may trade away the guarantee of an optimal solution (provided by exhaustive search), in return for an exponential decrease in overall design time.

How can a knowledge-based system control its search of a large design space so that a satisfactory solution is produced in a reasonable amount of time? Good *control heuristics* help.

Control heuristics may either be domain-specific or domain-independent. "Spend much of the available design time optimizing the component that is a bottleneck with respect to the most tightly restricted resource" is an example of a domain-independent heuristic, while "Spend much of the available design time optimizing the datapath" is a domain-specific version of this heuristic that applies to certain situations in the microprocessor design domain. Control heuristics may address different control questions. Some address the question: "Which area of the design should be worked on next?" while others address the question, "What should I do there? How should I refine that area of the design?"

Automatically improving performance and automated reuse of design experience. At this stage in the evolution of design automation in a design area, most of the burden of routine design has been lifted from the end user; this has been accomplished by *reformulating* this burden as one for the knowledge engineers and system programmers. In turn, techniques from machine learning can make life easier for the system builders themselves. In particular, they can build a design tool that is *incomplete* or *inefficient*; the design tool can be augmented by machine learning and case-based reasoning techniques that can extend the knowledge in the system, or use its knowledge with ever greater efficacy.

1.2.3.2. The differing goals of CAD tool and AI researchers

A misunderstanding frequently arises between AI researchers who develop experimental Computer-aided Design (CAD) tools, and traditional CAD tool developers in a particular design area (e.g., VLSI or mechanical design) who specialize in developing new design tools that will be usable in production mode in the near-term future. The CAD tool developers accuse the AI researchers of being too general, and of creating inefficient or toy knowledge-based systems. On the other hand, the AI researchers criticize the traditional CAD tool researchers of creating overly brittle systems.

Confusion arises because these two types of researchers (each of whom is likely to be reading this book) do not share quite the same research goals, and each tends to judge the other with respect to their own community's values. Traditional CAD tool developers seek to reduce the effort in creating *new designs*. Most AI researchers aim at reducing the effort in developing *new design tools*.

Both research programs are worthy enterprises. The former goal requires the design tools to be powerful. The latter requires the methodology for constructing the tool (e.g., instantiation of a particular shell) to be general, and thus sometimes requires the design tool itself to be an instance of a general form rather than a custom-built tool. This book describes results from both enterprises.

1.2.4. A Methodology for Building a Knowledge-based Design Tool

In Section 1.2.1, we described the problem of design, and mentioned features of the problem that indicate design is generally an *ill-structured problem*. We then described AI as a three-level, software engineering methodology for developing knowledge-based systems for solving ill-structured problems. In the last section, we identified specific design automation tasks where such a methodology can be most usefully applied. We now describe what the general methodology looks like, when restricted to building knowledge-based design systems.

The steps involved in the development of AI tools for engineering design are shown in Table 1-3. The rest of this chapter will go into these steps in greater detail. We indicate which levels are involved in each step (knowledge, function, or program level), and which sections of this chapter will elaborate on that step.

The next few sections flesh out basic ideas relevant to understanding the phases of this methodology. They also relate the later chapters of this book to this methodology.

1.3. FORMALIZING THE DESIGN SPACE AND THE DESIGN KNOWLEDGE BASE

Algorithms can be decomposed into *passive* data structures and *active* access and update operations on these data structures. Similarly, models of design can be partitioned into passive components -- the design space and the knowledge base; and an active component -- the process that (efficiently) navigates through that space, guided by the knowledge in the knowledge base. This section

Table 1-3: Phases of Knowledge-based Tool Construction

PHASE	LEVEL	SECTION
Identify design task	knowledge level	1.5.1
Formalize design space	algorithm level	1.3
Formalize knowledge base	algorithm level	1.3
Configure appropriate model of design process, based on properties of design task and design space	algorithm level, knowledge level	1.4, 1.5.2
Instantiate by acquiring and operationalizing knowledge	knowledge level, algorithm level	1.5.2
Implement	algorithm level, program level	1.5.3
Test (validate and verify)	all levels	covered in individual chapters
Deploy		covered in individual chapters
Improve	all levels	covered in individual chapters

focuses on the nature and organization of design spaces and design knowledge bases, while the next section explores the spectrum of design processes that search such a space.

1.3.1. What Distinguishes a Design Search Space?

In order to characterize a (dynamically generated) search space, we must define the nature of the points in that space, the relationships that can exist between points in the space, and how to generate new points from old ones.

Points in the design space. In a *design space*, the points can be design specifications[1] or implementations. They can be at varying levels of abstraction. Some points may only correspond to parts of a design (specification or implementation). A single such point P1 might have associated with it:

- its parts: {P11,...,P1n}. In the simplest case, these parts are simple parameters; in general, they can be arbitrarily complex structures.

- constraints on it and its parts.

- information about how its parts are connected.

Chapter 3 in Volume I considers the case where a design can be represented as a *constraint graph*, whose nodes are parameters, and whose arcs represent constraint relationships. Several design operations are easy to implement (in a domain-independent manner), given such a representation: automatic generation of parameter dependencies; evaluation of a constraint network; detection of over- and under-constrained systems of constraints, and the identification and correction of redundant and conflicting constraints. A few commercial tools, such as Cognition's MCAE^{TM} and DesignView^{TM} (see Volume III, Section 4.3.1), incorporate variations of Serrano's constraint management system. Chapter 4 in Volume I goes on to discuss how such a constraint network representation can be used to design automobile transmissions. The application of interval calculus methods to constraint satisfaction problems is treated in Volume I, Chapter 5. These interval methods are used in a mechanical design compiler, which accepts generic schematics and specifications for a wide variety of designs, and returns catalog numbers for optimal implementations of the schematics.

The design space as a whole. Some of the most basic relationships that can exist between points in the design space include:

- P2 is a part of P1.

- P2 is a refinement of P1 (where P1 and P2 are both specifications). P2 consequently may be at a lower level of abstraction than P1.

- P2 is an implementation of P1 (where P1 is a specification for and P2 is a description of an artifact in the target technology).

---

[1]We use the word *specification* to denote a *function* or a *goal* that needs to be realized or satisficed in the final design, e.g., "Design a land vehicle capable of going at least 100 mph over sand."

- P2 is an optimization of P1 (i.e., P2 is better than P1 with respect to some evaluatable criterion).

- P2 is a patch of P1 (i.e., P1 contains a constraint violation that P2 does not).

These points can also be clustered into multiple levels of abstraction; for example, in VLSI design, there might be a system level, a logic level, and a geometric layout level. Figure 1-2 illustrates some of these relationships.

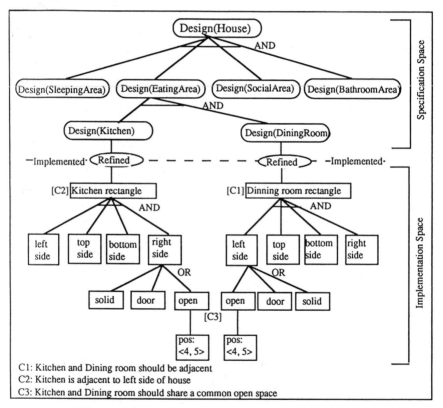

Figure 1-2: The Design Space as an AND/OR Tree

Dynamically generating the design space. Some of the most basic operations for generating new points in the design space from old ones include:

- refining P1 into P2.
- implementing P1 as P2 in target technology T.
- decomposing P1 into {P11,...,P1n}.
- optimizing P1 into P2 with respect to criteria O.
- patching constraint violation V in P1, yielding P2.

Chapter 2 in Volume I discusses the issues involved in representing all these aspects of a design space. The points are illustrated in the context of VLSI design.

1.3.2. What Distinguishes a Design Knowledge Base?

Often the parts that occur in designs (at any level of abstraction) can be viewed as *instances* of a generic class. For example, microprocessors are usually composed of generic parts such as ALUs, registers, busses, etc.

Such regularity can be exploited by maintaining a knowledge base of *design object classes*, and then viewing designs as configurations of instances of particular classes (e.g., a new microprocessor instance is constructed by creating an instance of ALU5, Datapath3, Bus4, etc. and then connecting these object instances together in a particular fashion). Design objects are also often *parameterized*. A complete instance of such a parameterized object class is created by assigning values to all the parameters.

In the standard object-oriented fashion, such design object classes may be organized hierarchically, thus reaping the standard benefits of inheritance. Design process operations (such as refinement, optimization, etc.) may also be indexed in a class-specific fashion (as methods), and thus, may also be inheritable.

The relation between a design space, a design knowledge base (of the kind just described), and a design process is as follows. A *design process* operation such as refinement, patching, or optimization may generate a new point in the *design space* from one or more old ones; the operation itself may involve creating new instances of design object classes from the *design knowledge base*.

Based on such an object-oriented representation of a design knowledge base, Chapter 2 (Volume I) discusses how to represent parameterized designs, design histories, and task-specific experts. As examples of desirable properties for design representations, it suggests modularity, compactness, flexibility permitted in the design process (e.g. in allowing both top-down and bottom-up design, and concurrent execution of design tasks), and extensibility; it describes how these properties may be achieved.

How does the design process know which design object class(es) should be instantiated to carry out a particular design operation (e.g., refinement of part P1)? One answer is to hardcode the association. For example, a specific *refinement rule* might express the knowledge that whenever a part of type P1 is being refined, it should be decomposed into parts of type {P11,...,P1n}. Or a specific *patching rule* might fix a specific type of constraint violation that commonly occurs in a specific kind of object. The design process models in Part II of this book take this hardcoded approach.

Another answer is to treat this question as a problem that must be solved explicitly by the design process. For example, the process of patching a constraint violation might actually involve solving the problem of *recognizing* that a particular object in the design is an instance of (or similar to) some object in the knowledge base, and then *recognizing* that the specified function of that object has been disabled in some way (by the context of the object). Available patching methods associated with that object class can then be applied (or adapted). Chapter 6 (Volume I) discusses how to organize a design knowledge base so that this kind of "innovative" patching can occur.

1.4. MODELS OF THE DESIGN PROCESS

1.4.1. The Nature of Design Tasks

1.4.1.1. Design task dimensions

Design tasks can be classified along several dimensions, including:

- available methods and knowledge;
- amount of unspecified (physical) structure;
- gap in abstraction levels between specification and implementation;
- complexity of interactions between subproblems; and
- amount and type of knowledge a system user can provide.

Available methods and knowledge. Is an appropriate method and/or sufficient knowledge always available for choosing what task to address next in the design process (e.g., what part to refine, what bug to fix, etc.)? Is knowledge or a method available for executing that next task? If there is more than one way of executing that task, is knowledge or a method available for selecting the alternative that will have the (globally) best outcome? The more (appropriate) knowledge and methods are available, the more *routine* the design task is. We will focus our discussion on two basic types of knowledge and methods: *generative* knowledge and methods, for generating new points in the design space; and *control* knowledge and methods, for helping the design process to converge efficiently on an acceptable design solution.

If sufficient knowledge and methods are available for always *directly* (i.e., without problem-solving) generating the next point in the design space and for converging on an acceptable design with little or no search, we will call the task a *routine* design task.

If the available knowledge and methods do allow for fairly rapid generation of an acceptable solution, but only by:

- *indirect* generation of new points in the design space -- i.e., finding a way to generate the next point in the design space involves a problem-solving process; and/or

- *indirect* control of the search, i.e., via problem-solving.

that is -- by itself, the available (directly applicable) knowledge generates unacceptable designs -- we will call the task an *innovative* design task.

Finally, if a problem-solving process is required to construct the design space in the first place, or if the best method available (given our current understanding) is an unguided search through a very large space, we will call the task a *creative* design task.

We will call design process models capable of handling these three types of design tasks routine, innovative, and creative design process models, respectively. We discuss routine design processes in Section 1.4.2, and innovative design processes in Section 1.4.3. We feel that creative design models, such as they are, are still at too preliminary a stage to be included here. However, [11] contains an interesting collection of workshop papers on this subject. Since we have tied creative design to the creation of the proper design space, creative design can also be viewed as a search through a space of design space representations, and thus work on problem reformulation and representation design can be seen as relevant here (see, e.g., [1]).

The terms "routine", "innovative", and "creative design" were introduced in [3], but were used in a somewhat different sense. Note that we use these terms in reference to the *task* and the *process*, but not the *product*. Thus, an innovative design process (e.g., replay of design plans) might not necessarily produce a product that is innovative with respect to the current market.

Amount of unspecified structure. Design maps function into (physical) structure. A design task often provides part of the (physical) structure of the design.

Since the design process involves creating a complete (physical) structure, it is also useful to identify what of the physical structure is left to be determined as a measure of design task complexity [39]. Design tasks are usefully distinguished according to what the *unspecified* structure looks like [40].

In *structure synthesis tasks*, the unspecified structure could potentially be any composition of primitive parts, which may not exist in the knowledge/data base. For example, the specified function might be a boolean function such as (and (or x y) (not z)). The physical structure might be any gate network that implements the boolean function; no part of the gate network is given *a priori*.

In *structure configuration tasks*, the unspecified structure is a configuration of parts of pre-determined type, and connectors of pre-determined type. For example, the physical structure might be a house floorplan containing some number of rooms, that can be connected by doors. For a particular floorplanning problem, the number of rooms and the size of the house might be given. In this case, the unspecified structure would be the configuration of rooms and doors, plus the values for room and door parameters.

Finally, in *parameter instantiation tasks*, the unspecified structure is the set of values for the parameters of each part. For example, the physical structure might be the part decomposition for all air cylinders (Volume I, Chapter 7). For a particular air cylinder design problem, the values for particular parameters (e.g., the length of the cylinder) might be given. Then the unspecified structure would be the values for all the remaining parameters.

Gap in abstraction levels between specification and implementation. In the simplest case, the design specification and the design implementation are at the same level of abstraction. This occurs, for example, when the only unspecified structure is parameter values. In other cases, a single level separates the functional specification from the target implementation level. That is, knowledge and methods are available for directly mapping the pieces of the specification into implementations; implementing a boolean function as a gate network is a simple example. In the worst case, the design may have to be driven down through several levels of abstraction before it is completed. For instance, in VLSI design, the initial specification might be of a digital system (e.g., a calculator or a microprocessor), which is first refined into a "logic level" description (a gate network), and then into a "layout level" description (of the actual geometry of the chip).

Complexity of interactions between subproblems. On one extreme (independent subproblems), the subproblems can all be solved independently, the solutions can be composed easily, resulting in an acceptable global design. On the other extreme, the subproblems strongly interact: a special (relatively rare) combination of solutions to the subproblems is required, and combining these solutions into an acceptable global solution may not be easy or quick. Complexity increases when the number of interactions increases or when the type of interaction becomes more complex.

Two major types of design interactions are worth distinguishing. *Compositional interactions* arise when not all choice combinations (for refining or implementing the different parts of the design) are (syntactically) composable. For example, in VLSI design, the output of one part may be "serial", while the input of another may be "parallel"; if the output of the one must feed the input of the other, then the parts are not syntactically composable. Syntactic interactions may be further subdivided into *functional interactions* index(Functional interactions) among parts of a functional decomposition (e.g., in VLSI design, the "serial output/input" interaction) and *physical interactions* among parts of the implementation (e.g., in VLSI design, wire1 and wire3 on the chip must be at least 3 lambda units apart).

Resource interactions arise when different choice combinations lead to different overall usage of one or more global resources (e.g., delay time, power, or area in VLSI design). Different resources "compose" in different ways: e.g., global part counts are related to local part counts by simple addition; global delay time involves critical path analysis; etc.

Each interaction can be represented by a *constraint*. A *local* constraint only constrains a single part; a *semi-local* constraint constrains a relatively small number of parts; and a *global* constraint constrains a relatively large number of parts. Compositional interactions tend to be represented by semi-local constraints (because the syntax rules for correctly composing parts tend to refer to a small number of parts). Resource interactions tend to be represented by global constraints (since the global resource usage tends to be a function of the whole design).

Compositional interactions are typically *weak* interactions; they are usually representable by semi-local constraints. In contrast, resource interactions are typically *strong* interactions, representable by global constraints.

Amount and type of knowledge a system user can provide. In considering the nature of a design task, we will consider human users as knowledge sources, and thus classify the design tasks addressed by a particular knowledge-based design system as "routine" or "innovative" depending on how much knowledge (and method) the system and the user *together* can provide during the overall design process. Thus, even if the design system itself has no directly applicable control knowledge, if the user makes choices at every decision point in a manner that leads to rapid convergence on an acceptable solution, then the task is "routine".

1.4.1.2. Design task decomposition

While sometimes the terms we have just introduced are appropriately applied to the design task as a whole, it is often the case that "the design task" is a collection of (themselves sometimes decomposable) subtasks. Whether a task is considered a "routine design task" really depends on whether the subtasks are all routine and on how strongly the subtasks interact; the same design task may have relatively more and less routine parts to it. A category such as "parameter instantiation task" may be aptly applied to one subtask, and be inappropriate for another. Reference [5] makes some further points about task decomposition and associating different methods with different types of subtasks.

1.4.2. Models of Routine Design

1.4.2.1. Conventional routine design

In many cases, knowledge-based models of design are simply inappropriate, or would constitute overkill; conventional methods suffice for solving the task (or subtask). Some design tasks can be cast as a set of linear constraints C(s) on a set of real-valued variables, plus an objective function O(s) on these variables; for such problems, the methods of *linear programming* apply. Other simple design tasks can be cast as *constraint satisfaction problems* (CSPs) when: only parameter values are left unspecified; each parameter has a discrete, finite range of values; the constraints are unary or binary predicates on these parameters; and there are no optimization criteria. In such a case, the constraint satisfaction methods of [9] apply. Similarly, other types of design tasks are well-fitted to other standard methods (integer programming, multi-objective optimization techniques, AND/OR graph search [26], numerical analysis techniques, etc.). Many of these conventional methods have performance guarantees of various sorts: linear programming and AND/OR graph search are guaranteed to find a global optimum; if the constraint network is a tree, constraint satisfaction methods are guaranteed to run in polynomial time; etc.

1.4.2.2. Knowledge-based routine design

Viewed as a knowledge-based search, a routine design process is comprised of several different types of basic operations: refinement, constraint processing, patching and optimization. *Refinement* and *implementation* operations generate new, and less abstract points in the search space; *constraint processing* operations prune inconsistent alternatives from consideration by the search; *patching* operations convert incorrect or sub-optimal designs into correct or more nearly optimal designs; *optimization* operations convert sub-optimal designs into designs that are more nearly optimal, with respect to some optimization criterion. Such operations might be stored as rules whose application requires pattern-matching (e.g., as in the VEXED system -- Volume I, Chapter 8); or as plans or procedures that are directly indexed by the type of design part to which they apply (e.g., as in the AIR-CYL system -- Volume I, Chapter 7).

1.4.2.3. Non-iterative, knowledge-based routine design

For some design tasks, sufficient knowledge or methods are available that a single pass (more or less) of top-down refinement -- possibly aided by constraint processing, patching, and directly applicable control knowledge -- is generally sufficient for converging on an acceptable design. This kind of design process model is demonstrated in several systems discussed in this book, including AIR-CYL (Volume I, Chapter 7) and VEXED (Volume I, Chapter 8). In the best case, applying this model requires running time linear in $p*l$, where p is the number of parts in the original specification, and l is the number of levels of abstraction through which each such part must be refined. However, constraint processing can slow things down, particularly if relatively global constraints are being processed [13].

1.4.2.4. Iterative, knowledge-based routine design

In other cases, the same kind of basic operations (refinement, constraint processing, etc.) are involved, but several (but not an exponential number of) iterations are generally required before an acceptable design is found. The need for iteration often arises when *multiple* constraints and objectives must be satisfied. A move in the design space that is good with respect to one constraint or objective may impair the satisfaction of another; tradeoffs may be necessary, and quickly finding a reasonable tradeoff (e.g., something close to a pareto-optimal solution) generally requires extensive domain-specific knowledge.

Several forms of iteration are possible:

- *Chronological backtracking.* A knowledge-poor method that is generally not acceptable for guaranteeing rapid convergence unless the density of solutions in the design space is very high, or the design space is very small. (Note, though, that "very small" need not mean a space of tens of designs, but -- given the speed of modern-day computing -- could be one containing thousands of designs. See, e.g., Volume I, Chapter 4, where an acceptable design for an automobile transmission is found using chronological backtracking.

- *Knowledge-directed backtracking.* Dependency-directed backtracking possibly aided by advice or heuristics. PRIDE   (Volume I, Chapter 9) and VT (Volume I, Chapter 11) both illustrate this kind of iteration.

- *Knowledge-directed hillclimbing.* Iterative optimization or patching of a design until all constraint violations have been repaired, and an acceptable tradeoff has been met among all global optimality criteria (e.g., area, power consumption, delay time, in VLSI design). The knowledge used to select among different possible modifications could be an evaluation function, or a set of domain-specific heuristics (CHIPPE, Volume I, Chapter 12), or the choice could be made by the user (DESIGNER, Volume I, Chapter 14).

- *Knowledge-directed problem re-structuring.* It is not only possible to change the design solution but also the design problem, e.g., by adding new constraints or objectives, or retracting or relaxing old ones. As the original problem poser, the user is often made responsible for such changes [BIOSEP (Volume I, Chapter 10) and WRIGHT (Volume I, Chapter 13)].

In the best case, applying this model requires running time *polynomial* in $p*l$, where p is the number of parts in the original specification, and l is the number of levels of abstraction through which each such part must be refined; i.e., the number of iterations is polynomial in $p*l$. In the worst case, the number of iterations is exponential because whatever knowledge is guiding the search turns out to be inadequate or inappropriate.

1.4.2.5. Routine design systems covered in this volume

Table 1-4 classifies along the dimensions we have been discussing the various routine design systems described in later chapters of this book. Notice that most of these routine design systems address design tasks involving parameter value assignment or structure configuration (but not "from scratch" synthesis of the entire structure).

Table 1-4: Categorization of Systems and Methods for Performing Routine Design

SYSTEM OR METHOD	DESIGN TASK	CHAPTER (VOL. I) OR PAPER	UNSPECIFIED STRUCTURE	DIRECTLY APPLICABLE KNOWLEDGE	SUBPROBLEM INTERACTIONS	ABSTRACTION LEVEL GAP
conventional optimization techniques	many simple tasks	--	parameter values	generative; control	algebraic constraints (global)	0
CSP methods	many simple tasks	Ref. [8]	parameter values	generative; some control	works best for semi-local constraints	0
AIR-CYL	air cylinders	7	parameter values	generative; patching	weak interactions	1
VT	elevators	11	parameter values	generative; knowledge-directed backtracking	strong interactions	0
PRIDE	copier paper paths	9	structure configuration	generative; knowledge-directed backtracking	works best for weak interactions	n
VEXED	circuits	8	entire structure	generative	weak interactions	n
BIOSEP	protein purification processes	10	structure configuration	generative	weak interactions + cost function	n
CHIPPE	VLSI	12	structure configuration	generative; knowledge-directed hillclimbing	weak interactions + global resource budgets	n
WRIGHT	spatial layouts	13	structure configuration	generative; user control	algebraic constraints + evaluation function	1
DESIGNER	graphic interfaces	14	structure configuration	generative; user control	mostly semi-local constraints	1

1.4.3. Models of Innovative Design

In innovative design tasks, routine design is not possible because of *missing design knowledge*. The missing knowledge might either be knowledge for directly generating new points in the design space, or knowledge for directly controlling the design space search. In this section, we will examine four different classes of innovative design. The first three focus (primarily) on missing generative knowledge, while the last deals with missing control knowledge:

- Innovation via case-based reasoning

- Innovation via structural mutation

- Innovation by combining multiple knowledge sources

- Search convergence by explicit planning of the design process

The first three approaches can be used to create innovative *designs*; the last approach involves creating innovative *design plans*, or innovative reformulations of the *design problem*.

1.4.3.1. Missing design knowledge

Why might relevant design knowledge be missing? One reason is that the most naturally acquirable knowledge might not necessarily be in a directly applicable form. This is often so in *case-based reasoning*; old designs and design process traces can be stored away fairly easily (if stored verbatim) in a case database, but then this leaves the problem of how to use these old cases to help solve a new design problem.

A second reason is that it generally is impossible to store the large amount of specific knowledge that would be necessary to adequately deal with all possible design variations (e.g., varying functional specifications, objective criteria, etc.). While some of this knowledge could be generalized, generalization often incurs a price of some sort; e.g., the generalized knowledge is not quite operational and must be made so at run-time; the (overly) generalized knowledge is not quite correct in all the circumstances to which it appears to be applicable; etc. Additionally, some of the knowledge simply is idiosyncractic, and thus not generalizable.

For this reason, deliberate engineering tradeoffs usually must be made in how much directly applicable design knowledge to build into the system, and how much to leave out, letting the system (or the user) cope with the missing knowledge.

A third reason is that human beings themselves may not have the relevant knowledge. Sometimes this is because the "structure to function" mapping is too complex to invert; methods may be available for analyzing the behavior and function of a given device, but not for taking a specified function and directly producing a structure that realizes that function. A case-based approach is often taken for such design tasks.

1.4.3.2. Case-based reasoning

Any case-based model of design must address the following issues:

- design case representation and organization
- design case storage
- design case retrieval
- design case adaptation and reuse

We will now say how three systems described in Volume II -- the BOGART circuit design system (Chapter 2), the ARGO circuit design system (Chapter 3), and the CADET system for designing fluid-mechanical devices (Chapter 4) -- handle these different issues. Chapter 5 (Volume II) analyzes case-based models of design in greater detail.

Design case representation. In BOGART, the stored cases are *design plans*, i.e., the steps used to incrementally refine a functional specification of a circuit into a pass transistor network are recorded *verbatim*. In ARGO, the same design session can yield several design cases, each at a different level of generality. Cases are stored as rules ("macrorules"), wherein the precise conditions for reuse of that case are stated explicitly. In CADET, each case involves four different representations: linguistic descriptions (i.e., <object attribute value> tuples); functional block diagramming; causal graphs; and configuration spaces.

Design case storage. In BOGART, the cases were automatically stored verbatim (when the user so chose) after a session with the VEXED design system (Volume I, Chapter 8). In ARGO, the design plan (a network of design steps and dependencies among them) is partitioned into levels. By dropping away more levels, more general plans are produced. Explanation-based generalization [19] of these design plans is used to determine the conditions under which each of these plans is applicable (which are then cached, along with the corresponding plans). In CADET, the cases were manually entered (since the focus of the CADET research was on case retrieval, and not case storage).

Design case retrieval. Because ARGO stores cases in such a way that the conditions for precise re-use are associated with them, retrieval of *applicable* cases is not an issue; ARGO uses a heuristic to restrict its retrieval to maximally specific cases. In BOGART, the *user* selects a case conceived as being similar to the current problem. In CADET, if no case directly matches the current specification, transformations are applied to the specification of device behavior until it resembles some case in the case database (e.g., some previously design artifact actually produces the desired behavior or something similar to it). In CADET, the specification may also be transformed in such a way that different parts of it correspond to different cases in the case database; all these cases are then retrieved (and the designs are composed).

Design case adaptation and reuse. In ARGO, reuse is trivial; a macrorule that matches is guaranteed to be directly applicable to the matching context. The transformations performed by CADET prior to retrieving a design permit direct use of the designs in the retrieved cases. In a case retrieved by BOGART (a design plan), some steps may apply to the current problem, while other parts may not; *replay* of the design plan is used to determine which steps apply. [23] is worth reading as a framework for case-based models of design such as BOGART, whose *modus operandi* is design plan replay.

Summary. BOGART's main innovation is in its method for design case reuse (via replay); ARGO's is in design case storage (macrorules with conditions of applicability); CADET's contribution is its method for design case retrieval (via transforming the design problem). All of these systems make contributions to the representation and organization of design cases that support their primary contribution.

1.4.3.3. Innovation via structural mutation and analysis

Most directly applicable knowledge for generating new points in the design space (either via refinement or modification) guarantees that something is being held invariant; most commonly, the functionality of the old design is preserved. If functionality-preserving transformations are not available, a weaker approach is to apply transformations that modify the artifact's (physical) structure in some manner, and then analyze the resulting functionality. Such analysis may then suggest further directions for modification until the desired functionality is (re)achieved. Such modifications are also guided by performance criteria and resource limitations.

One such approach is described in Volume II, Chapter 6. Here the problem is to find a way to simplify a given, modular design (modular in that each structural part implements a different function) by identifying and exploiting structure-sharing opportunities (i.e., ways to make a given structure achieve multiple functions). Here the transformation for modifying the artifact's structure is one that deletes some part of the structure. After a part has been deleted (and hence a function has been unimplemented), other features of the remaining structure are identified that can be perturbed to achieve the currently unimplemented function (while not ceasing to achieve the function(s) they are already implementing). The identified features are then perturbed in the direction of better achieving the unimplemented function. For example, the handle of a mug could be safely deleted if the remaining cylinder were sized and shaped in such a way that it could be grasped by a human hand easily, and were made of a material that was heat-insulating (and hence would not burn the hand) -- e.g., a styrofoam cup. Essential to this approach is knowledge that associates changes in particular physical features of an artifact to the functions these (might) achieve.

If associations between (change of) physical structure and (change of) function are not hardcoded, then they may have to be derived. Qualitative modeling and reasoning of various kinds (e.g., qualitative simulation: see Volume II, Chapter 10) can sometimes be used to derive such associations.

1.4.3.4. Exploiting multiple knowledge sources

We have just described systems that use a case database to generate new designs, and other systems that use associations between structure and function to do the same. For some design tasks, multiple sources of (such indirectly usable) knowledge may be available, and all potentially useful; it might even be the case that solving the design problem *requires* integrating the advice of several knowledge sources.

Chapter 7 (Volume II) describes the ALADIN system, which helps design new aluminum alloys that meet specified properties. ALADIN draws on several sources of expertise to generate new points in the design space:

- a case database of previously designed alloys and their properties.

- if-then rules which associate structural changes (e.g., adding magnesium to the alloy) with functional changes (e.g., the value of the "strength" property increases).

- mathematical models of physical properties.

- statistical methods for interpolation and extrapolation.

1.4.3.5. Planning the design process

In a simple *routine design* scenario, the control questions that must be answered along the way take relatively simple forms: which part of the design to work on next? What to do there (refine, implement, optimize, patch)? Of several possible ways to do that, which to pick? Acquirable control knowledge may be sufficient for answering the control questions as they arise.

However, for several reasons, a design process model can be more complex, thus giving rise to new control questions, and hence to the need for a more complex controller:

- *More methods and knowledge sources.* Innovative design systems can involve a diverse range of activities and draw on many sources of knowledge. For example, the ALADIN system draws on multiple knowledge sources, and consequently must also answer new control questions: which knowledge source to consult next? How to combine the outputs of several knowledge sources? etc.

- *Multiple objectives.* Another source of control problems arises when multiple objectives must be satisfied. New control questions include: With respect to which objective should the design be improved next? Which part of the design should be redesigned to effect the improvement?

- *Expensive design operations.* Operations such as simulation (e.g., VLSI chip simulation) or analysis (e.g., finite element analysis) can be sufficiently costly that their use should be carefully planned.

A global view: Control as planning. To be operational, any control strategy must provide answers to specific, *local* control questions of the kind just described. However, the problem of control has a *global* goal in mind: Utilize knowledge and methods so as to most rapidly converge on an acceptable solution. Hence we can think of the problem of control as a *planning problem*: construct a relatively short design plan whose steps invoke various design methods and draw on design knowledge, and which, when completely executed, results in the creation of an acceptable design.

Stefik [36, 37] and Wilensky [45] gave the name *meta-planning* to this approach to control, since the design process itself is being explicitly represented and reasoned about. Stefik's MOLGEN system represented the design (a plan for a molecular genetics experiment) at multiple levels of abstraction. MOLGEN took a least commitment approach to refining the design through these levels of abstraction. It also used a multi-layered control strategy, explicitly representing and modifying the design plan. The ALADIN system (Volume II, Chapter 7) uses a very similar approach to managing the navigation through its multiple spaces for designing aluminum alloys.

Control as top-down refinement of design plans. When design operations (such as VLSI simulation) are expensive, one response is to create abstractions of these operations and much more cheaply construct plans for the design process in the space of abstract operations, pick the best abstract plan, and then refine it into an actual design plan (one whose execution would produce complete designs, and accurate analyses). This approach can be viewed as a special kind of meta-planning in which the planning method is top-down refinement (often also called "hierarchical planning"). This approach has been applied to VLSI design in the ADAM system (Volume II, Chapter 8).

But what is the "best" abstract plan? In ADAM, "best" means the one which when executed, creates a design that comes closest to satisfying all of several resource limitations (on area, speed, power, and design time). ADAM uses a single weighted evaluation function of all the resource usages:

```
w1 * area + w2 * speed + w3 * power + w4 * design time


where w1+w2+w3+w4=1
```

to guide its search. ADAM first finds plans that construct designs which are optimal with respect to each of the individual resources; for instance, to do so for "area" would involve setting $w1 = 1$, and $w2 = w3 = w4 = 0$. Based on the the difference between the costs of the resulting designs and the specified budgets, ADAM uses *linear interpolation* to readjust the weights on the evaluation function. It then replans.

Exploratory design: Control as hillclimbing in the space of problem formulations. The following hypothesis (we will call it the *routine design hypothesis*) is one way of viewing the relationship between an innovative design problem and a routine design problem:

> If the design problem is appropriately structured and contains enough detail (i.e., if we are "looking at the problem right"), then a single pass of a simple routine design process should produce an acceptable design (if one exists).

The control strategy we will next describe, called *exploratory design*, is appropriate for those problems where the initial design problem is *not* appropriately structured or annotated (i.e., it is an *innovative* design problem). We call this "exploratory design" because our intuition is that human designers handle problems that are complex in novel ways by spending their initial time finding a good way to look at the problem.

Models of routine design involve a search purely in the space of designs. In exploratory design, the problem and the solution co-evolve. Exploratory design hillclimbs in the space of problem formulations (the "outer loop" of the method), getting feedback for adjusting the problem formulation from analyzing how the candidate designs generated so far (by the "inner loop" of routine design) fail to be acceptable.

The DONTE system (Volume II, Chapter 9) performs such hillclimbing in the space of circuit design problem formulations using top-down refinement, constraint processing, and design patching operations in its "inner loop". The kind of problem reformulation operations it performs there are: macro-decision formation, which imposes a hierarchical structure on a relatively flat problem decomposition; budgeting, which adds a new budget constraint to every design component; re-budgeting, which may adjust such constraints in several components; rough design, which assigns estimates of resource usage to various parts of the design; and criticality analysis which (re)assesses how (relatively) difficult the various subproblems are to solve (given their current budgets, etc.).

1.4.3.6. Innovative design systems covered in this volume

Table 1-5 classifies along the dimensions we discussed earlier the various innovative design systems described in later chapters of this book. Notice that most of these innovative design systems address design tasks involving synthesis of the entire structure.

1.4.4. Qualitative Reasoning about Artifacts during Design

The mapping of a knowledge level specification of a design system into am algorithm level search algorithm can draw on formally represented bodies of generally useful "common sense" knowledge and procedures relevant to reasoning about the physical artifacts being designed. We now describe two kinds of such knowledge: knowledge about physical systems; and knowledge about geometry. With respect to codification of "common sense" knowledge, the CYC project [14] represents an alternate and possibly complementary approach to those described here.

Table 1-5: Categorization of Systems and Methods
for Performing Innovative Design

SYSTEM OR METHOD	DESIGN TASK	CHAPTER (VOL. II)	UNSPEC. STRUC.	ABSTR. LEVEL GAP	GENERATION PROBLEMS ADDRESSED	CONTROL PROBLEMS ADDRESSED	WHAT IS INN-OVATIVE
BOGART	circuits	2	entire structure	1	how to replay retrieved case		design
ARGO	circuits	3	entire structure	1	how to store cases so generation is easy		design
CADET	fluid-mechanical devices	4	entire structure	n	how to identify similar cases		design
FUNCTION SHARING	fluid-mechanical devices	6	none	0	how to identify function-sharing possibilities		design
ALADIN	aluminum alloys	7	entire structure	n spaces	how to use multiple knowledge sources to generate new design		design
ADAM	VLSI	8	entire structure	n		how to find promising design plan	design plan
DONTE	circuits	9	entire structure	n		how to find good problem decomposition, budget allocation, resource usage estimations	design problem reformula-tion

1.4.4.1. Qualitative reasoning about physical systems during design

Functional specifications for *physical systems* often take the form of stipulating a particular relationship between behavioral parameters, e.g., the output rotation of a rotation transmitter must be 30 times as fast as the input rotation. It is rarely the case that a single part (e.g., a single gear pair) is capable of directly achieving the specified relationship. Instead, a series of interacting components may be needed. This is especially the case when the type of the behavioral parameter changes: e.g., the input is a rotational speed, but the output is a rate of up-and-down movement. The network of interacting behavioral parameters may necessarily include feedback loops, e.g., when the specified relationship defines a self-regulating device (e.g., a change in one variable should result in a corresponding change in the other).

Williams has proposed a design process model for such problems called *interaction-based invention*:

> Invention involves constructing a topology of interactions that both produces the desired behavior and makes evident a topology of physical devices that implements those interactions [46].

One of the key steps in this process is verifying that the interactions in the constructed interaction topology actually "compose" to produce the specified interaction. Carrying out this step (and satisfying its representational needs, i.e., providing an adequate representation of the causal and temporal features of each interaction) is particularly difficult when the topology is complex (e.g., as in most circuits that contain feedback loops). Chapter 10 (Volume II) discusses how to adequately represent such interactions in complex physical systems (such as analog circuits with feedback loops), and how to qualitatively analyze the global behavior of these systems.

1.4.4.2. Qualitative reasoning about geometry in design

Geometry-constrained synthesis. Many design tasks involve geometry in one way or another in their functional specifications or domain knowledge. In the simplest of cases, the role geometry plays is purely static, placing restrictions on the boundaries of the artifact, points of attachment of parts of the artifact, etc. The WRIGHT system described in Chapter 13 (Volume II) handles a subclass of such spatial placement problems.

The synthesis of small load-bearing structures illustrates a more complex role of geometry: *forces* (i.e., the loads) are positioned at certain points in space; a single structure must be synthesized that is both stable and capable of bearing the loads (and that does not occupy any "obstacle" regions of space). Chapter 11 (Volume II) describes the MOSAIC system, which synthesizes such load-bearing structures using a design process model that performs problem abstraction, problem decomposition, and iterative re-design.

Another geometric complication shows up in *kinematic synthesis*, the synthesis of physical structures that *move* in ways that satisfies certain restrictions on motion in space. Chapter 12 (Volume II) considers the problem of designing linkages (e.g., door hinges, aircraft landing gear, cranes, etc.), given constraints on specific points through which the linkage must pass (perhaps in a particular order), number of straight line segments in the path of motion, etc. In the TLA system, the user selects a linkage from a case database of four-bar linkages, looking for those that have features resembling the problem specifications. Optimization techniques are then used to adapt the known case to the current problem; user intervention helps such techniques avoid getting stuck in local minima.

Joskowicz (Volume II, Chapter 13) also describes an approach to kinematic synthesis. Mechanisms, retrieved from either a catalog or a case database, are considered during artifact redesign. Retrieved mechanisms should ideally be *kinematically equivalent* to the current design. Joskowicz describes a method for comparing two mechanisms for kinematic equivalence, that involves trying to find a common abstraction of both. This same mechanism comparison technique is used to organize the case database (for the purpose of efficient retrieval) into classes of kinematically equivalent mechanisms.

Geometry-based analysis. That designed artifacts have geometric features means that some of the analysis processes performed during design will involve geometric reasoning, including: static and dynamic analysis of stresses (based on shape), and kinematic simulation of mechanisms.

The conventional approach to analyzing stress is finite element analysis. However, this method requires a grid as an input, and which grid is best varies with the problem. In contrast, Chapter 14 (Volume II) describes an approach to stress analysis that geometrically partitions an object into regions in such a way that the object parts have shapes (e.g., a plate with a hole in it) resembling known cases (e.g., a plate without a hole in it). These known cases have associated (pre-computed) stress analyses, which are then used as part of the stress analysis data for the overall object.

One method for *kinematic simulation* is described in Chapter 13 (Volume II). First, local behaviors are computed from two-dimensional configuration spaces, defined by the objects' degrees of freedom. Global behaviors are then determined by composing pairwise local behaviors.

1.5. BUILDING A KNOWLEDGE-BASED DESIGN TOOL

The actual construction of a new knowledge-based design tool goes through three basic phases:

- Identify the design task
- Configure and instantiate the design process model

• Implement the design process model

1.5.1. Identifying the Design Task

Identifying the design task involves defining the task and classifying it.

1.5.1.1. Knowledge acquisition to define the design task

To define a design task, we must acquire knowledge defining:

- the class of *problems* that can be solved;

- the class of *candidate solutions* that contains a set of acceptable solutions to the problem;

- the *domain theory*, the body of domain-specific knowledge that is accessed in solving such problems, and constrains what is considered to be an acceptable solution.

How can such design knowledge be either easily acquired from domain experts, or otherwise automatically added to the knowledge base?

Graphical interfaces. Chapter 2 (Volume III) discusses the advantages of using graphical interfaces in acquiring design knowledge from experts. In particular, the knowledge is acquired in the form of decision trees. These trees are then mapped into expert rules in OPS5. The complete process is illustrated by acquiring and compiling knowledge from experts for bearing selection.

Knowledge acquisition for specific design process models. Another way to simplify knowledge acquisition is to tailor a particular knowledge acquisition method to a specific design model. For example, the SALT system (Volume I, Chapter 11) specializes in acquiring knowledge for a design system that iteratively modifies a design.

SALT first acquires a graph whose nodes are design inputs, design parameters, or design constraints and whose edges express various relationships between these. SALT then acquires three types of knowledge that are indexed off the graph nodes: knowledge for proposing a design extension (specifying a design parameter), knowledge for identifying a constraint, and knowledge for proposing a fix to a constraint violation. SALT has a schema for each type of knowledge, and prompts the user with questions whose answers fill in the appropriate schema. SALT also has techniques for analyzing the completeness and consistency of the knowledge base. The SALT system was used to acquire the knowledge in the VT system.

Case-based reasoning. In Section 1.4.3.2, we described case-based reasoning as a particular model of innovative design. Because case-based reasoning involves storage of design cases from previous design system sessions, it represents another way of adding "new" knowledge to the knowledge base.

As mentioned previously, the stored knowledge can range in generality from design plans that are stored verbatim (as in the BOGART system, Volume II, Chapter 2), to automatically generalized knowledge (as in the ARGO system of Volume II, Chapter 3).

1.5.1.2. Classifying a design task

As mentioned earlier, design tasks can be classified along several dimensions, including:

- available methods and knowledge

- gap in abstraction levels between specification and implementation

- amount of unspecified (physical) structure

- complexity of interactions between subproblems; and

- amount and type of knowledge a system user can provide

1.5.2. Configuring and Instantiating the Design Process Model

Classification of a design task identifies important features of that task. Different features suggest different design process models. Tables 1-4 and 1-5 suggest, by example, some of the correspondences.

1.5.3. Implementing the Design Process Model

Once a design process model is determined, the next step is to map the design process model onto the program level (see Figure 1-1). "Maxims" pertinent to carrying out this mapping include:

1. Code in an appropriate programming language, such as C++, LISP, OPS5, KEE^{TM}. Most of the papers in Volume I and Volume II, as well as Chapter 7 in Volume III, take this approach.

2. Use a commercial tool that provides some support for design artifact representation; implement appropriate extensions. Chapters 3, 4, 5, and 6 in Volume III follow this path.

3. Develop a domain-independent shell that implements the design process model(s) and instantiate the shell for a particular application.

4. Use a knowledge compiler to generate special-purpose procedures for efficiently processing particular (and generally domain-specific) subtasks of the overall design task.

1.5.3.1. Commercially available tools

There are two kinds of tools available in the commercial market place for civil/mechanical engineering applications (see Table 1-2):

1. **Parametric modelers**, which provide constraint processing capabilities to geometric modelers. An application utilizing a parametric modeler (DesignView^{TM}) and a knowledge-based programming tool (NEXPERT^{TM}) for designing a product and forming sequence for cold forging is described in Chapter 4 (Volume III). We have included a list of commercial tool vendors in Appendix A at the end of this chapter.

2. **Design representation frameworks**, which provide additional layers over knowledge representation languages. Typically these layers support the following activities:

   • Representation of engineering entities, including composite objects;
   • Geometric modeling;

- Constraint management;
- Access to external programs, such as engineering databases;
- Programming language support (current tools are implemented in LISP); and
- Rule-based inferencing.

Applications implemented in three commercially available tools are described in Volume III, Chapters 3 (ICAD^{TM}), 4 (DesignView^{TM} and NEXPERT Object^{TM}), 5 (Design++^{TM}), and 6 (Concept Modeller^{TM}).

1.5.3.2. Domain-independent shells

Domain-independent shells, in addition to representation and programming language support, provide design process models as problem solving strategies. Applications can be built by adding domain-specific knowledge. Many of the routine design systems described in Volume I have evolved into domain-independent shells. These systems view design as:

```
Hierarchical Refinement + Constraint Propagation + ..
```

and provide knowledge editing facilities for inputting design plans, goals, artifacts, and constraints. Table 1-6 summarizes several domain-independent shells, developed in the United States. Several organizations in other countries are attempting to build such tools, e.g., LEOSYS^{TM} , developed by Olivetti Computers, Italy.

1.5.3.3. Knowledge compilers

In principle, *knowledge compilers* can be used to create (at compile time) those components of the design system that are not easily viewable as instantiations of domain-independent "shell" components, and that are not one of the commercially available tools (e.g., parametric modellers or design representation frameworks). Often the compiled components handle particular, domain-specific tasks such as maze routing [32], house floorplanning [44], or synthesis of gear chains [24]. It is also possible to use knowledge compilers to optimize components that originated as shell instantiations.

Some compilers are quite specialized; for example, the ELF system

Table 1-6: Domain-Independent Shells that Implement
Hierarchical Refinement and Constraint Propagation

SHELL/ REFERENCE	PREDECESSOR/ DOMAIN	REP. LANGUAGE/ BASE LANG.	MACHINE OR OS	DEPARTMENT/ PLACE
DESCRIBE [20]	PRIDE Paper Handling	LOOPS LISP	XEROX	Only Inhouse
EDESYN [16]	HI-RISE Buildings	FRAMEKIT LISP	Unix	Civil Engrg. CMU
DSPL [4]	AIR-CYL Air Cylinders	LISP	Unix	Comp. Sci. OSU & WPI
EVEXED [38]	VEXED VLSI	STROBE LISP	XEROX	Comp. Sci. Rutgers
DIDS [2]	MICON Computers	C++ C	Unix	EECS Univ. Michigan
CONGEN [34]	ALL-RISE Buildings	C++ C	Unix	Civil Engrg. M.I.T.

[32] specializes in compiling global routers, for varying VLSI technologies.
The KBSDE compiler [44] and the constraint compiler of the WRIGHT system
(Volume I, Chapter 13) address a different and somewhat broader class of
knowledge-based systems for spatial configuration tasks. The DIOGENES
compiler [24] addresses the still broader class of heuristic search algorithms.
These compilers appear to obey the standard power/generality tradeoff. The
models of knowledge compilation also grow progressively weaker as the breadth
widens, culminating in such weak (i.e., relatively unrestricted) models as: a
transformational model of knowledge compilation [22] or a model of knowledge
compilation as formal derivation.

All the compilers just mentioned are research prototypes, and are thus not
commercially available. Nonetheless, we mention this technology because of its
potential importance in the not too distant future. In the meantime, human programming skills will have to suffice.

1.6. DESIGN AS PART OF A LARGER ENGINEERING PROCESS

It is important to view design in the perspective of the overall engineering process, which involves several phases: market studies, conceptualization, research and development, design, manufacturing, testing, maintenance, and marketing (see Figure 1-3). In this process people from various disciplines interact to produce the product.

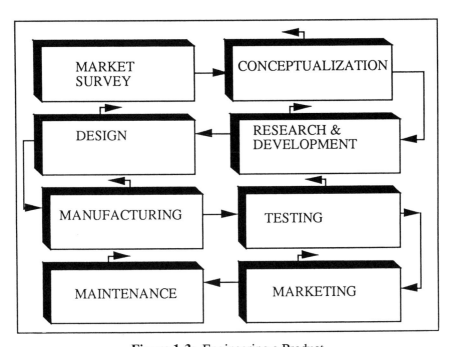

Figure 1-3: Engineering a Product

(Bent arrows indicate that the process is iterative)

In traditional product development, the lack of proper collaboration and integration between various engineering disciplines poses several problems, as expounded by the following Business Week (April 30, 1990, Page 111) clip [see Figure 1-4 for a typical scenario in the AEC industry].

The present method of product development is like a relay race. The research or marketing department comes up with a product idea and hands it off to design. Design engineers craft a blueprint and a hand-built prototype. Then, they throw the design "over the wall" to manufacturing, where production engineers struggle to bring the blueprint to life. Often this proves so daunting that the blueprint has to be kicked back for revision, and the relay must be run again - and this can happen over and over. Once everything seems set, the purchasing department calls for bids on the necessary materials, parts, and factory equipment -- stuff that can take months or even years to get. Worst of all, a design glitch may turn up after all these wheels are in motion. Then, everything grinds to a halt until yet another so-called engineering change order is made.

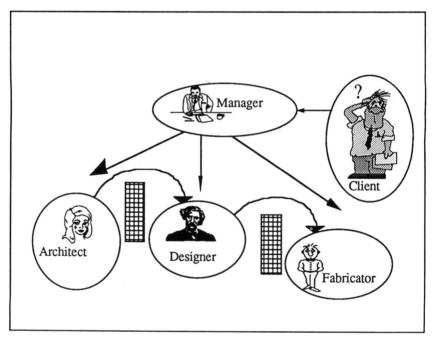

Figure 1-4: Over the Wall Engineering

Several companies have addressed the above problem by resorting to a more flexible methodology, which involves a collaborative effort during the entire life cycle of the product. It is claimed (Business Week, April 1990) that this approach[2] results in reduced development times, fewer engineering changes, and better overall quality. The importance of this approach has been recognized by the Department of Defense, which initiated a major effort -- the DARPA Initiative in Concurrent Engineering (DARPA DICE) -- with funding in the millions of dollars.

It is conceivable that the current cost trends in computer hardware will make it possible for every engineer to have access to a high performance engineering workstation in the near future. The "over the wall" approach will probably be replaced by a network of computers and users, as shown in Figure 1-5; in the figure we use the term *agent* to denote the combination of a human user and a computer.

The following is a list of issues that we consider important for computer-aided integrated and cooperative product development.

1. **Frameworks**, which deal with problem solving architectures.

2. **Organizational issues**, which investigate strategies for organizing engineering activities for effective utilization of computer-aided tools.

3. **Negotiation techniques**, which deal with conflict detection and resolution between various agents.

4. **Transaction management issues**, which deal with the interaction issues between the agents and the central communication medium.

5. **Design methods**, which deal with techniques utilized by individual agents.

6. **Visualization techniques**, which include user interfaces and physical modeling techniques.

Several papers in Volume III address some of the above issues; [33] contains additional papers in this area. Chapters 7 and 8, Volume III, discuss the DFMA and the ECMG frameworks, respectively, that bring manufacturability knowledge into the early design phases. The manufacturing knowledge is tightly integrated into the the design framework. The Engineous system, described in Volume III, Chapter 9, is a generic shell that combines knowledge-

---

[2]"Concurrent engineering", "collaborative product development", "cooperative product development", "integrated product development" and "simultaneous engineering" are different phrases used to connote this approach.

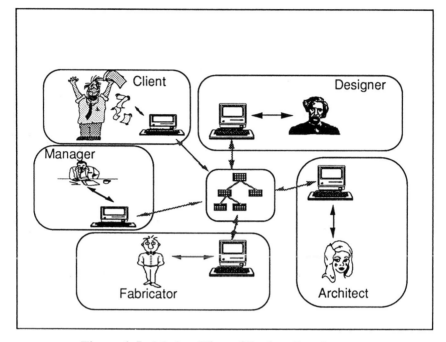

Figure 1-5: Modern View of Product Development

based expert systems, numerical optimization, and genetic algorithms for product design.

While the above systems are closely coupled architectures, the systems described in Chapters 10, 11, and 12 (Volume III) are loosely coupled and reflect the architecture shown in Figure 1-5. A multi-level and a multi-modal architecture, DMA, that supports easy integration of various design/manufacture CAD systems is proposed in Chapter 10 (Volume III). The design module supports an axiomatic approach to design [41]. The manufacture module contains manufactability knowledge, such as assembly sequencing, etc.

A dual design partner scheme is proposed in Chapter 11 (Volume III). This scheme supports two competing system behaviors. One expert machine -- the stabilizer -- resists change and always presents a conservative hypothetical model of the product. The other expert machine -- the innovator -- strives for well calculated and justified alternative hypothetical models of the product. The dual partner scheme is being implemented using the blackboard architecture [25].

The DICE project (Volume III, Chapter 12) implements a blackboard architecture over an object-oriented database management system; thus the blackboard and the object-store are tightly integrated. In addition, the objects in the blackboard have behavior associated with them. Hence, the need for a sophisticated scheduler -- as provided in the traditional blackboard systems -- is obviated. The DICE project also incorporates comprehensive transaction and version management mechanisms. The DICE version described in this volume was implemented in Common LISP. Other implementations also exist in the OPAL/GEMSTONE and C++/ONTOS environments.
Table 1-7 summarizes the various efforts in integrated design systems.

Table 1-7: Summary of Integrated Design Frameworks

SYSTEM	CHAPTER (VOL. III)	FEATURES	NO. LEVELS	STATUS
DFMA	7	Tightly coupled	1	In-house use
ECMG	8	Tightly coupled; Domain-independent	1	Commercially available
Engineous	9	Tightly coupled expert systems; genetic algorithms; optimization	1	In-house use
Dual Partner	11	Loosely coupled; Blackboard; database	n	Prototype
DMA	10	Loosely coupled	n	Prototype
DICE	12	Loosely coupled; Blackboard; object-oriented databases; negotiation; transaction management	n	Prototype

1.7. SUMMARY

In this overview chapter, we have presented a framework for helping to understand the field of "AI in Engineering Design" in general, and the papers in this collection, in particular.

Applying AI software engineering methodology to Engineering Design problems. We first considered "Engineering Design" and "Artificial Intelligence" as separate disciplines, the former providing special kinds of ill-structured problems, and the latter providing a methodology for developing knowledge-based systems that effectively solve certain types of ill-structured problems.

Design problems are *ill-structured* in that the mapping of desired functionality onto a (physical) structure that correctly implements it is generally not straightforward. Furthermore, most design problems call for not only a *correct* design but a *good* design -- good with respect to one or more (possibly ill-defined) metrics (e.g., cost, area, volume, power consumption, etc.); this further complicates the mapping, thereby decreasing the likelihood that a simple (polynomial time) algorithm will suffice for carrying out the mapping, and increasing the likelihood that some degree of search (e.g., generate-and-test) will be necessary. Finally, the design problem representation itself may begin its life as an ill-structured set of "requirements" and only gradually (enabled by feedback from actual design experience) evolve into a set of formal "specifications".

For the purposes of this book, we have described Artificial Intelligence as a discipline that provides a multi-level methodology for engineering knowledge-based problem-solving systems. In particular, a *knowledge level* specification of the system (and the class of problems it must solve) is mapped into an *algorithm level* description of an efficient search algorithm for efficiently and acceptably solving that class of problems. That (simulatable) algorithm description is then mapped into an actual piece of code at the *program level,* using one or more programming paradigms (e.g., procedural programming, rule-based programming, object-oriented programming), shells (e.g., VP-EXPERT^{TM}), or commercially available subsystems (e.g., an ATMS in KEE^{TM}). The application of AI to Engineering Design thus looks like a specialization of this software engineering methodology to: design tasks (specified at the "knowledge level"); design process models (described at the "algorithm level"); and design programs built from shells, commercially available design subsystems, and manually constructed code (implemented at the "program level").

Mapping a knowledge level specification for a design system into a algorithm-level search algorithm. In considering mapping a knowledge level specification for a design system into an algorithm-level search algorithm, it is useful to decompose the algorithm into passive and active components. One passive component is the *design space* to be searched. The active design components are the various *functional components of the design process model* (e.g., refinement, hillclimbing, constraint propagation, backtracking, etc.), which, in effect, generate the design space and navigate through it. These active components draw upon another passive component, declaratively represented *design knowledge*, interpreting this knowledge at run time (e.g., to estimate the cost of a particular design, to choose between several design alternatives, etc.).

The same piece of knowledge can be embedded into an algorithm in a variety of ways, with varying degrees of effectiveness. The most effective way to map available design knowledge into the algorithm-level search algorithm is to carefully engineer the design space itself, so that it -- *a priori* -- will contain (when generated at run-time) as few incorrect or poor designs as possible. The next most effective way to use design knowledge is to *compile* it into the active components of the search algorithm (e.g., creating customized routines for efficiently performing special tasks such as routing, placement, estimation, simulation, etc.) The least effective (though sometimes easiest, and sometimes necessary) way to use design knowledge is to represent it declaratively (e.g., as is often the case in shells), and then *interpret* it at run time.

Other factors also come into consideration when mapping a knowledge level specification of a design system into an algorithm-level search algorithm. Design tasks can be categorized along various dimensions; different search algorithms will be appropriate for different types of design tasks. Useful dimensions for taxonomizing design tasks include: available methods and knowledge (addressing that task); gap in abstraction levels between specification and implementation; amount of unspecified (physical) structure; and amount and type of knowledge a system user can provide.

Of primary importance in distinguishing types of design tasks is the amount and types of available knowledge (and the form in which the knowledge is available). The more design knowledge available in the right form, the more *routine* (or "direct") a design process can be used (involving a top-down refinement and/or hillclimbing process that converges on an acceptable design with little or no search). Any missing knowledge or knowledge in the wrong form or incorrect knowledge must be compensated for. Such *innovative* design problems can be addressed by various "indirect" techniques such as case-based reasoning, structural mutation, combining multiple knowledge sources, and explicit planning of the design process.

Design processes can be non-routine and *indirect* in the sense that generating new points in the design space may require an explicit problem-solving process, rather than the direct application of a single procedure or the direct interpretation of a single piece of knowledge. Using case-based reasoning to generate new points in the design space is usually indirect in that it requires nontrivial processes of design case selection, adaptation, and reuse. Using structural mutation to generate new points can be indirect in the sense that the quality and even the functionality of the mutations may not be knowable *a priori*, may require a problem-solving process (e.g., qualitative or numerical simulation) to determine, and may lead to a search through the space of possible mutations for a correct and good one. Using multiple knowledge sources to generate new points in the design space is usually indirect in that integrating partial solutions is a nontrivial problem-solving process.

Design processes can also be non-routine and indirect in the sense that *control* of the search is indirect -- it requires an explicit problem-solving process, rather than merely the direct application of a simple control procedure or the direct interpretation of a single piece of control knowledge to decide what to do next. The design search control problem can be usefully viewed as a *planning problem*, and various planning techniques can be applied: forward or backward planning, "hierarchical planning" (i.e., top-down refinement of design plans), or "exploratory design" (i.e., hillclimbing in the space of problem formulations).

The mapping of a knowledge level specification of a design system into an algorithm-level search algorithm can draw on formally represented bodies of generally useful "common sense" knowledge and procedures relevant to reasoning about the physical artifacts being designed. Much has been learned regarding qualitatively reasoning about *physical systems* in general. We have initial answers to such questions as: how to qualitatively simulate certain classes of physical systems; how to derive aggregate system behavior from the behavior of the parts; how to determine the function of the system given its aggregate behavior and a description of the system's context; etc. Much also has learned about (qualitatively) reasoning about the *geometry* of physical objects in general: how to satisfy placement and sizing constraints; how to satisfy constraints involving forces being applied at various points in space; how to satisfy kinematic constraints on how physical structures can move; how to analyze stresses based on shape; and how to simulate a mechanism's movement through space.

Mapping an algorithm-level search algorithm into a program. Implementing a design search algorithm can involve several types of tasks: coding in an appropriate programming language, such as C++, LISP, OPS5, KEE^{TM}; using commercially available tools for representing design artifact representations (e.g., parametric modellers) and for processing common tasks (e.g., constraint managers, geometric modellers and constraint managers, engineering databases); instantiating a domain-independent, design process shell (e.g., for hierarchical refinement and constraint propagation); and creating customized procedures or algorithms for special purpose tasks, either by hand, or by running a knowledge compiler.

Design as part of a larger engineering process. Design is only one phase or aspect of a larger engineering process that also includes market studies, conceptualization, research and development, manufacturing, testing, maintenance and marketing. The more the design process can be integrated with the other engineering phases, the more cost-effective the entire process will be. Approaches to computer-aided support of an integrated engineering process can range from loose couplings of the phases (facilitated by electronic mail, or shared files, or blackboard architectures), to tight couplings that constrain earlier phases (e.g., design) with requirements anticipated in later phases (e.g., manufacturing constraints) and reformulated so that they are expressed in the language of the earlier phases.

Other summary references. We have intended this chapter as a brief but complete summary of the state of the field of AI in Engineering Design. Other useful summary references worth reading include [3] (which introduced the "routine", "innovative", and "creative" design distinction), [21] (which distinguishes different design process models on the basis of types of design goal interactions), and [43] (which introduced the distinction between the "program level" and the "algorithm level", which was called the "function level" in that paper).

1.8. APPENDIX A: VENDORS OF SOME AI-BASED TOOLS FOR COMPUTER-AIDED ENGINEERING

Ashlar, Inc.
1290 Oakmead Pkwy.
Sunnyvale, CA 94806
Tool: Vellum^{TM}

Integraph Corp.
Mail Stop WYLE3
Huntsville, AL 35894-0001
Tool: MicroStation^{TM}

Cognition Inc.
900 Tech Park Drive
Bellerica, MA 01821
Tool: ECMG^{TM} and MCAE^{TM}

Mentor Graphics
8500 South West Creek Side Place
Beaverton, OR 97005
Tool: ADE^{TM}, Logic Synthesizer^{TM}

ICAD Inc.
1000 Massachusetts Avenue
Cambridge, MA 02138
Tools: ICAD^{TM}

Parametric Technology Corp.
128 Technology Sr.
Waltham, MA 02154
Tool: Pro/ENGINEER^{TM}

ComputerVision
55 Wheeler Street
Cambridge, MA 02138
Tool: DesignView™

Spatial Technology
2425, 55th Street, Bldg. A
Boulder, CO 80301
Tool: ACIS™

Wisdom Systems
Corporate Circle
30100 Cagrin Blvd.
Suite 100
Pepper Pike, OHIO 44124
Tool: Concept Modeller™

1.9. BIBLIOGRAPHY

[1]   Benjamin, P., Ed., *Change of Representation and Inductive Bias,* Kluwer
        Publishing, 1990.

[2]   Birmingham, W. and Tommelin, I., "Towards a Domain-Independent
        Synthesis System," in *Knowledge Aided Design,* Green, M., Ed.,
        Academic Press, 1991.

[3]   Brown, D. and Chandrasekaran, B., "Expert systems for a class of
        mechanical design activity," *Proc. IFIP WG5.2 Working Conf. on
        Knowledge Engineering in Computer Aided Design,* IFIP, September
        1984.

[4]   Brown, D. and Chandrasekaran, B., *Design Problem Solving: Knowledge
        Structures and Control Strategies,* Morgan Kaufmann, San Mateo, CA,
        1989.

[5]   Chandrasekaran, B., "Design Problem Solving: A Task Analysis," *AI
        Magazine,* 1990.

[6]   Clancey, W., "Classification problem-solving," *AAAI,* August 1984.

[7]   De Kleer, J., "An assumption-based TMS," *Artificial Intelligence,*
        Vol. 28, No. 2, pp. 127-162, March 1986.

[8]   Dechter, R. and Pearl, J., "Network-based heuristics for constraint satisfaction problems," *Artificial Intelligence*, Vol. 34, pp. 1-38, 1988.

[9]   Dechter, R., "Enhancement Schemes for Constraint Processing: Backjumping, Learning, and Cutset Decomposition," *Artificial Intelligence*, Vol. 41, pp. 273-312, January 1990.

[10]   Feigenbaum, E. and Feldman, J., Ed., *Computers and Thought*, McGraw-Hill, New York, 1963.

[11]   Gero, J., Ed., *Preprints of the international round-table conference on modelling creativity and knowledge-based creative design*, University of Sydney, 1989.

[12]   Coyne, R., Rosenman, M., Radford, A., Balachandran, M., and Gero, J., *Knowledge-Based Design Systems*, Addison-Wesley, Reading, Mass., 1990.

[13]   Kelly, Kevin M., Steinberg, Louis I., and Weinrich, Timothy M., *Constraint Propagation in Design: Reducing the Cost*, unpublished working paper, March 1988, [Rutgers University Department of Computer Science AI/VLSI Project Working Paper No. 82].

[14]   Guha, R. and Lenat, D., "Cyc: A Mid-Term Report," *The AI Magazine*, Vol. 11, No. 3, pp. 32-59, Fall 1990.

[15]   Lowry, M. and McCartney, R., Ed., *Automated Software Design*, MIT Press, Cambridge, MA 02139, 1991.

[16]   Maher, M. L., "Engineering Design Synthesis: A Domain-Independent Approach," *Artificial Intelligence in Engineering, Manufacturing and Design*, Vol. 1, No. 3, pp. 207-213, 1988.

[17]   McCarthy, J. and Hayes, P., "Some philosophical problems from the standpoint of artificial intelligence," in *Readings in artificial intelligence*, Webber, B. and Nilsson, N., Ed., Morgan Kaufmann, Los Altos, CA., 1981.

[18]   Meyer, E., "Logic Synthesis Fine Tunes Abstract Design Descriptions," *Computer Design*, pp. 84-97, June 1 1990.

[19]   Mitchell, T. M. and Keller, R. M. and Kedar-Cabelli, S. T., "Explanation-Based Generalization: A Unifying View," *Machine Learning*, Vol. 1, No. 1, pp. 47-80, 1986.

[20]   Mittal, S. and Araya, A., "A Knowledge-based Framework for Design," *Proceedings AAAI86*, Vol. 2, Philadelphia, PA, pp. 856-865, June 1986.

[21]   Mostow, J., "Toward better models of the design process," *AI Magazine*, Vol. 6, No. 1, pp. 44-57, Spring 1985.

[22]   Mostow, J., "A Preliminary Report on DIOGENES: Progress towards Semi-automatic Design of Specialized Heuristic Search Algorithms," *Proceedings of the AAAI88 Workshop on Automated Software Design*, St. Paul, MN, August 1988.

[23]   Mostow, J., "Design by Derivational Analogy: Issues in the Automated Replay of Design Plans," *Artificial Intelligence*, Elsevier Science Publishers (North-Holland), Vol. 40, No. 1-3, pp. 119-184, September 1989.

[24]   Mostow, J., "Towards Automated Development of Specialized Algorithms for Design Synthesis: Knowledge Compilation as an Approach to Computer-Aided Design," *Research in Engineering Design*, Amherst, MA, Vol. 1, No. 3, 1989.

[25]   Nii, P., "The Blackboard Model of Problem Solving: Part I," *AI Magazine*, Vol. 7, No. 2, pp. 38-53, 1986.

[26]   Nilsson, N., *Principles of Artificial Intelligence (second edition)*, Morgan Kaufmann, 1984.

[27]   Ohr, S., *CAE: A Survey of Standards, Trends, and Tools*, John Wiley and Sons, 1990.

[28]   Pentland, A., "ThingWorld: A Multibody Simulation System with Low Computational Complexity," in *Computer-Aided Cooperative Product Development*, Sriram, D., Logcher, R., and Fukuda, S., Ed., Springer-Verlag , pp. 560-583, 1991.

[29]   Requicha, A. and Voelcker, H., "Solid Modeling: Current Status and Research Directions," *Solid Modeling: A Historial Summary and Contemporary Assesment*, pp. 9-24, March 1982.

[30]   Rich, C. and Waters, R. C., Eds., *Readings in Artificial Intelligence and Software Engineering*, Morgan Kaufmann, Los Altos, CA, 1986.

[31]   Rychener, M., Ed., *Expert Systems for Engineering Design*, Academic Press, Inc., Boston, 1988.

[32]   Setliff, D. and Rutenbar, R., "ELF: A Tool for Automatic Synthesis of Custom Physical CAD Software," *Proceedings of the Design Automation Conference*, IEEE, June 1989.

[33]   Sriram, D., Logcher, R., and Fukuda, S., Eds., *Computer-Aided Cooperative Product Development*, Springer Verlag, Inc., 1991.

[34]   Sriram, D., Cheong, K., and Kumar, M. L., "Engineering Design Cycle: A Case Study and Implications for CAE," in *Knowledge Aided Design*, Green, M., Ed., Academic Press, 1992.

[35] Steele, G., *The Definition and Implementation of a Computer Programming Language Based on Constraints,* unpublished Ph.D. Dissertation, Massachusetts Institute of Technology, August 1980.

[36] Stefik, M., "Planning and Meta-Planning (MOLGEN: Part 2)," *Artificial Intelligence 16:2,* pp. 141-169, May 1981.

[37] Stefik, M., "Planning with Constraints (MOLGEN: Part 1)," *Artificial Intelligence 16:2,* pp. 111-140, May 1981.

[38] Steinberg, L., Langrana, N., Mitchell, T., Mostow, J., Tong, C., *A Domain Independent Model of Knowledge-Based Design,* unpublished grant proposal, 1986, [AI/VLSI Project Working Paper No. 33, Rutgers University].

[39] Steinberg, L., "Dimensions for Categorizing Design Tasks," *AAAI Spring 1989 Symposium on AI and Manufacturing,* March 1989, [Available as Rutgers AI/Design Project Working Paper Number 127.].

[40] Steinberg, L. and Ling, R., *A Priori Knowledge of Structure vs. Constraint Propagation: One Fragment of a Science of Design,* unpublished Working paper, March 1990, [Rutgers AI/Design Group Working Paper 164].

[41] Suh, N., *The Principles of Engineering Design,* Oxford University Press, 200 Madison Ave., NY 10016, 1990.

[42] Sussman, G., *A Computer Model of Skill Acquisition,* American-Elsevier, New York, 1975.

[43] Tong, C., "Toward an Engineering Science of Knowledge-Based Design," *Artificial Intelligence in Engineering, special issue on AI in Engineering Design,* Vol. 2, No. 3, pp. 133-166, July 1987.

[44] Tong, C., "A Divide-and-Conquer Approach to Knowledge Compilation," in *Automating Software Design,* Lowry, M. and McCartney, R., Eds., AAAI Press, 1991.

[45] Wilensky, R., *Planning and Understanding,* Addison-Wesley, Mass., 1983.

[46] Williams, B, "Interaction-based Invention: Designing novel devices from first principles," *Proceedings of the Seventh National Conference on Artificial Intelligence (AAAI90),* Boston, MA, pp. 349-356, 1990.

[47] Winograd, T., *Understanding Natural Language,* Academic Press, New York, 1972.

PART I: REPRESENTATION: STRUCTURE, FUNCTION & CONSTRAINTS

Chapter 2
REPRESENTATION AND CONTROL FOR THE EVOLUTION OF VLSI DESIGNS: AN OBJECT-ORIENTED APPROACH (EXTENDED SUMMARY)

P. A. Subrahmanyam

Abstract

The information involved in the development of hardware (and software) designs is both vast and conceptually complex. This paper summarizes an object-based representation of the information needed to support design development processes. In this representation, attributes that are invariant under certain classes of design operations are identified and grouped into objects. The resulting structure allows different implementations to be simultaneously and compactly maintained; it also supports parameterized designs. Although we believe that the representation applies quite generally, the specific examples presented are concerned with the design of VLSI systems.

2.1. INTRODUCTION

The information involved in the development of VLSI designs (and more, generally, software and hardware designs) is both vast and conceptually complex. This paper summarizes an object-based representation for the information needed to support design development processes, while allowing for a mix of tools that span the spectrum from rule-based to algorithmic. Although we believe that the representation applies quite generally, the specific examples presented are concerned with the design of VLSI systems. In particular, the taxonomy and vocabulary of the representation is taken from the VLSI arena. We first present an overview of the representation in order to establish a context for the summary in Section 2.4.

Artificial Intelligence in Engineering Design
Volume I
Design Representation and Models of Routine Design

57

This chapter is a revised summary of 'Representation and Control for the Evolution of VLSI Designs,' by John D. Gabbe and P.A. Subrahmanyam, in *Artificial Intelligence in Engineering* (1987), 2, 4, pp. 204 – 223.

Design is the process of converting a set of functional (behavioral) and performance specifications for an artifact into an acceptable *realization* (or implementation). Transformation-based design converts the specifications into realizations through a series of incremental refinement steps, each of which produces a description of the artifact. The descriptions are called *versions*.

The versions may be arranged in a hierarchy, as shown in Figure 2-1. The *architectural* level determines the way in which the function or artifact is decomposed into subfunctions or parts (*modules*). The *environmental* level imposes additional specifications (such as technological characteristics or geometrical placement constraints) that restrict the implementation. For example, the environmental level may be used to specify that a standard cell layout must be used for a submodule that appears in several places in a design. The final *realization* level contains various (possibly partial) implementations (*e.g.*, mask layouts) of the modules and the constraints that they satisfy. Thus, each module, as shown in Figure 2-2, contains *decompositions*, which are associated with architectures; decompositions contain *contexts*, which are associated with environments; and contexts contain *refinements*, which are associated with realizations of the artifact.

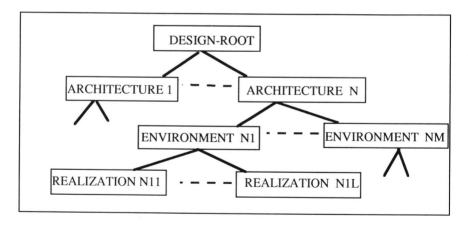

Figure 2-1: The Hierarchy of Versions of a Design

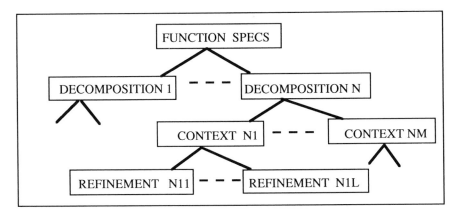

Figure 2-2: Components of a Module
(Versions of Designs are made of these Pieces)

Starting with the overall functional and performance specifications, the design process builds architectures (hierarchies of decompositions), environments (corresponding hierarchies of contexts), and realizations (corresponding hierarchies of refinements) that constitute acceptable implementations. In the object-oriented programming paradigm [6]adopted in this work, these hierarchies are made up of *objects*. Objects are data abstractions that contain both values and the operations that transform the values. The interface among objects is defined by the messages through which they communicate. Objects are created during the design process. Modules (and their component decompositions, contexts, and refinements) are created from defining objects -- *disembodied modules* and *module superclasses* -- that contain appropriate structures, operations, and default values. These defining structures and operations are part of the knowledge of the design domain (*e.g.,* VLSI design techniques) built into the representation.

To provide flexibility in the control of the design process, it is broken down into rather general tasks; and operations in the objects are specified in terms of these tasks. The selection of the *agent*, the procedure that executes the task, is the province of the *tasker*, which has at its disposal a control object (*controller*) for each task. The controller has access to the agents, to information about the agents and the state of the design, and to the user. This arrangement provides the opportunity for separately customizing and preserving control regimes; for maintaining, massaging, and analyzing information about the design process; and for dynamically manipulating the design process itself.

Design information is separated into three categories by the representation. The first category provides for the various aspects of artifact description; from functional specifications through architectural descriptions, circuits, and topological layouts to the details of masks; and assertions about design states, design goals, design history, etc. This *design-value* information is contained in the instances of the modules that make up artifacts. The second category provides the structures and default values for the modules and the various procedures that convert specifications to realizations (e.g., masks). The items (disembodied modules, module superclasses, and agents) in this category comprise the *domain knowledge*. The last category contains the procedures that decide which task to perform and which agent to designate to perform the selected task. This category, which comprises the *control knowledge*, contains the tasker and the controllers (one for each task).

In addition to providing a basic structure, it is essential for any useful representation to provide the ability to expand gracefully. Thus, the representation has been designed keeping in mind support for the acquisition of domain and control knowledge (*i.e.*, the long term development of a design methodology) as well as for the transformation-based design (and redesign) of artifacts. The first activity implies support for the abstraction of information during the design process (*e.g.*, the creation of disembodied modules); the modification of module superclasses; the tailoring, abstraction, and preservation of control regimes; the addition of agents during design; and the collection, analysis, and application of information regarding the design process. The second activity implies support for the maintenance and utilization of design histories as well as the entry, display, transformation, and storage of specifications and realizations.

2.1.1. Evolution of the Representation

The basic concepts underlying both the representation and its derivation do not depend on the language in which the objects are implemented. However, the computing environment that prevailed, Lisp machines with objects implemented both as flavors provided in Common Lisp [5] and as frames provided in the KEE[TM] system [4],[2] influenced some of the details of the representation. Another concern was our desire to support an interface to variants of formal methods and tools.

---

[2]KEE[TM] is a trademark of IntelliCorp.

Reference [3] enunciates the use of the invariance of attributes over design operations as a primary factor influencing representational considerations. The representation focuses primarily on the design development process itself, rather than the underlying artifact values, *i.e.*, the designed objects. Among other salient features of the current representation are its use of the object-based paradigm and associated inheritance mechanisms, and the attempt at modularizing the control involved in design. The module superclass hierarchy that allows design techniques to be inherited is similar in spirit to [2]. The representation supports design paradigms that are top-down, bottom-up, and combinations thereof ([1] and [7])

Section 2.2 describes the general design process, notes the role played by modules, and categories design information as specifications or results. Reference [3] elaborates on the motivation for the rather complex representation that has been constructed. This was done by evolving the representation rather than presenting it as a *fait accompli*. The evolution begins with the assumption of a one-pass, non-iterative design process and a correspondingly simple representation. An iterative design process is then considered, and the representation is expanded accordingly. As the design process is made more realistic, the representation evolves to keep pace. Issues of consistency, design history, and the propagation of specifications are also addressed. Changes in the representation are then introduced that allow a module to be used in more than one context. The next major expansion of the representation, provides means for dealing with more than one architecture for a module. Multiple architectures imply that the representation should also provide for parameterized modules. The resulting representation is summarized in Section 2.4.

2.2. MODULES AND DESIGN PHILOSOPHY

A *module* realizes a function. It is composed of other (typically simpler) modules or primitive modules. A *root module* is a module that is not contained in any other module. In the VLSI arena a module is composed of a network of other modules and/or primitives (*e.g.*, transistor, input-output pads, wires). Modules are represented by objects.

Figure 2-3.1(a) is a diagram of a root module, showing its composition structure. Every module in the example is regarded as being distinct, so the structure corresponds to the tree shown in Figure 2-3.1(b). When describing trees and (later) directed acyclic graphs, the usual meanings are ascribed to root, ancestor, parent, child, descendant, sibling, cousin, and leaf modules.

Two basic kinds of information arise in the process of design: *specifications*

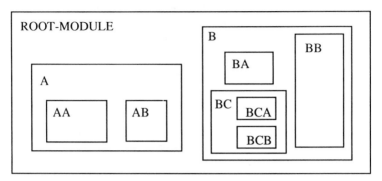

(a) Block Representation

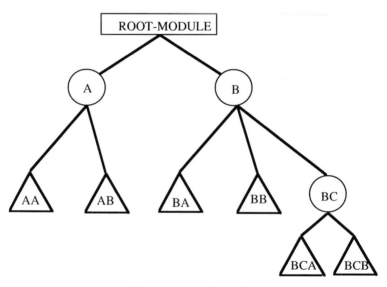

(b) Tree Representation

Figure 2-3: Example of a Root Module

and *results*. Specifications are the *input* to a particular step in the design process and results are the *output*. Some of the results of one step may be the specifications for another. Aside from identifying its children, a module contains explicit information only about itself and its parents, that is, about only two levels in the overall hierarchy. The representation is built by separating this information into categories that are associated with various operations in the design process. This is done by identifying the information that is invariant during different design steps.

The representation depends on the design philosophy as well as on the structure of artifacts of which Figure 2-3.1 is a simple example. While developing the representation, we begin with a top-down design paradigm. Later, to resolve the situation that arises when a design step cannot produce results that meet its specifications, we extend the design paradigm to allow iterations, *e.g.*, by introducing methods that attempt to negotiate new specifications by making local adjustments. (Some specifications, such as the external specification of the root module, may be considered non-negotiable.) More global changes come into play only if local adjustments are ineffective, or if experiments with different solutions seem desirable. The structure of the resulting representation is layered, with layers corresponding to information that is invariant over their substructures. It accords well with the structure of artifacts, stores information compactly, and is easily manipulated by the design process.

2.3. THE MODULE STRUCTURE: A SUMMARY

This section briefly summarizes the module structure, as well as some notational and representational issues. Motivations for these may be found in [3].

An artifact is composed of *modules*, that is, of subassemblies and parts. Viewed externally, a module is a named instance of a class of objects. It responds to messages and may also send messages. Internally, a module is a compound object, and many of the messages sent it will have to specify the substructure for which they are ultimately intended. The concept of a world allows much of this substructure identification to be done automatically.

The structure of a compound module object is shown in Figure 2-4. It is composed of a tree whose root is the module-kernel. *Module-kernels* hold the functional specifications for the module and certain performance and interface specifications. The second level of the tree contains one or more decompositions; the third level contains one or more contexts, and subsequent levels contain refinements.

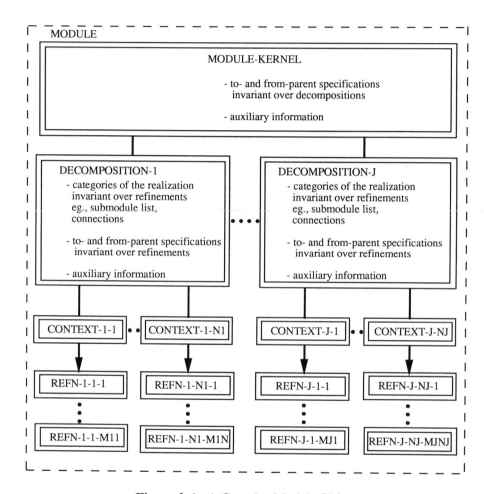

Figure 2-4: A Complex Module Object

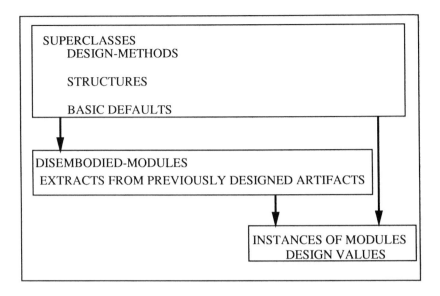

Figure 2-5: The Module-Classification Hierarchy

Decompositions are concerned with the division of a module into submodules and, ultimately, primitives. An instance of a module may have several decompositions (associated with different architectures). In addition to specifying a set of submodules that implements the module and the connections among them, the decomposition provides for specifying the to- and from-parent specifications associated with the architectural level. *Architectures* are closures of decompositions that have compatible to- and from-parent specifications.

Contexts are concerned with the environment in which a module will be used. A decomposition may have several contexts each of which specifies different sets of to- and from-parent specifications that all the subordinate refinements must meet. Contexts include provision for the coordination of from-parent specifications from multiple parents, and thus allow for replication (*i.e.*, the use of a refinement in more than one parent module). *Environments* are closures of contexts that belong to the same architecture and have compatible to- and from-parent specifications. Thus each context must also provide for the specification of the parent and child contexts in the environmental hierarchy.

Refinements are concerned with the realization of a module. A refinement contains an implementation (*e.g.*, floorplan, layout) and the realization-dependent to- and from-parent interface specifications associated with it. A context may have many refinements, proposing different (possibly incomplete) implementations for the module. The to- and from-parent interface specifications of a refinement apply to specific refinements in the same environment. A *realization* of an artifact is composed of a set of consistent refinements (*i.e.*, one for every context in the environment). A set of refinements is consistent when their to- and from-parent interface specifications are compatible.

A realization contains the values generated by the design process when it attempts to satisfy a particular set of interface specifications. Protection categories in the representation provide for transactionalizing the design process. Narrowly applied, this allows design steps to be aborted, more broadly applied it allows modules to be designed concurrently. The history categories provide data that can be used to prevent the repetition of unsuccessful design paths in the current design, and unsuccessful design strategies in general.

The design process, which creates module-kernels, decompositions, contexts and refinements, is concerned with resolving conflicts (both obvious and subtle) among their to- and from-parent specifications. This conflict resolution may lead to the creation of additional module-kernels, decompositions, and contexts before producing those refinements that constitute the end product of a successful design process.

2.4. AN OBJECT-ORIENTED REPRESENTATION: A SUMMARY

Reference [3] examined the general design problem with particular emphasis on the development of a representation for the evolution of custom VLSI designs. A number of orthogonal perspectives associated with the design problem were considered, that we briefly recapitulate below:

- Nonprimitive circuit functions are decomposed into subfunctions, which may be in turn decomposed. The functions correspond to modules in the hardware implementation. Modules are related through a directed acyclic graph that specifies the inclusion of modules within other modules.

- The design process is partitioned into transactions. Each transaction represents a major step (*e.g.*, floorplan, layout) in the design of a module. The design philosophy is similar to that of CADRE [1]. That is: design specifications come from the parents and children of the module; the children are not designed in the transaction; if the specifications cannot be met, they are negotiated with the parent;

ancestor modules may have to be redesigned to arrive at mutually satisfactory sets of specifications; and previously designed children of redesigned ancestors may have to be reworked. The purpose of transactionalizing the design process is to allow modules to be designed concurrently, and to maintain the integrity of the data base when errors or a user decision terminate a design step.

• Transactions are partitioned into tasks. Tasks are design operations, and there may be more than one way of performing a task.

• Tasks are performed by agents. There are two kinds of agents: design agents carry out the actual design operations; control agents (meta-agents) select the appropriate design agents. The selection of the appropriate agent depends on the state of the design process, the details of the specifications, and the goals of the user.

• Each task is associated with a controller. Configuring the controllers allows the design process to be customized.

• Modules are composed of a module-kernel, decompositions, contexts, and refinements. This partitioning uses the principle of collecting together attributes that are invariant under a class of design operations.

  • A module-kernel (1) contains the (decomposition independent) module behavior, which specifies the relation between the inputs and outputs, and (2) identifies the inferior decompositions (i.e., the existing set of decompositions for the module).

  • A decomposition delineates a particular implementation of the module in terms of elements (child modules) and the relations (connections) among them, contains the architectural constraints associated with the decomposition, and identifies the inferior contexts. A set (graph) of compatible decompositions constitutes an architecture. Thus decompositions allow for different architectures for a module.

  • A context specifies a set of constraints that apply to all the inferior refinements. A set (graph) of compatible contexts constitute an environment. Different (sets of) contexts may specify different replications (of modules) that are to be used when implementing an architecture; thus contexts allow a particular refinement to be incorporated into many parts of a realization. A context provide for merging constraints collectively imposed on the module by its parents, and identifies the refinements that depend upon it.

- A refinement contains the details of a proposed implementation at the level of the module as well as to- and from-parent constraints imposed on the implementation. Successive refinements represent successive proposed (possibly partial) solutions to the design problem. The details of a proposed implementation may depend (through the constraints) on particular proposed implementations for the parents and children. Thus a refinement must be associated with the parent and child refinements with which it is consistent. Consistent sets of refinements (one for each context in the environment) comprise a realization of the artifact.

- Disembodied modules contain module-kernels, decompositions, contexts, and refinements that have been stripped of the information that associates them with a particular artifact. These collections of specifications and (partial) implementations form a pool of knowledge that can be inherited to serve as a starting point for the design process.

- Module superclasses provide a hierarchy of structures and defaults from which modules may be constructed, and supply design strategies in the form of methods that initiate design tasks.

- Design knowledge is decomposed into three categories, which are stored separately. The domain knowledge contains the module-superclass hierarchy, disembodied modules, and the agents that carry out design operations. The artifact values contains the instance modules that specify the architectures, environments, and realizations of particular designs, the goals that they fulfill, and their development history. Control knowledge contains the task control knowledge that guides the design process by selecting particular agents (or meta-agents) to accomplish various design tasks.

An outcome of these considerations has been the development of an object-base representation of information that supports general transformation-based incremental design paradigm; is modular, compact, flexible, transparent, and uniform; provides for separation of categories of knowledge, modification of design strategy and classification structure, customization of control; and contains facilities on which to base redesign, planning, and learning. An initial version of the representation has been implemented in Common Lisp and KEE (a frame-based object-oriented expert-system shell), and interfaced to tools that include a leaf cell layout program, and a floorplanner. It is intended for use in experimental VLSI design tools that are simultaneously evolving.

2.5. ACKNOWLEDGMENTS

This paper is a summary of the paper that appeared under the title "An Object-Based Representation for the Evolution of VLSI Designs" in *Artificial Intelligence in Engineering*,(4), pp. 204-223, 1987. For copyright reasons, it could not be reproduced here.

We would like to thank Bryan Ackland, Allen Ginsberg and Chris Tong for helpful feedback on an earlier version of this paper, as well as D. Sriram for his patience.

2.6. BIBLIOGRAPHY

[1]   Ackland, B., Dickenson, A., Ensor, R., Gabbe, J., Kollaritsch, P., London, T., Poirer, C., Subrahmanyam, P., and Watanabe, H., "CADRE: A system of cooperating VLSI design experts," *1985 IEEE International Conference on Computer Design: VLSI in Computers*, IEEE, pp. 99-104, October 1985.

[2]   Brown, H., Tong, C. and Foyster, G., "Palladio: An exploratory environment for circuit design," *IEEE Computer Magazine*, pp. 41-56, December 1983.

[3]   Gabbe, J. and Subrahmanyam, "An Object-Based Representation for the Evolution of VLSI Designs," *International Journal for Artificial Intelligence in Engineering*, Vol. 2, No. 4, pp. 204-223, 1987.

[4]   IntelliCorp, "KEE Version 3.0 Software Manuals," 1986.

[5]   Steele, G. L., *Common Lisp - The Language*, Digital Press, 1987.

[6]   Stefik, M. and Bobrow, D., "Object-oriented programming: themes and variations," *AI Magazine*, Vol. 6, No. 4, pp. 40-62, Winter 1986.

[7]   Subrahmanyam, P. A., "SYNAPSE: An Expert System for VLSI Design," *IEEE Computer*, Vol. 19, No. 7, pp. 78-89, July 1986.

Chapter 3
TOOLS AND TECHNIQUES
FOR CONCEPTUAL DESIGN

David Serrano and David Gossard

ABSTRACT

Engineering design is constraint-oriented; much of the design process involves the recognition, formulation and satisfaction of constraints. Constraints are continually being added, deleted and modified throughout the development of a new device. Of particular interest are the constraints that relate to a design's performance (i.e., function), physical laws it must obey (i.e., physics) and to its geometrical and topological properties (i.e., form). The management of these constraints throughout the evolving design is a non-trivial task and existing computational tools are not adequate.

Effective tools for constraint management will be of great importance in knowledge-based systems for conceptual design. They will provide designers with assistance during the early stages of design and will help close the gap between novice and experienced designers.

This paper presents a graph-theoretical approach to constraint management. Constraint networks are represented as directed graphs, where nodes represent parameters and arcs represent constraint relationships. Parameter dependencies are generated automatically. Techniques are presented for the evaluation of constraint networks, the detection of over- and under-constrained systems of constraints, as well as the identification and correction of redundant and conflicting constraints.

The constraint management techniques were implemented in The Concept Modeler, a system for conceptual design. The Concept Modeler allows the designer to interactively construct models of a design using iconic abstractions of common machine elements.

Artificial Intelligence in Engineering Design
Volume I
Design Representation and Models of Routine Design

3.1. INTRODUCTION

Design is constraint-oriented; much of the design process involves the recognition, formulation and satisfaction of constraints. There are many sources of constraints ranging from "soft" constraints imposed by aesthetic or economic considerations to "hard" constraints imposed by physical laws. Of particular interest are constraints that relate to a design's performance (i.e., function), physical laws it must obey (i.e., physics) and to its geometrical and topological properties (i.e., form).

Constraints are continually being added, deleted and modified throughout the development of a new product. Design begins with a functional specification of the desired product: a description of properties and conditions that the product should satisfy (i.e. constraints). The original set of functional requirements are augmented, changed and/or refined as the design solution evolves. The resulting constraint set may contain conflicting and/or unrealizable requirements.

The management of these constraints throughout the evolving design is a non-trivial task. The constraints are often numerous, complex and contradictory. Particularly in more complex designs where form, function and physics interact strongly, it is difficult to keep track of all relevant constraints and parameters, and to understand the basic design relationships and tradeoffs.

Effective tools for constraint management will be of great importance in knowledge-based system for conceptual design. They will provide designers with assistance during the early stages of design. In addition, they will help close the gap between novice designers and experienced designers.

This paper presents a framework for a highly-automated conceptual design system and requisite techniques for constraint management. These computational methods have proven to be very effective for the management and visual feedback of constraints during design. The following sections will present an overview on previous work on constraints highlighting the requirements for a constraint manager for design, and then present the framework for a constraint manager in the context of a constraint-based system for conceptual design.

3.2. RELATED WORK ON CONSTRAINTS

One of the first attempts to manage constraints for automation of computation in engineering applications was the work done by Harary [15] and Steward [30, 31]. Their primary concern was the partitioning (i.e., "tearing") of large systems of equations to reduce computational effort. They assumed the systems of equations were self-consistent and did not consider inequalities. Friedman and Leondes [9], [10, 11] provide a mathematical basis for a constraint theory. Other work followed in the area of chemical process design. Soylemez [26], Sutherland [33], Steele [27], deKleer and Sussman [6], Borning [3], among others, describe computational implementations in domains of geometry, computation, electronics and simulation. Stefik's MOLGEN system was developed to aid in the design of molecular genetic experiments [28]. MOLGEN is a hierarchical planner; it propagates constraints arising at different levels of planning abstraction to generate plans for gene-splicing experiments. MOLGEN also meta-plans, i.e., it reasons about its own reasoning plan.

A substantial amount of work has dealt exclusively with geometric constraints. Sutherland [33] was one of the first to use a system of constraint equations to compute changes in geometry corresponding to changes in a set of dimensional parameters. Light [18, 19] used row and column operations on the jacobian of the constraint equations to detect overconstrained and underconstrained dimensioning schemes. Given a dimensional change, Lin's method [20] attempted to reduce computation by segmenting the system of constraints into two groups; one group contained those constraints affected by a dimensional change and the second containing the remaining constraints. He accomplished this by two different methods: one an extension of Light's approach, which used the jacobian to determine the sensitive constraints in an iterative fashion; and the second, a constraint propagation approach which found constraints sensitive to a dimensional change. Since the main objective of Lin's work was to reduce computation, the issue of maintaining consistency by detecting redundancies and conflicts was not addressed. Chyz [5] proposed a 2D constraint manager for geometric constraints. His constraint manager would make use of the structure of a limited number of geometric constraints in order to resolve conflicts and maintain consistency in the system; it therefore lacked the generality required in a general constraint manager for design.

Chang [4] and Pabon [21] dealt with the problem of re-design, i.e., modifying an existing design to meet new requirements by reevaluating its constraint relationships. Using standard optimization techniques, their systems could handle inequalities, and cases in which there were more unknowns than constraints. Garret [13] focussed on the problem of selecting selecting applicable constraints to a design situation, using a rule-based approach. Once the set of applicable constraints was selected, he used numerical optimization techniques to solve the constraints. The systems lacked facilities for modifying the causality of constraint relationships or determining the existence of a solution space (i.e., identifying problems with a null solution space).

Gosling [14] and Holtz [16] developed constraint-based systems based on symbolic algebraic manipulations. Gosling's system, MAGRITTE, was an an editor for line drawings and his treatment of constraints was similar to that presented by Steele. Holtz developed a system called CONMAN, which included inequality constraints as well as equalities and was capable of performing interval arithmetic. The system provided no interactive facilities nor means for design iteration; its primary function was to evaluate and check designs using standard design codes. No work was reported on identifying redundant or conflicting constraints.

In all of these systems, it was not possible to change the geometry and evaluate the resulting change in dimensional parameters (i.e., to reverse the causality of the constraint equations). Serrano [23, 24, 25] developed a system called MATHPAK for preliminary design which included non-geometrical "engineering" constraints as well as geometric constraints. Serrano's MATHPAK allowed the user to reverse causality in the constraint relationships. Gallagher's system [12] and a commercial system developed by Steinke [29] are based on the MATHPAK concept. This past work made clear the need for efficient constraint management methods in more advanced design tools, and identified some of the more important functions of a general constraint manager.

3.3. CONSTRAINT MANAGEMENT FUNCTIONS IN CONCEPTUAL DESIGN

The key features of the constraint manager include: consistency (detection of conflicts and redundancies), completeness (identification of missing information, i.e., unconstrained degrees of freedom), efficient evaluation of the constraint networks (selection of applicable sets of constraints for evaluation), and providing guidance and support for the decision-making process (qualitative analysis). The next sections present the graph-based representation for constraints as well as constraint networks. The major advantages of such a representation are: it is a very general domain independent representation; and it allows both qualitative and quantitative operations. An additional advantage of choosing a graph representation is that it has allowed us to draw upon a number of existing graph-theoretic algorithms.

A constraint manager with the above functionality is the foundation of a knowledge-based system for conceptual design currently being developed by the authors. A typical display from the system is shown in Figure 3-1. The system provides the user with a menu of predefined concept models of common mechanical engineering components. The components of the system may be added to the database as needed and may include power sources (e.g. electric motors, internal combustion engines, hydraulic motors), power transmission elements (e.g. gears, belts, chains, ropes) and other basic machine elements (e.g. springs, dampers, shafts, bearings, couplings).

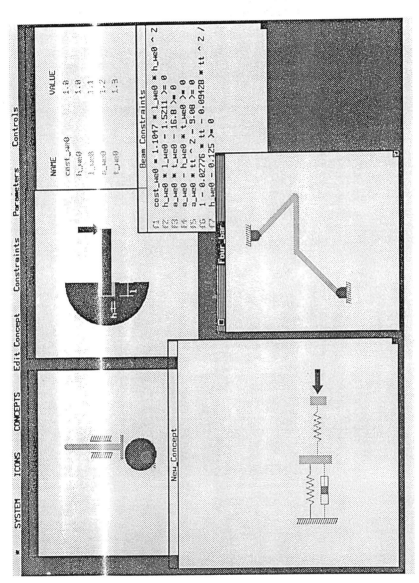

Figure 3-1: Sample Screen for Concept Modeller

Adapted from 'Constraint Management in Conceptual Design,' by David Serrano, © 1987 Massachusetts Institute of Technology.

Each model is an object with the following properties: a set of constraints which predict its performance, establish its physical limits, and define its topological (connectivity) restrictions. In addition each object has an iconic representation for user interaction.The user can interactively select individual components from the menu, and then specify the connectivity and the causality among these components in the resulting aggregate "concept model." The system creates the aggregate model by fusing the individual models. It evaluates the aggregate model given the known parameters and identifies redundant or conflicting constraints. Concepts may be stored and retrieved, and may be used as components in higher-level concepts.

This finite set of common machine elements restricts the scope of the system so as to be manageable, yet retains the essential characteristics of the generic design process. While the individual machine elements are well understood, they offer the possibility for interesting combinations, and they may be used in a variety of conceptual design situations.

Section 3.4 presents the general definitions of the graph representation. Terminology will be defined as needed and simple examples will be used to demonstrate the key issues. Section 3.5 discusses the representation of constraint networks. Evaluation of these constraint networks is described in Section 3.6. Detection of redundant constraints and conflict resolution are addressed in Section 3.7. Section 3.8 illustrates this strategy on a cantilever beam example. The integration of the constraint manager in a MCAE system is described in Section 3.9.

3.4. GRAPH THEORY TERMINOLOGY

A brief introduction to the terminology used in the paper follows. For more details see [8, 17, 22].

A directed graph (digraph) is the ordered pair $D = \{ V, E \}$, where V is a non-empty set of nodes (points, vertices) and E is a set of ordered pairs, which are called arcs (also known as edges, lines, or pointers). Directed graphs are also called networks. If certain members of E can be placed in the sequence $P=\{(v_1,v_2),(v_2,v_3),....,(v_{n-1},v_n)\}$, then the set P is a path from v_1 to v_n in D. For example, $P=\{(a,b)(b,c)(c,d)\}$ is a path in Figure 3-2.

A node is said to be reachable from another node if their exists a path from the second to the first. A path becomes a cycle when the starting node and the last node correspond to the same node. The path P is a cycle if v_1 and v_n are the same. The nodes on a cycle are mutually accessible (reachable) in the sense that there exists a path from every node in the cycle to any other node in the cycle.

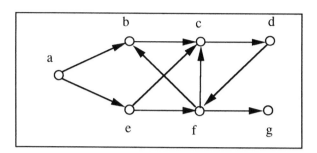

Figure 3-2: A Directed Graph

Adapted from 'Constraint Management in Conceptual Design,'
by David Serrano, © 1987 Massachusetts Institute of Technology.

The nodes of a graph may be partitioned into sets called strongly connected components. A strongly connected component of a digraph is a maximal strongly connected subgraph. Strongly connected components in a digraph have the property that all nodes within a strong component are mutually accessible, but not all nodes belonging to different strong components are mutually accessible. Nodes that are not part of a cycle are strong components because they satisfy the definition as well. A formal definition follows [2]:

- *Definition 1:* A digraph is strongly connected if every node in the digraph is reachable from every other node in the digraph.

- *Definition 2:* Subdigraph $D' = \{ X, (X \, 4 \, X) \, G \, E'\}$ of $D = \{ V, E \}$ is a strongly connected component (strong component) of D if it is strongly connected and there exists no pair of nodes $a \in X, b \notin X$ such that a and b lie on the same cycle, where X is a nonempty proper subset of V and E is the set of edges in D.

The paths $P_1=\{(c,d)(d,f)(f,c)\}$ and $P_2=\{(b,c)(c,d)(d,f)(f,b)\}$ shown in Figure 3-2 are cycles; P_2 is a strong component as well. It is maximal because it contains both P_1 and P_2. The node a is a strong component by Definition 2; because it is possible to go from $S_1 = \{a\}$ to $S_2 = \{ b,c,d,f \}$ but not from S_2 to S_1, each is a distinct strong component of the digraph.

Directed graphs with no directed cycles are called directed acyclic graphs (DAGs). A tree is a special case of a digraph; trees are acyclic graphs in which exactly one node has indegree of zero and every other node has indegree of one. The indegree of a node is defined as the number of arcs entering the node. The node with indegree of zero is the root of the tree and nodes with zero outdegree are terminal nodes (the "leaves" of the tree). The outdegree of a node is defined as the number of arcs leaving the node. Node x is the root for the tree in Figure 3-3. Nodes **t, u, v,** and **w** are the terminal nodes for the tree. Forests are sets of trees.

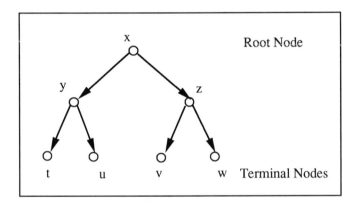

Figure 3-3: Tree (Directed Acyclic Graph)

Adapted from 'Constraint Management in Conceptual Design,'
by David Serrano, © 1987 Massachusetts Institute of Technology.

A bipartitle graph is a graph $D = \{V, E\}$ which has its set of nodes V as the union of two subsets B and C such that $B \cap C = \Phi$ and E is a set of arcs such that every member of E has one element in B and the other in C. Bipartite graphs are useful in constraint management and will be used as an auxiliary aid to transform the undirected graphs into directed graphs. Figure 3-4 shows a bipartite graph, where **V** =**B** ∪ **C** = **{a,b,c}** ∪ **{f1,f2,f3}** and **E** = **{(a,f1)(a,f2)(b,f3)(c,f1)(c,f3)}**

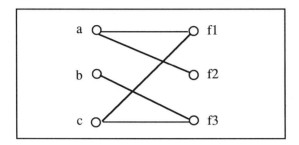

Figure 3-4: Bipartite Graph

Adapted from 'Constraint Management in Conceptual Design,'
by David Serrano, © 1987 Massachusetts Institute of Technology.

3.5. CONSTRAINT NETWORK REPRESENTATION

A constraint, as defined previously, is a relation among several objects stating something that should be true among them. This broad definition allows constraints to take on a large number of forms. The constraints of interest in this article are equalities, inequalities, and functions or procedures. The following are valid constraints:

```
x2 + y2 - c2 = 0  (f1)
3x + y < 0        (f2)
g = F( x y z)     (f3)
```

where (f1) and (f2) are equality and inequality constraints respectively; in general, these constraints may be any nonlinear algebraic expression. (f3)

represents a constraint which is defined in terms of a lisp function, or a procedure in any language. The scope of our implementation was limited to these
three basic types of relationships, but the theory applies to other representations.
For example, if the constraints were differential or integral relations, they can be
included as well in the graph representation. Functional constraint (f3) was
selected to demonstrate the generality of the approach. A constraint may also
have multiple inputs and multiple outputs (MIMO), such as those found in
database queries. As an example, consider the case where, in (f3), $g = S_0 = \{ a_1,$
..., $a_n\}$; S_0 is a set of n parameters which depend on the set $S_i = \{ x, y, z \}$. S_i is
the input set and S_0 is the output set for the constraint. An example of this may
be the selection of a standard component from a database, which is chosen given
a set of parameters S_i and that its description is given by the set S_0. The treatment of MIMO constraints is analogous to that of the supernodes discussed in
Section 3.6.2. The graph representation is general and productions can be encoded as a graph structure. In the graph representation, the actual functional
relationship among the parameters in a constraint is not explicitly represented.
However, the fact that they are related or "connected" by the constraint depicts
this relationship abstractly. For example, (f1), (f2), and (f3) may be represented
as in Figure 3-5 [(a),(b) and (c), respectively]. The nodes represent the
parameters and the arcs (or edges) represent the existence of a constraint between the parameters. The arcs are labeled according to the constraint.

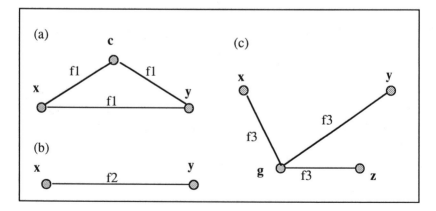

Figure 3-5: Graph Representation for Constraints (f1),(f2) and (f3)

Adapted from 'Constraint Management in Conceptual Design,'
by David Serrano, © 1987 Massachusetts Institute of Technology.

A set of constraints may form a network relating a larger set of parameters. If the parameters **x**, **y** and **z** are common to (f1),(f2) and (f3) then the constraint set may be represented as a network, as shown in Figure 3-6. The nodes and the arcs retain their original meaning. A constraint network is therefore a declarative structure which expresses the existence of relations among the parameters of more than one constraint. The declarative structure, such as that in Figure 3-6, is an undirected graph (because its edges have no direction associated to them). This implies that information may flow or propagate in either direction. Therefore, a single representation may be used to solve a large number of problems depending on the desired flow of information.

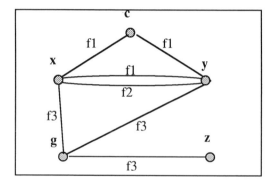

Figure 3-6: Network Graph Representation for a Constraint Set

Adapted from 'Constraint Management in Conceptual Design,' by David Serrano, © 1987 Massachusetts Institute of Technology.

A particular problem is defined by selecting a set of parameters with known values { K } and a set of parameters with unknown values { U }. The set of parameters with known values may be thought of as the inputs to the system and the set of parameters with unknown values as the desired outputs from the system (Figure 3-7). The status of a parameter is defined by its membership in one of these two sets. Therefore a parameter may have a status of known or unknown depending on whether it is given or it is to be computed. By defining and redefining the status of the parameters, various aspects of a given design situation may be studied, with a minimum of data manipulation from the user.

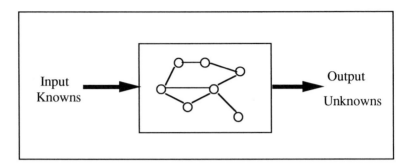

Figure 3-7: Defining a Problem using a Constraint Network

Adapted from 'Constraint Management in Conceptual Design,'
by David Serrano, © 1987 Massachusetts Institute of Technology.

3.5.1. Causality and Dependency

Initially the constraint network or graph is undirected, that is, information is
allowed to flow in any direction. In order to obtain a particular solution from
the constraint network, the user specifies the input parameters { K } and the output parameters { U }. This choice of inputs and outputs converts the network
into a directed graph. The direction of the flow of information is known as the
causality of the constraint network. For example, suppose x is a member of { K
}, y is a member of { U }, and they are related by a constraint. If changing the
value of x causes that of y to change, the causality is directed from x to y. The
dependency relationship is the inverse of the causality relationship, therefore it
may be said that y "depends on" x, and the dependency is directed from y to x.
Throughout the paper only the dependency notation will be used, unless stated
otherwise. Therefore, a directed arc will denote "depends on" and is read from
tail to head; for example "y ---> x", is read "y depends on x."

3.5.2. Representing Constraint Networks as Directed Graphs

Before we can check for consistency or evaluate a constraint network, we must determine the interdependencies among the various parameters. The dependencies establish the flow of information, and allow us to detect abnormalities in the topology of the network. Existing rule-based systems generally require that the dependency information be coded as part of the rules, requiring the user to figure them out beforehand. The method that follows generates the dependency information automatically. Once the status of the parameters is defined, the dependency relationships can be determined (as well as the causality). This requires an assignment or matching of every unknown parameter to a constraint. This assignment is the key to the automatic dependency generation, which is required for constraint propagation and constraint management.

A bipartite graph $G=\{V,E\}$ is constructed from a constraint set where $V = N \cup F$ is the set of vertices. $N = \{ n_1,...,n_p \}$ is a set of p nodes (which correspond to the parameters which have been defined as unknowns), and $F = \{ f_1, ..., f_r \}$ is the set of r edges (which correspond to the constraints). E is the bipartite edge set wherein no member of N is connected to another member of N and no member of F is connected to another member of F. The set of edges $E = \{ e_1,...., e_k \}$ connect the elements of N with those of F. Therefore each edge $e_i = (n_l\ f_j)$ in E corresponds to a node (variable) in the original network and a corresponding edge leaving it. In other words, the edges in the bipartite graph indicate which unknown parameters are present in each constraint; therefore constraints are not directly related among themselves and cannot be connected in a bipartite representation. Similarly, the unknown parameters are not directly connected among themselves but through the constraints.

Given the above representation, we would like to find a maximum matching between the elements of N and those of F, subject to E; that is, find the largest subset of E with the property that no two pairs have the same n or f in common. A maximum matching is complete when its cardinality (number of matchings) equals $|N| = |F|$, where $|N|$ is the number of nodes in the parameter set and $|F|$ is the number of nodes in the constraint set of the bipartite graph. For example, consider the simple network consisting of constraints (f1),(f2) and (f3) and the parameters $\{c,g,x,y,z\}$. If the system status were defined such that $U = \{c,g,y\}$ and $K = \{x,z\}$, then we can construct the bipartite graph in Figure 3-8 a. The assignment is created in such a way that a maximum number of connections is made between the sets N and F. In this example, the maximum number of matchings is three and the resulting assignments are shown in Figure 3-8 b as the bold lines. The dotted lines indicate the assignments which were not used. Once the assignments are made, we can apply the results to the original network; all nodes which have been defined as knowns are shown as squares, while those nodes defined as unknowns are represented as circles, and only those edges incident on their assigned node are kept. For example, both **f1** and **f2** are incident on node **y** (see Figure 3-6) before the matching; after the matching **y** is assigned to f2. Hence the edge f1 is removed (Figure 3-8 b), and only the edge corresponding to the assigned constraint f2 is used. In general, only those edges which connect their assigned node to another node are kept. The directions on the arcs are assigned using the following rule: nodes defined as unknowns have the arcs labeled with the matched constraint, with the arrow pointing away from the node. For example, in Figure 3-8 b, **g** was matched to **f3** therefore the arrows on **f3** point away from **g**. Similarly **y** was matched to **f2**; therefore the arrow on **f2** is away from **y**. Using this rule, all knowns (terminal nodes) have all edges incident on them with the arrow pointing at the node. This assignment makes sense, because the direction of the arrow was defined to read "depends on." Therefore no known quantities (terminal nodes) have any dependencies, and all other nodes adjacent to the terminal nodes depend on them.

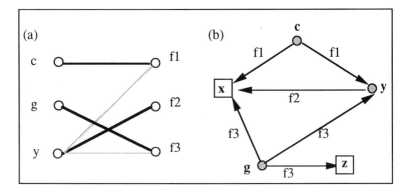

Figure 3-8: Bipartite Matching and Directed Graph

Adapted from 'Constraint Management in Conceptual Design,'
by David Serrano, © 1987 Massachusetts Institute of Technology.

Consider a different status for the same simple network of Figure 3-6. Let **U** = {**g,x,y**} and **K** = {**c,z**}. The bipartite matchings are shown in Figure 3-9 (a, c). Notice that there exists more than one possible solution to the assignment problem, a situation which is generally true except in the most trivial cases.

Therefore the matchings are not unique; if the system is consistent, it does not matter which set of assignments is chosen because the final result will be the same. In cases where the constraint network is not consistent or complete, the matching process may be used to identify redundant and conflicting constraints, as well as unspecified parameters required in order to solve the problem. In particular, when the constraint network contains inequalities, the results from the matching can be used to generate multiple feasible solutions. Another feature that shows up in the resulting directed graph is the presence of cycles, e.g., **x** depends on **y** which in turn depends on **x**. The next section is dedicated to the evaluation of constraint networks and some more examples.

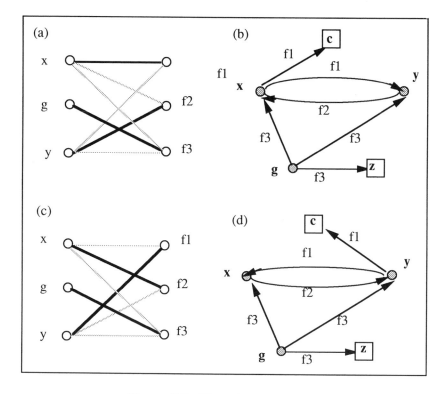

Figure 3-9: Nonunique Matchings

Adapted from 'Constraint Management in Conceptual Design,'
by David Serrano, © 1987 Massachusetts Institute of Technology.

The matching problem (or the marriage problem as it is also known) seems straightforward at first but subtleties quickly become apparent [1, 2, 6]. Algorithms which solve the problem can be considered as an application of the concept of augmentation used in the solution of network flow problems. However, in the case of matching, detecting and performing augmentations efficiently can become extremely subtle. There are, in general, too many pairings to try all possibilities, and the solution algorithm must be carefully designed to try as few possibilities as possible. The problem has been studied extensively [1, 7, 8, 17] and a number of solution techniques exist. The majority are network flow techniques, either heuristic (Ford-Fulkerson) or based on optimization techniques such as linear programming. The matching problem is conceptually simple and the details are described in the literature [1, 7, 8, 17, 25]. In order to avoid distractions in the discussion, we have presented only the basic ideas of the matching process and its use in generating parameter dependencies.

3.6. CONSTRAINT NETWORK EVALUATION

After matching, the resulting network is a tree-like structure which may or may not have cycles. For many applications involving directed graphs, cyclic subgraphs do arise. Areas in which directed graphs appear naturally include manufacturing process planning, general problem solving strategies, design and causal reasoning. These are areas in which plans are sought and events are sorted based on their interdependencies. In some cases, cyclic behavior is not allowed, while in other situations there is a physical explanation for the phenomenon. For example, if a graph modeled a manufacturing line, a cycle would be inconsistent and therefore is not allowed. In an analytic constraint network, a cycle represents a set of parameters (specified by the nodes on the path) which are coupled and must be solved simultaneously. Therefore they must be allowed. The presence of cycles cause problems in local constraint propagation and the use of backtracking techniques during the solution process does not solve the constraint propagation problem when the cycles are inherent to the behavior of the system being modelled by the constraint. The strategy is to locate the cycles before any propagation is attempted and then collapse them into a supernode, rendering the network acyclic. For constraint propagation and many other applications, such as manufacturing, directed graphs with no directed cycles are called for. Such graphs are called directed acyclic graphs (DAGs).

This section presents the details of the evaluation process for constraint networks. The first subsection presents the traversal techniques used on directed graphs. The second subsection discusses the process of rendering a cyclic graph acyclic by identifying strong components and collapsing them into supernodes. The third subsection presents how the evaluation plan is generated given the acyclic digraph, and the fourth subsection presents how the digraph can be used to perform a sensitivity analysis on a constraint network. Finally the last section presents some special cases and limitations of the evaluation procedure.

3.6.1. Topological Sorts on DAGs

Although graphs, DAGs behave very much like trees. Their special structure may be used efficiently in their processing. Viewed from any vertex, a DAG looks like a tree in the sense that the depth-first search forest for a DAG has no return edges to a visited node (cycles). A fundamental operation on DAGS is to process the vertices of the graph in such an order that no vertex is processed before any vertex that points to it is processed. This operation is called topological sorting. The sorting may be based on either a depth-first search or a breadth-first search. In general, the vertex order produced by a topological sort is not unique. The nonuniqueness is because one task or event may have no direct or indirect dependence on another and can be processed in any order. Figure 3-10 shows a typical directed acyclic graph, for which two valid topological orderings may be: (i) Topological ordering based on a depth-first search: **b-a-d-c-g-f-e**, and **b-g-f-e-d-c-a**, (ii) Reverse topological ordering based on a breadth-first search: **e-f-g-c-a-d-b** and **e-f-c-g-a-d-b**.

It is useful to find an ordering with the property that every term (assigned to a constraint) is defined (evaluated) before it is used in any other definition. This particular ordering corresponds to an inverse topological sort. Performing a reverse topological sort on a graph is equivalent to performing a topological sort on a graph obtained by reversing all the edges. For example e-f-g-c-a-d-b, is obtained by performing a breadth-first search in the DAG of Figure 3-10, as follows: start with node **b**, expand its dependents in a breadth first fashion **a-d-g**, expand a (no dependents-nil), expand **d**: a-c-g, expand **g**: f. Expand the descendents of the next level (i.e. **c** and **f**) , expand c (no dependents-nil), expand f: e. Expand e (no dependents-nil). Thus we have visited: **b-a-d-g-nil-a-c-g-nil-f-e-nil**; reverse the order and remove repeated elements: **e-f-g-c-a-d-b**. This ordering will be used in determining the solution sequence for a constraint network.

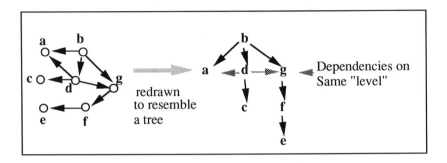

Figure 3-10: Directed Acyclic Graph

Adapted from 'Constraint Management in Conceptual Design,'
by David Serrano, © 1987 Massachusetts Institute of Technology.

3.6.2. Cycles and Strong Components

Constraint networks may have cycles imbedded within, as mentioned previously. This section describes how to detect cycles and what is done with them when they are detected. A graph contains a directed cycle if we can get from a node back to itself by following edges in the indicated direction. A graph containing a cycle cannot be topologically sorted. It was mentioned previously that in some applications, cycles indicate inconsistencies (e.g., in the manufacturing process line), but in others (e.g., in constraint networks and causal networks), they imply that a subset of the constraints need to be solved simultaneously or that a subset of the events happen in parallel with certain level of interaction. In order to process a constraint network, it is necessary to eliminate the cyclic nature. This may be accomplished by identifying the cycles in the network and collapsing them into "super nodes" forming a new digraph which has no cycles. The nodes on a cycle are mutually accessible in the sense that that there is a way to get from every node on the cycle to another node on the cycle and back. Therefore the nodes may be partitioned into sets called strongly connected components. A strongly connected component of a digraph is a maximal strongly connected subgraph. Strongly connected components have the property that all nodes within a component are mutually accessible, but there is no way to get from a node in one component to a node in another, and back. Hence nodes in a DAG also satisfy these conditions and by considering a set of nodes belonging to a strong component as a super node it is possible to render a graph acyclic for topological sorting.

Figure 3-11 a shows an example of a cyclic directed graph representing a constraint network, $G = \{V,E\}$. Figure 3-11 b shows its strong components S_i, $S_1 = \{D,E,F\}$, $S_2 = \{K\}$, $S_3 = \{B\}$, $S_4 = \{A,C,G,J,L,M\}$ and $S_5 = \{H,I\}$ and Figure 3-11 c shows the equivalent condensed graph $G' = \{V', E'\}$, where V' has five elements and the edge S_iS_j is in E' if and only if there is an edge in E from some vertex in S_i to some vertex in S_j.

Strong components are located essentially by search-based algorithms which traverse the network labelling the visited nodes and storing the cycles as they are encountered. The details of the algorithm that generates the strong components given the directed graph are presented in [1, 7, 8, 17, 25].

3.6.3. Solution Plan

The plan for a solution sequence which solves for the unknowns in the network is determined by a reverse topological sort on the resulting network with the strong components collapsed. Figure 3-11 shows the subsets $S_1 = \{D,E,F\}$, $S_2=\{K\}$, $S_3=\{B\}$, $S_4 = \{A,C,G,J,L,M\}$ and $S_5=\{H,I\}$ which form the strong components for the network. Each subset corresponds to a set of constraints that must be solved simultaneously. The subsets are collapsed and the resulting DAG with super nodes is shown in Figure 3-11 c.

An inverse topological sort based on a breadth-first search yields the desired solution sequence for the cyclic network as follows: S_1-S_2-S_3-S_4-S_5. This indicates that the constraints matching the set { D,E,F } are to be solved simultaneously then along with the evaluation of B and K the set of constraints belonging to {A,C,G,J,L,M} are to be solved simultaneously and finally the set {H,I } is to be solved for. In terms of the parameters it would look like {{D,E,F},{B},{K},{A,C,G,J,L,M},{H,I}}. Notice that the order in which S_3,S_2 and S_1 are processed is not important because they are independent components; therefore another valid solution would be {{B},{K},{D,E,F}, {A,C,G,J,L,M},{H,I}}.

Actually the components S_3,S_2 and S_1 may be evaluated in parallel. Consider the example presented in Figure 3-8. The directed acyclic graph for the defined status is a tree. Therefore no cycles or strong components are present and a topological sort can be readily applied. Figure 3-12 shows the tree and the solution sequence is **y-g-c**, obtained by expanding the dependents in a breadth-first manor as shown by the dotted line. Note that the unknown parameters are the circle nodes and the known parameters are the square nodes. Square nodes do

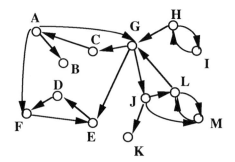

(a) Cyclic Directed Network

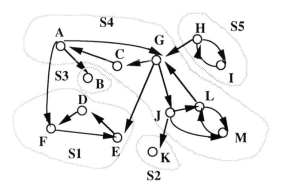

(b) Strong Components for Digraph

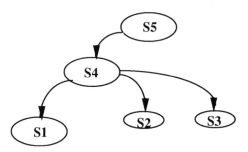

(c) Equivalent Network with the Strong Components Collapsed

Figure 3-11: Examples of Directed Graphs

Adapted from 'Constraint Management in Conceptual Design,'
by David Serrano, © 1987 Massachusetts Institute of Technology.

not expand, because they are terminal nodes and therefore are not included in the resulting topological sort. When the same network has a different status, such as shown in Figure 3-9, the resulting directed graph is not acyclic and the strong components must be identified before a solution sequence is generated, as shown in Figure 3-13. Notice that, for a consistent system (i.e., one where the number of constraints equals number of unknowns and there are no redundancies or conflicts) the solution sequence is effectively the same no matter what the matching assignments. The solution sequence for the network in Figure 3-13 is **(x,y)-g** regardless of the matching selected.

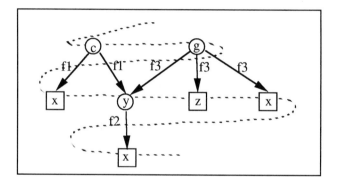

Figure 3-12: Solution Sequence for a Cyclic Network

Adapted from 'Constraint Management in Conceptual Design,'
by David Serrano, © 1987 Massachusetts Institute of Technology.

In addition to providing a degree of parallelism, the directed graph representation allows the computation mechanism to be efficient as well. Consider once again the network of Figure 3-12. If the value of z were changed, it is not necessary to reevaluate the complete network because z only affects (causes) g. Therefore by looking at the causality, it is possible to determine the exact number of parameters that need be recomputed for given change (or changes). In large sparse networks, the advantages of this capability are of great value. Similarly consider the network of Figure 3-11. If either **B** or **K** need to be recomputed, the simultaneous set within S_1 need not be evaluated, saving computation time. In addition, the solution sequence may be stored and used as long

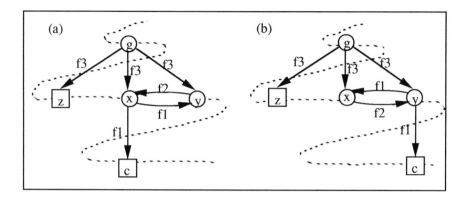

Figure 3-13: Solution Plan for a Consistent Constraint Network with
Multiple Matchings

Adapted from 'Constraint Management in Conceptual Design,'
by David Serrano, © 1987 Massachusetts Institute of Technology.

as the network status is not changed (that is, the sets **U** and **K** are not redefined);
this saves the computational time in the reevaluation as well. This approach is
applicable regardless of the nature of the constraints, i.e., whether they are linear
or nonlinear.

The solution sequence is of help not only to the computational efficiency of
the system, but it may also be used as an explanation facility to inform the user
of the solution procedure for a given problem. Using the information from the
matching, each unknown parameter is assigned a constraint, which is used in its
evaluation. Therefore if the solution sequence is augmented with this information it is possible to inform the user which constraints were selected for
evaluation, the order in which the constraints were used and for which parameter
was each constraint used. For example, using the example of Figure 3-12, the
solution trace for the reverse topological sort may look like:

```
solved for y using f2
solved for g using f3
solved for c using  f1.
```

For the example in Figure 3-13, the solution trace may look like:

```
solved for (x,y) using (f1,f2) simultaneously
solved for g using f3
```

For the example in Figure 3-14, the solution trace may look like:

```
solved for j using f8
solved simultaneously for (f,g) using (f6,f7)
solved for e using f5
solved for d using f4
solved for c using f3
solved for b using f2
solved for a using f1
```

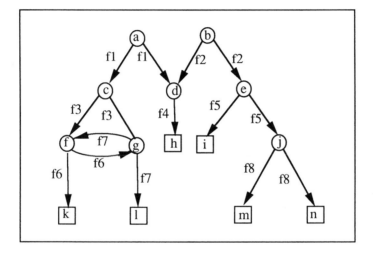

Figure 3-14: Directed Graph, Solution Sequence: j-(f,g)-e-d-c-b-a

Adapted from 'Constraint Management in Conceptual Design,'
by David Serrano, © 1987 Massachusetts Institute of Technology.

The dependency information is useful for the designer as a qualitative aid as well; it is possible to query the network for dependency information in order to help the designer's decision-making process. It is also possible to inform the designer of which known parameters directly or indirectly affect an unknown parameter he is trying to evaluate. For example, in Figure 3-14, it might be desirable to determine which known parameters affect **b**. By traversing the tree starting at node b in a breadth-first fashion until the terminal nodes are reached, it is found that the set {h,j,m,n} affects b. This is important when the number of constraints increases beyond a reasonable number and it is not possible to mentally keep track (bookkeeping) of all the dependencies and associations among the parameters. Similarly, it is possible to inform the user of the system which unknown parameters depend on a given input parameter of his selection. For example if j is to be changed, the user may want to know which parameters get affected. This may be accomplished by performing a traversal as before, but using the parents of the nodes rather than the children in the expansion. A change in j will affect only e and b in the network.

3.6.4. Sensitivity Analysis

It is sometimes not enough to know which parameters affect others but also desirable to have an order of magnitude sensitivity analysis indicating how one or more parameters affect another. The dependency information may be used in the sensitivity analysis of a system of constraints as well. Therefore when setting up the sensitivity analysis, the only input that is required is the parameter of interest. The dependencies are used to generate all the input parameters which affect it, and to determine all those intermediate constraints which need to be included as well.

For a single constraint $f_i(x_1,x_2) = 0$ in two variables, the sensitivity analysis is performed by taking the partial derivatives with respect to x_1 and x_2:

$$\frac{\partial f}{\partial x_1}dx_1 + \frac{\partial f}{\partial x_2}dx_2 = 0$$

Then if it is desired to know how x_1 varies with respect to x_2, use the expression:

$$\frac{dx_1}{dx_2} = - \frac{\dfrac{\partial f}{\partial x_2}}{\dfrac{\partial f}{\partial x_1}}$$

In general, for a constraint in m parameters:

$$\sum_{i=1}^{m} \frac{\partial f}{\partial x_i}dx_i = 0$$

The constraint may have various known and unknown parameters and it may be rewritten as:

$$\sum_{j=1}^{n} \frac{\partial f}{\partial u_j} du_j = \sum_{k=1}^{c} \frac{\partial f}{\partial x_k} dx_k$$

where the du_j are the unknown parameters and the dx_k are the known parameters. The dx_k are set to one if the variation with respect to x_k is of interest, and to zero otherwise. When the variations of one parameter with respect to another is not direct (i.e., they are not members of the same constraint), or the value is dependent on highly coupled constraints, it is necessary to take into account the effect of other constraints. In this case, the last expression is better written in terms of matrices:

$$J_{nxn} \, du = - J'_{nxc} \, dx$$

where du is the vector of the unknown parameters found in the n constraints and dx is the vector of the c parameters which have been defined as knowns.

In general, when the sensitivity of a parameter is requested, two lists are generated. The first list contains all the terminal nodes under the node corresponding to the desired parameter. The second list contains all the intermediate nodes between the desired parameter and the terminal nodes. The intermediate parameters form the du vector and the associated n constraints are used to generate the jacobians J and J'. The terminal nodes form the dx vector. By assigning a value of one to each parameter k in dx and zero to all others, it is possible to determine the sensitivity of any parameter j in du. The results are returned qualitatively in the form of a sign. If the variation is increasing then (+) is returned, else if it is decreasing, then (-) is returned.

Using the dependency information, it is possible to determine all the relevant constraints that must be included in the analysis automatically, thus avoiding the need to include the entire network in the analysis. As an example, consider the network in Figure 3-14. If we are interested in the sensitivities for parameter c, we first find terminal nodes for c, i.e., $\{k,l\}$. Next, we determine all other dependents of c excluding the terminal nodes $\{f,g\}$. Then, from the set $\{c\} \cup \{f,g\} = \{c,f,g\}$ the appropriate constraints are determined using the results of the matching, in such a way that the constraint set is $\{f3,f6,f7\}$. Therefore the vectors are: $du = \{dc \; df \; dg\}^T$ and $dx = \{dk \; dl\}^T$.

The jacobians become:

$$\mathbb{J} = \begin{bmatrix} \dfrac{\partial f3}{\partial c} & \dfrac{\partial f3}{\partial f} & \dfrac{\partial f3}{\partial g} \\[2ex] \dfrac{\partial f6}{\partial c} & \dfrac{\partial f6}{\partial f} & \dfrac{\partial f6}{\partial g} \\[2ex] \dfrac{\partial f7}{\partial c} & \dfrac{\partial f7}{\partial f} & \dfrac{\partial f7}{\partial g} \end{bmatrix} \qquad \mathbb{J}' = \begin{bmatrix} \dfrac{\partial f3}{\partial k} & \dfrac{\partial f3}{\partial l} \\[2ex] \dfrac{\partial f6}{\partial k} & \dfrac{\partial f6}{\partial l} \\[2ex] \dfrac{\partial f7}{\partial k} & \dfrac{\partial f7}{\partial l} \end{bmatrix}$$

The jacobians for the sensitivity analysis as well as those required for the Newton-Raphson iterative solution are generated symbolically. An overview of symbolic manipulation of constraints is available in the literature. For more information see [23, 25, 32, 35].[2]

3.6.5. Evaluation of Constraints: Some Special Cases

In Section 3.5, it was mentioned that the graph representation can accomodate constraints of the form: $g = F(x,y,z)$, where F may be computed represent using a lookup table or any other procedure. This is indeed true for all the representational issues presented so far, but care must be taken at the evaluation stage because it is possible that the functions described by these functional or procedural constraints are not differentiable and will cause problems when they are part of a strong component. In many cases, these "procedural constraints" have a fixed flow of information and the causality may not be reversed. When they are present outside a strong component they behave exactly as any other node. The treatment of these types of constraints in a domain-independent, generic fashion is still to be resolved. However, our approach can handle such constraints, so long as they are used with the above restriction.

Finally a few words on Multi-Input, Multi-Output (MIMO) nodes. It may be possible to define functions or procedures with multiple outputs. An example of a MIMO function is the selection of a standard component from a database. When such a selection is made, the result is a complete description of the component, in general, consisting of multiple parameters and corresponding values. For example, in bearing selection, the function may return all the bearing's dimensions (e.g., its inside diameter (ID), outside diameter (OD), and width). Once again these may be dealt with readily, as long as they are not part of a strong component.

---

[2]Editors' note: For related work on matrix evaluation of constraints see [34].

3.7. DETECTION OF REDUNDANT AND CONTRADICTORY CONSTRAINTS

For any given constraint set, we would like to find a *maximum matching*, i.e., to find the largest possible subset of E. A maximum matching is complete when the cardinality of N and F are equal, i.e. $|N| = |F|$, and no elements remain unmatched in either N or F.

Although a complete matching is obviously not possible when $|N| \neq |F|$, a maximum matching may not be complete even when $|N| = |F|$; unmatched variables and unmatched constraints may arise.

An unmatched subset in N indicates an underconstrained subsystem in which there are more variables than constraints on those variables. It should be noted that this situation cannot be identified by simply considering the number of constraints and unknowns, since a system may be underconstrained with respect to a particular subset of its variables even when $|F| \geq |N|$. An important benefit of the matching process is that it identifies unconstrained variables, bringing to the attention of the designer (or of the knowledge-based system) areas in which additional (constraint) information is required.

An unmatched subset in F indicates an overconstrained system in which there are unmatched constraints. The importance of these unmatched constraints can be determined by first evaluating the constraints which were successfully matched. The parameter values resulting from this evaluation can then be used to evaluate the unmatched constraints. If an unmatched constraint is satisfied, then it does not affect the solution or the other constraints and is said to be *redundant*. If the unmatched constraint is not satisfied, it is in conflict with (violates) the matched constraints and is said to be *contradictory constraints*.

Redundant constraints are common in handbooks and other sources of engineering knowledge and they usually appear as constraints which are combinations of other constraints, rewritten for the user's benefit. In general they are harmless; although they provide no new information they should not hinder the solution process if the overall system is not underconstrained. Redundant constraints are troublesome when they occur within a strong component (set of simultaneous equations) because they cause singular jacobians, which are sources of numerical difficulties. Contradictory (conflicting) constraints not only cause numerical difficulties but require modifications in the constraint set before evaluation. This situation will be discussed more fully in the following section.

3.7.1. Redundancies and Conflicts within Strong Components

As mentioned previously both redundant and conflicting constraints cause numerical difficulties when simultaneous constraints must be solved; therefore it is necessary to check the strong components for redundancies and conflicts due to functional interactions between constraints. Two alternatives exist for this checking. The first method depends on explicit symbolic manipulations on the constraints; the second method linearizes the constraints and requires the use of the jacobian matrix.

Using the symbolic approach, the different constraints represented in the strong component are combined, eliminating variables until either one variable's value may be determined and propagated back to find all others (in which case the set of constraints is consistent), or an invalid result is obtained.

The second approach is a modification of that presented by Light and Gossard [19]. The method uses Newton-Raphson's method for solving nonlinear equations in conjunction with a variation of Gaussian elimination.

If the set of constraint equations constituting a strong component is solved by the Newton-Raphson technique, we obtain the system of equations shown below:

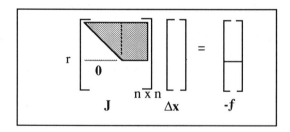

where J_i, the jacobian, is the matrix of partial derivatives of the constraint equations with respect to their matching unknown parameters evaluated at x_0, Δx_i is the vector (x_i- x_0), x_i is the vector of unknowns, x_0 is the initial estimate, and f_i is the vector of the constraints evaluated at x_0.[3]

The system of equations is then solved using Gaussian elimination. The jacobian is reduced to upper triangular form. If it is non-singular, the strong component is consistent and the equations may be solved simultaneously. If on the other hand, the jacobian is singular, the constraints in the set are not consistent and must be corrected by the user before they can be solved.

It is also important to know whether the constraints corresponding to rows r+1 to n are in conflict with the rest of the set or are merely redundant. Any row of

---

[3]In the constraint manager, the jacobian is generated symbolically.

the jacobian containing all zeros represents a redundant constraint if its residual is also zero. The problem may be corrected in one of two ways: by replacing the constraints in rows r+1 through n with unmatched constraints (if any exist) containing the variables represented by the corresponding columns; or by specifying values for the variables represented by columns r+1 through n.

If the residuals corresponding to the constraint with zero coefficients are not zero, the constraint conflicts with the other constraints in the strong component. When such a conflict is encountered, the unknown parameters associated with the strong component can be presented to the user instead of simply signalling failure. The user may then resolve the conflict by examining the conflicting set and eliminating one or more constraints.

Both methods have advantages and disadvantages. The first requires a relatively sophisticated symbolic algebra package which may not be able to solve all possible cases, i.e., it may not be possible to explicitly solve for a given variable in a particular constraint. The second method is relatively straightforward to implement but is subject to numerical difficulties. The second method requires a good initial guess for the variables. It is possible that a particular set of starting values may initially produce a nonsingular jacobian (indicating no problems within the strong component) but as the iterative numerical process continues, the jacobian may become singular. Conversely, the starting values may indicate problems within a strong component when a solution to the subsystem actually exists.

The principal difference between the method presented here and the method described by Light and Gossard [19], is that the method presented here uses the jacobian only for the smallest set of constraints which must be solved simultaneously. This is possible because the search for conflicting constraints is limited to constraints which are members of strong components. The strong components also guarantee that the jacobian is square.

3.8. AN EXAMPLE

The purpose of this section is to illustrate the various techniques presented in this paper with a complete example. The following example uses the familiar cantilever beam formulae to demonstrate the process of transforming an undirected network to a directed graph using the bipartite matching approach. The solution sequence plan will be generated for more than one variation of the constraint network. The geometry and the constraints are shown in Figure 3-15 a. The constraints are shown in Figure 3-15b where: σ is the bending stress in the beam, I is the cross sectional area moment of inertia, M is the maximum bending moment due to the load F, Y is the distance from the neutral axis to a fiber on the surface of the beam and K is the stiffness of the beam. L, H and B are the length, height and width of the beam. The undirected graph corresponding to the constraints and all the parameters is shown in Figure 3-15 c. The nodes correspond to the parameters and the arcs are labelled with the corresponding constraint they represent. Initially the graph is undirected because the status of the system is not specified. There is an arc for each constraint relating any two parameters. Constraint f1 relates σ, M, Y and I, therefore there is an arc labelled f1 between (σ,M), (σ,Y), (σ,I), (M,Y), (M,I) and (Y,I).

In order to evaluate the constraint network the status must be defined. The status specifies which parameters will be used as inputs (knowns) and which parameters are to be evaluated (unknowns). The same constraint network can be used to solve various different problems by redefining the status of the parameters in the constraint network. To illustrate the formulation of the bipartite matching problem and the solution sequence given a constraint network and a status consider the status defined by the sets $U = \{I, L, H, B, Y\}$ and $K = \{\sigma, F, K, M, E\}$. The matching problem in this example is formulated in terms of $G = \{V,E\}$ such that $V = N \cup F$, where $N = \{I, L, H, B, Y\}$ and $F = \{f_1, f_2, f_3, f_4, f_5\}$ and $E = \{(I,f_1),(I,f_3),(I,f_5),(H,f_3),(H,f_4),(B,f_3),(L,f_2),\ (I,f_5),\ (Y,f_1),\ (Y,f_4)\}$. Figure 3-16 a shows the bipartite matching graph where the bold lines are the maximum matching assignments. The dotted lines are the assignments not used by the matching. In this example there is only one possible matching assignment and no parameters or constraints are left unmatched. Using the results of the matchings, the dependencies are created, which transforms the undirected graph into a directed graph. The dependencies are assigned such that only the arcs incident on matching nodes are kept. For example, Y was assigned to f_1; therefore only the edges labelled f_1 with one end on Y are kept and the arrows are directed away from the node, indicating that Y depends on the adjacent nodes M, σ, and I through constraint f_1. The resulting directed graph is shown in Figure 3-16 b and redrawn in a tree-like fashion in Figure 3-16 c. The solution plan may be generated using an inverse topological sort on the digraph. The breadth-first search (without including the terminal nodes in the list) is: **B-I-H-L-Y-I-L**. Reversing the BFS and removing repetitions from left to right yields the solution plan: **L-I-Y-H-B**.

Consider a second example using the same constraint network of Figure 3-15 as follows; in this example rather than specifying the stress level σ and calculating the dimensions B, H and L, the dimensions will be given and the stress will be computed. The status of the system is defined by $K = \{F,L,H,B,E\}$ and $U = \{\sigma,M,I,Y,K\}$. The bipartite matching is shown in Figure 3-17 a and the directed graph is shown in Figure 3-17 b. The tree-like digraph is shown in Figure 3-17 c from which the solution plan is obtained using a reverse topological sort as before. The BFS is σ-**K-M-Y-I**, reversing yields the order **I-Y-M-K-**σ which is the evaluation order required to solve for the unknowns.

(a)

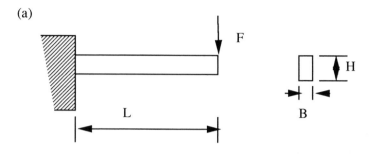

(b)

$$f_1 \quad \sigma - \frac{MY}{I} = 0$$

$$f_2 \quad M - F L = 0$$

$$f_3 \quad I - \frac{B H^3}{12} = 0$$

$$f_4 \quad Y - \frac{H}{2} = 0$$

$$f_5 \quad K - \frac{3\,EI}{L^3} = 0$$

(c)

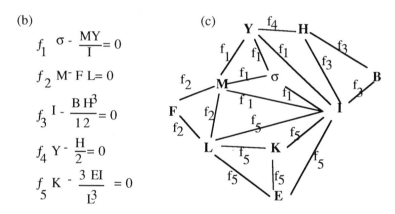

Figure 3-15: Cantilever Beam Example:
(a) Geometry (b) Constraints (c) Constraint Graph

Adapted from 'Constraint Management in Conceptual Design,'
by David Serrano, © 1987 Massachusetts Institute of Technology.

The constraints used in the evaluation are f_3-f_4-f_2-f_5-f_1, corresponding to I-Y-M-K-σ according to the matchings. If the designer is interested in which parameters affect another, the affecting parameters can be determined using a search in the digraph. For example in order to determine which parameters affect the stiffness K, a search for the terminal nodes below K is made. From Figure 3-17 c using a breadth-first search starting at K and only reporting the terminal nodes yield the list {H,B,E,L}. The elements of the list are the parameters which the designer has specified as inputs which affect the stiffness K.

The parameter sensitivities are determined by selecting the set of constraints and parameters which affect the desired parameter. For example, in the case of the stiffness K, only constraints f_5 and f_3 are required. The required constraints are determined by listing all the nodes descendants of the desired parameter (terminal nodes excluded); the constraints matching these nodes are the constraints that must be included in the sensitivity analysis. For K the nodes are K (itself) and I; the corresponding constraints are f_5 and f_3 (from the matching). The parameters to be included in the analysis are all those parameters corresponding to nodes that are descendants of the desired parameter. For example, the sensitivity analysis for the stiffness involves the parameters K,I,H,B,E and L. And the jacobians are:

$$
\mathbb{J} = \begin{bmatrix} \dfrac{\partial f5}{\partial K} & \dfrac{\partial f5}{\partial I} \\[2mm] \dfrac{\partial f3}{\partial K} & \dfrac{\partial f3}{\partial I} \end{bmatrix} \qquad \mathbb{J}' = \begin{bmatrix} \dfrac{\partial f5}{\partial H} & \dfrac{\partial f5}{\partial B} & \dfrac{\partial f5}{\partial E} & \dfrac{\partial f5}{\partial L} \\[2mm] \dfrac{\partial f3}{\partial H} & \dfrac{\partial f3}{\partial B} & \dfrac{\partial f3}{\partial E} & \dfrac{\partial f3}{\partial L} \end{bmatrix}
$$

As a final example, to demonstrate the solution process when the digraph is cyclic, an additional constraint is added to the constraint network of Figure 3-15. The new constraint f_6 introduces the slope of the beam ϕ. The constraints are shown in Figure 3-17 a, and the new undirected graph is shown in Figure 3-17 b. Figure 3-17 shows two possible matchings. The matchings are not always unique. For a consistent system, as in this example, the matching selected does not affect the solution, but in inconsistent systems or systems with $|N| \neq |F|$ each matching may represent a different solution. The first matching of Figure 3-17 c is used in the current example, and the resulting digraph is shown in Figure 3-17 d. The digraph is redrawn in a tree-like form in Figure 3-17 e, where the cycles are clearly shown. The strong component is composed of the cycles L-F-L and I-L-F-I. If the strong component is collapsed (meaning that it will be solved

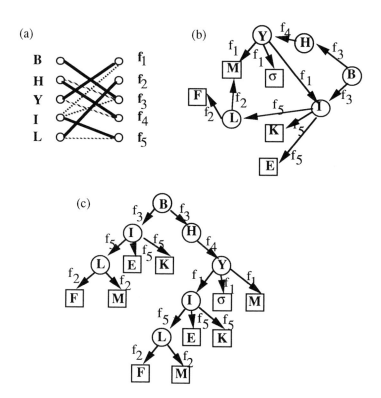

Figure 3-16: Cantilever Beam Example:
Knowns (L,H,B,I,Y), Unknowns (σ,F,K,M,E)
(a) Bipartite Matching (b) Digraph (c) Tree

Adapted from 'Constraint Management in Conceptual Design,'
by David Serrano, © 1987 Massachusetts Institute of Technology.

(a)

$$f_1 \quad \sigma - \frac{MY}{I} = 0$$

$$f_2 \quad M - FL = 0$$

$$f_3 \quad I - \frac{BH^3}{12} = 0$$

$$f_4 \quad Y - \frac{H}{2} = 0$$

$$f_5 \quad K - \frac{3EI}{L^3} = 0$$

$$f_6 \quad \varnothing - \frac{FL^2}{EI} = 0$$

(b)

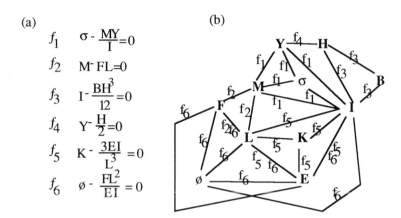

(c)

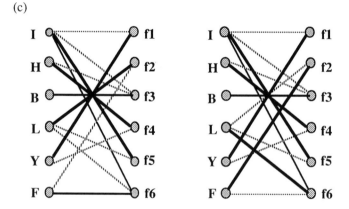

Figure 3-17: Coupled Constraints:
(a) Constraints (b) Undirected Graph (c) Non-unique Matchings

Adapted from 'Constraint Management in Conceptual Design,'
by David Serrano, © 1987 Massachusetts Institute of Technology.

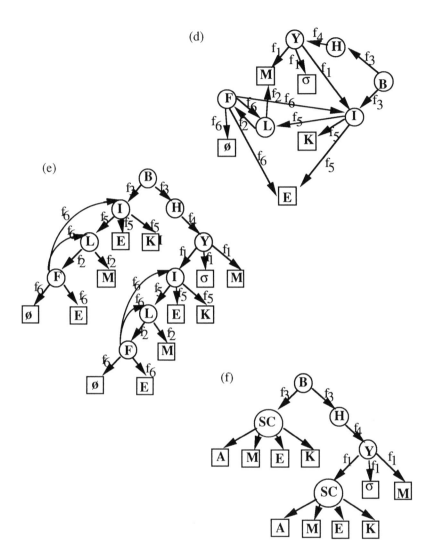

Figure 3-17, Coupled Constraints (Continued):
(d) Directed Graph (e) Tree-like Representation (f) Directed Acyclic Graph
with Strong Components Collapsed

Adapted from 'Constraint Management in Conceptual Design,'
by David Serrano, © 1987 Massachusetts Institute of Technology.

simultaneously), the digraph is rendered acyclic as shown in Figure 3-17 f. The reverse topological sort may be applied to the DAG and the solution plan is: SC-Y-H-B or (I,L,F)-Y-H-B. The parentheses indicate that the set will be solved simultaneously. The constraints to be used in the simultaneous solution are those matching (I,L,F): (f_5, f_2, f_6).

3.9. CONCEPT MODELLING: DESIGNPAK

The constraint management techniques form part of a MCAE system which allows the designer to interactively construct models of his/her design using a "building block" metaphor.[4] In this metaphor, a chest contains elementary building blocks and a work bench. Each of the building blocks contains its own set of properties which describe its physical nature (form, size, materials, etc.) and its behavior (physical laws, possible interactions, etc.). Each object or building block will be referred to as an *icon*. The building blocks may be combined to form more complex objects defined as **concepts**. The resulting object inherits properties of its constituent building blocks.

In DESIGNPAK, the components or building blocks are common machine elements and other engineering abstractions which form the natural language of engineers. Machine elements include, but are not limited to: shafts, gears, bearings, kinematic links, springs, motors, concentrated loads, edge supports, grounds, vectors, etc. Each element is represented as a frame. Each frame encodes a set of constraints which predict its performance, establish its physical limits, and define its topological (connectivity) restrictions. In addition, graphical icons and other physical properties (e.g., geometrical characteristics) are included in each frame. The implementation of a building block metaphor allows the interactive creation of design concepts by assembling a concept using basic elements. The connectivity between mating icons is specified interactively. Figure 3-1 shows various concepts constructed from the basic icons. The concept is represented graphically as an aggregation of icons and normally correspond to the contents of a window. Computationally, the concept is also a frame and it is represented as a hierarchical structure of a concept and its subcomponents which may either be concepts themselves or icons. The icon-concept window is an attempt to implement the building block metaphor.

Figures 3-18 through 3-20 show sample screens in the process of constructing a gear reducer concept using icons. Figure 3-18 shows the selection of a gear

---

[4]See also chapter 6, which relies on a similar metaphor.

element to be connected to the previously selected shaft. Figure 3-19 shows the gear connected to the shaft and Figure 3-20 shows the completed gear reducer concept. In addition, Figure 3-20 illustrates some of the characteristics of the user interface which include multiple windows for text and graphics, scroll bars (input valuators), thermometers (output valuators), plots and menus. Figure 3-21 shows the solution plan for the gear reducer example. The solution plan was presented in Section 3.6.3. Figure 3-22 shows the results of the sensitivity analysis with respect to the shaft diameter (OD_sh1) and Figure 3-23 shows the advice for correcting a constraint violation (f34). Sensitivity analysis and constraint violations were discussed in Sections 3.6.4 and 3.7, respectively.

3.10. SUMMARY

A digraph representation for constraint networks was presented. Methods for the evaluation both qualitative and quantitative of constraint networks was also presented and examples given.

One of the advantages of the directed graph representation is that the topological properties of digraphs may be used to identify certain conditions in the constraint model (such as highly coupled constraints). The information on the topology of the constraint network is useful in planning a solution sequence for the evaluation of the network; for example, by locating and collapsing the strong components in the graph a cyclic graph is rendered acyclic and a standard topological sort may be applied. Topological information is useful for efficiency because it allows the selection of the relevant constraints for evaluation and sensitivity analysis. Another advantage of the digraph representation is that the same constraint network may be used to focus on various aspects of the problem depending on the designer's designation of known and unknown parameters. Bipartite matching not only provides the information required to assign the dependencies, but also provides useful information about the constraints before a solution is requested. The bipartite matching will identify parameters which need to be constrained and constraints which are not included in the matching are possible sources of conflict.

DESIGNPAK allows the interactive generation and evaluation of engineering concepts. Incomplete, inconsistent and redundant constraint sets are handled and assistance is provided in order to resolve conflicts. Causal order may be reversed while maintaining consistency in the constraint set. DESIGNPAK provides an interactive environment which supports multiple objectives, alternative designs, iteration, evolution, and refinement. The system provides both qualitative and quantitative support.

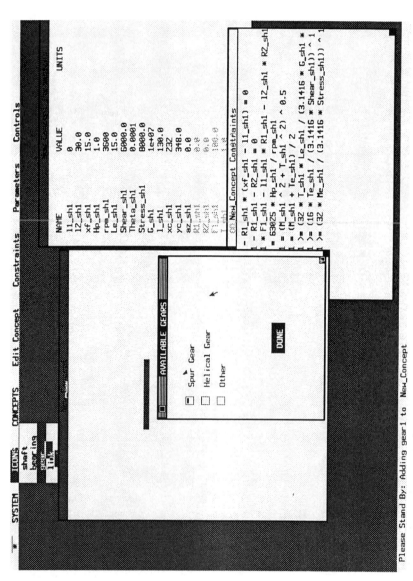

Figure 3-18: Selecting Gear from Concept-Base

Adapted from 'Constraint Management in Conceptual Design,' by David Serrano, © 1987 Massachusetts Institute of Technology.

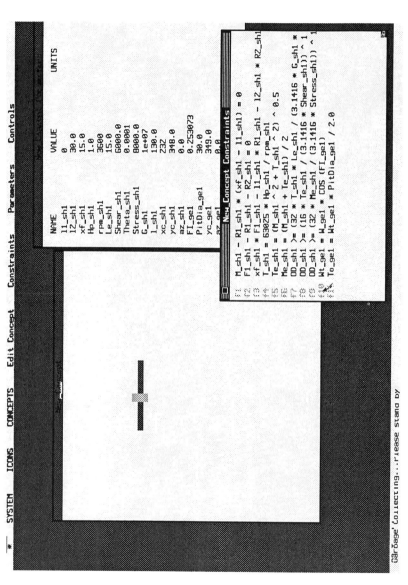

Figure 3-19: Shaft1-Gear1 Connection

Adapted from 'Constraint Management in Conceptual Design,' by David Serrano, © 1987 Massachusetts Institute of Technology.

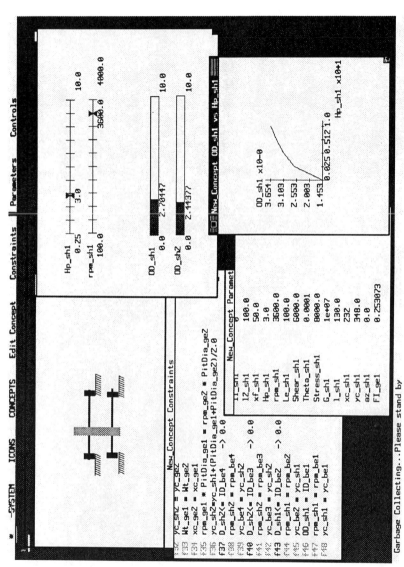

Figure 3-20: Completed Gear Reducer Concept

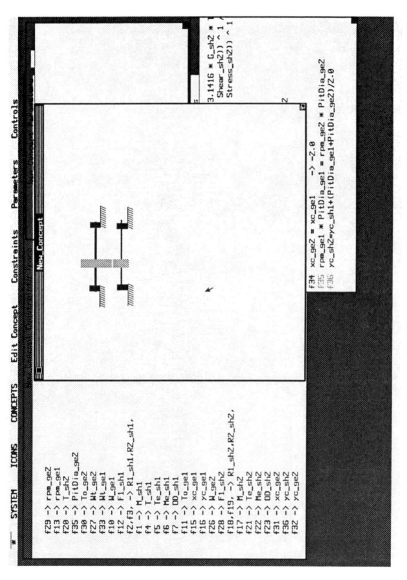

Figure 3-21: Solution Plan

Adapted from 'Constraint Management in Conceptual Design,' by David Serrano, © 1987 Massachusetts Institute of Technology.

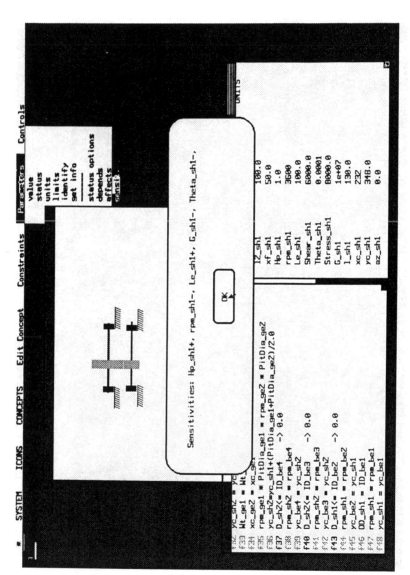

Figure 3-22: Sensitivity Analysis with Respect to Shaft Diameter (OD_sh1)

Adapted from 'Constraint Management in Conceptual Design,' by David Serrano, © 1987 Massachusetts Institute of Technology.

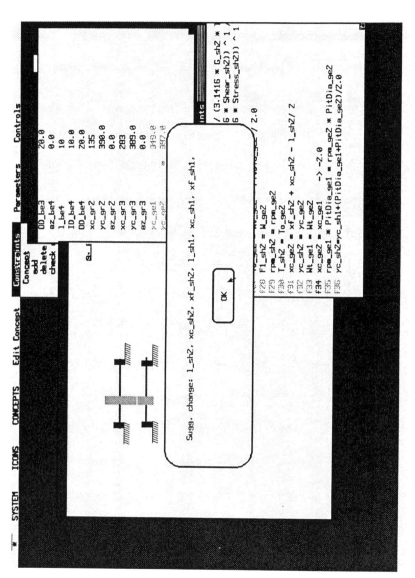

Figure 3-23: Suggested Parameter Modifications to Correct Constraint Violation in f34

Adapted from 'Constraint Management in Conceptual Design,' by David Serrano, © 1987 Massachusetts Institute of Technology.

The system has potential as a design tool, an educational tool, and asa research vehicle in design methodology.

3.11. ACKNOWLEDGMENTS

The authors gratefully acknowledge the financial support from the National Science Foundation, the Control Data Corporation and the University of Puerto Rico during various stages of this work.

3.12. BIBLIOGRAPHY

[1]   Baase, S., *Computer Algorithms: Introduction to Design and Analysis*, Addison-Wesley, Reading, MA, 1978.

[2]   Berztiss, A. T., *Data Structures: Theory and Practice*, Academic Press, New York, 1975.

[3]   Borning, A., "Thinglab - An Object-Oriented System for Building Simulations using Constraints," *Proc. Fifth International Joint Conference on Artificial Intelligence*, Morgan Kaufman, pp. 497-498, 1977.

[4]   Chang, D., "Automatic Scaling of Assemblies for Computer-Aided Design," M. S. Thesis, Dept. of Mechanical Eng., M.I.T., Cambridge, MA 02139, 1983.

[5]   Chyz, G. W., "Constraint Management for Constructive Geometry," M. S. Thesis, Dept. of Mechanical Eng., M.I.T., Cambridge, MA 02139, 1985.

[6]   de Kleer, J. and Sussman, G.J., *Propagation of Constraints Applied to Circuit Synthesis*, Technical Report AI Memo 485, AI Laboratory, M.I.T., September 1978.

[7]   Even, S. and Tarjan, R.E., "Network Flow and Testing Graph Connectivity," *SIAM J. Comput.*, pp. 507-518, December 1975.

[8]   Even, S., *Graph Algorithms*, Computer Science Press, 1979.

[9]   Friedman, G.J., and Leondes, C.T., "Constraint Theory, Part I: Fundamentals," *IEEE transactions on Systems Science and Cybernetics,* Vol. SSC-5, pp. 48-56, January 1969.

[10]   Friedman, G.J., and Leondes, C.T., "Constraint Theory, Part II: Model Graphs and Regular Relations," *IEEE transactions on Systems Science and Cybernetics,* Vol. SSC-5, No. 2, pp. 132-140, April 1969.

[11]   Friedman, G.J., and Leondes, C.T., "Constraint Theory, Part III: Inequality and Discrete Relations," *IEEE transactions on Systems Science and Cybernetics,* Vol. SSC-5, No. 3, pp. 191-200, April 1969.

[12]   Gallagher, D., "Variational Systems in Computer Aided Design," M. S. Thesis, Dept. of Mechanical Eng., M.I.T., Cambridge, MA 02139, 1984.

[13]   Garrett, J. and Fenves, S. J., *A Knowledge-Based Standards Processor for Structural Component Design,* R-86-157, Dept. Civil Engineering, CMU, Pittsburgh, PA 15213, September 1986, [See also AI in Engineering Journal, Vol. 1, No. 1, 1986].

[14]   Gosling, J., *Algebraic Constraints,* unpublished Ph.D. Dissertation, Dept. of Computer Science, CMU, Pittsburgh, PA 15213, 1983.

[15]   Harary, F., "A Graph Theoretic Approach to Matrix Inversion by Partitioning," *Numerische Mathematik,* Vol. 4, pp. 128-135, 1962.

[16]   Holtz, N., *Symboloc Manipulation of Design Constraints,* unpublished Ph.D. Dissertation, Dept. of Civil Engineering, CMU, Pittsburgh, PA 15213, 1982.

[17]   Hopcroft, J.E., and Karp, R.M., "An N**5/2 Algorithm for Maximum Matchings in Bipartite Graphs," *SIAM J. Comput.,* Vol. 2, No. 4, pp. 225-231, 1973.

[18]   Light, R., "Symbolic Dimensioning in Computer-Aided Design," M. S. Thesis, Dept. of Mechanical Eng., M.I.T., Cambridge, MA 02139, 1980.

[19]   Light, R.A. and Gossard, D.C., "Variational Geometry: A New Method for Modifying Part Geometry for Finite Element Analysis," *Computers and Structures,* Vol. 17, No. 5-6, pp. 903-909, 1983.

[20]   Lin, V. C., "Variational Geometry in Computer Aided Design," M. S. Thesis, Dept. of Mechanical Eng., M.I.T., Cambridge, MA 02139, 1981.

[21]   Pabon, J., "Basic Steps Towards Computer Aided Scaling of Assemblies," M. S. Thesis, Dept. of Mechanical Eng., M.I.T., Cambridge, MA 02139, 1985.

[22] Sedgewick, R., *Algorithms*, Addison-Wesley Publishing Co., 1984.

[23] Serrano, D., "MATHPAK: An Interactive Preliminary Design Package," M. S. Thesis, Dept. of Mechanical Eng., M.I.T., Cambridge, MA 02139, 1984.

[24] Serrano, D. and Gossard, D. C., "Combining Mathematical Models with Geometric Models in CAE Systems," *ASME, Proceedings of 1986 International Computers in Engineering Conference*, July 1986.

[25] Serrano, D., *Constraint Management in Conceptual Design*, unpublished Ph.D. Dissertation, Dept. of Mechanical Eng., M.I.T., Cambridge, MA 02139, 1987.

[26] Soylemez, S. and Seider, W. D., "A New Technique for Precedence-Ordering Chemical Process Equation Sets," *AIChE*, Vol. 19, No. 5, 1973.

[27] Steele, Jr., G. L., *The Definition and Implementation of a Computer Programming Language Based on Constraints*, Technical Report AI-TR-595, AI Laboratory, August 1980.

[28] Stefik, M., "Planning with Constraints (MOLGEN 1)," *Artificial Intelligence*, Vol. 16, pp. 111-140, 1981.

[29] Steinke, G. C. and Shussel, M. D., "Engineering by the Book ... And On-line," *Mechanical Engineering*, pp. 56-59, November 1985.

[30] Steward, D. V., "On an Approach to Techniques for the Analysis of the Structure of Large Systems of Equations," *SIAM Review*, Vol. 4, No. 4, 1962.

[31] Steward, D. V., "Partitioning and Tearing Systems of Equations," *J. SIAM Numer. Anal.*, Vol. 2, No. 2, 1965.

[32] Sussman, G.J. and Abelson, H., *Structure and Interpretation of Computer Programs*, McGraw Hill/MIT Press, 1985.

[33] Sutherland, I., *Sketchpad -A Man -Machine Graphical Interface*, unpublished Ph.D. Dissertation, Dept. of Computer Science, M.I.T., Cambridge, MA 02139, 1963.

[34] Wang, P. T. R., *Bandwith Minimization, Reducibility Decomposition, and Traiangularation of Sparse Matrices*, unpublished Ph.D. Dissertation, Computer and Information Science Research Center, The Ohio State University, Columbus, Ohio 43210, 1973.

[35] Winston, P. H. and Horn, B. K. P., *LISP*, Addison-Wesley Publishing Company, Massachusetts, 1984.

Chapter 4
AUTOMOBILE TRANSMISSION DESIGN AS A CONSTRAINT SATISFACTION PROBLEM: FIRST RESULTS

Bernard A. Nadel and Jiang Lin

ABSTRACT

This paper describes our preliminary results with a system we call TRANS-FORM that uses constraint satisfaction techiques in automating the process of designing automatic automobile power transmissions. The work is being conducted in collaboration with the Ford Motor Company Advanced Transmission Design Department in Livonia, Michigan. Our current focus is on the design of the mechanical subsystem, but we anticipate extending this later to the electrical and hydraulic subsystems as well. In this paper we concentrate on the particular problem of designing a transmission of four forward speeds and one reverse speed, using two planetary gearsets, cross-connected by two permanent links. Results to date indicate that design of the mechanical subsystem is an application very naturally formulated as a constraint satisfaction problem. So far, two classic transmissions, known as Axod and HydraMatic, have been rediscovered by our program. Future extensions to more general versions of the search space are expected to lead to the discovery of totally new transmissions.

4.1. INTRODUCTION

The Constraint Satisfaction Problem (CSP) is ubiquitous in Artificial Intelligence. It has received intensive study from many researchers and many algorithms have been developed for solving this class of problems. Surveys of these algorithms appear in [7] and [9]. Mathematical complexity analyses of some of these algorithms appear in [4] and [15]. The importance of CSP is due to the wide range of practical problems it can be used to model. A survey of some of these applications appears in [12]. A variety of natural CSP formulations are in fact usually possible for a given real-world application. This is discussed in [10].

This paper presents our preliminary results with a system we call TRANS-FORM that uses the CSP framework for the apparently new application of designing automatic automobile power transmissions. This is a project we have now been pursuing for about six months in collaboration with Ford Motor Company. In particular, we are working with the Ford Advanced Transmission Design Department in Livonia, Michigan, where our principal "domain expert" is Robert Roethler. Our basic result is that we have been able to rediscover (somewhat abstracted versions of) two well-known 4R-speed[2] automatic transmissions, Axod [1] and HydraMatic 700 [2].

Section 4.2 presents background material for this work, Section 4.3 describes the variables and their domains that we use in formulating transmission design as a constraint satisfaction problem, and Section 4.4 describes the corresponding constraints we use. The results of our current preliminary study are given in Section 4.5. Expected future extensions are discussed in Section 4.6. A fuller presentation of the engineering aspects of this work is available in [13]. A discussion of the implementation of our system in Prolog appears in [14]. An analysis of the complexity of solving arbitrary constraint satisfaction problems in Prolog appears in [11].

4.2. BACKGROUND

Our work involves the application of constraint satisfaction techniques to transmission design. In this section we present background material for both components: (i) the constraint satisfaction problem and (ii) the transmission design problem.

---

[2]We call a transmission nR-speed if it has n forward speeds (or gear ratios or "gears") and 1 reverse speed. The description n-speed, without an R, refers to a transmission with n forward speeds but no reverse.

4.2.1. Constraint Satisfaction Problem

Constraint satisfaction problems involve three components: *variables, values* and *constraints*. The goal is to find *all* assignments of the values to the variables such that all the constraints are simultaneously satisfied. More specifically, there is a set $Z = \{ z_1\, z_2 \dots z_n \}$ of n variables z_i. Each variable takes values from an associated finite domain d_{z_i} of values. There is a set $C = \{ C_1\, C_2 \dots C_c \}$ of c constraints. A constraint C_j is some way of specifying for a given set $Z_j \subseteq Z$ of argument variables, which values for those variables together "satisfy" the constraint − where values for a variable are chosen only from the corresponding domain. Thus each constraint C_j specifies a subset $T_j \subseteq D_j$ of satisfying-tuples from the cartesian product $D_j = \times_{z_i \in Z_j} d_{z_i}$ of the domains of the constraint's arguments. A constraint may thus be specified canonically as a pair of the form $C_j = (Z_j\ T_j)$. Formally, the goal in solving a given CSP instance is to find all value-tuples in the overall cartesian product $\times_{z_i \in Z} d_{z_i}$ that (have projections which) satisfy all c constraints.

4.2.2. The Transmission Design Problem

4.2.2.1. Planetary gearsets

An automobile must deliver *torque* or "turning power" from the engine, via what is called the *drive train*, to the driving wheels. The main component of the drive train is the transmission. It acts as a torque multiplier (and divider) for adjusting the amount and direction of torque delivered from the engine to the drive wheels under varying engine operating conditions and driving conditions. The torque multiplication factor is known as the transmission's *gear ratio* ρ.

Most automatic automobile transmissions are made from various combinations of *planetary gearsets*. A planetary gearset is a combination of *sun, ring* and *planet* gears arranged somewhat like a miniature solar system. Good introductions to automatic transmissions and planetary gearsets are found in [2] and [5]. A more advanced treatment can be found in [8]. Figure 4-1 shows an example of a simple planetary gearset with four planets. The planets p are attached to an arm a which can rotate with the planets about a central sun gear s. Each planet rotates about its own center as the group of planets on the arm revolves about the sun. At the perimeter of the gearset is a ring gear r whose teeth are on the inside so as to mesh with the planets.

An important parameter for our purposes will be the ratio of the number of teeth T_r on the ring to the number T_s on the sun in a gearset,

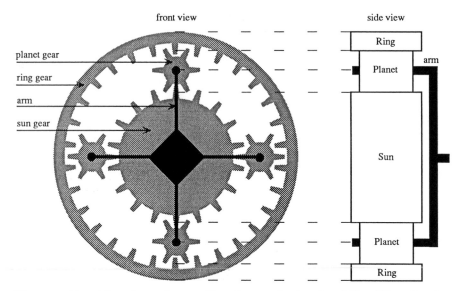

There are $T_s = 18$ teeth on the sun, $T_p = 6$ on each planet and $T_r = 30$ on the ring.

Figure 4-1: A Planetary Gearset with 4 Planet Gears.

$$\beta = T_r / T_s. \tag{4.1}$$

The assumptions we make in the current formulation of the transmission design problem (see [13] for details) allow gearsets corresponding to

$$7/5 \le \beta \le 7/2. \tag{4.2}$$

A basic requirement in meshing gears is that the tangential velocities of the points of contact must be equal. From this one can derive [5] the following kinematic equation relating ω_s, ω_a and ω_r, the angular velocities of the sun gear, arm and ring gear respectively

$$\omega_s - (\beta + 1)\,\omega_a + \beta\,\omega_r = 0 \tag{4.3}$$

A planetary gearset provides the basis for a remarkably flexible mechanism for changing angular velocity (and torque). Each of the three parts – sun s, arm a and ring r – may be conveniently linked to an *input*, *output* or *ground*, so as to act respectively as a *driving*, *driven* or *fixed* member of the gearset. These choices can be modeled as linear equations, which, in conjunction with equation (4.3), allow one to solve for the corresponding gear ratio, $\rho = \omega_{Out} / \omega_{In}$, the ratio of the angular velocity of the output part to that of the input part. Seven different types of gear ratios are found to be possible for a single planetary gearset: a *direct drive* ratio ($\rho = 1$) and six non-direct drive ratios, two being *reverse* ratios ($\rho < 0$), two being *underdrive* ratios ($0 < \rho < 1$) and two being *overdrive* ratios ($\rho > 1$). We will see examples of such ratios and their derivation below in connection with Table 4-1, for the 2-gearset case.

The classic Sturmey Archer bicycle transmission [3] was the first to take advantage of this capability. It is a 3-speed transmission which, by allowing switching between three of the seven kinematic states achievable with a planetary gearset, is able to incorporate an underdrive, a direct drive and an overdrive ratio. Not all seven ratios of a planetary gearset could be incorporated into the Sturmey Archer transmission because topological constraints on the network needed to switch between the corresponding states make this impossible.

4.2.2.2. Two linked planetary gearsets

Coupling together two or more planetary gearsets provides a wider range of achievable kinematic states and gear ratios and hence more flexibility in overcoming topological, and other, constraints in designing a transmission. In automobiles, transmissions with two and three gearsets are common. For our present initial study we restrict ourselves to two gearsets, which we distinguish as gearset 1 and gearset 2. Their relevant component sets are respectively $Parts_1 = \{s1, a1, r1\}$ and $Parts_2 = \{s2, a2, r2\}$, where si, ai and ri of course denote respectively the sun, arm, and ring of gearset i. For the purposes of ordering our computer search we assume that these six components of our two gearsets have the following (purely arbitrary) relative ordering:

$$s1 < a1 < r1 < s2 < a2 < r2. \tag{4.4}$$

In linking two gearsets together, it is possible to use various numbers of hard (or permanent) links. We currently restrict ourselves to exactly two hard links. Such a pair of hard links may be configured in many ways. It turns out that of these, there are only 18 pairs that satisfy the constraints of our domain. Table 4-1 shows the kinematic states achievable for one of these 18 cases using output part $Out = r2$. The hard link pair shown is $L1 = (a1, r2)$ and $L2 = (r1, a2)$, where $Li = (x, y)$ denotes a link between components x and y.

The diagrams used to denote planetary gearsets in Table 4-1 (and in Table 4-2) below, are intended as schematics of the *top half* of the side view of a planetary gearset such as shown at the right in Figure 4-1. Note however that, unlike what is depicted in such a top-half gearset side view, the middle squares of our schematic diagrams do not denote a planet *per se*, but rather the arm which connects to planets. The schematic diagrams use inwards and outwards arrows to denote the input and output components respectively, and use gray shading to denote the braked component.

Note the six kinematic equations given (in matrix form) for each state in Table 4-1. Each state involves six relevant unknowns: the angular velocities

Table 4-1: Gear Ratios Achievable Using Two Planetary Gearsets with two Links $L1 = (a1, r2)$ and $L2 = (r1, a2)$, and Fixed Output $Out = r2$ (or $a1$).

State	In	Braked	Out	Diagram	Kinematic Equations	Gear Ratio $\rho = \dfrac{\omega_{Out}}{\omega_{In}}$	Ratio Type
1†	s1	r1 (a2)	r2 (a1)	Gearset 1 (r1, a1, s1) — Gearset 2 (r2, a2, s2)	$\begin{bmatrix} 1 & -\beta_1-1 & \beta_1 & 0 & 0 \\ 0 & 0 & 0 & -\beta_2-1 & \beta_2 \\ 0 & 1 & 0 & 0 & -1 \\ 0 & 0 & 1 & 0 & 0 \\ 1 & 0 & 0 & 0 & 0 \end{bmatrix}\begin{bmatrix}\omega_{a1}\\\omega_{r1}\\\omega_{a2}\\\omega_{r2}\end{bmatrix}=\begin{bmatrix}0\\0\\0\\0\\1\end{bmatrix}$	$\dfrac{1}{1+\beta_1}\approx 1/3$	under drive
2†	s1	s2	r2 (a1)	(gearset schematic)	$\begin{bmatrix} 1 & -\beta_1-1 & \beta_1 & 0 & 0 \\ 0 & 0 & 0 & -\beta_2-1 & \beta_2 \\ 0 & 1 & 0 & 0 & -1 \\ 0 & 0 & 1 & 0 & 0 \\ 1 & 0 & 0 & 0 & 0 \end{bmatrix}\begin{bmatrix}\omega_{a1}\\\omega_{r1}\\\omega_{a2}\\\omega_{r2}\end{bmatrix}=\begin{bmatrix}0\\0\\0\\0\\1\end{bmatrix}$	$\dfrac{1+\beta_2}{1+\beta_1+\beta_2}\approx 3/5$	under drive
3*	r1 (a2)	s1	r2 (a1)	(gearset schematic)	$\begin{bmatrix} 1 & -\beta_1-1 & \beta_1 & 0 & 0 \\ 0 & 0 & 0 & -\beta_2-1 & \beta_2 \\ 0 & 1 & 0 & 0 & -1 \\ 0 & 0 & 1 & 0 & 0 \\ 1 & 0 & 0 & 0 & 0 \end{bmatrix}\begin{bmatrix}\omega_{a1}\\\omega_{r1}\\\omega_{a2}\\\omega_{r2}\end{bmatrix}=\begin{bmatrix}0\\0\\0\\0\\1\end{bmatrix}$	$\dfrac{\beta_1}{1+\beta_1}\approx 2/3$	under drive
4*†	r1 (a2)	s2	r2 (a1)	(gearset schematic)	$\begin{bmatrix} 1 & -\beta_1-1 & \beta_1 & 0 & 0 \\ 0 & 0 & 0 & -\beta_2-1 & \beta_2 \\ 0 & 1 & 0 & 0 & -1 \\ 0 & 0 & 1 & 0 & 0 \\ 1 & 0 & 0 & 0 & 0 \end{bmatrix}\begin{bmatrix}\omega_{a1}\\\omega_{r1}\\\omega_{a2}\\\omega_{r2}\end{bmatrix}=\begin{bmatrix}0\\0\\0\\0\\1\end{bmatrix}$	$\dfrac{1+\beta_2}{\beta_2}\approx 3/2$	over drive
5*	s2	s1	r2 (a1)	(gearset schematic)	$\begin{bmatrix} 1 & -\beta_1-1 & \beta_1 & 0 & 0 \\ 0 & 0 & 0 & -\beta_2-1 & \beta_2 \\ 0 & 1 & 0 & 0 & -1 \\ 0 & 0 & 1 & 0 & 0 \\ 1 & 0 & 0 & 0 & 0 \end{bmatrix}\begin{bmatrix}\omega_{a1}\\\omega_{r1}\\\omega_{a2}\\\omega_{r2}\end{bmatrix}=\begin{bmatrix}0\\0\\0\\0\\1\end{bmatrix}$	$\dfrac{\beta_1}{1+\beta_1+\beta_2}\approx 2/5$	under drive
6*†	s2	r1 (a2)	r2 (a1)	(gearset schematic)	$\begin{bmatrix} 1 & -\beta_1-1 & \beta_1 & 0 & 0 \\ 0 & 0 & 0 & -\beta_2-1 & \beta_2 \\ 0 & 1 & 0 & 0 & -1 \\ 0 & 0 & 1 & 0 & 0 \\ 1 & 0 & 0 & 0 & 0 \end{bmatrix}\begin{bmatrix}\omega_{a1}\\\omega_{r1}\\\omega_{a2}\\\omega_{r2}\end{bmatrix}=\begin{bmatrix}0\\0\\0\\0\\1\end{bmatrix}$	$-\dfrac{1}{\beta_2}\approx -1/2$	reverse under drive

ω_{si}, ω_{ai} and ω_{ri} for the sun, arm and ring respectively of both gearsets $i = 1$ and $i = 2$. Since there are six variables, we require six equations for a well-defined system. Equation (4.3) provides the first two of these for each state, one version for each of the two gearsets, giving:

$$\omega_{s1} - (\beta_1 + 1)\,\omega_{a1} + \beta_1\,\omega_{r1} = 0 \qquad\qquad (4.5)$$

$$\omega_{s2} - (\beta_2 + 1)\,\omega_{a2} + \beta_2\,\omega_{r2} = 0. \qquad\qquad (4.6)$$

The β_1 and β_2 here are, of course, just $\beta_1 = T_{r1}\,/\,T_{s1}$ and $\beta_2 = T_{r2}\,/\,T_{s2}$, the respective gearset 1 and 2 counterparts of β, the single gearset tooth-ratio defined in (4.1). Equations (4.5) and (4.6) apply to all states of Table 4-1 since the corresponding two gearsets are present in each case. The next two equations for each state reflect its pair of hard links. The first link $L1 = (a1, r2)$ restricts the angular velocity of $a1$ to equal that of $r2$, which contributes equation $\omega_{a1} - \omega_{r2} = 0$. Similarly the second hard link $L2 = (r1, a2)$ contributes equation $\omega_{r1} - \omega_{a2} = 0$. All states of Table 4-1 also have these two as their third and fourth equations because all these states are for the same hard link pair. The remaining two equations for a state reflect its unique combination of input part and braked part. For instance, since state 1 of Table 4-1 has braked and input parts $r1$ and $s1$ respectively, we add the corresponding equations $\omega_{r1} = 0$ and $\omega_{s1} = 1$. The latter value of 1 is convenient here since we are only interested in the *ratio* of output to input velocity.

In the above manner, we can model any state of a pair of linked gearsets using a set of six simultaneous linear equations in six unknowns. Solving these equation sets allows us to obtain symbolic expressions for the transmission states' gear ratios $\rho = \omega_{Out}\,/\,\omega_{In}$ in terms of β_1 and β_2, as seen for example in the rightmost column of Table 4-1. Our algorithm dynamically generates the equation set and obtains the corresponding symbolic expression for ρ for each kinematic state that it generates in its search. Note the numerical approximations for ρ given in the right column of Table 4-1. These are based on a nominal value of 2 for β_1 and β_2, which is within our assumed range (4.2). We now look at how the design of two-planetary transmissions is made possible by formulating it as a constraint satisfaction problem.

4.3. VARIABLES AND THEIR DOMAINS

This section describes the variables and their domains of candidate values that we have employed in formulating transmission design as a constraint satisfaction problem. The section after this will treat the corresponding constraints used. The domains and constraints given in these two sections correspond to common practice in designing full-sized passenger vehicles in the United States. In the interest of brevity, detailed explanations of the domains and constraints are not provided. Fuller explanation appears in [13]. Here we are interested in the design of 4R-speed transmissions. We use index 0 to denote reverse speed, and indices 1, 2, 3 and 4 for the four forward speeds, in increasing order of gear ratio. Speed $i = 3$ will be the direct drive speed, which in the general case we denote by index value d. At this stage of the formulation we in fact ignore the direct drive state, and concentrate on finding only compatible states for speeds $i = 0, 1, 2$ and 4. We will see that ten CSP variables suffice for our present formulation.

Hard Links (2 variables): A *hard,* or *permanent,* link is a link built into the transmission so as to remain permanently in effect at all speeds. A *soft,* or *clutchable* or *temporary* link is one that may be established via clutch changes just to achieve a specific speed, and is not in effect at all speeds. We assume here that the transmissions we are designing have exactly two planetary gearsets linked by exactly two hard links, $L1$ and $L2$, and have no soft links. For each of the hard links, we need to decide what gearset components it joins together. The parts of gearset 1 that may constitute an end of a link are $Parts_1 = \{ s1, a1, r1 \}$, and the parts of gearset 2 are $Parts_2 = \{ s2, a2, r2 \}$. The two ends of a hard link must be in different gearsets. The domains for link variables $L1$ and $L2$ are thus

$$d_{L1} = d_{L2} = Parts_1 \times Parts_2 =$$

$$\{(s1,s2),(s1,a2),(s1,r2),(a1,s2),(a1,a2),(a1,r2),(r1,s2),(r1,a2),(r1,r2)\}.$$

Outputs (0 variables): In general, for each of the n forward speeds (in our case, $n = 4$) and the 1 reverse speed that we want our transmission to realize, we need to decide on the part to output from. This would introduce $n +1$ new variables, Out_i for $0 \leq i \leq n$, into our CSP formulation. Since we ignore the direct drive case $i = d$, this gives n variables. But actually it is common practice in automobile transmissions to have the same output component for each speed. Thus a single output variable Out will suffice.

The domain of Out might a priori be thought to be $d_{Out} = Parts_1 \cup Parts_2 = \{s1, a1, r1, s2, a2, r2\}$. However, output from a sun is not used in practice due to stress considerations [13]. Thus the domain of Out is reduced to $d_{Out} = \{a1, r1, a2, r2\}$. Symmetry considerations allow us to reduce this further to $d_{Out} = \{a2, r2\}$, and for simplicity in this initial formulation, we restrict ourselves even further to simply $d_{Out} = \{r2\}$. Since *Out* is thus allowed only a single value, it is actually no longer a CSP variable as such, and need not be explicitly instantiated at some given level of the search tree. It thus will not appear in the trace of Figure 4-2 below, where *Out* = $r2$ is assumed to hold globally.

Inputs (4 variables): For each of the non-direct-drive speeds that we want our transmission to realize, we need to decide on the part to which we input. This introduces n new variables In_i for $0 \leq i \neq d \leq n$, into our CSP formulation. A priori, any of the combined six parts of the two gearsets is a potential input at each speed so that the domain of each variable In_i is thus

$$d_{In_i} = Parts_1 \cup Parts_2 = \{s1, a1, r1, s2, a2, r2\} \quad \text{for } 0 \leq i \neq d \leq n.$$

Brakes (4 variables): For each of the non-direct-drive speeds that we want our transmission to realize, we need to decide on the braked part. (Direct drive speed is usually achieved without resort to a braked part, but this is irrelevant here since we are ignoring the direct drive speed.) This introduces n new variables Br_i for $0 \leq i \neq d \leq n$, into our CSP formulation. As with the inputs, any of the combined six parts of the two gearsets is a priori a potential braked component at each speed. The domain of each variable Br_i is thus

$$d_{Br_i} = Parts_1 \cup Parts_2 = \{s1, a1, r1, s2, a2, r2\} \quad \text{for } 0 \leq i \neq d \leq n.$$

4.4. CONSTRAINTS

This section describes the constraints that we use in connection with the variables of the previous section, in obtaining a CSP formulation of the transmission design problem. The constraints are labeled below as C_j for various j values. These C_j labels will be useful in our later sample trace in Figure 4-2, to identify which constraint is being applied where in the search process. The states in Table 4-1 above (and in Table 4-2 below) all satisfy the constraints of this section, and thus provide useful examples to help in understanding the constraints better.

Non-Connecting Links: The two hard links joining our two gearsets are not allowed to have a common end. If the two hard links are $L1 = (x_1, y_1)$ and $L2 = (x_2, y_2)$ then we can express this constraint as

$$x_1 \neq x_2 \quad \text{and} \quad y_1 \neq y_2. \tag{C_1}$$

Link Renaming Equivalence: In linking gearsets using two links it does not matter which link we call $L1$ and which we call $L2$. That is, having two links $L1 = (x_1, y_1)$ and $L2 = (x_2, y_2)$ is physically the same as having the two links $L1 = (x_2, y_2)$ and $L2 = (x_1, y_1)$. This kind of redundancy can be avoided by requiring say link $L2$ to be lexographically greater than link $L1$, with respect to the underlying order of parts given in (4.4). For hard links $L1 = (x_1, y_1)$ and $L2 = (x_2, y_2)$ we write this constraint as

$$(x_1, y_1) < (x_2, y_2). \tag{C_2}$$

Using constraints C_1 and C_2 reduces the a priori $81 = 9 \times 9$ possible pairs of links for two planetaries down to only 18 pairs (one of which was seen in Table 4-1).

Link End Equivalence: Since two parts joined by a link are by definition constrained to move together, braking one end of a link also brakes the other end. Similarly, inputing to one end of a link is like inputing to the other end, and the same applies for outputing. This kind of functional redundancy can be avoided by choosing say the gearset 1 end of a link as the preferred part, and not allowing the gearset 2 end as legal for the input In_i or brake Br_i at any speed i. If the two hard links are $L1 = (x_1, y_1)$ and $L2 = (x_2, y_2)$, then we can express these constraints as

$$In_i \notin \{ y_1, y_2 \} \quad \text{for } 0 \le i \le n. \tag{C_3}$$

$$Br_i \notin \{ y_1, y_2 \} \quad \text{for } 0 \le i \le n. \tag{C_4}$$

Don't Brake the Output: It is obvious that a brake should not be applied to the output part, else we get no output torque. Thus we have the constraints

$$Br_i \ne Out \quad \text{for } 0 \le i \le n. \tag{C_5}$$

Since braking a part that is linked to the output causes the same problem – no output torque – we interpret C_5 to mean that neither the output part, nor a part joined to it by a link, may be braked.

Don't Brake the Input: As with not braking the output above, we also cannot brake the input, else we effectively get no input torque. Thus we have:

$$Br_i \ne In_i \quad \text{for } 0 \le i \le n. \tag{C_6}$$

Don't Input to the Output: When the input part is the same as the output part, the gear ratio $\rho = \omega_{Out} / \omega_{In}$ must of course be $\rho = 1$, so we get a direct drive speed. Thus for all non-direct-drive speeds $i \neq d$ this possibility must be excluded. We therefore have:

$$In_i \neq Out \quad \text{for } 0 \le i \neq d \le n. \tag{C_7}$$

Since inputing to a part that is linked to the output causes the same result − a direct drive ratio − we interpret C_7 to mean that neither the output part, nor a part joined to it by a link, may be the input part.

Different Ratios in Different Gears: By definition, different speeds or "gears" must have different gear ratios. Since we are assuming a fixed output Out in each speed i, the gear ratio in speed i (for a given pair of hard links) varies only with the input In_i and the braked element Br_i. To avoid the same ratio at different speeds i and j, we thus require at least one of these variables to be different, so that

$$(In_i \neq In_j) \text{ or } (Br_i \neq Br_j) \quad \text{for } 0 \le i < j \le n. \tag{C_8}$$

Gear Ratio Ranges: The most basic attributes of a transmission are how many speeds it provides and the corresponding gear ratio values at those speeds. As mentioned, we are assuming here a transmission with 1 reverse speed ($\rho < 0$) and $n = 4$ forward speeds consisting of two underdrives ($0 < \rho < 1$), a direct drive ($\rho = 1$) and an overdrive ($\rho > 1$) speed. The following constraints specify the ranges we will consider acceptable for the gear ratios ρ_i at these speeds.

Reverse Gear Ratio:	$-2/5 \le \rho_0 \le -1/5$	(C_9)
First Gear Ratio:	$1/3 \le \rho_1 \le 1/2$	(C_{10})
Second Gear Ratio:	$3/5 \le \rho_2 \le 4/5$	(C_{11})
Third Gear Ratio:	$\rho_3 = 1$	(C_{12})
Fourth Gear Ratio:	$5/4 \le \rho_4 \le 5/3$	(C_{13})

Our algorithm computes ρ symbolically as a function of β_1 and β_2, for each kinematic state it generates. (Examples were seen in Table 4-1.) Thus once we have assigned specific values to β_1 and β_2 we can obtain the corresponding value for a given $\rho(\beta_1, \beta_2)$ as a way of testing for the given speed under consideration, whether the applicable constraint from C_9 to C_{13} is satisfied. But like the gear ratios ρ_i themselves, the teeth ratios β_1 and β_2 are not CSP variables per se, whose values are known directly by instantiation. Rather, the latter are functions of the teeth numbers T_{r1}, T_{r2}, T_{s1} and T_{s2}. Thus values for β_1 and β_2, and hence for ρ_i, could be obtained by instantiating those teeth number variables. This would be a natural approach, but in our current formulation we do not wish to go to this level of detail and corresponding search complexity. So teeth numbers on gears are not features (CSP variables) of our design, and the above ratio-range constraints must be tested less directly.[3]

The indirect test we use is based on the work of Ward [16] (see also Chapter 5). Given a function $z = f(x,y)$, which is monotonic in both x and y, it is possible to bound the variation in z given bounds on the variation in x and y. In particular, if $a \leq x \leq b$ and $c \leq y \leq d$ then

$$\min\{f(a,c),f(a,d),f(b,c),f(b,d)\} \leq z \leq \max\{f(a,c),f(a,d),f(b,c),f(b,d)\}. \quad (4.7)$$

Given that we have bounds on β_1 and β_2 from (4.2), we can use (4.7) to bound the value of $\rho(\beta_1, \beta_2)$ for a given kinematic state. If there is no overlap between this derived range for ρ and that required by the ratio-range constraint above for a given speed i, then the ratio-range constraint is violated and the corresponding state cannot serve to provide that speed.

Simplicity-of-Switching Constraints: An important class of constraints are what we call the simplicity-of-switching constraints. These are to ensure that only simple changes of braking and clutching are required in switching between adjacent speeds i and $i + 1$. We ensure this by requiring that at most one of the braked part and the input part may change in an adjacent-speed transition. This gives us the following simplicity-of-switching constraints:

$$(In_{i+1} = In_i) \text{ or } (Br_{i+1} = Br_i) \quad \text{for } 1 \leq i \leq n - 1. \quad (C_{14})$$

4.5. OUR RESULTS

The previous two sections showed how the transmission design problem can be formulated as a constraint satisfaction problem. In particular, Section 4.3 specified the CSP variables and domains which we use, and Section 4.4 specified the CSP constraints. Part of the Backtrack tree [9, 15] corresponding to our formulation of the previous two sections is given in Figure 4-2. The ten CSP variables we use correspond to the ten levels of the search tree, with correspondences as indicated in the "Variables" column at the left of the figure. At a given level the figure shows all possible assignments of that level's variable, corresponding to all values from the domain of that variable as described in Section 4.3.

---

[3] Even if we did consider teeth numbers, it would be preferable in terms of combinatorial explosion to postpone instantiation of the corresponding variables till the last levels of the search tree — and an initial application of our indirect scheme for testing the ratio-range constraints would still be desirable to allow some earlier pruning higher up in the tree.

For extra clarity we include, in the "Constraints" column at the left of the figure, the list of constraints (using the constraint labels of Section 4.4) that are checkable at each level. These are listed top to bottom in the order in which they are checked by our algorithm. Under each tree node, we show for each of the checkable constraints whether the corresponding constraint test succeeds (shown by a check mark) or fails (shown by a cross). As an aid to the reader, at nodes in Figure 4-2 where the processing gets as far as checking a ratio-range constraint (C_9 to C_{13}), we precede the result of that check by a row, shown enclosed in a rectangle, giving the corresponding symbolic expression computed by our algorithm for the ratio ρ_i. Of course, once the first constraint-check failure occurs down the list of constraints at a node, no further constraints need be checked and the corresponding path through the tree is "pruned off." Only nodes at which all checkable constraints are satisfied can be used to sprout descendant nodes at the next level.

Figure 4-2 shows two branches leading to solutions in our search tree. The left branch shown leads to the discovery of a 4R-speed extension of the classic 3R-speed Simpson transmission [2, 5] and the right branch leads to discovery of the well-known 4R-speed Axod transmission [1]. Interestingly, these two transmissions, although made up of different sets of states, have the same gear ratios at corresponding speeds.

The full set of solutions found by our search is shown in Table 4-2. Ten solutions are found. In fact, only the last two actually correspond to known transmissions, the HydraMatic 700 and Axod. It is possible that some of the other eight solutions we found are actually new discoveries (we haven't had time to check thoroughly), but it is more likely they will all be eliminated when the other applicable constraints are added.

For instance, the switching network (which we are ignoring here) required to build the "extended Simpson" transmission, solution 5, is known to not be topologically realizable. Also, solution 7 is obviously unacceptable because no matter what are the values for β_1 and β_2, the ratio for speed 2, $\rho_2 = (\beta_1\beta_2 - 1) / (\beta_2 + \beta_1\beta_2)$, will be less than the ratio obtained for speed 1, $\rho_1 = (\beta_1\beta_2 - 1) / \beta_1\beta_2$, because of the extra β_2 in the denominator of the former. Solution 7 slips by here because we have not yet implemented the class of "step" constraints, which ensure acceptable ratios between the gear ratios. The closest we get are the ratio-range constraints, C_9 to C_{13}. The symbolic (non-numeric) way we are testing these, using (4.7), ensures only that for each speed tested independently, there are possible values for β_1 and β_2 that allow the gear ratio to be in the necessary range. This does not ensure proper relative sizes of ratios at different speeds, nor even that the desirable ranges for the set of ratios are achievable using the *same* pair of β_1 and β_2 values, as is of course required since the gears in our gearsets (and hence β_1 and β_2) do not change with speed for a given transmission. The latter problem will disappear once we start

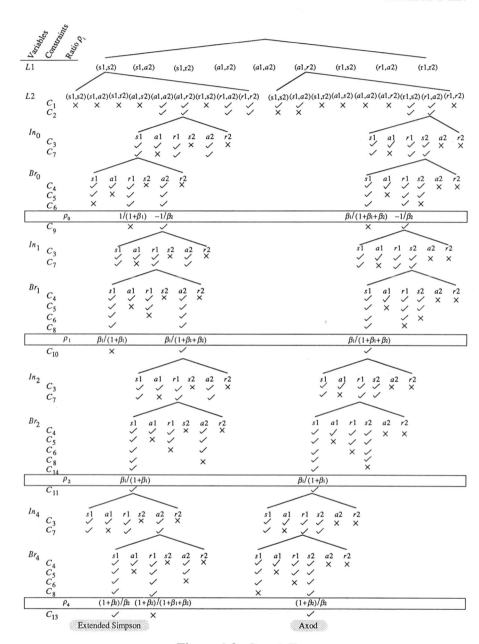

Figure 4-2: Search Tree

Table 4-2: Solution Table

Solution	L1	L2	Out	Diagram	Speed 0 (reverse) In_0	Br_0	ρ_0	Speed 1 (low underdrive) In_1	Br_1	ρ_1	Speed 2 (high underdrive) In_2	Br_2	ρ_2	Speed 4 (overdrive) In_4	Br_4	ρ_4
1	$(s1,s2)$	$(a1,a2)$	$r2$		$s1$	$a1$	$-\dfrac{1}{\beta_2}$	$r1$	$a1$	$\dfrac{\beta_1}{\beta_2}$	$r1$	$s1$	$\dfrac{\beta_1+\beta_1\beta_2}{\beta_2+\beta_1\beta_2}$	$a1$	$s1$	$\dfrac{1+\beta_2}{\beta_2}$
2					$s1$	$r1$	$\dfrac{\beta_2-\beta_1}{\beta_2+\beta_1\beta_2}$	$r1$	$a1$	$\dfrac{\beta_1}{\beta_2}$	$r1$	$s1$	$\dfrac{\beta_1+\beta_1\beta_2}{\beta_2+\beta_1\beta_2}$	$a1$	$s1$	$\dfrac{1+\beta_2}{\beta_2}$
3					$a1$	$r1$	$\dfrac{\beta_2-\beta_1}{\beta_2}$	$r1$	$a1$	$\dfrac{\beta_1}{\beta_2}$	$r1$	$s1$	$\dfrac{\beta_1+\beta_1\beta_2}{\beta_2+\beta_1\beta_2}$	$a1$	$s1$	$\dfrac{1+\beta_2}{\beta_2}$
4	$(s1,s2)$	$(a1,r2)$	$r2$		$s1$	$a2$	$-\dfrac{1}{\beta_2}$	$s1$	$r1$	$\dfrac{1}{1+\beta_1}$	$a2$	$r1$	$\dfrac{1+\beta_2}{1+\beta_1+\beta_2}$	$a2$	$s1$	$\dfrac{1+\beta_2}{\beta_2}$
5 (Extended Simpson)					$s1$	$a2$	$-\dfrac{1}{\beta_2}$	$r1$	$a2$	$\dfrac{\beta_1}{1+\beta_1+\beta_2}$	$r1$	$s1$	$\dfrac{\beta_1}{1+\beta_1}$	$a2$	$s1$	$\dfrac{1+\beta_2}{\beta_2}$
6	$(a1,a2)$	$(r1,s2)$	$r2$		$r1$	$a1$	$-\dfrac{1}{\beta_2}$	$s1$	$a1$	$\dfrac{1}{\beta_1\beta_2}$	$s1$	$r1$	$\dfrac{1+\beta_2}{\beta_2+\beta_1\beta_2}$	$a1$	$r1$	$\dfrac{1+\beta_2}{\beta_2}$
7					$r1$	$a1$	$-\dfrac{1}{\beta_2}$	$a1$	$s1$	$\dfrac{\beta_1\beta_2-1}{\beta_1\beta_2}$	$r1$	$s1$	$\dfrac{\beta_1\beta_2-1}{\beta_2+\beta_1\beta_2}$	$a1$	$r1$	$\dfrac{1+\beta_2}{\beta_2}$
8					$r1$	$a1$	$-\dfrac{1}{\beta_2}$	$r1$	$s1$	$\dfrac{\beta_1\beta_2-1}{\beta_2+\beta_1\beta_2}$	$a1$	$s1$	$\dfrac{\beta_1\beta_2-1}{\beta_1\beta_2}$	$a1$	$r1$	$\dfrac{1+\beta_2}{\beta_2}$
9 (HM 700)	$(a1,r2)$	$(r1,a2)$	$r2$		$s2$	$r1$	$-\dfrac{1}{\beta_2}$	$s1$	$r1$	$\dfrac{1}{1+\beta_1}$	$s1$	$s2$	$\dfrac{1+\beta_2}{1+\beta_1+\beta_2}$	$r1$	$s2$	$\dfrac{1+\beta_2}{\beta_2}$
10 (Axod)					$s2$	$r1$	$-\dfrac{1}{\beta_2}$	$s2$	$s1$	$\dfrac{\beta_1}{1+\beta_1+\beta_2}$	$r1$	$s1$	$\dfrac{\beta_1}{1+\beta_1}$	$r1$	$s2$	$\dfrac{1+\beta_2}{\beta_2}$

131

to explicitly consider teeth number for gears. We will then be able to use the corresponding fixed numerical values for β_1 and β_2 in testing the set of ratio-range constraints. Being able to test the step constraints also depends on having numerical values for β_1 and β_2. A recent preliminary run of an extended formulation allowing explicit consideration of teeth numbers does, in fact, result in removal of about half of the eight unlikely solutions of Table 4-2.

4.6. EXTENSIONS

There are many ways in which our work to date may be extended. The following is a partial list.

A. As mentioned in Section 4.5, eight of the ten transmission design solutions found by our program (Table 4-2) are probably not physically realizable. This is because we have not yet formulated the problem at a sufficient level of detail nor incorporated all relevant constraints even for the current level of detail. Among other things, our future formulations will need to consider (i) teeth number on gears and the corresponding *gearing* constraints, (ii) the specific nature of the transmission's switching network and the corresponding *topological* constraints, (iii) the *step* constraints on the ratios between gear ratios, and (iv) the nature of the transmission's direct drive and neutral states with corresponding full use of the applicable *simplicity-of-switching* constraints.

B. Apart from adding detail to our designs, as discussed in item A, we also need to broaden the design space being searched. The current search is restricted to transmissions of four forward speeds and one reverse speed, made of two simple planetary gearsets joined by two hard links and no soft (or clutchable) links. In our future formulations we expect to allow (i) an arbitrary number g of gearsets, rather than just two as here, (ii) an arbitrary number h of hard links, rather than just two as here, (iii) an arbitrary number s of soft (or clutchable) links, rather than none as here, (iv) an arbitrary number n of (forward) speeds, rather than just four as here, and (v) "compound" planetary gearsets, rather than just simple planetary gearsets. A description of compound gearsets is beyond the scope of this paper. See for example [5] or [6].

C. Automobile automatic transmissions consist of three interacting subsystems: mechanical, hydraulic and electronic, the latter two being needed to control the former. Our present work concentrates exclusively on the mechanical subsystem. In the long run we expect to extend our transmission design task to include the integrated design of all three subsystems.

Basically the present "first pass" at transmission design has been encouraging. We have been able to automate the rediscovery of the known transmissions within the class we have delimited, and to avoid the discovery of most unacceptable solutions. The space we have used has been relatively well explored manually by human designers in the past. However, the space corresponding to the above anticipated refinements and extensions has not been manually explored to the same extent. The distinct possibility exists of discovering new and better transmissions in an automated search of such broader design spaces.

4.7. ACKNOWLEDGMENTS

This work has been made possible by a research grant, and generous cooperation, from the Ford Motor Co. In particular, thanks to Bob Roethler and the rest of the Ford Advanced Transmission Design Department in Livonia, Michigan, for extensive discussions on the engineering aspects of this work. Access to the Ford library in Dearborn, Michigan, was also very helpful.

4.8. BIBLIOGRAPHY

[1] "AXOD Automatic Overdrive Transaxle – Operation and Diagnosis," Ford Parts and Service Division, Training and Publications Dept., 1985 [order no. 1701-205].

[2] Ellinger H. E., *Automechanics*, Prentice Hall, Englewood Cliffs, New Jersey, 1983 (third edition).

[3] Hadland T., *The Sturmey Archer Story*, Pinkerton Publishing Co., London, England, 1987.

[4] Haralick R. M. and Elliot, "Increasing Tree Search Efficiency for Constraint Satisfaction Problems," *Artificial Intelligence*, Vol. 14, pp. 263-313, 1980.

[5] Husselbee W. L., *Automatic Transmissions: Fundamentals and Service*, Prentice-Hall, Englewood Cliffs, New Jersey, 1986 (second edition).

[6] Lynwander P., *Gear Drive Systems: Design and Application*, Marcel Dekker Inc., New York, NY, 1983.

[7]   Mackworth A. K., "Constraint Satisfaction," in *Encyclopedia of Artificial Intelligence*, S. Shapiro, Ed., Wiley, New York, 1987.

[8]   Muller H. W., *Epicyclic Drive Trains – Analysis, Synthesis and Applications*, Wayne State University Press., Detroit, Michigan, 1982.

[9]   Nadel B. A., "Constraint Satisfaction Algorithms," *Computational Intelligence*, Vol. 5, No. 4, pp. 188-224, November 1989, [A preliminary version appeared as 'Tree search and arc consistency in constraint satisfaction algorithms', in *Search in Artificial Intelligence*, edited by L. Kanal and V. Kumar, Springer-Verlag, New York, 1988].

[10]   Nadel B. A., "Representation Selection for Constraint Satisfaction: a case study using *n*-queens," *IEEE Expert*, Vol. 5, No. 3, June 1990.

[11]   <Nadel B. A., "The Complexity of Constraint Satisfaction in Prolog," *Proc. Eighth Nat. Conf. on Artificial Intelligence (AAAI-90)*, Boston, Mass., pp. 33-39, August 1990, [An expanded version is available as technical report CSC-89-004, 1989, Dept. Computer Science, Wayne State University, Detroit, Michigan].

[12]   Nadel B. A., "Some Applications of the Constraint Satisfaction Problem," 1990 [in review. Available as technical report CSC-90-008, Dept. Computer Science, Wayne State University, Detroit, Michigan].

[13]   Nadel B. A. and Lin J., "Automobile Transmission Design as a Constraint Satisfaction Problem: Modeling the Kinematic Level," *Artificial Intelligence for Engineering Desing, Analysis and Manufacturing (AI EDAM)*, Vol. 5, No. 2, 1991.

[14]   Nadel B. A. and Lin J., "Automobile transmission design: a constraint satisfaction formulation and Prolog implementation," 1991 [in review].

[15]   Nudel B. A., "Consistent-labeling Problems and their Algorithms: Expected-complexities and Theory-based Heuristics," *Artificial Intelligence (special issue on search and heuristics)*, Vol. 21, nos. 1 and 2, pp. 135-178, March 1983, [Also in *Search and Heuristics*, North-Holland, Amsterdam, 1983].

[16]   Ward A. C., "A Theory of Quantitative Inference for Artifact Sets, Applied to a Mechanical Design Compiler," Dept. Mechanical Engineering, MIT, 1988, Doctor of Science dissertation (See also Chapter 5, Volume I).

Chapter 5
DESIGN COMPILERS AND THE LABELED INTERVAL CALCULUS: A TUTORIAL

Daisie D. Boettner and Allen C. Ward

Abstract

Compilers accept descriptions of wide range of designs in high level, easy to use languages, and translate them into detailed, implementable descriptions. They have been proven useful in software and digital hardware design. The mechanical design compiler discussed here appears to be the first of its kind: it accepts a schematic, specifications and a utility function, and returns catalog numbers for an implementation.

The mechanical domain involves a high degree of interaction between parts, and a strong requirement for near optimal performance and cost. These issues are addressed in the compiler through the use of a novel mathematical formalism, the labeled interval calculus, which enables the compiler to draw inferences about sets of possibilities. This chapter provides a tutorial introduction to the theory underlying both the compiler and the calculus.

5.1. INTRODUCTION

5.1.1. Background

The "compiler" metaphor is a natural way to think about automating design. Compilers provide the human designer with a high-level language in which to describe the design. They can then transform this high-level description into a detailed, implementable description. This approach has had great success in computer programs and Very Large Scale Integrated (VLSI) circuits (see, e.g., Chapter 12).

In the mechanical domain it is natural to think of this "high-level language" as being composed in part of "components" and/or "features": abstract or generalized parts of machines which are to be connected to form the complete machine. However, in the programming and VLSI domains, the instantiation (transformation from high level to detailed level) of the elements of the high-level language is relatively independent of the circumstances. In the mechanical domain, there are normally many possible instantiations, and a major function of the program is to choose the right one. This choice is largely quantitative -- a matter of selecting the lowest "cost" (by some measure) of the possible instantiations which is satisfactory under the circumstances. The machine code produced by a programming language compiler may be a few times less efficient than that produced by hand, but remains acceptable. Such losses are rarely acceptable in mechanical design.

Figure 5-1: Design Schematic

Hence, a mechanical design compiler must focus at least as much on the relationships between components (as in the example design schematic shown in Figure 5-1) as on the transformation or formulation of the individual component. It is natural to think in terms of the propagation of constraints between the components; and equally natural to consider propagating real number values through algebraic equations. Once a system of equations has been defined for each component, the equations can be connected to one another by the identifying interface variables when the components are connected. This characterizes (in part) the work of Serrano (Chapter 3), Popplestone [4], and Bahler [1]. See Figure 5-2.

When the designer or some other mechanism has decided a sufficient number of the values for the variables in the equations, these programs can compute the remaining values.   They are in themselves analysis rather than synthesis programs. Bahler [1] has annotated such programs with optimization suggestions, which change the variable values to try new combinations based on the results of the current analysis. S. Tong has constructed an environment for such heuristic optimization which relies on general analysis codes rather than equations; it is discussed in Volume 3, Chapter 9. However, it is not clear to us

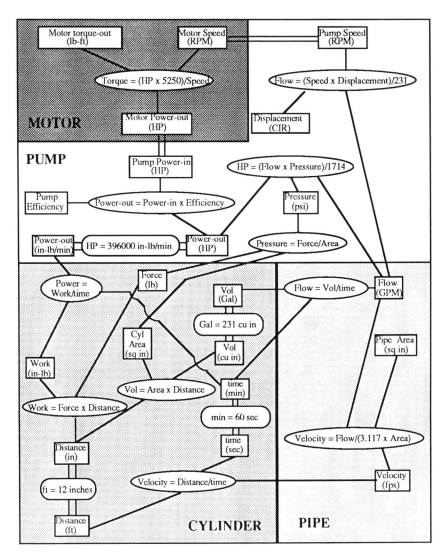

Figure 5-2: Connection-of-Variables

whether such distributed and heuristic optimization procedures can perform significantly better than traditional, formal optimization techniques. In particular, it is not clear how such a program could be confident of finding the best available solution rather than a purely local optimum.

5.1.2. Purpose

This paper describes a tool for making choices, rather than for analyzing the consequences of the choices. In order to accomplish this, we have changed the way the equations are used. That is, instead of propagating single values, we propagate information about sets of values; these sets are most commonly intervals of real numbers. The "constraint propagation of intervals" or the "interval arithmetic" is fairly well understood; see Davis [2] and Moore [3]. Somewhat to our surprise, this standard notion of interval constraint propagation is by no means sufficient for even simple design problems. Treating these problems formally requires expanding the interval constraint propagation ideas so dramatically as to constitute a new formalism, which we have dubbed the "labeled interval calculus."

In particular, we hold that design descriptions represent sets of components functioning under sets of operating conditions. Traditionally, reasoning about sets has been quantitative, but informal. The Labeled Interval Calculus (LIC) formalizes a system for reasoning about sets.

LIC defines a number of operations on intervals and equations, some of which can be thought of as inverses to the usual notion of interval propagation. These are discussed in Section 5.2.2.

Section 5.2.3 turns to the question, "What do the intervals mean?" or more precisely, "What kinds of relationships are possible between a set of values, a variable, and a set of artifacts, each subject to a set of operating conditions?" We will find that the usual notion of an interval constraint must be supplemented in the design context by a system of labels to indicate which is meant of several possible relationships between the interval and the set.

Section 5.2.4 then defines a set of inferences that use the operations defined in Section 5.2.2 and the labeled intervals of Section 5.2.3 to reason about sets of artifacts and operating conditions.

Finally, Section 5.3 discusses how these inferences are employed in a mechanical design compiler, which accepts generic schematics and specifications for a wide variety of designs, and returns catalog numbers for optimal implementations of the schematics.

5.1.3. Unanswered Issues

The LIC raises issues of causality and independence of variables still not fully understood. This lack of full understanding is apparent when considering some of the inference rules under development. The problems with this issue are addressed more fully in Section 5.2.4.

5.2. LABELED INTERVAL CALCULUS

5.2.1. Introduction

In order to examine LIC more closely, LIC can be subdivided into three areas: operations, labels, and inferences. Ordinary arithmetic operations manipulate numerical values. LIC operations manipulate assignment intervals (variable features with their corresponding interval of values). Three kinds of LIC labels describe how a variable feature is constrained with respect to its interval of values, represent information about entire sets of artifacts, and show causality. LIC inferences are rules based on operations and labels. The MDC uses inferences to draw conclusions about sets of artifacts under consideration for a design.

This is an informal introduction to the LIC. For a more rigorous exposition, see Ward [5].

5.2.2. Operations

LIC operations are analogous to ordinary mathematical operations. For example, the operation, plus, takes two numerical values, 2 and 3, and produces a numerical value, 5. On the other hand, the operations of LIC take two assignment intervals (each consisting of a variable and an interval of numerical values) and produce a new assignment interval.

5.2.2.1. Some basic operations definitions

1. LIC involves intervals of assignments, consisting of a variable feature and an interval of values. For example, let P be the interval of pressures, p (psi). We will write this interval as P = <p 1000 3000>. Other intervals used in subsequent examples describing operations are F, the interval of forces, f (lb), and A, the interval of areas, a (sq in). The following examples demonstrate the mathematical manipulation of the LIC operations. The design aspect of these operations is discussed in later sections.

2. G is an implicit relationship among three variables; for example pressure (p) - force (f)/area (a) = 0. Throughout this tutorial, we

assume that the relationships are continuous and satisfy "uniqueness" throughout the intervals of interest; that is $G(x_1, y_1, z_1) = 0$ and $G(x_2, y_1, z_1) = 0$ implies $x_1 = x_2$ (and similar for y and z).

3. $g_x(y, z) = x$ is relationship G solved for x, given y and z. For example:

$$G \equiv p - f/a = 0, p = 1000 \text{ psi, and } a = 5 \text{ sq in; } g_f(p,a)=f=5000lb.$$

The uniqueness property implies that G always can be solved for any of the three variables, and that the resulting functions are strictly monotonic, that is, the partial derivatives are never zero and have the same sign throughout the interval of interest.

5.2.2.2. LIC operations

LIC has nine operations. They are Intersection ($\cap$), Subset ($\subseteq$), Union ($\cup$), Filled-Union ($\cup$), Corners, Central, Range, Domain, and Sufficient Points (SufPt). The first three operations listed are described in elementary set theory.

Filled-Union combines two intervals X_1 and X_2 into a new interval X_3 such that the endpoints of X_3 are the overall lowest value and the highest value from intervals X_1 and X_2. For example, given: $X_1 = < x \ 2 \ 4 >$ and $X_2 = < x \ 6 \ 8 >$, then $(X_1 \cup X_2) = X_3 = < x \ 2 \ 8 >$.

The five remaining operations require a relationship G and two known intervals. Detailed discussion of these operations follows.

5.2.2.3. Corners operation

Given a relationship G, an interval X, and an interval Y, the Corners operation determines 4 discrete values. Substitution of all combinations of the endpoints of the given intervals X and Y into relationship G produces 4 discrete values for the variable z.

By definition, Corners $(G, X, Y) = \{z_1, z_2, z_3, z_4\} = \{g_z(x_l, y_l), g_z(x_h, y_l), g_z(x_l, y_h), g_z(x_h, y_h)\}$,

```
where  x_l = lowest value of x in interval X.
       x_h = highest value of x in interval X.
       y_l = lowest value of y in interval Y.
       y_h = highest value of y in interval Y.
```

Example: Corners (G, A, F)

Given:

1. G: $p = f/a$, a relationship among pressure, force, and area.

2. A = < a 2 5 >, interval of areas (sq in).

3. F = < f 1000 3000 >, interval of forces (lb).

Computation:

$a_l = 2$ sq in, $a_h = 5$ sq in, $f_l = 1000$ lb, $f_h = 3000$ lb

Corners (G, A, F) = $\{p_1, p_2, p_3, p_4\}$ = { 1000/2, 1000/5, 3000/2, 3000/5} (psi)

Corners (G, A, F) = {500, 200, 1500, 600} (psi)

5.2.2.4. Central interval operation

The Central Interval is defined as the interval bounded by the two middle values obtained from the result of the Corners operation. From the previous Corners example, Central (G, A, F) = < p 500 600 > (psi).

5.2.2.5. Range operation

Given the relationship G, an interval X, and an interval Y, the Range operation determines an interval Z. Z is the interval containing all possible values of z which can be obtained by computing $g_z(x, y)$ for every choice of value x in interval X and every choice of value y in interval Y. Range (G, X, Y) always exists.

Computation of Range. The Range is computed by applying the Corners operation to X and Y and forming an interval bounded by the lowest and the highest values obtained from the result of the Corners operation.

It is shown in Ward [5] that Range (G, X, Y) = Z = < min (Corners (G, X, Y)) max (Corners (G, X, Y)) >.

Example: Range (G, A, F)
Given:

1. G: $p = f/a$

2. A = < a 2 5 > (sq in)

3. F = < f 1000 3000 > (lb)

Computation:
Corners (G, A, F) = {500, 200, 1500, 600} (psi)
Range (G, A, F) = P = < p 200 1500 > (psi)
This is shown graphically in Figure 5-3.

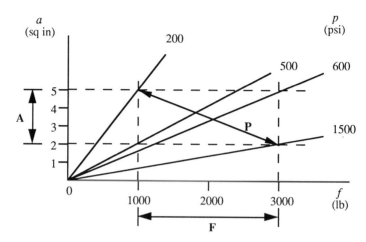

Figure 5-3: Range (G, A, F) = P

5.2.2.6. Domain operation

Given a relationship G, an interval Z, and an interval X, the Domain operation determines an interval Y. Y is the smallest continuous interval such that for every value x in interval X there is a value z in interval Z which satisfies relationship $g_y(x, z) = y$. The Domain operation is a partial inverse of the Range operation. By definition, Domain (G, Z, X) = Y if and only if Range (G, X, Y) = Z.

Computation of Domain. Domain (G, Z, X) is computed in two steps. First, apply the Central Interval operation to Z and X to form interval Y. Check whether Range (G, X, Y) = Z: if so, then Domain (G, Z, X) = Y; if not Domain (G, Z, X) does not exist.

Example 1: Domain (G, P, A)
  Given:

  1. G: $p = f/a$

  2. P = < p 200 1500 > (psi)

3. A = < a 2 5 > (sq in)

Computation:
Corners (G, P, A) = {(200 × 2), (1500 × 2), (200 × 5), (1500 × 5)} (lb)
Corners (G, P, A) = {400, 3000, 1000, 7500} (lb)
Central (G, P, A) = F = < f 1000 3000 > (lb)
Now check whether Range (G, A, F) = P = < p 200 1500 >.
Given:

1. G: $p = f / a$

2. A = < a 2 5 > (sq in)

3. F = < f 1000 3000 > (lb)

Computation:
Corners (G, A, F) = {500, 200, 1500, 600} (psi)
Range (G, A, F) = < p 200 1500 > (psi)
Since Range (G, A, F) = < p 200 1500 > = P, Domain (G, P, A) = F.
Domain (G, P, A) = F is shown graphically in Figure 5-4.

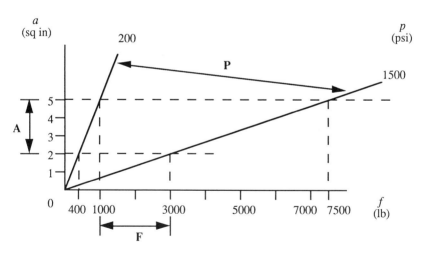

Figure 5-4: Domain (G, P, A) = F

Verification that Range (G, A, F) = P is shown graphically in Figure 5-5.

Example 2: Domain (G, A, P)

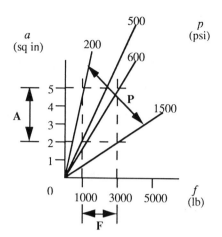

Figure 5-5: Range (G, A, F) = P

Given:

1. G: $p = f/a$

2. A = $< a\ 2\ 5 >$ (sq in)

3. P = $< p\ 200\ 1500 >$ (psi)

Computation:
Corners (G, A, P) = {(2 × 200), (5 × 200), (2 × 1500), (5 × 1500)} (lb)
Corners (G, A, P) = {400, 1000, 3000, 7500} (lb)
Central (G, A, P) = F = $< f\ 1000\ 3000 >$ (lb)
Now check whether Range (G, P, F) = A = $< a\ 2\ 5 >$.
Given:

1. G: $p = f/a$

2. P = $< p\ 200\ 1500 >$ (psi)

3. F = $< f\ 1000\ 3000 >$ (lb)

Computation:
Corners (G, P, F) = {5, .67, 15, 2} (sq in)
Range (G, P, F) = $< a\ .67\ 15 >$ (sq in)

Since Range (G, P, F) does not equal A = < a 2 5 >, Domain (G, A, P) does not exist.
Central (G, A, P) = F is shown graphically in Figure 5-6.

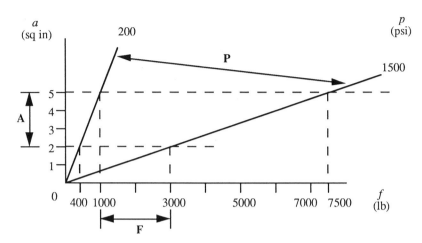

Figure 5-6: Central (G, A, P) = F

Verification showing that Range (G, P, F) does not equal < a 2 5 > is shown graphically in Figure 5-7.

5.2.2.7. Sufficient points operation

Given the relationship G, an interval X, and an interval Z, the Sufficient Points operation determines an interval Y. For each y in Y, computation of $g_x(y, Z)$ using every value z in interval Z produces an interval X_1 which includes the entire interval X as a subset.

By definition, SufPt (G, X, Z) is the set of assignments y such that X is a subset of Range (G, Z, y). SufPt (G, X, Z) exists only if X is a subset of X_1 = Range (G, Z, y).

Computation of Sufficient Points. Sufficient Points is computed in two steps. First, apply the Central Interval operation to X and Z to form interval Y. Check whether X is a subset of Range (G, Z, y) for y = each endpoint of interval Y. If so, then SufPt (G, X, Z) = Y; otherwise, SufPt (G, X, Z) does not exist.

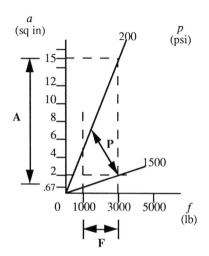

Figure 5-7: Range (G, P, F) Does Not Equal < a 2 5 >

Example 1: SufPt (G, A, P)
Given:

1. G: $p = f/a$

2. A = < a 2 5 > (sq in)

3. P = < p 200 1500 > (psi)

Computation:
Corners (G, A, P) = {(2 × 200), (5 × 200), (2 × 1500), (5 × 1500)} (lb)
Corners (G, A, P) = {400, 1000, 3000, 7500} (lb)
Central (G, A, P) = F = < f 1000 3000 > (lb)
For any value f in interval < f 1000 3000 >, interval P = < p 200 1500 >, and relationship $p = f/a$, A = < a 2 5 > must be a subset of Range (G, P, f) for SufPt (G, A, P) to exist.

We can verify this by checking both endpoints of F. Let f = 1000. Range (G, P, f) = A_1 = < a .67 5 > which includes the entire interval A = < a 2 5 > as a subset. Similarly, let f = 3000. Range (G, P, f) = A_1 = < a 2 15 > which includes the entire interval A = < a 2 5 > as a subset.

In this example, for any value f in the interval < f 1000 3000 >, the resulting interval A_1 = Range (G, P, f) always contains at least the interval A = < a 2 5 >. Consequently, SufPt (G, A, P) = F.

SufPt (G, A, P) = F is shown graphically in Figure 5-8.

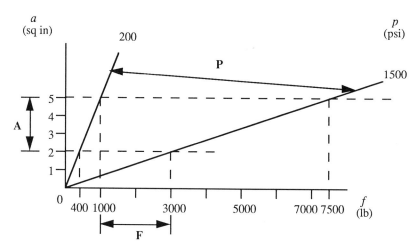

Figure 5-8: SufPt (G, A, P) = F

Verification that A = < a 2 5 > is a subset of each endpoint of interval F is shown graphically in Figure 5-9.

Example 2: SufPt (G, P, A)
Given:

1. $p = f/a$

2. P = < p 200 1500 > (psi)

3. A = < a 2 5 > (sq in)

Computation:
Corners (G, P, A) = {(200 × 2), (1500 × 2), (200 × 5), (1500 × 5)} (lb)
Corners (G, P, A) = {400, 3000, 1000, 7500} (lb)
Central (G, P, A) = F = < f 1000 3000 > (lb)
For any value f in interval < f 1000 3000 >, interval A = < a 2 5 >, and relationship $p = f/a$, P = < p 200 1500 > must be a subset of Range (G, A, f) for SufPt (G, P, A) to exist.
Check both endpoints of F. Let f = 1000. Range (G, A, f) = P_1 = < p 200 500 > which does not include the entire interval P = < p 200 1500 >. Similarly, let f = 3000. Range (G, A, f) = P_1 = < p 600 1500 > which also does not include the entire interval P = < p 200 1500 >.

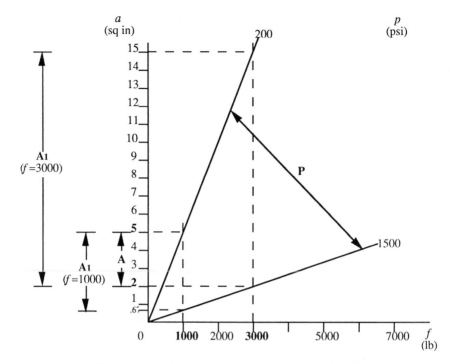

Figure 5-9: A is a subset of Range (G, P, *f*) = A₁

In this example, for any value *f* in interval < *f* 1000 3000 >, interval A = < *a* 2 5 >, and relationship *p* = *f* /*a*, the resulting interval P₁ = Range (G, A, *f*) does not contain at least the interval P = < *p* 200 1500 >. Consequently, SufPt (G, P, A) does not exist.

Central (G, A, P) = F is shown graphically in Figure 5-10.

Verification that P = < *p* 200 1500 >is not a subset of each interval P₁ formed using each endpoint of interval F is shown graphically in Figure 5-11.

5.2.3. LIC Labels

LIC uses a system of labels to describe relationships between variable features and value intervals, relationships among sets of assignment intervals, and

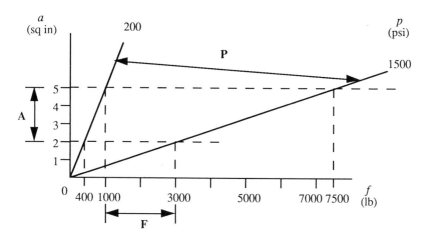

Figure 5-10: Central (G, P, A) = F

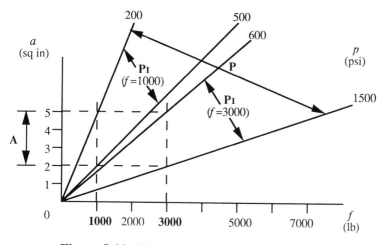

Figure 5-11: P is not a subset of Range (G, A, *f*) = P₁

causality or origin of value intervals for a variable feature. There are three types
of labels used in LIC. They are constraint labels, set labels, and causality labels.

5.2.3.1. Some basic label definitions

1. A = a set of artifacts or objects under consideration for a design.

2. A_s = a selectable subset of artifacts or objects in set A.

   Note: In design, there is a distinguishable difference between a selectable subset, A_s, and a non-selectable subset. The following examples demonstrate this point.

   a. The ACME Gear Pump Catalog contains a list of several different gear pumps,   each with its own part number and description. The set of gear pumps contained in the ACME Gear Pump Catalog is the set of artifacts, A, being considered. Gear pump Part #GP100 is a selectable subset, A_s, of ACME Gear Pump Catalog, A. Each A_s is unique because each gear pump listed in catalog A has a different part number and description.   Each part number in a catalog represents a smallest selectable subset, A_s.

   b. In the ACME Warehouse there is a bin which contains the gear pumps with Part #GP100. Each part in the bin is unique due to manufacturing tolerances.   The set of gear pumps in the bin is the set of artifacts, A. The gear pump in the front right corner of the bin is a subset of the set of gear pumps in the bin, but it is not a selectable subset, A_s, for the designer.   Individual parts are non-selectable because the designer cannot select individual parts when he creates his design.   Since designers cannot select individual parts, designers cannot reason about individual parts.

3. A Variable feature is a component physical or operational characteristic which can have different values (i.e., pressure range of a gear pump, diameter of a cylinder considering tolerances, etc.).

4. A State Set, S, is the set of states or conditions, s, under which a component operates (i.e., normal operation, start-up, stall, etc.). S = $\{s\}$.

5.2.3.2. Constraint labels

The constraint label describes how the variable feature is constrained with respect to the given interval of values. The constraint label describes what is known about the values that a variable feature of an artifact or object can have under a single set of operating conditions such as a gear pump (Part #GP100) which operates under normal operating conditions at pressures ranging from 200 to 1500 psi. There are four constraint labels: only, every, some, and none.

Only. < only *p* **200 1500** > means that the pressure, under the specified operating conditions, takes values only in the interval of 200 psi to 1500 psi. Pressure does not take any values outside this interval. **Only** can be represented graphically as shown in Figure 5-12.

Figure 5-12: < only *p* 200 1500 >

Every. < every *p* **200 1500** > means that the pressure, under the specified operating conditions, takes every value in the interval 200 psi to 1500 psi. Pressure may or may not take values outside the given interval; that information is not available from this labeled interval. **Every** can be represented graphically as shown in Figure 5-13.

Figure 5-13: < every *p* 200 1500 >

Some. < some *p* **200 1500** > means that the pressure, under the specified operating conditions, takes at least one of the values in the interval 200 psi to 1500 psi. Pressure may or may not take values outside the given interval. **Some** can be represented graphically as shown in Figure 5-14.

None. < none *p* **200 1500** > means that the pressure, under the specified

Figure 5-14: < some p 200 1500 >

operating conditions, never takes any of the values in the interval 200 psi to 1500 psi. **None** can be represented graphically as shown in Figure 5-15.

Figure 5-15: < none p 200 1500 >

In design practice, the **none** constraint label is not used since it is redundant with respect to the **only** label. < only x x_l x_h > implies < none x x_h ∞ > and < none x $-\infty$ x_l >. Consequently, further discussion of LIC will not include the none constraint label.

5.2.3.3. Set labels

The set label consolidates information about the variable feature values for the entire set of artifacts or objects under consideration. There are two set labels: All-Parts and Some-Part.

All-Parts. All-Parts means the constraint interval is true for every artifact (manufactured part) in each selectable subset (part number) of the set of artifacts (catalog) under consideration.

For example, for a pump catalog we have < All-Parts only pressure 0 3000 >. Every pump manufactured for each part number in the catalog operates only under pressures between 0 and 3000 psi under the specified operating conditions.

Some-Part. Some-Part means the constraint interval is true for at least some artifact (some manufactured part) in each selectable subset (part number) of the set of artifacts (catalog) under consideration.

For example, for a shaft catalog we have < Some-Part every diameter 49.99 50.01 >. At least one shaft manufactured for each part number in the catalog has a diameter between 49.99 and 50.01 inches under the specified operating conditions.

The catalog writer uses the some-part label to describe part numbers which may have tolerances on some variable features.

Example: Set Labels. To describe the set of shafts represented in Figure 5-16, we could use either the All-Parts label or the Some-Part label depending on the information we wish to represent.

If we wish to describe the interval of diameters of the shafts in the entire catalog, we write < All-Parts only diameter 49 51 >. None of the shafts has a diameter less than 49 inches or a diameter greater than 51 inches.

If we wish to describe the precision of the diameters of the shafts in the entire catalog, we write < Some-Part every diameter 49.99 50.01 >. We cannot from this catalog obtain any shaft with a diameter more precisely specified than between 49.99 inches and 50.01 inches.

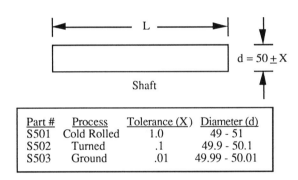

Part #	Process	Tolerance (X)	Diameter (d)
S501	Cold Rolled	1.0	49 - 51
S502	Turned	.1	49.9 - 50.1
S503	Ground	.01	49.99 - 50.01

Figure 5-16: Catalog of Shafts

5.2.3.4. Causality labels

Causality labels describe how the values that the variable feature takes are achieved. There are two causality labels: parameter and state-variable:

1. **Parameter** means that the value of the variable feature is set at manufacture and does not change during operation of the entire system (i.e., the diameter of a cylinder).

2. **State-Variable** means that the value of the variable feature is not fixed and may change during the operation of the entire system (i.e., pressure in a cylinder under varying loads).

5.2.4. Labeled Interval Inferences

We have defined a method (labeled intervals) for describing sets of artifacts being considered for a design. We have also defined operations that can be applied to these intervals. We can use these labeled intervals and operations to create inference rules which draw conclusions about the sets of artifacts under consideration.

There are five types of inferences used in LIC: Abstraction Rules, Elimination Conditions, Redundancy Conditions, the Translation Rule, and Propagation Rules. Based on specifications built into its catalogs, connections defined by a schematic, and user specifications, the Mechanical Design Compiler (MDC) uses the five kinds of labeled interval inferences to reach a conclusion about a design.

5.2.4.1. Some basic inferences definitions

1. A **Catalog-Entry-Level** labeled interval is a labeled interval created by the catalog writer for an individual set of selectable artifacts, A_s. The catalog writer creates these intervals when he writes labeled intervals describing variable features for specific part numbers in a catalog.

2. A **Component-Level** labeled interval is a labeled interval which describes a complete set of artifacts, A. The designer creates these intervals when he enters a specification for a component in his design. The MDC also creates these intervals when it abstracts the catalog-entry-level labeled intervals for part numbers into a labeled interval describing the entire catalog.

The following example distinguishes catalog-entry-level labeled intervals from component-level labeled intervals.
Given:

Gear Pump Catalog

Part Number	min RPM	max RPM
GP100	1000	4000
GP200	900	3600
GP300	700	3000

From the catalog data, the catalog writer creates the following catalog-entry-level labeled intervals:

```
< All-Parts  only  rpm  1000  4000 >
< All-Parts  only  rpm   900  3600 >
< All-Parts  only  rpm   700  3000 >
```

To describe the interval of RPM's at which the gear pumps in the entire catalog operate, the MDC (using Abstraction Rule 1 below) creates the component-level labeled interval < All-Parts only rpm 700 4000 >.

5.2.4.2. Abstraction rules

Abstraction rules take information about individual catalog entries and form a description of the entire catalog. The MDC applies the abstraction rules to catalog-entry-level labeled intervals to create a component-level labeled interval for the entire set of selectable artifacts (the catalog). These component-level descriptions can then be used to reason about the design at a high level, before decisions on particular catalog numbers have been made.

These rules apply either to All-Parts inputs to produce All-Parts outputs or to Some-Part inputs to produce Some-Part outputs. If the rules produce a false interval such that the "lowest" value is greater than the "highest" value, then the MDC does not make an abstraction. There are three abstraction rules.

Abstraction Rule 1.

$\langle$ only $X_i \rangle (A_{s,i}, S_i) \rightarrow \langle$ only x $\min_i x_{l,i}$ $\max_i x_{h,i} \rangle (A, \cap_i S_i)$
where
i = index over the set of catalog entries.
X represents a variable feature or operational quality interval.
X_i = X interval for the ith catalog entry.
A = catalog of items being examined (i.e., gear pump catalog).
$A_{s,i}$ = ith selectable subset within catalog A (i.e., gear pump #GP100).
S_i = set of states or conditions under which the ith catalog entry operates (i.e., normal operating conditions, start-up conditions, etc.).
x represents a variable feature or operational quality.
$x_{l,i}$ = the lowest value of x in interval X of the ith entry.
$\min_i x_{l,i}$ = the minimum lowest value of x over all entries i.
$x_{h,i}$ = the highest value of x in interval X of the ith entry.
$\max_i x_{h,i}$ = the maximum highest value of x over all entries i.
$\cap_i S_i$ = the intersection over all entries i of the set of states under which catalog entries operate.
Example: Abstraction Rule 1
Given:

Gear Pump Catalog

i	Part Number	min RPM	max RPM
1	GP100	1000	4000
2	GP200	900	3600
3	GP300	700	3000

From the catalog data, the catalog writer creates the following catalog-entry-level labeled intervals:

X_i	Labeled Interval	S_i
X_1 =	< All-Parts only rpm 1000 4000 >	(normal)
X_2 =	< All-Parts only rpm 900 3600 >	(normal)
X_3 =	< All-Parts only rpm 700 3000 >	(normal)

Computation:

$$x_{l,1} = 1000 \qquad x_{h,1} = 4000$$
$$x_{l,2} = 900 \qquad x_{h,2} = 3600$$
$$x_{l,3} = 700 \qquad x_{h,3} = 3000$$

$$\text{min } x_{l,i} = 700 \qquad \text{max } x_{h,i} = 4000$$

Abstraction Rule Result:
< All-Parts only rpm 700 4000 > (normal)
A graphical interpretation is shown in Figure 5-17.

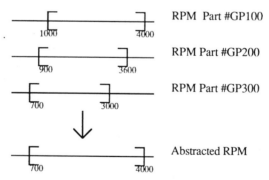

Figure 5-17: Abstraction Rule 1

Physical Interpretation:
The gear pumps in this catalog under normal conditions will only operate at an RPM between 700 RPM and 4000 RPM. The MDC creates this new

component-level labeled interval to describe the RPM interval for the entire catalog of gear pumps.

Abstraction Rule 2

$\langle$ every $X_i \rangle$ $(A_{s,i}, S_i) \rightarrow \langle$ every x max$_i$ $x_{l,i}$ min$_i$ $x_{h,i} \rangle$ $(A, \cap_i S_i)$
Example: Abstraction Rule 2
Given:

X_i	Labeled Interval	S_i
X_1 =	< All-Parts every efficiency .75 .90 >	(normal)
X_2 =	< All-Parts every efficiency .80 .95 >	(normal)
X_3 =	< All-Parts every efficiency .70 .85 >	(normal)

Computation:
max$_i$ $x_{l,i}$ = .80   min$_i$ $x_{h,i}$ = .85
Abstraction Rule Result:
< All-Parts every efficiency .80 .85 > (normal)
A graphical interpretation is shown in Figure 5-18.

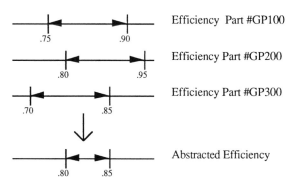

Figure 5-18: Abstraction Rule 2

Physical Interpretation:
Regardless of the pump catalog number selected, the pump may exhibit, and the design must work at, every efficiency between 80% and 85%. The MDC creates this new component-level LI to describe the efficiency interval for the entire catalog of gear pumps; this LI can be used to make design decisions before the pump is selected.

Abstraction Rule 3

$\langle$ some $X_i \rangle$ $(A_{s,i}, S_i) \rightarrow \langle$ some x min$_i$ $x_{l,i}$ max$_i$ $x_{h,i} \rangle$ $(A, \cap_i S_i)$
Example: Abstraction Rule 3
Given:

$\underline{X_i}$	Labeled Interval	$\underline{S_i}$
X_1 = < Some-Part some rpm 998 4005 >		(normal)
X_2 = < Some-Part some rpm 890 3595 >		(normal)
X_3 = < Some-Part some rpm 701 3000 >		(normal)

Computation:
min$_i$ $x_{l,i}$ = 701   max$_i$ $x_{h,i}$ = 4005
Abstraction Rule Result:
< Some-Part some rpm 701 4005 > (normal)
A graphical interpretation is shown in Figure 5-19.

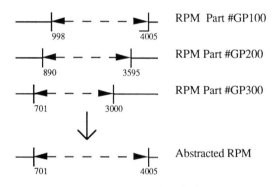

RPM Part #GP100
998   4005

RPM Part #GP200
890   3595

RPM Part #GP300
701   3000

Abstracted RPM
701   4005

Figure 5-19: Abstraction Rule 3

Physical Interpretation:
Under normal conditions some of the gear pumps designated by each catalog number in this catalog will operate at at least one RPM between 701 RPM and 4005 RPM. The MDC creates this new component-level labeled interval to describe the RPM interval for the entire catalog of gear pumps.

5.2.4.3. Elimination conditions

The elimination conditions redefine catalogs by determining individual catalog entries which do not meet given specifications (whether user specifications or internally generated specifications) and eliminating those entries. In order for these conditions to apply, at least one interval must have an All-Parts label and the state sets must intersect. There are three elimination conditions. Each condition is formatted such that there are two labeled intervals and a condition. One labeled interval is a variable feature requirement placed on the entire catalog (component-level LI) while the other labeled interval describes a variable feature of a selectable subset or individual catalog entry within the catalog (catalog-entry-level LI). The MDC looks for conflicts between the given requirement and the known information about the individual entry by applying the condition to the two labeled intervals. If the condition is true, the MDC eliminates the catalog entry from the catalog.

Elimination Condition 1

$\langle$ only $X_1 \rangle$ and $\langle$ every $X_2 \rangle$ and Not $(X_2 \subseteq X_1)$

Example 1:
Given:
Gear Pump Requirement: < All-Parts only efficiency .80 1.00 >
Gear Pump Part #GP100: < All-Parts every efficiency .75 .90 >
Computation:
X_1 = < efficiency .80 1.00 >
X_2 = < efficiency .75 .90 >
Condition: Not $(X_2 \subseteq X_1)$ ==> true for this example
Elimination Condition Result:
Eliminate Part #GP100 from the gear pump catalog since X_2 is not a subset of X_1 (the condition is met).
A graphical representation is shown in Figure 5-20.

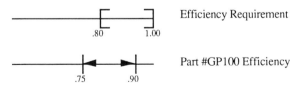

Figure 5-20: Example 1, Elimination Condition 1

Physical Interpretation:
When the efficiency of gear pump part #GP100 is .75 to .79, the gear pump requirement is not met. Since it is known that part #GP100 will not meet the requirement, the MDC eliminates it from further consideration for the design.
Example 2:
Given:
Gear Pump Requirement: < All-Parts every efficiency .70 .90 >
Gear Pump Part #GP400: < Some-Part only efficiency .60 .90 >
Computation:
X_1 = < efficiency .60 .90 >
X_2 = < efficiency .70 .90 >
Condition: Not $(X_2 \subseteq X_1)$ ==> false for this example
Elimination Condition Result:
Do not eliminate Part #GP400 from the gear pump catalog since X_2 is a subset of X_1 (the condition is not met).
A graphical representation is shown in Figure 5-21.

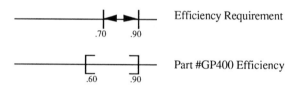

Figure 5-21: Example 2, Elimination Condition 1

Physical Interpretation:
Since gear pump part #GP400 only has efficiencies in the interval .60 to .90, it may meet the requirement that the efficiency have every value in the interval .70 to .90. The specific efficiency values within the interval .60 to .90 that Part #GP400 takes are not known. Since information available does not prove that Part #GP400 will not meet the requirement, the MDC does not eliminate this part from consideration at this point in the design process.

Elimination Condition 2

⟨ only X_1 ⟩ and ⟨ only X_2 ⟩ and Not $(X_1 \cap X_2)$
Example 1:
Given:
Cylinder Requirement: < All-Parts only diameter 1 3 >
Cylinder Part #C400: < All-Parts only diameter 3.25 3.25 >
Computation:

X_1 = < diameter 1 3 >
X_2 = < diameter 3.25 3.25 >
Condition: Not $(X_1 \cap X_2)$ ==> true for this example
Elimination Condition Result:
Eliminate Part #C400 from the cylinder catalog since X_1 and X_2 do not intersect (the condition is met).
A graphical representation is shown in Figure 5-22.

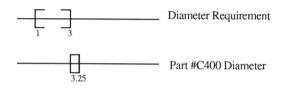

Figure 5-22: Example 1, Elimination Condition 2

Physical Interpretation:
The diameter of part #C400 is too large for the given requirement. The MDC eliminates it from further consideration for the design.
Example 2:
Given:
Gear Pump Requirement: < All-Parts only pressure 0 2900 >
Gear Pump Part #GP100: < All-Parts only pressure 0 3000 >
Computation:
X_1 = < pressure 0 2900 >
X_2 = < pressure 0 3000 >
Condition: Not $(X_1 \cap X_2)$ ==> false for this example
Elimination Condition Result:
Do not eliminate Part #GP100 from the gear pump catalog since X_1 and X_2 do intersect (the condition is not met).
A graphical representation is shown in Figure 5-23.

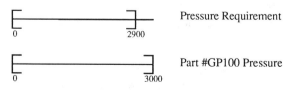

Figure 5-23: Example 2, Elimination Condition 2

<u>Physical Interpretation</u>:

Part #GP100 may meet the requirement to operate at pressures only between 0 and 2900 psi since it only operates at pressures between 0 and 3000 psi. The specific pressures within the interval 0 and 3000 at which it will operate are not known; the values may fall in the interval 0 to 2900. Since information available does not prove that Part #GP100 will not meet the requirement, the MDC does not eliminate this part from consideration at this point in the design process.

Elimination Condition 3

$\langle$ only $X_1 \rangle$ and $\langle$ some $X_2 \rangle$ and Not $(X_1 \cap X_2)$

   <u>Example 1</u>:

   <u>Given</u>:

   Cylinder Requirement: < All-Parts only diameter 1 3 >

   Cylinder Part #C400: < Some-Part some diameter < 3.15 3.35 >

   <u>Computation</u>:

   X_1 = < diameter 1 3 >

   X_2 = < diameter 3.15 3.35 >

   Condition: Not $(X_1 \cap X_2)$ ==> true for this example

   <u>Elimination Condition Result</u>:

   Eliminate Part #C400 from the cylinder catalog since X_1 and X_2 do not intersect (the condition is met).

   A graphical representation is shown in Figure 5-24.

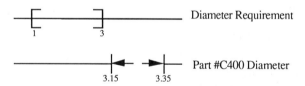

Figure 5-24: Example 1, Elimination Condition 3

<u>Physical Interpretation</u>:

   The diameter of part #C400 takes some value that is too large for the given requirement. The MDC eliminates it from further consideration for the design.

   <u>Example 2</u>:

   <u>Given</u>:

   Gear Pump Requirement: < All-Parts only pressure 0 2900 >

   Gear Pump Part #GP100: < Some-Part some pressure 0 3000 >

   <u>Computation</u>:

X_1 = < pressure 0 2900 >
X_2 = < pressure 0 3000 >
Condition: Not ($X_1 \cap X_2$) ==> false for this example
Elimination Condition Result:
Do not eliminate Part #GP100 from the gear pump catalog since X_1 and X_2 do intersect (the condition is not met).
A graphical representation is shown in Figure 5-25.

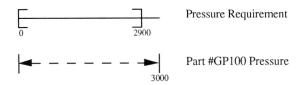

Figure 5-25: Example 2, Elimination Condition 3

Physical Interpretation:
Part #GP100 may meet the requirement to operate at pressures only between 0 and 2900 psi since it operates at some pressure between 0 and 3000 psi. The specific pressure within the interval 0 and 3000 at which it will operate is not known; the value may fall in the interval 0 to 2900. Since information available does not prove that Part #GP100 will not meet the requirement, the MDC does not eliminate this part from consideration at this point in the design process.

5.2.4.4. Redundancy conditions

Redundancy conditions determine if a newly generated component-level labeled interval (X_1) is not needed because its information is contained in another component-level labeled interval (X_2) that has already been processed by the MDC. If the newly generated labeled interval is redundant, the MDC does not process it.

In order for the redundancy conditions to apply, the artifact set and the state set of the newly generated labeled interval (X_1) must be subsets of the artifact set and the state set of the previously processed labeled interval (X_2). X_1 having either an All-Parts label or a Some-Part label can be redundant with respect to X_2 having an All-Parts label; X_1 having a Some-Part label can be redundant with respect to X_2 having a Some-Part label. Redundancy conditions do not apply, however, to X_1 having an All-Parts label while X_2 has a Some-Part label.

There are five redundancy conditions. Each condition is formatted such that there are two component-level labeled intervals and a condition. The first labeled interval refers to the newly generated labeled interval (X_1) while the second labeled interval refers to the previously processed labeled interval (X_2). The MDC applies the condition to the two labeled intervals. If the condition is true, the MDC does not process X_1 since X_1 is redundant with respect to X_2.

Redundancy Condition 1

⟨ every X_1 ⟩ and ⟨ every X_2 ⟩ and ($X_1 \subseteq X_2$)
  Example 1:
  Given:
  X_1: < All-Parts every efficiency .80 .85 >
  X_2: < All-Parts every efficiency .75 .90 >
  Computation:
  Condition: ($X_1 \subseteq X_2$) ==> true for this example
  Redundancy Condition Result:
  X_1 is redundant with respect to X_2 since X_1 is a subset of X_2 (the condition is met).
  A graphical representation is shown in Figure 5-26.

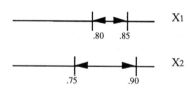

Figure 5-26: Example 1, Redundancy Condition 1

Physical Interpretation:
  Any part which satisfies requirement X_2 (efficiency takes every value in the interval .75 to .90) automatically satisfies requirement X_1 (efficiency takes every value in the interval .80 to .85). The MDC does not process the X_1 requirement since X_1 is redundant with respect to X_2.
  Example 2:
  Given:
  X_1: < All-Parts every efficiency .70 .85 >
  X_2: < All-Parts every efficiency .75 .90 >
  Computation:
  Condition: ($X_1 \subseteq X_2$) ==> false for this example

Redundancy Condition Result:
X_1 is not redundant with respect to X_2 since X_1 is not a subset of X_2 (the condition is not met).
A graphical representation is shown in Figure 5-27.

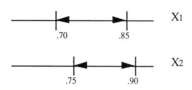

Figure 5-27: Example 2, Redundancy Condition 1

Physical Interpretation:
Any part which satisfies requirement X_2 (efficiency takes every value in the interval .75 to .90) does not necessarily satisfy requirement X_1 (efficiency takes every value in the interval .70 to .85). X_2 does not require the part to have efficiency values in the interval .70 to .74. Consequently, the MDC processes the X_1 requirement since X_1 places a requirement additional to that of X_2 on the chosen part.

Redundancy Condition 2

$\langle$ some $X_1 \rangle$ and $\langle$ every $X_2 \rangle$ and $(X_1 \cap X_2)$
Example 1:
Given:
X_1: < All-Parts some rpm 3000 5000 >
X_2: < All-Parts every rpm 0 4500 >
Computation:
Condition: $(X_1 \cap X_2)$ ==> true for this example
Redundancy Condition Result:
X_1 is redundant with respect to X_2 since X_1 and X_2 intersect (the condition is met).
A graphical representation is shown in Figure 5-28.
Physical Interpretation:
Any part which satisfies requirement X_2 (rpm takes every value in the interval 0 to 4500) automatically satisfies requirement X_1 (rpm takes some value in the interval 3000 to 5000). The MDC does not process the X_1 requirement since X_1 is redundant with respect to X_2.
Example 2:

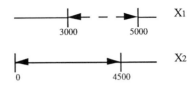

Figure 5-28: Example 1, Redundancy Condition 2

Given:
X_1: < Some-Part some rpm 3500 4000 >
X_2: < All-Parts every rpm 0 3000 >
Computation:
Condition: $(X_1 \cap X_2)$ ==> false for this example
Redundancy Condition Result:
X_1 is not redundant with respect to X_2 since X_1 and X_2 do not intersect (the condition is not met).
A graphical representation is shown in Figure 5-29.

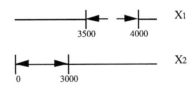

Figure 5-29: Example 2, Redundancy Condition 2

Physical Interpretation:
Any part which satisfies X_2 (rpm takes every value in the interval 0 to 3000) does not necessarily satisfy requirement X_1 (rpm takes some value in the interval 3500 to 4000). X_2 does not require the part to have any rpm values in the interval 3500 to 4000. Consequently, the MDC processes the X_1 requirement since X_1 places a requirement additional to that of X_2 on the chosen part.

Redundancy Condition 3

$\langle$ only $X_1 \rangle$ and $\langle$ only $X_2 \rangle$ and $(X_2 \subseteq X_1)$
Example 1:
Given:

X_1: < All-Parts only rpm 700 4000 >
X_2: < All-Parts only rpm 1000 3000 >
Computation:
Condition: $(X_2 \subseteq X_1)$ ==> true for this example
Redundancy Condition Result:
X_1 is redundant with respect to X_2 since X_2 is a subset of X_1 (the condition is met).
A graphical representation is shown in Figure 5-30.

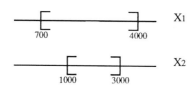

Figure 5-30: Example 1, Redundancy Condition 3

Physical Interpretation:
Any part which satisfies requirement X_2 (rpm takes only values in the interval 1000 to 3000) automatically satisfies requirement X_1 (rpm takes only values in the interval 700 to 4000). The MDC does not process the X_1 requirement since X_1 is redundant with respect to X_2.
Example 2:
Given:
X_1: < All-Parts only rpm 1500 4000 >
X_2: < All-Parts only rpm 1000 3000 >
Computation:
Condition: $(X_2 \subseteq X_1)$ ==> false for this example
Redundancy Condition Result:
X_1 is not redundant with respect to X_2 since X_2 is not a subset of X_1 (the condition is not met).
A graphical representation is shown in Figure 5-31.
Physical Interpretation:
Any part which satisfies requirement X_2 (rpm takes only values in the interval 1000 to 3000) does not necessarily satisfy requirement X_1 (rpm takes only values in the interval 1500 to 4000). Any part which satisfies X_2 by having an rpm value anywhere in the interval 1000 to 1499 would not satisfy X_1. Consequently, the MDC processes the X_1 requirement since X_1 places a requirement additional to that of X_2 on the chosen part.

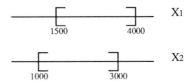

Figure 5-31: Example 2, Redundancy Condition 3

Redundancy Condition 4

⟨ some X_1 ⟩ and ⟨ only X_2 ⟩ and $(X_2 \subseteq X_1)$
Example 1:
Given:
X_1: < All-Parts some rpm 700 4000 >
X_2: < All-Parts only rpm 1000 3000 >
Computation:
Condition: $(X_2 \subseteq X_1)$ ==> true for this example
Redundancy Condition Result:
X_1 is redundant with respect to X_2 since X_2 is a subset of X_1 (the condition is met).
A graphical representation is shown in Figure 5-32.

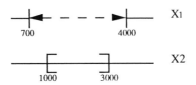

Figure 5-32: Example 1, Redundancy Condition 4

Physical Interpretation:
Any part which satisfies requirement X_2 (rpm takes only values in the interval 1000 to 3000) automatically satisfies requirement X_1 (rpm takes some value in the interval 700 to 4000). The MDC does not process the X_1 requirement since X_1 is redundant with respect to X_2.
Example 2:
Given:
X_1: < All-Parts some rpm 3000 5000 >

X_2: < All-Parts only rpm 1000 3000 >
<u>Computation:</u>
Condition: $(X_2 \subseteq X_1)$ ==> false for this example
<u>Redundancy Condition Result:</u>
X_1 is not redundant with respect to X_2 since X_2 is not a subset of X_1 (the condition is not met).
A graphical representation is shown in Figure 5-33.

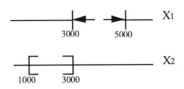

Figure 5-33: Example 2, Redundancy Condition 4

<u>Physical Interpretation:</u>
Any part which satisfies requirement X_2 (rpm takes only values in the interval 1000 to 3000) does not necessarily satisfy requirement X_1 (rpm takes some value in the interval 3000 to 5000). Any part which satisfies X_2 by having an rpm value anywhere in the interval 1000 to 2999 would not satisfy X_1. Consequently, the MDC processes the X_1 requirement since X_1 places a requirement additional to that of X_2 on the chosen part.

Redundancy Condition 5

$\langle$ some X_1 $\rangle$ and $\langle$ some X_2 $\rangle$ and $(X_2 \subseteq X_1)$
<u>Example 1:</u>
<u>Given:</u>
X_1: < All-Parts some rpm 700 4000 >
X_2: < All-Parts some rpm 1000 3000 >
<u>Computation:</u>
Condition: $(X_2 \subseteq X_1)$ ==> true for this example
<u>Redundancy Condition Result:</u>
X_1 is redundant with respect to X_2 since X_2 is a subset of X_1 (the condition is met).
A graphical representation is shown in Figure 5-34.
<u>Physical Interpretation:</u>
Any part which satisfies requirement X_2 (rpm takes some value in the interval 1000 to 3000) automatically satisfies requirement X_1 (rpm takes some value in the interval 700 to 4000). The MDC does not process the X_1 requirement since X_1 is redundant with respect to X_2.

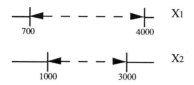

Figure 5-34: Example 1, Redundancy Condition 5

Example 2:
Given:
X_1: < All-Parts some rpm 3000 5000 >
X_2: < All-Parts some rpm 1000 3000 >
Computation:
Condition: $(X_2 \subseteq X_1)$ ==> false for this example
Redundancy Condition Result:
X_1 is not redundant with respect to X_2 since X_2 is not a subset of X_1 (the condition is not met).
A graphical representation is shown in Figure 5-35.

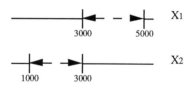

Figure 5-35: Example 2, Redundancy Condition 5

Physical Interpretation:
Any part which satisfies requirement X_2 (rpm takes some value in the interval 1000 to 3000) does not necessarily satisfy requirement X_1 (rpm takes some value in the interval 3000 to 5000). Any part which satisfies X_2 by having an rpm value anywhere in the interval 1000 to 2999 would not satisfy X_1. Consequently, the MDC processes the X_1 requirement since X_1 places a requirement additional to that of X_2 on the chosen part.

5.2.4.5. Translation rule

The translation rule generates new labeled intervals from old based on the interrelationships among components. When ports are connected in a schematic, the connecting ports establish equivalence between matching variables in each component. Then, when a labeled interval is created for one of the variables in one port, a matching labeled interval in the other port is created by the translation rule.

Some components have variable features which are directional (i.e., torque: a motor produces torque-out while a transmission accepts torque-in; RPM: a motor produces RPM-out while a pump accepts RPM-in; HP: a motor produces HP-out while a transmission accepts HP-in). When a component (i.e., motor) has a labeled interval being processed, the translation rule determines whether this labeled interval should be translated to a connected component (i.e., transmission).

If:

1. The connected components (i.e., motor and transmission) have a matching variable name (i.e., torque); and

2. The labeled interval (for the motor) is new information for the connected component (transmission). Note: Information is new if the labeled interval was not previously translated from the connected component (transmission) to the component under consideration (motor).

then
Translate the labeled interval to the connected component.
Example:
Given:
Transmission: < All-Parts every input-rpm 0 1800 >
Transmission is connected to a motor.
Translation Rule Result:
Create LI for motor: < All-Parts every rpm 0 1800 >

5.2.4.6. Propagation rules

Propagation rules generate new labeled intervals based on previously processed labeled intervals and a given relationship G, which is implicit among three variables. Each rule is formatted such that there are two antecedant component-level labeled intervals, a given relationship G, and a resultant

component-level labeled interval. There may be additional causality requirements. The resultant labeled interval contains a constraint label and labeled interval calculus operation -- one of Range, Domain, or Sufficient Points.

The MDC determines the resultant labeled interval by applying the operation
to the variables. If the operation on the variables produces a labeled interval, the
MDC propagates this new labeled interval. If the operation on the variables
does not produce a labeled interval (i.e., the labeled interval does not exist), the
propagation rule is not valid.

The artifact set and the state set of the new labeled interval are the intersection
of the artifact set and the state set of the two antecedant labeled intervals. If
both of the antecedant labeled intervals have an All-Parts set label, the new
labeled interval will have an All-Parts set label. If the two antecedant labeled
intervals have any other combination of set labels (i.e., one with a Some-Part set
label and the other with an All-Parts set label or both with a Some-Part set
label), then the new labeled interval will have a Some-Part set label.

Propagation Rule 1

⟨ only X ⟩ and ⟨ only Y ⟩ and G ==> ⟨ only Range (G, X, Y) ⟩
Example: Hydraulic Pump
Given:
G: flow (GPM) = (displacement × rpm)/231
< All-Parts only displacement .32 3.80 > (CIR)
< All-Parts only rpm 700 4000 > (RPM)
Displacement is the volume of fluid that moves through a hydraulic line per
revolution of the pump motor. RPM is the speed of the motor driving the pump.
The flow is the rate at which the fluid moves through the lines.
Computation:
Corners (G, Displacement, RPM) = {.97, 11.52, 5.54, 65.80} (GPM)
Range (G, Displacement, RPM) = < flow .97 65.80 > (GPM)
Propagation Rule Result:
< All-Parts only flow .97 65.80 >
A graphical representation is shown in Figure 5-36.
Physical Interpretation:
We know that the pumps run at an rpm only in the interval 700 to 4000 RPM
and that the pumps have a displacement capability only in the interval .32 to
3.80 cubic inches per revolution. Consequently, the pumps can only produce
flows in the interval .97 to 65.80 GPM.

Propagation Rule 2

Independent (⟨ **every X** ⟩, ⟨ **every Y** ⟩) and G ==> ⟨ **every Range (G, X, Y)** ⟩
We define X and Y as **Independent** unless:

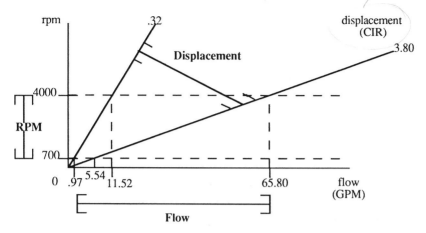

Figure 5-36: < only Range (G, Displacement, RPM) > = < only flow
.97 65.80 >

1. The designer designates X and Y as dependent

2. The process determines that the labeled intervals, X and Y, have a
   common source in their histories.

Example: Transmission
Given:
G: t_o = ratio × t_i
< All-Parts every ratio 2 4 >
< All-Parts every t_i 1 2 > (ft-lb)
t_i is the torque that the transmission accepts from the motor. t_o is the torque
that the transmission provides to its load. Ratio is a parameter fixed by the
transmission design.
Computation:
Corners (G, Ratio, T_i) = {2, 4, 4, 8} (ft-lb)
Range (G, Ratio, T_i) = < t_o 2 8 > (ft-lb)
Propagation Rule Result:
< All-Parts every t_o 2 8 >
A graphical representation is shown in Figure 5-37.
Physical Interpretation:
We know that the ratio will take every value in the interval 2 to 4. We also
know that the transmission will receive every torque in the interval 1 to 2 ft-lb,
independent of the ratio. Consequently, the transmission will provide every
torque in the interval 2 to 8 ft-lb.

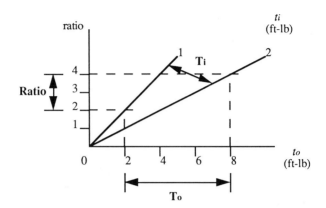

Figure 5-37: $<$ every Range (G, Ratio, Ti) $>$ = $<$ every t_o 2 8 $>$

Propagation Rule 3

⟨ **every X** ⟩ **and** ⟨ **only Y** ⟩ **and (State-variable (z) or Parameter (x)) and G** ==> ⟨ **every Domain (G, X, Y)** ⟩
Example 1: Head Loss in a 90° Bend Pipe
Given:
G: hl (Head Loss) = [k_b × (velocity)^2]/64.4
$<$ All-Parts every velocity 4 8 $>$ (ft/sec)
$<$ All-Parts only k_b .16 .35 $>$

k_b is the bending coefficient for a 90° smooth bend pipe. The value of k_b is based on the ratio between the radius of curvature of the pipe to the diameter of the pipe. As such, the value for k_b is fixed when the pipe is manufactured and is a parameter. K_b corresponds to Y in the rule. The head loss (hl) depends on the velocity of the fluid which can change as the system operates. Consequently, hl varies as the system operates and is a state-variable. hl corresponds to z in the rule.
Computation:
Corners (G, Velocity, K_b) = {.04, .16, .09, .35} (ft)
Central (G, Velocity, K_b) = $<$ hl .09 .16 $>$ (ft)
Verify Range (G, K_b, HL) = Velocity.
Corners (G, K_b, HL) = {5.9, 4, 8, 5.4} (ft/sec)
Range (G, K_b, HL) = $<$ velocity 4 8 $>$ (ft/sec)
Since Range (G, K_b, HL) = $<$ velocity 4 8 $>$, Domain (G, Velocity, K_b) = HL.
Propagation Rule Result:
$<$ All-Parts every hl .09 .16 $>$

A graphical representation is shown in Figure 5-38.

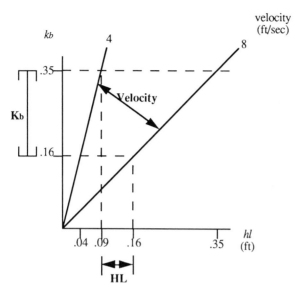

Figure 5-38: < every Domain (G, Velocity, K_b) > = < every hl .09 .16 >

Physical Interpretation:
We know that velocity in the pipe will take every value between 4 and 8 ft/sec. We also know that the pipes available have bending coefficients only between .16 and .35. Since hl varies as the system operates, hl will take every value in the interval .09 to .16 ft. No matter which pipe is chosen, the hl still takes every value in the interval .09 to .16 ft.

Example 2: Fitting a Shaft in a Hole
Given:
G: $d_h - d_s = c$
< All-Parts only c .000875 .002 > (in)
< Some-Part every d_s 5.9995 6.0005 > (in)
d_s is the diameter of the shaft to be put in a hole. The value for d_s is fixed when the shaft is manufactured and is therefore a parameter. D_s corresponds to X in the rule. d_h is the diameter of the hole. The value for d_h is fixed when the hole is created and is therefore a parameter. D_h corresponds to Z in the rule. c is the clearance between the hole and the shaft. c is a parameter because it is fixed by the diameter of the shaft in combination with the diameter of the hole. C corresponds to Y in the rule.

Computation:

Corners $(G, D_s, C) = \{6.00125, 6.0035, 6.00225, 6.0045\}$ (in)
Central $(G, D_s, C) = \ <\ d_h\ 6.00225\ 6.0035\ >$ (in)
Verify Range $(G, C, D_h) = D_s$.
Corners $(G, C, D_h) = \{6.0005, 6.00175, 5.99825, 5.9995\}$ (in)
Range $(G, C, D_h) = \ <\ d_s\ 5.99825\ 6.00175\ >$ (in)
Since Range (G, C, D_h) does not equal D_s, Domain (G, D_s, C) does not exist--
however, see Propagation Rule 4, Section 5.2.4.6.
Propagation Rule Result:
No propagation occurs.

Propagation Rule 4

⟨ **every X** ⟩ **and** ⟨ **only Y** ⟩ **and Parameter** (z) **and G** ==> ⟨ **only SufPt (G, X, Y)** ⟩
Example 1: Fitting a Shaft in a Hole
Given:
G: $d_h - d_s = c$
$<$ All-Parts only c .000875 .002 $>$ (in)
$<$ Some-Part every d_s 5.9995 6.0005 $>$ (in)
d_s is the diameter of the shaft to be put in a hole. The value for d_s is fixed
when the shaft is manufactured and is therefore a parameter. D_s corresponds to
X in the rule. d_h is the diameter of the hole. The value for d_h is fixed when the
hole is created and is therefore a parameter. D_h corresponds to Z in the rule. c
is the clearance between the hole and the shaft. c is a parameter because it is
fixed by the diameter of the shaft in combination with the diameter of the hole.
C corresponds to Y in the rule.
Computation:
Corners $(G, D_s, C) = \{6.00125, 6.0035, 6.00225, 6.0045\}$ (in)
Central $(G, D_s, C) = \ <\ d_h\ 6.00225\ 6.0035\ >$ (in)
Verify Range (G, C, d_h) contains at least $<\ d_s\ 5.9995\ 6.0005\ >$
Let $d_h = 6.00225$. Range $(G, C, d_h) = (D_s)_1 = \ <\ d_s\ 5.99825\ 6.0005\ >$ which
contains $<\ d_s\ 5.9995\ 6.0005\ >$ as a subset. Similarly, let $d_h = 6.0035$. Range $(G,
C, d_h) = (D_s)_1 = \ <\ d_s\ 5.9995\ 6.00175\ >$ which contains $<\ d_s\ 5.9995\ 6.0005\ >$ as
a subset. Consequently, SufPt $(G, D_s, C) = D_h$.
Propagation Rule Result:
$<$ Some-Part only d_h 6.00225 6.0035 $>$ (in)
A graphical representation is shown in Figure 5-39.
Physical Interpretation:
Due to manufacturing tolerances, we know that the 6 inch shafts have a
tolerance of $\pm$ .0005 inch indicating that some shaft diameter has every value in
the interval 5.9995 to 6.0005 inches. We also know that the clearance is only in
the interval .000875 to .002 inch. Since the diameter of the hole is a parameter
and every shaft must fit in the hole, we can only have holes with a diameter in

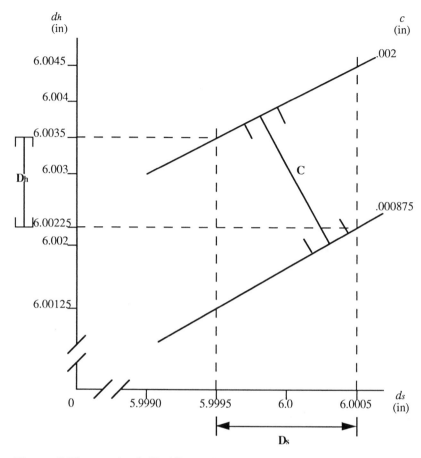

Figure 5-39: < only SufPt (G, D_s, C) > = < only d_h 6.00225 6.0035 >

the interval 6.00225 to 6.0035 inches. If we have a hole diameter outside the interval 6.00225 to 6.0035 inches, the clearance requirement will not be met.

Example 2: Cylinder with Load

Given:

G: $p = f/a$

< All-Parts every f 9000 12000 > (lb)

< All-Parts only p 1500 3000 > (psi)

f is the force of the load the hydraulic cylinder is required to lift. p is the pressure at which the system operates. a is the cross-sectional area of the piston.

Computation:

Corners (G, F, P) = {6, 8, 3, 4} (sq in)
Central (G, F, P) = $< a\ 4\ 6 >$ (ft-lb)
Verify Range (G, P, a) contains at least $< f\ 9000\ 12000 >$.
Let $a = 4$; Range (G, P, a) = F_1 = $< f\ 6000\ 12000 >$ which contains $< f\ 9000\ 12000 >$ as a subset. Similarly, let $a = 6$; Range (G, P, a) = F_1 = $< f\ 9000\ 18000 >$ which contains $< f\ 9000\ 12000 >$ as a subset. Consequently, SufPt (G, F, P) = A.

Propagation Rule Result:
$<$ All-Parts only $a\ 4\ 6 >$
A graphical representation is shown in Figure 5-40.

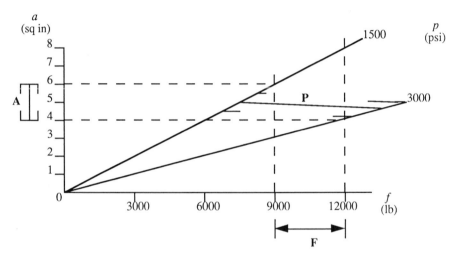

Figure 5-40: $<$ only SufPt (G, F, P) $> = <$ only $a\ 4\ 6 >$

Physical Interpretation:
We know that the cylinders can operate under pressures only between 1500 and 3000 psi. We also know that the the cylinders must lift loads at every value between 9000 and 12000 lb. The diameter and thus the area of our cylinder does not vary as the cylinder functions. Consequently, any cylinder that will operate within the specified pressure interval and will handle the loads given must have an area only in the interval 4 to 6 in.

Propagation Rule 5

⟨ every X ⟩ and ⟨ only Y ⟩ and G ==> ⟨ some SufPt (G, X, Y) ⟩
Example: Variable Speed Transmission
Given:

G: t_o = ratio × t_i
< All-Parts every ratio 2 4 >
< All-Parts every t_i 1 8 > (ft-lb)
t_i is the torque that the transmission accepts from the motor. t_o is the torque
that the transmission provides to its load. The ratio is determined by the trans-
mission setting.
Computation:
Corners (G, Ratio, T_i) = {2, 4, 16, 32} (ft-lb)
Central (G, Ratio, T_i) = < t_o 4 16 > (ft-lb)
Verify Range (G, T_i, t_o) = at least < ratio 2 4 >.
Let t_o = 4; Range (G, T_i, t_o) = (Ratio)$_1$ = < ratio .5 4 > which contains < ratio
2 4 > as a subset. Similarly, let t_o = 16; Range (G, T_i, t_o) = (Ratio)$_1$ = < ratio 2
16 > which contains < ratio 2 4 > as a subset. Consequently, SufPt (G, Ratio,
T_i) = T_o.
Propagation Rule Result:
< All-Parts some t_o 4 16 >
A graphical representation is shown in Figure 5-41.

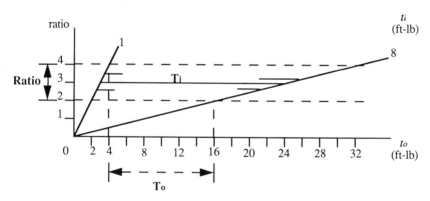

Figure 5-41: < some SufPt (G, Ratio, T_i) > = < some t_o 4 16 >

Physical Interpretation:
We know that the transmission will be adjusted over every ratio in the interval
2 to 4. We also know that the transmission will receive torques only in the interval 1 to 8 ft-lb. Consequently, the transmission must produce some torque in the
interval 4 to 16 ft-lb.

Propagation Rule 6

⟨ only X ⟩ and ⟨ some Y ⟩ and G ==> ⟨ some Range (G, X, Y) ⟩

Example: Fluid Flow in Hydraulic Line
Given:
G: flow = 3.117 × velocity × area
< All-Parts only area 1 2 > (sq in)
< Some-Part some flow 12.5 100 > (GPM)
Area is the cross-sectional area of the hydraulic line. Flow is the rate at which
fluid flows from the hydraulic pump. Velocity is the speed at which the fluid
moves through the lines.
Computation:
Corners (G, Diameter, Flow) = {4.0, 2.0, 32.1, 16.0} (ft/sec)
Range (G, Diameter, Flow) = < velocity 2 32.1 > (ft/sec)
Propagation Rule Result:
< Some-Part some velocity 2 32.1 > (ft/sec)
A graphical representation is shown in Figure 5-42.

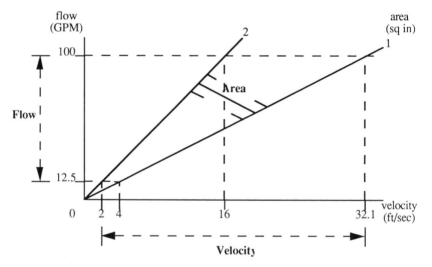

Figure 5-42: < some Range (G, Area, Flow) > = < some velocity 2 32.1 >

Physical Interpretation:
We know that we have pipe cross-sectional areas only in the interval 1 to 2 sq
in. The flow into the pipe will take at least some value in the interval 12.5 to
100 GPM. We know then that the velocity of the fluid in the pipe will take at
least some value in the interval 1 to 32.1 ft/sec.

5.2.4.7. Issues of causality

We have used the Parameter and State-Variable labels to describe how variable features achieve their operating values. We initially assumed that we captured all of the information that we need about causality by representing variable features with either of these two labels. However, problems with some examples for Propagation Rules currently under development indicate this description of causality is not complete. Research on this problem continues.

5.3. THE MECHANICAL DESIGN COMPILER (MDC)

5.3.1. Introduction

Based on a schematic, component specifications, and a cost expression provided by the user, the MDC uses the operations and inference rules of labeled interval calculus to produce an optimal design. It progressively narrows the space containing possible designs down to one design rather than testing every possible design.

This is a recursive process. The question, "What is the best feasible design in this set of designs?" is answered by first asking, "What subsets can we easily and correctly eliminate as infeasible?" The remaining set is split into subsets, and attention is focused on the subset with the best design regardless of feasibility. The same process of elimination and splitting continues until the subset containing the best design has only the best design -- this is the best feasible design in the original set.[2]

More precisely, it achieves the optimal design by first reasoning about component-level specifications in order to determine which catalog-entry level specifications will not work. Once the MDC eliminates all catalog-entry-level specifications which will not work, the MDC conducts a search for the optimal design. It searches by splitting component catalogs and creating "daughter designs." The MDC uses the cost expression to determine the more promising daughter design. Pursuing the most promising design, the MDC again identifies catalog-entry-level specifications that will not work. This iterative process con-

---

[2]This is a form of A^* search -- it is guaranteed to find the optimum design provided estimates of the best design are always optimistic and never become less accurate as the design space is divided.

tinues until the MDC either determines that no design will work or identifies the optimal design.

5.3.2. Operation of the MDC

5.3.2.1. General operation

The general operation of the MDC consists of the following steps:
1. *Formulate* the initial *Design*, and add it to the (empty) list of active designs.

2. Until

Active designs is empty (the design problem is shown to be impossible, or

A single solution remains for each component of the Most Promising active design and it has no pending specifications

Do for the most promising of the active designs

If

The design has *Pending Specifications*,

Then

Process Specifications to eliminate catalog entries which can be proven active not to work.

Else

Split the *Design* into daughter designs; add the daughter designs to the active designs; remove the design from the active designs.

5.3.2.2. Formulate design

1. Until the schematic is complete, Do

a. User enters the name of a component type,

1. Create an "in-box" for the component.

2. Create a "component-level specification table" for the component.

and

b. If there is a previous component,

    1. Verify common port types of connected components.

    2. Verify complementary port directions of connected components.

2. User enters cost expression.

3. User enters specifications for components, which are placed in their in-boxes.

5.3.2.3. Pending specifications

Specifications are pending if

    The MDC has eliminated catalog-entry-level specifications from any component catalogs.

or

    The MDC has split a component and formed "daughter designs."

or

    Any component has a specification in its in-box.

5.3.2.4. Process specifications

While there are pending specifications, Do

1. Abstract any component catalogs which have been split or undergone eliminations since the last abstraction to formulate component-level specifications. Place the resulting (abstracted) specifications in the in-box.

2. While any in-box is not empty, pick a component with a non-empty in-box. Call it *comp*. Pop one specification from *comp's* in-box. Call it *spec*.

    Check *spec* for redundancy with respect to specifications in *comp's* component-level specification table.

        If redundant, then discard *spec*.

Else if *spec* conflicts with a specification in *comp's* component-level specification table, remove the design from active designs.

Else,

a. For each equation in *comp's* equation table with the same variable as in *spec*,

For each specification contained in *comp's* component-level specification table with another variable in the equation chosen

For each propagation rule pattern that matches the specifications.

If

The propagation rule produces a new specification,

Then

Put the new specification in *comp's* in-box.

b. Eliminate part numbers that do not work using elimination conditions to check if any catalog-entry-level specifications conflict with the *spec*.

c. For each connected component, apply the translation rule, and place any resulting specifications in the connected component's in-box.

d. Add *spec* to the *comp's* component-level specification table.

5.3.2.5. Split design

1. The user designates which component to split. The component designated must have more than one part number remaining.

2. Split the component's catalog into two sub-catalogs.

3. Create two "daughter designs" using only one sub-catalog in each daughter design for this component; the remaining parts of the daughters are copies of the parent.

5.3.2.6. Most promising

1. Determine for each component in each design the maximum and minimum possible values for all variables appearing in the cost expression.

2. Determine the minimum possible value of the cost expression for each component based on these values.

3. Sum the minimum values for the components in each design to form a value for each design.

4. Pick the design with the minimum value.

5.3.3. Guide for Use of the Mechanical Design Compiler

This section describes how a user interacts with the MDC to create a design.

5.3.3.1. Background

Once the MDC has been loaded, the screen should look like the screen in Figure 5-43.

The menu bar contains the menu title, "Design", which has the following menu commands:

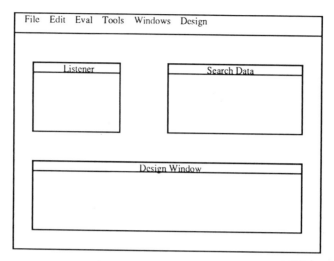

File   Edit   Eval   Tools   Windows   Design

Listener

Search Data

Design Window

Figure 5-43: Initial Screen

```
New Design
Form-Cost-Expression
Add Specifications
Search
```

5.3.3.2. Procedure

Step 1:
Highlight the menu command, "New Design", within the "Design" menu title
and click once. "Select an Item" window as shown in Figure 5-44.
Step 2:
Highlight "Electrical Supply" and click "OK." The electrical supply appears
in the "Design Window" as shown in Figure 5-45.
Step 3:
Double click on the port of the electrical supply to add another item to the
design. The "Select an Item" window as shown in Figure 5-46 appears.
Step 4:
Highlight the desired item in the "Select an Item" window and click "OK."
The MDC adds the item selected to the design in the "Design Window" as
shown in Figure 5-47.
Step 5:
Double click on the port of the last item in the design to add another item to
the design. The "Select an Item" window appears. Highlight the desired item in
the "Select an Item" window and click "OK." The MDC adds the item selected

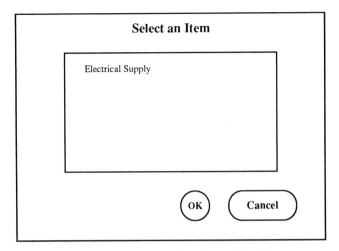

Figure 5-44: Select an Item Window - Initial Component

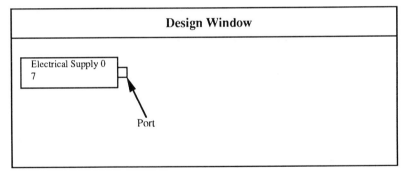

Figure 5-45: Design Window with First Component

to the design in the "Design Window." Continue this process until the complete design desired appears in the "Design Window" as shown in Figure 5-48.

Step 6:

Highlight the menu command, "Form-Cost-Expression", within the "Design" menu title and click once. The "Enter the Utility Function" window as shown in Figure 5-49 appears.

Step 7:

Enter the desired utility function. Click "OK."

Example: For a utility function based on price, enter (+ (* price 1) (* 0 1)). This is interpreted as (price x 1) + (0 x 1) = price.

Step 8:

Highlight the menu command, "Add Specifications", within the "Design" menu title and click once. The screen remains the same.

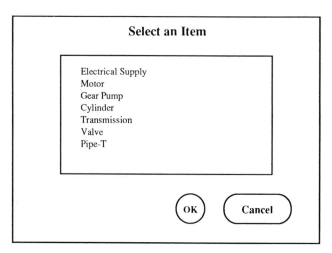

Figure 5-46: Select an Item Window - Additional Components

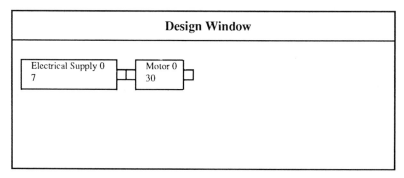

Figure 5-47: Design Window with Second Component

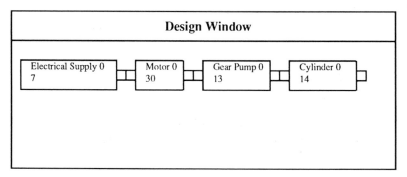

Figure 5-48: Design Window with All Components

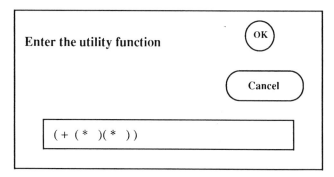

Figure 5-49: Utility Function Window

Step 9:
Within the "Design Window", place the cursor on the item for which you have a specification. Click once on that item. The "Select Keys and Bounding Values" window as shown in Figure 5-50 appears.

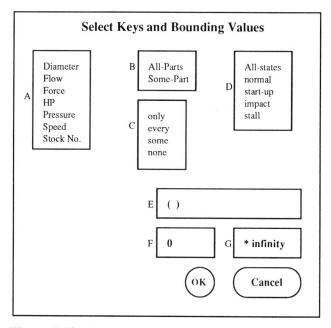

Figure 5-50: Select Keys and Bounding Values Window

Step 10:
Refer to Figure 5-50, "Select Keys and Bounding Values Window." With the cursor highlight the appropriate one item in each area, A, B, C, and D. If the

specification has only discrete values, enter these values separated by a comma in area E. If the specification does not have discrete values, leave area E blank. If the specification has only a continuous range of values, enter the lowest value in area F and the highest value in area G. If the specification does not have a continuous range of values, leave areas F and G blank. Click "OK." The "Listener" window will list any parts killed along with the labeled interval conflicts causing elimination of the part number. The "Design Window" displays the number of part numbers of the item remaining and the cost interval of those part numbers within the box for each item. If only one part number remains for an item, the item box contains a "1", the cost of the remaining part number, and the part number of that part. See Figure 5-51.

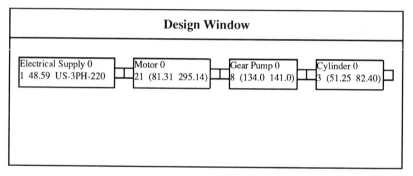

Figure 5-51: Design Window Showing Components with Several
Part Numbers Remaining

Step 11:
To add another specification, within the "Design Window" place the cursor on the item for which you have a specification. Click once on that item. The "Select Keys and Bounding Values" window appears. Repeat Step 10.
Repeat Step 11 until all specifications for any parts have been entered.
Step 12:
Highlight the menu command, "Search", within the "Design" menu title and click once.
Step 13:
Within the "Design Window", you can search (split the design into daughter designs) on any item with more than one part number remaining. Place the cursor on the item to be searched and click once. It does not matter which item is searched first. The results of the search appear in the form of daughter designs (with the most promising daughter design in bold face type) in the "Search Data"

window. Any parts killed during the search process appear in the "Listener" window along with the labeled interval conflicts causing elimination of the part number. The updated status of the number of part numbers remaining for each item is contained in the box for each item within the "Design Window." Repeat Step 13 for each item with more than one part number remaining until each item has only one part number remaining.

Upon completion of this process, the design in the "Design Window" is the optimal design. Each item within the design appears with a "1", the price of the item, and the part number for the item. See Figure 5-52.

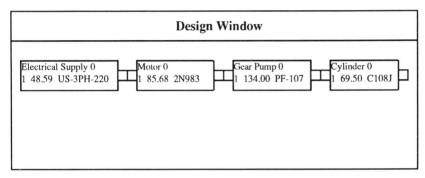

Figure 5-52: Design Window Showing Final Design

The daughter design in bold face type in the "Search Data" window is the same optimal solution listing the price range in parentheses for the overall design. See Figure 5-53.

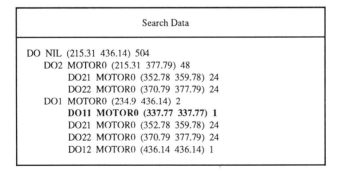

Figure 5-53: Search Data Window

5.4. BIBLIOGRAPHY

[1]   Bahler, D., Bowen, J., O'Grady, P. and Young, R., *Constraint Networks for Life-Cycle Engineering: Project Summary*, Technical Report, LIS-DEM Technical Report, 1990.

[2]   Davis, E., "Constraint propagation with interval labels," *Artificial Intelligence*, Vol. 32, pp. 281-331, 1987.

[3]   Moore, R., *Methods and Applications of Interval Analysis*, SIAM, Philadelphia, 1979.

[4]   Popplestone, R. J., "The Edinburgh Designer system as a framework for robotics: the design of behavior," *AI EDAM*, Vol. 1, pp. 25-36, 1987.

[5]   Ward, A. C., Lozano-Perez, T. and Seering, W. P., "Extending the Constraint Propagation of Intervals," *AI EDAM*, Vol. 4(1), pp. 47-54, 1990.

Chapter 6
KNOWLEDGE REPRESENTATION FOR DESIGN IMPROVISATION

Jack Hodges, Margot Flowers, and Michael Dyer

ABSTRACT

This chapter briefly reports on the representational strategy used in EDISON, a program currently being designed to (1) invent novel mechanical devices through heuristic strategies of mutation, combination and analogy, and (2) to comprehend descriptions of invented device representations. The representational constructs required to support these tasks include: (a) intentional structures such as goals, plans and settings, which organize relationships between device use and context, (b) physical entities such as regions and materials, (c) behavioral process relationships, such as object motion, connection and deformation, which relate objects to their physical states, (d) function relationships, which relate primitive devices to expected applications, and (e) mechanical dependencies and inferences. Invented and comprehended device representations are indexed and generalized into a memory of design episodes. The organization of such a memory supports the use of cross-contextual reminding and analogy during problem solving.

6.1. INTRODUCTION

EDISON is a project created to explore the processes of comprehension [15] and creativity [8, 9] in naive mechanics [6]. These tasks require basic research in: the representation of physical knowledge, memory organization, inference and dependency structures, planning, problem-solving, and learning. The overall approach has been to build a prototype process model and to test the limitations of various comprehension and invention heuristics, along with the representational constructs over which they operate.

Artificial Intelligence in Engineering Design
Volume I
Design Representation and Models of Routine Design

193

The situations we are interested in are those relating to the development of a preliminary design, resulting from an idea or goal and the associated context, rather than design optimization or performance. This approach is exemplified by the following scenario:

Example 1: Swinging Door

Joe Pizzamaker finds himself repeatedly having to carry pizzas through a doorway in both directions. In one direction he merely pushes the door while in the other he must open the door. At some point of discomfort Joe might say "surely there must be a better way!". He already knows the ease of door use in one direction and so he might have the idea to redesign the door into a swinging door by modifying the existing door to "close" in both directions. The problem-solving for this scenario utilizes memory retrieval and combinational strategies.

Swinging Door is an example of naive invention, a design methodology which uses naive, or common sense mechanical reasoning to solve problems and generate novel devices. Common Sense reasoning is particularly suited to the representation and processing of **Swinging Door** for three reasons. The first is *motivation*. Joe is motivated to invent, and his idea originates from a need to reduce his discomfort. The second is *feasibility*. Joe is first interested in whether the idea will work in general, rather than how well it works. His understanding of door use, function, and behavior need only be detailed enough to associate the door with the context of its use, recognize the conditions which will enable and disable its functionality, and predict resulting door behavior. The third is *naive evaluation*. Joe is interested in a simple solution, and evaluates the new door by comparison to other (known) devices.

Common Sense reasoning supports invention in situations such as **Swinging Door** through the application of experiential knowledge, which requires the integration of intentional and physical knowledge constructs organized into a memory of design episodes.A process model for naive invention is comprised of two major components: a representation and memory which support common sense reasoning, and a creative component which both recognizes serendipitous situations for change and can follow through with a first-cut design approach.

6.2. SYSTEM ARCHITECTURE

The EDISON system is composed of eleven elements (Figure 6-1). In this figure thin lines with arrows indicate flow of information through the system; thin dotted lines without arrows indicate semantic links between knowledge structures; thick lines indicate knowledge access between knowledge bases (squares) and interpretation subsystems (squares with rounded corners). EDISON accepts three types of natural language input: (a) a device description, (b) a question, or (c) a goal specification and context. A detailed discussion of natural language (NL) comprehension in the EDISON system can be found in Reference [15].

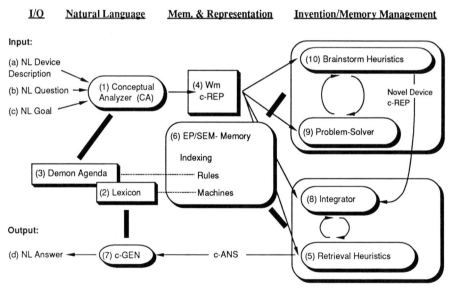

Figure 6-1: EDISON Process Model

Briefly, a goal specification given as input to EDISON is passed to the conceptual analyzer ((1) in Figure 6-1).

The CA coordinates the analysis of input text and generates a conceptual representation (c-REP in Figure 6-1) of the goal statement. The c-REP is then utilized by the invention management subsystem to interpret the goal and invent a device.

If the goal is to create a novel device of a given type, then the c-REP is handed directly to the brainstorming component ((10) in Figure 6-1). Brainstorming consists of heuristics which attempt to create novel devices by four general strategies: (1) interpretation of setting and actor intentions to generate design constraints, (2) retrieval and combination of known devices which satisfy, or partially satisfy design constraints, (3) analogy, where some attribute of the device representation is generalized and a device is retrieved (from another episode and/or context) which shares features with the given device at the abstract level, and (4) mutation, where a given device representation is altered along some device property. The door redesign in **Swinging Door** exemplifies the use of mutation in EDISON.

If the goal specification already includes design constraints, the c-REP is passed first to the problem-solving component of the invention management subsystem ((9) in Figure 6-1). The problem-solver attempts to apply rules and principles of mechanics to satisfy physical constraints. When the problem-solver cannot recall a solution from memory, it calls upon the brainstorming heuristics to improvise a solution to the planning failure.

6.3. NAIVE MECHANICS REPRESENTATION

A naive mechanics representation (NMR) must support comprehension, problem-solving, learning and invention. The general approach of the EDISON representation is to represent physical, relational, behavioral, and functional device attributes as conceptual dependencies, focusing on how device characteristics support device function in the different contexts in which devices are used.

6.4. THE NEED FOR INTENTIONAL KNOWLEDGE IN PROBLEM SOLVING

Consider the doors in Figure 6-2. Most people easily recognize that the door in Figure 6-2(a) simply won't work, and that the door in Figure 6-2(b) cannot be opened in the direction shown. It takes a little longer to realize exactly *why* the normal function of these doors is disabled. This comprehension process often requires that they re-examine how a working door actually functions.

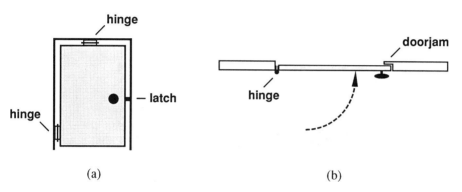

(a)   (b)

Figure 6-2: Examples of Non-functional Doors:
a) attribute-based, and b) process-based motion disablements

Comprehending the bugs in Figure 6-2 requires that EDISON be able to (1) receive a conceptual representation of a door as input, (2) recognize it as a door (either from a label or by comparing its representation to that of a device in memory), and (3) realize that this particular representation disables a door function. Figures 6-2(a) and 6-2(b) illustrate two ways in which motion can be disabled. In Figure 6-2(a) motion *capability* is disabled from the placement of hinges. In Figure 6-2(b) existing door motion is disabled by a path restraint (doorjam).

We believe that the processes of invention and comprehension share high-level, abstract features across a variety of task domains. In order to detect device errors, EDISON must be able to analyze a device in terms of the goals its use accomplishes. In story understanding and invention domains the relevant goals are those of the characters and include hunger, health, achievement, etc.

In the naive mechanics domain, goals involve physical transformations, such as connection and separation. Physical goals are achieved by the *use* of devices. For example, use of the door represented in Figure 6-3 is instrumental to achieving the intentional goal (D-PROX [18]) of moving (PTRANSing) between rooms. Door use, and the function with which a use is associated, thus depends on the context of actor goals.

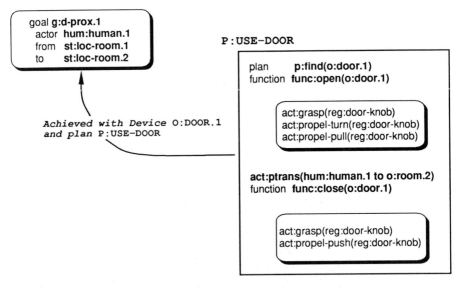

Figure 6-3: Use of Intentional Representation in Device Comprehension

The intentional use of objects is represented as a series of events,[2] and how those events achieve particular goals. For example, door function (e.g. opening) is initiated by a combination of actions: GRASPing the knob and turning it (a PROPEL resulting in door latch release from the door jam), and pushing the door (a PROPEL resulting in door rotation about its hinges).

---

[2]Dyer views an event as an action-state pair, or causal primitive [7]

In story domains, goals are achieved through the application of plans, and a number of plans may exist which are able to achieve a single goal. Likewise, in naive mechanics, goals are also achieved through the application of abstract plans, but here realized through the operation of physical devices. For example, using the door of Figure 6-3 requires release of an (implied) door latch. Door mobility can be realized by executing the processes used to achieve latch release (e.g. unbolting and untying are acceptable plans for un-restraining parts).

6.5. DEVICE TAXONOMY FOR REPRESENTING FUNCTIONAL COMPREHENSION

A simple door is comprised of many devices (a doorslab, doorway, latch and hinges). Each device is used for different purposes, and functions in different manners. If every device has a unique representational form, EDISON would never be able to distinguish one device from another, nor recognize similarities. On the other hand, if all devices are decomposed to a primitive set of devices, then similarities can easily be traced, supporting both device retrieval and analysis. In the mechanical domain, all basic machines [2, 3] manifest the principle of mechanical advantage [19]; and all devices in EDISON decompose to the interaction of simple mechanisms, called machine primitives [14], which exhibit mechanical advantage.

Notice that one can understand the function of a door and recognize when a door will fail to work (such as those in Figure 6-2) without knowing the exact principles behind leverage. We only need a shallow model of what components do, and not exactly why they do it. In terms of door hinges we need only know that hinges realize mechanical advantage, how their use is enabled and disabled, and how hinges interact with other devices. In EDISON, the representation of device physical and relational properties directly supports the comprehension of (a) physical behavior which the device exhibits, (b) the device function which describes sequenced behavior and produces observable states,and (c) device use and interaction.

Mechanical comprehension and representing behavioral processes. Each mechanical device interacts with other devices, objects, and the environment. In EDISON mechanical *interactions*, (e.g. motion and connection) are represented as qualitative behavioral processes similar to Forbus' Qualitative Process (QP) theory [11]. Processes represent causal state sequences relating perturbations to physical state changes, and are used to predict and comprehend device behavior. There are two differences between process representation in EDISON and QP theory.

First, EDISON has no relationships or influences that can be used to explicitly simulate device behavior. Instead, processes are represented as frames: by their behavioral and quantity enablements, and by the states an enabled process results in. A process can be used to predict the resutling state given the proper enabling conditions, or to explain a failed process, but not to simulate spatial behavior. Nor can EDISON processes by used to simulate or predict transient behavior. Second, in EDISON all mechanical behavior can be decomposed to one of five behavioral process primitives: BPP-Motion, BPP-Restrain, BPP-Transform, BPP-Store, or BPP-Deform. Each BPP results in a unique change in state: BPP-Motion to location, BPP-Restrain to restraint, BPP-Transform to force, BPP-Store to stored energy, and BPP-Deform to size/shape. Moreover, BPPs can be combined to describe arbitrarily complex mechanical behavior, so analysis of mechanical behavior is somewhat simplified.

Despite differences in representational detail, the EDISON methodology is directed at understanding function through context. The approach is best suited to integrating a device with the context of its use; for conceptual or preliminary design, rather than optimization. Clearly both points of view play significant roles in a complete representational model, and one intention of this project has been to maintain predictive continuity with qualitative representation models.

To illustrate how a theory of mechanisms and processes can be useful in creative device interpretation (and generation), let us decompose the representation of door-use that was introduced in Figure 6-3. Early intentional (object) models, e.g. Lehnert [16], represented device use in context but didn't associate use and function, or use and behavior. The Lehnert representation could infer what the device was used for, but not how or why. We are interested in how the door actually behaves as a result of an intentional act, and how device behavior is interpreted. Figure 6-4 shows how the open and close *functions* of a door-use plan are represented in EDISON. Device function is represented as the observable input to a device, as perturbations, and by the observable states which the device produces. Device function can be described as a sequence of behavioral processes which causally relate user/device input to the function terminating states. The function terminating state is the state associated with the original purpose for which the device was chosen. Each device may have multiple functions, associated with different properties, mechanisms, or combinations therein, and these may be used together or separately in different contexts. A door has two simple functions: open and close. Each door function consists of an initial action, a motion (or motions), and a resulting position (state).

The *close* function shown in Figure 6-4 describes a simplified (black box) version of the key steps in door closing. The contact between latch (reg:linkage-doorknob) and doorway, sliding and compressing of the spring, and the resulting linkage containment in the doorway have been omitted. The *open* function shown, on the other hand, describes enough detail so that all but the most specific relationships are represented. Decomposing door-use representation to

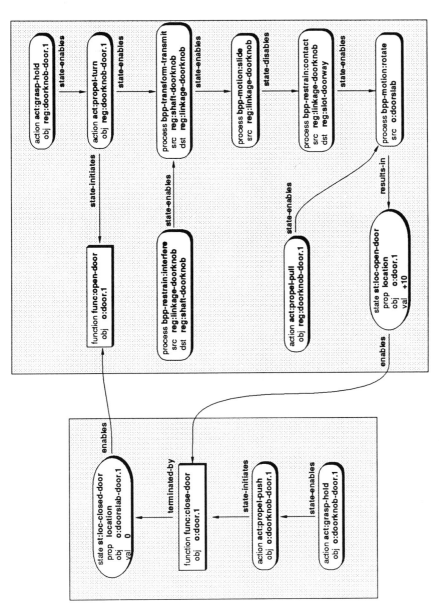

Figure 6-4: Representing Door Functions: Opening and Closing

this level is useful for (a) constraining processing, (b) making inferences and predictions about gross device behavior, (c) integrating the intentional and physical representations, and (d) presenting limiting, or bounding, information for device function. The information obtained from Figure 6-4 enables EDISON to recognize motion of the door toward (direction is not shown in the figure) the doorway as a closing function, and to predict that the door will very likely reach a closed state (processes are scriptal). EDISON can also make the inference that someone, or some thing, was responsible for the motion of the door, and that its closing will satisfy one of their goals. (This is only implied in the figure through reference to the actions of actors, and hence to their higher level goals and plans; see [12, 13] for complete examples and taxonomy.)

Although Figure 6-4 shows how processes interact in a device function, nothing specific has been said about what processes do, or how. Bounding the door-use plan enables some inference and prediction for cyclic behavior, however, predicting and explaining door behavior requires some representation at the process level. Figure 6-5 details the process representation level representation in EDISON, and how it supports understanding the *BPP-Restrain* processes in Figure 6-4.

Figure 6-5 shows the representational form for EDISON processes and how different BPP-Restrain processes are realized by different role bindings. The representation of processes is very similar to that of Schank's actions [18], but there are three differences: (a) processes have no agent, (b) processes are context-free, and (c) processes are more predictive. The rationale for introducing processes over new actions is that processes occur in a physical world which parallels the intentional world. To illustrate, consider an action such as push (propel) as applied by an actor to a ball. The action may result, at the intentional level, in the ball flying through the air (ptrans) from one location (the actor) to another. People generally do not think of the lower level processes of how the impulse is transmitted from the actor to the ball, the storage of energy in the ball, the restraints on the ball, whether or not the ball can move, or what path the ball will take. However, these processes all occur as the object is propelled. Processes have been introduced to maintain the ability to address both representational levels independently. Processes do not have an agent because the forcing function can be supplied by another mechanism (such as a device, or gravity). Processes are context-free because they have specific conditions which, when met, result in their expected behavior. These conditions are situation independent, and do not index directly to any intentional knowledge structures. Finally, processes are more predictive because the physical world (process dependencies) is well defined. That is, states resulting from enabled behavioral processes are true physical states.

In EDISON, all mechanical behavior is represented with five behavioral process primitives: *BPP-Motion, BPP-Restrain, BPP-Transform, BPP-Store*, and *BPP-Deform*. The process BPP-Restrain describes object interactions

BPP-Restrain Representation

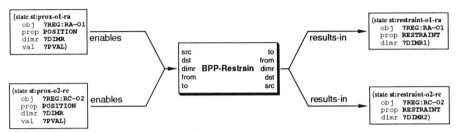

Specializations to BPP-Restrain

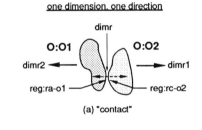

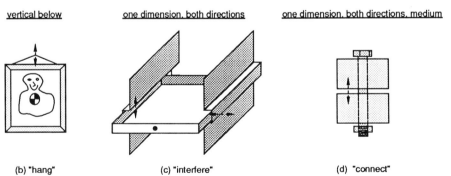

Figure 6-5: Representing BPP-Restrain Process in EDISON

which produce mutual restraint states, thus disabling motion, which is represented with the process BPP-Motion. BPP-Motion and BPP-Restrain are sufficient to enable the transmission and transformation of force between objects, represented with the process BPP-TRANSFORM, the storage of elastic energy in objects, represented with the process BPP-STORE, and the plastic deformation of objects, represented with the process BPP-DEFORM. From Figure 6-5, BPP-Restrain can be seen to require two parts, a dimension and direction, and potentially some medium (e.g. a connector) for holding the objects together. All processes have enablements, and BPP-Restrain requires that the parts be in physical contact to one another. Processes, like actions, cause state changes. Once enabled, BPP-Restrain results in a restraint state on each object, in equal dimensions but opposite directions.

BPP-Restrain:Interfere describes object contact in which object motion is disabled along an entire dimension axis.[3] The meaning of *BPP-Restrain:Interfere* can now be interpreted. O:Linkage-DoorKnob and Reg:Slot-DoorWay instantiate the process roles *src* (the source or reference object) and *dst* (the destination object). The object which fills the *src* role determines the process dimension. The dimension (ALONG-RADIUS) refers to the O:Linkage-DoorKnob radial dimension. The process *from* and *to* roles refer to the state change produced by the enabled process. BPP-Restrain processes describe restraint states, which are defined by the process dimension and direction, so the *from* and *to* roles are uninstantiated. The interference between O:Linkage-DoorKnob and Reg:Slot-DoorWay causes a set of restraint states for each: along the O:Linkage-DoorKnob radial dimension.

Two basic process assumptions are made in the EDISON representation approach: (a) parts are free to move unless specifically restrained, and (b) enabled processes will continue unless otherwise acted upon. These assumptions, and other basic knowledge for processes and process interactions, are formulated as process enablements, and take the place of more formalized relations and influences in QP theory, the intention being to make a reasonable accounting for a depth of representation which is beyond the scope of the EDISON project. The assumptions do, however, enable similar types of reasoning, and support limited process prediction, diagnosis, and explanation.

Machine primitives and function comprehension. Behavioral Process Primitives underlie the representation of complex device behavior and device function. Nevertheless, devices, as physical objects, play the central representational role in EDISON, because they index directly to both why the device is used (intentional representation), and how it produces the desired effect (function and

---

[3]As compared to BPP-Restrain:Contact or BPP-Restrain:Support, which act on specific directions along a dimension.

behavior representation). The more compact the device representation, the easier it is to associate device use and behavior, and less computational effort will be required to do so. Because we are indexing devices by their use, it is inappropriate to decompose devices to the most primitive known physical mechanisms [1]. Instead, we decompose all devices to a set of eleven commonly accepted basic machines [2], called Machine Primitives: MP-Linkage, MP-Lever, MP-Wheel-Axle, MP-Gear, MP-Pulley, MP-Bearing, MP-Spring, MP-Container, MP-Plane, MP-Blade, and MP-Screw. Machine primitives represent simple devices which have a single expected function. For example, MP-Linkage is associated with objects which are used to extend force over some distance by transmission. The objects which can be involved in this function are those which can transmit force in at least one dimension and direction. The roles of the primitive are those regions where applied forces are applied, called *appl*, and reacted, called *react*. All mechanical devices can be decomposed to combinations of machine primitives, and by understanding them EDISON has the capacity to understand, reason about, and generate, more complex devices.

Figure 6-6(a) presents the EDISON representation for BPP-Lever, which is instantiated by simple lever-objects. A lever-object is a linkage-object with the addition of a pivot location. Thus MP-Lever specializes MP-Linkage with the addition of a *pivot* role (i.e., MP-Lever has three roles; appl, pivot, and react). The pivot location, as with the locations associated with the appl and react MP roles, represents a generalized location directly associated with device function. Generalized locations are represented with a physical characteristic called a *region* [10]. Whereas MP-Linkage is used to transmit or translate forces and velocities, the function of MP-Lever (Figure 6-6(b)) is to magnify force or speed; both of which enable specializations of the process BPP-Transform.[4] MP-Lever is realized in different ways depending on how the remaining MP-Lever roles are instantiated: (a) type of applied input, (b) relative locations (represented as *relations*) of the input, fulcrum, and reaction regions, and (c) relative magnitudes of input and reaction (whether velocity or force). The resulting state change is effected through the representation of BPP-Transform, and BPP-Transform:Magnify in particular. The bindings for *door-hinge* in Figure 6-6(c) are shown as they apply to the function representational form. The doorhinge is really two simple lever-objects *pinned* together. However, the effect of the MP-Lever instantiated by O:Plate1-DH is nullified because BPP-Motion enables MP-Lever use, and the doorway is grounded.

The significance of physical and relational characteristics is that all device-related knowledge structures index directly to device use, device function, or to a process which the characteristic enables. The representation for a device thus

---

[4]All EDISON machine primitives, except MP-Spring and MP-Container, enable BPP-Transform. MP-Spring enables BPP-Store, and MP-Container enables BPP-Restrain.

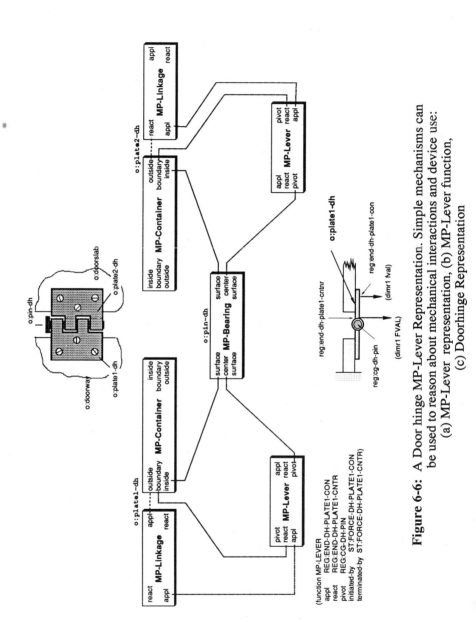

Figure 6-6: A Door hinge MP-Lever Representation. Simple mechanisms can be used to reason about mechanical interactions and device use: (a) MP-Lever representation, (b) MP-Lever function, (c) Doorhinge Representation

indexes into both intentional (e.g plans) and physical (e.g processes) knowledge types. EDISON will always be able to say which device characteristic is responsible for a particular use, or why an intended use failed. For example, regions describe generalized locations on a device, and instantiate the roles of a machine primitive. By representing only those device regions which directly affect a particular device function, the complexity of spatial descriptions is reduced, thereby aiding in differentiating uses and processes. How do we recognize the futility of trying to cut a metal rod with a rolling pin? People recognize that cutting requires an object with a sharp edge, where edge is a region, and sharp is called a *property attribute*. An attribute describes a simple comparison between the property values of objects used in a particular context. Both the edge and its sharpness are associated with the cutting of objects by the machine primitive *MP-Blade* and the process *BPP-Deform*. A rolling pin simply doesn't have a sharp edge, so most people do not consider it in the light of cutting. The door-hinge fulcrum (instantiated by the object O:Pin-DH) is a pivot region which allows the hinge plates to rotate relative to one another. The fulcrum location and implementation are actually unimportant in relation to the knowledge that either plate can carry the door weight.

The combination of process and device knowledge, with primitives, enables a broad view of physical interactions. EDISON can now make predictions and explanations of device behavior given only limited knowledge. For example, when a door is mentioned in text we *expect* some reference to dooor open or door close. Given an event in either the open or close function of door-use, we can *predict* the processes, and events within the processes, which are temporally local to the known event. EDISON can also *explain* behavior which deviates from that expected either at the device or process level. This kind of behavioral, and functional, analysis is used during comprehension of text describing mechanical situations. Consider the inferences required to understand the text of **Broken Foot**(figure 6-7).

The inferences required in building a conceptual representation of **Broken Foot** utilize knowledge in the door-closing function not ;explicitly mentioned in the text. The lexical entry for "door" sets up expectations for the functions associated with door use [15]. The phrase "would have...but" indicates a failure to achieve a given state, followed by an explanation. An explanation for the failure leads to a consideration of how the door-closing function is disabled. Closing is disabled either by restraining door motion or by eliminating the propelling force (see Figure 6-4). The conjunction "but" is a causal indicator linking foot placement with the disabled closing function. "Would have" and "closed" enable the inference that the door was being closed. Foot placement is thus assumed to restrain door motion, since motion once enabled can only be disabled by direct behavioral interaction. Thus, the foot must be positioned somewhere along the door's path of motion.

The integration of process and machine knowledge from the last two sections

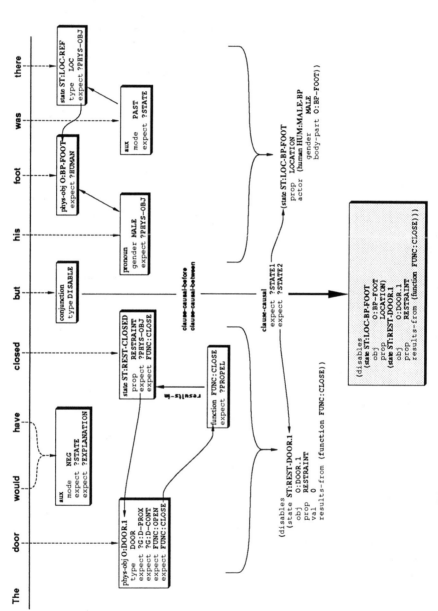

Figure 6-7: Comprehending Broken Foot using Process Theory

enables an explanation to be constructed for the buggy doors in Figure 6-2. Behavioral process primitives and machine primitives are instantiated to describe the configurations depicted. The knowledge captured by these representations can be formulated as rules such as **H1** and **C1-C4** below:

H1: If object O1 is a hinge, then the plates of O1 can rotate relative to each other about the long axis of O1.

C1: If two objects O1 and O2 are connected along direction D, then if one moves in D the other moves in D.

C2: If two objects O1 and O2 are in contact, then if either moves toward the other the other will also move.

C3: If two objects O1 and O2 are connected in multiple points, then the global restraint on the objects is the union of restraints along each dimension.

C4: If two objects O1 and O2 are connected in more than one location but do not share a common axis, then the connection is rigid.

H1 is a simple statement that hinges transmit forces in all dimensions except about their longitudinal axis. That is, relative rotation between the plates is the only motion that a hinge is capable of. H1 is loaded onto a rule agenda when a hinge is recognized and retrieved from memory. When the agenda is cycled the rule is applied to knowledge in working memory. C1-C4 can all be derived from the simple relationship that two objects connected along a dimension share the restraints of the connection type, minimally along that dimension. Process rules are applied in the same manner as device rules. The result of applying these rules to the devices in Figure 6-2 is a global (device) restraint state which disables motion.

Device representation and episodic comprehension. Naive mechanics reasoning in EDISON is experience-based. The potential for making interesting device comparisons and combinations is directly related to (a) the amount of experience, and (b) the number of possible connections between representational constructs. However, representational complexity, which is directly related to the number of possible connections, is inversely related to comprehension, and to the ease of comparison. EDISON organizes device knowledge behaviorally, functionally and intentionally to account for this contrast. Behaviorally, device characteristics, represented as states, index to behavioral processes. Functionally, device behavioral sequences index to the observed behavior associated with device use. Intentionally, device functions *must* index to the context which motivates device use. The relatively small number of machine and behavioral primitives, combined with the use/functional nature of the model, provide an environment where comprehension and diverse comparisons can coexist.

People tend to learn about, remember, and retrieve devices in terms of *attributes* associated with a situation. A device attribute is a comparison between a device property value and its boundary values, or with property values of other devices. For example, we may consider a faucet *leaky* if it won't close all the way. The comparative property is position, and the bounding values are open and closed. Were we to make the same kind of comparison, only w.r.t. the open position, then we might say that the faucet is clogged or restricted. The attribute thus tells us the point of view whereby device function is evaluated. Property attributes can index to any contextual component, and so device use can be interpreted in context. Also, because the physical property is directly associated with a behavioral process, EDISON can infer the function to which the situational context refers.

Design episodes in EDISON are comprised of four components: (1) an environmental context, represented as states, (2) a problem solver's goals, motivated by the environmental context, (3) the problem solver's planning, related to the goal, which includes the devices applied, and (4) the observable states resulting from the executed plans. Each component adds a contextual element to the episode and serves as a point of view for episodic interpretation. To illustrate this concept consider the doors in Figure6-8. One door may be used in a bank vault as security, while the other door is used in a flood for flotation.

The environmental state of flooding motivates a not-drown (G:Preserve-Health) goal. One way to avoid drowning is to stay-afloat, and staying afloat is associated with devices which float, and to materials capable of floating. Because the door is wooden, it may well be used to stay afloat. In contrast, a $banking script[5] builds expectations for money containment (G:D-Preserve-Wealth). This goal suggests a default (prototypical) door use with emphasis on material strength (for security), which is also met with a material (metal) property.

6.6. NAIVE INVENTION IN EDISON

In EDISON the point of view is taken that the creative process requires the ability to (a) address and interpret a situation from multiple perspectives, (b) select an interpretation among many, and (c) visualize the environmental effect of the interpretation. If a problem-solver resolves each new problem by simply recalling a past solution, then inventiveness should diminish as the number of

---

[5]The use of $ follows the convention used by Schank and Abelson [18] for scripts.

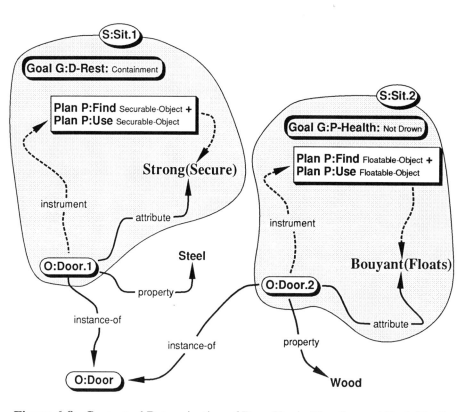

Figure 6-8: Contextual Determination of Door Use in Flooding and Bank Vault

xperiences grows. However, with human inventors the acquisition
evice serves as a platform for coming up with more devices.
_____d, in his research with children [5], extensive use of analogy and
combination when the task given to the children was to create novel devices.
Making device comparisons this way is supportive of the idea that growth in
episodic memory increases the potential of inventiveness rather than diminish-
ing it.

The representation presented uses design episodes to support the ability to
make and comprehend comparisons. The creative utilization of design episodes
introduces four issues important to the study of naive invention: (1) the motivation for invention, (2) preliminary design and invention, (3) methods for
generating new designs, and (4) assessing the ingenuity and worth of new
devices.

Failure motivates invention. The quote *"necessity is the mother of invention"*
has popularized a basic tenet in recognizing the potential for invention: goals are
significant motivators for change. Goal successes rarely lead to inventions, but
goal failures point out planning limitations, conflict, and/or competition between
goals. These are good indicators that an invention process will be useful. When
invention is initiated, past design failures can be reviewed in the light of new
knowledge, and may result in a successful design. Likewise knowledge
generated from remindings[6] may result in more goals being achieved by a single
design.

Invention and conceptual designs. Invention is customarily associated with the
early, conceptual, stages of design; inventors identify factors which are instrumental to a successful design, and build prototypes to demonstrate the concept. EDISON is a model of conceptual design. We seek contextual interpreta-
tions which lead to the understanding, and development, of design constraints.
The invention itself results from the interaction of constraint and relaxation
based methods applied to the design constraints. The device representation is
fundamental for interpreting context and developing constraints, and thus fits
into the creative strategy of this model.

Design generation. Devices can be generated by the application of three simple
invention heuristics, (1) combining known devices, each of which partially
satisfy a design constraint, (2) analogically mapping a known device (and source
domain) to a new device and target domain, and (3) mutating known devices.
Mindless generation of devices, however, is anything but creative. Each invention heuristic has its place, and the inventor knows when best to apply them. An

---

[6]Remindings are spontaneous similarity-based retrievals, see Schank [17].

example illustrating an appropriate use of analogy for invention is the door redesign in **Swinging Door**. Once Joe has decided to make a door which opens both ways he runs into the problem that standard door hinges only open in one direction. If Joe analogizes swinging horizontally to swinging in any dimension he can be *reminded* of a clock radio with numbers on flash cards which flap as their axis is turned. The cards use an axial hinge to enable swinging in both directions. Making the comparison between the two doors Joe can now consider whether the axial hinge will work on a door in the vertical dimension.

Design ingenuity and uselessness. Two kinds of knowledge constrain EDISON's processing. First, physical knowledge constrains the generation of novel but useless devices. A good example is the use of physical orientations between objects. In Figure 6-2 the door wouldn't secure were the linkage and slot not coaxial, a state which would render the device useless for door restraint. Second, the interaction of planning *metrics* constrains the design process.

Many problems arise in designing a door, including the selection of hinge type and placement, latch type and placement, even the material out of which the door is made. Each of these details is significant in arriving at an overall door design. Achieving the intended use, however, will generally have priority over satisfying more detailed design constraints. In EDISON new designs are created using simple heuristics such as mutation and combination. Similarly, the design process is both constrained and evaluated using invention planning *metrics*. EDISON has six invention metrics: (1) functional cost, (2) elegance (physical and functional simplicity), (3) utility, (4) performance, (5) novelty, and (6) efficiency. Invention metrics oversee the invention process and compete for priority in the design. A device is considered ingenious if multiple invention metrics are satisfied in its design.

In some cases only one planning metric may be activated, resulting in a natural focus. One such case arises in improvisation, in which the only metric involved is utility (i.e. will the device work). In such cases any invention heuristic resulting in a design contradicting the desired use will be avoided. In other cases competition between metrics forces the design process. **Swinging Door** is a good example of competition between planning metrics. Joe has a goal to get Pizzas from one room to the next; this involves utility. Simultaneously, Joe has a personal goal to maximize personal comfort; this involves ease and simplicity. The two goals conflict, the result of which is a conflict between the design metrics. Depending on the strength of Joe's goals the door design will vary.

6.7. FUTURE WORK IN EDISON

The EDISON representation is designed to support the creative process, but the creative capacity suggested by this model leaves many issues unanswered. Some of these issues have been addressed to some extent but remain unimplemented, others are just too difficult to consider at the present stage of model development. We present here a few interesting concepts which we would like to pursue further.

Throwing in the towel. Designers and inventors alike tend to get an idea and milk it to death, oftentimes ignoring simple and more elegant solutions. The issue of competing models, the importance which a creator gives to a partially-successful invention, and what the creator does with a partial invention when the evidence points against it (in terms of processing) is interesting. The same comments can be made of device interpretation. Often times there may be many mechanisms in a device, and understanding one may be requisite to understanding another. Perhaps some processing stack exists and invention (and comprehension) processes can be shuttled to and from the stack, depending on the context and available information.

Interpreting failure in an inventive memory. We have seen, above, that failures motivate invention scenarios. But what is the role of failure in memory? Schank [17] has argued that failures are important because learning occurs at failure points. Dyer [7] has shown that plan failures represented at an abstract level serve as an indexing structure to cross-contextual memories. If every trivially bad design is stored in EDISON's episodic memory, then problem-solving efficiency may suffer, as a result of recalling bad designs. However, if failures are never stored in memory, then EDISON will be doomed to repeat its mistakes. Therefore, along with design successes EDISON must store design failures. The generalization of specific instances, whether success or failure, leads to abstract experiences in memory. Situations which are not generalized remain salient as episodes. The overall effect is that EDISON will later be able to apply a bad design to resolve a different problem, or will be able to re-explore the bad design in lieu of new knowledge, in the same ways that successful designs are used.

Interference and invention. A conflict exists between the use of reminded experiences during invention and the interference [4] of reminded experiences upon invention. Creative people use their broad experience as a platform for creating new designs *because* their experience can be applied across domain boundaries when the context is similar. In this respect remindings aid invention. During invention, however, continual reminding of old solutions can detract from being creative. The inventor must be able to override reminded memory *in order* to invent. Inventors don't seem to block remindings but, rather, make decisions as to what knowledge is pertinent. The EDISON model is being designed to address this fundamental issue in design creativity. The current approach is to consider the active goals being processed. When an active goal is associated with device use, remindings are not used as direct solutions. Thus if EDISON is trying to invent a better bicycle, a bicycle may be retrieved for comparison purposes, or to generate new indices into memory, but won't be used as a solution. Nominally, if the bicycle is the only item retrieved, then mutation of some bicycle attribute would be applied. When remindings are associated with non-primary design goals direct use is acceptable. One example are the screws used to connect a hinge to a door/doorway. Why reinvent a screw unless the mode of connection is of interest. We hope that this initial approach will lead to further insight into the problem of interference in creative design.

6.8. CONCLUSIONS

Naive mechanics comprehension and invention can be modeled in terms of symbolic manipulations on representational constructs. Invention and creative design can be motivated from an interpretation of situational context in terms of actor goals and plans. Interpreting design episodes results in the development of conceptual design constraints. Invention heuristics then enable us to combine, analogize and/or mutate representations so as to achieve constraint driven goals; resulting in a preliminary design. The representational approach stresses the interaction of intentional and physical knowledge structures in memory, as applied to the creative process. The resulting designs are indexed into memory by features common across domains, increasing the amount of knowledge potentially applicable to future design goal achievement.

The model emphasizes the role of episodic memory in creativity, and lacks the ability to simulate device behavior as some qualitative, and all quantitative, representation models. The difference lies in the approach. EDISON is directed at reasoning about multiple device uses, and emphasizes a simple representation for behavior and function through the introduction of knowledge primitives associated with each. This limits the ability of EDISON to simulate device behavior, but enables us to describe entire problem-solving scenarios and to express similarities between devices used for different purposes, in different contexts. We believe that this representational outlook is a necessary component to an overall representational scheme which can support creativity.

6.9. ACKNOWLEDGMENTS

The research reported in this section was funded in part by a grant from the Office of Naval Research (contract no. N00014-86-0615)

6.10. BIBLIOGRAPHY

[1]   Alonso, Marcello and Finn, Edward J., *Physics, Series in Physics,* Addison-Wesley Publishing Company, Inc., Reading, MA, 1970.

[2]   Bureau of Naval Personnel, Ed., *Basic Machines and How They Work,* Dover Publications, Inc., 1971.

[3]   Bramwell, Martyn and Mostyn, David, *How Things Work,* Usborne Publishing, 1984.

[4]   Crowder, R.G., *Principles of Learning and Memory,* Lawrence Erlbaum Associates, Hillsdale, N.J., 1976.

[5]   DeBono, Edward, *Children Solve Problems,* Penguin, 1980.

[6]   Dyer, Michael G. and Flowers, Margot, "Automating Design Invention," Autofact 6, Anaheim, CA, 1984.

[7]   Dyer, Michael G., *In-Depth Understanding: A Computer Model of Integrated Processing For Narrative Comprehension, Artificial Intelligence Series,* MIT Press, Cambridge, MA, 1983.

[8]   Dyer, Michael G., Flowers, Margot, and Hodges, Jack, "Naive Mechanics Comprehension and Invention in EDISON," Tenth International Joint Conference on Artificial Intelligence, Morgan-Kaufmann, Milan, Italy, August 1987.

[9]   Dyer, Michael G., Flowers, Margot, and Hodges, Jack, "EDISON: An Engineering Design Invention System Operating Naively," *International Journal of Artificial Intelligence in Engineering,* Vol. 1, No. 1, July 1986.

[10]   Dyer, Michael G., Flowers, Margot and Hodges, Jack, "EDISON: An Engineering Design Invention System Operating Naively," *Applications of Artificial Intelligence in Engineering Problems,* Vol. 1, Sriram, D. and Adey, R., Eds., First International Conference, Springer Verlag, Southampton, United Kingdom, pp. 327-342, April 1986.

[11]   Forbus, Kenneth, "Qualitative Process Theory," *Artificial Intelligence,* Vol. 24, pp. 85-168, July 1983.

[12]   Hodges, Jack, "Device Representation for Modeling Improvisation in Mechanical Use Situations," Proceedings of the Eleventh Annual Conference of the Cognitive Science Society, Lawrence Erlbaum associates, Hillsdale, NJ, pp. 643 - 650, August 1989.

[13]   Hodges, J.B., "NAIVE MECHANICS: A Computational Model of Device Use and Function in Design Improvisation," *IEEE-Expert special track on Functional Representation,* Vol. , pp. , 1992.

[14]   Hodges, Jack, *Naive Mechanics: Computational Experiments in Representing and Reasoning about Simple Mechanical Devices,* unpublished Ph.D. Dissertation, University of California at Los Angeles, 1992.

[15]   Dyer, Michael G., Hodges, Jack, and Flowers, Margot, "Computer Comprehension of Mechanical Device Descriptions," in *Knowledge-Based Systems in Engineering and Architecture,* Gero, John, Ed., Addison-Wesley, 1987.

[16]   Lehnert, Wendy G., *The Process of Question Answering,* Lawrence Erlbaum Associates, 1978.

[17]   Schank, Roger, *Dynamic Memory,* Cambridge University Press, 1982.

[18]   Schank, Roger and Abelson, Robert, *Scripts, Plans, Goals, and Understanding, The Artificial Intelligence Series,* Lawrence Erlbaum, Hillsdale, NJ, 1977.

[19]   Weiss, Harvey, *Machines and How They Work,* Thomas Y. Crowell, 1983.

PART II: MODELS OF ROUTINE DESIGN

Chapter 7
INVESTIGATING
ROUTINE DESIGN PROBLEM SOLVING

David C. Brown and B. Chandrasekaran

ABSTRACT

We have been investigating the knowledge and control structures that characterize *design* as a generic problem-solving activity. In particular we have studied a subclass that we call *routine design*, and have constructed a high-level language called DSPL that allows task-level expression of design knowledge and makes appropriate control behaviors available. We have tested our approach by implementing a routine mechanical design expert system for air cylinders. We propose an architecture where a hierarchical collection of design "specialists" solve the design problem in a top-down distributed manner, where each specialist chooses from sets of design plans and "refines" the design. This paper provides a general introduction to the research, shows a trace from the expert system, and discusses ongoing DSPL research at OSU and WPI.

7.1. INTRODUCTION

7.1.1. Our Research

Most first-generation expert systems have been rule-based with a separate inference engine. A large unstructured collection of rules clearly lacks validity as a cognitively realistic model of design, as reducing all knowledge to a single form does not recognize that there are many different types of knowledge used in any design problem-solving activity. It also does not recognize that design knowledge forms into clusters, nor does it specify where or when this

Based on 'Knowledge and Control for the Mechanical Design of an Expert System,' by D. Brown and B. Chandrasekaran, which appeared in *IEEE Computer*; 19, 7, 92 – 100; July 1986. © 1986 IEEE.

knowledge is to be applied, as different clusters of knowledge are applicable at different times during design. Similarly, by using a single central "all purpose" inference engine, the richness of design problem-solving has been ignored. Another problem is that there is a potential for unfocused system behavior, as all the rules have equal status in the system and have equal potential for use.

Many systems structure rules into sets. These sets are based on domain-dependent subproblems rather than domain-independent types of knowledge [1, 18, 20]. In addition, the problem-solving method is uniform and not knowledge-based. The authors' claim is that the subproblems can be solved linearly with no backtracking between them and only minimal backtracking within them. This approach tells us more about the nature of their domain than about design, as it is clear that design decisions of any kind can often be wrong and, if so, will lead to attempts to recover from failure. The uniform rule representation and the lack of knowledge dependent structure does not provide us with any clear predictions about an expert's failure recovery behavior.

These problems stem mainly from a basic mismatch between the level of the tools available to build systems and the level of abstraction of the design task. Consequently, for handling more complex forms of expert problem solving, there is a need for tools that are at the "task" level. That is, tools related to the type of problem-solving being done, such as design (as opposed to diagnosis). Such tools will have to provide a rich set of design-related task-level constructs. They should be helpful in capturing more structured forms of knowledge and should be such that they help organize both knowledge and problem-solving behavior for more focused problem-solving.

The Laboratory for AI Research at Ohio State has been developing a framework in which investigation of *generic tasks* in knowledge-based reasoning plays a fundamental role. For a summary of the approach see [11]. For each generic task, appropriate families of knowledge structures and control regimes are constructed. In this perspective, design as a generic task calls upon and uses distinctly different types of knowledge and control from, say, diagnosis, prediction, or selection.

The above point of view naturally leads to families of high-level languages for the construction of expert systems. These languages have the property that domain knowledge can be captured much more perspicuously by using primitives appropriate to the task and that appropriate classes of control behavior are made available to the designer. For a subclass of design that we have called "routine design", we have developed a task-level language called DSPL [4].

Design itself is a complex activity and AI has relatively weak theories of it, especially for more creative design activity. In routine design the structure of the artifact under design is presumed fixed and standard methods of completing the design of various parts are known. However, there is still a complex problem-solving activity involving integrating and satisfying all the constraints of the particular design problem. Rough design and backtracking are observed in this design process, but much of the problem solving is piecing together the design, rather than creation of new methods. In our view, a substantial part of design activity in industry is of this type, and thus our approach could be of wide applicability.

We have use the domain of mechanical components (air cylinders in particular) to motivate our research. Our initial discussion of a simple prototype system is described in [2], while a more recent and more complete account is available in [8].

In this paper we present an outline of a theory of routine design, describe the types of knowledge involved, and briefly discuss the handling of failures during design. Air cylinder design is presented as an example of routine design problem-solving.

7.1.2. Other Work in Design

There has been considerable discussion in Artificial Intelligence about the nature of design. An analysis of this literature is outside the scope of this paper. Circuit design has been a domain where somewhat more sophisticated issues regarding the structure of knowledge and control in design have been discussed, but systems that consider design problems in a principled way are relatively few in number - see, for example, [15, 19, 21, 23] and the other chapters in this Volume. In the domain of mechanical systems we should mention the work of [13] and Chapter 9 as having interesting points of contact. In addition, an important view of design is presented in [22].

However, for the most part this other design research did not lead to generic languages and architectures to support design as a problem-solving activity, which is at least partly our aim. Because of this aim we have deliberately sought a level of design where the complexity of knowledge and control can be kept limited, but more powerful building blocks than are currently available can be provided in return. On the other hand the complexity of the design problems that can be solved by our framework is still higher than those that have been solved using the rule-based paradigm [18, 20].

7.2. DESIGN

7.2.1. Design in General

Design is a highly creative activity involving diverse problem-solving techniques and many kinds of knowledge. Clearly, as we don't know many of the problem-solving components of general design, and as we poorly understand those components we do know about, a comprehensive, detailed model of design is currently out of reach.

However, knowledge-based design researchers appear to agree about many components of design activity. Refinement is one such component. That is, descriptions get refined into less abstract forms. Plans are used in recognizable situations. Such plans are the result of past planning and validation by repeated use. Design activity often has a rough design phase followed by design proper. That is, an approximate or partial design is done first, before attempting to complete the design. Design activity is organized in ways that reflect the structure or functionality of the entity being designed. Similarly the representation of the design is also structured. During the design various restrictions on what is allowable for this kind of entity will be checked at appropriate points, and the initial conditions (i.e., requirements) form a starting set of restrictions.

7.2.2. Routine Design

We have been concentrating on routine design. However, we do not claim that all design problems are of this type. In routine design, the designer proceeds by selecting among previously known sets of well-understood design alternatives. At each point in the design the choices may be simple, but overall the task is still too complex for it to be done merely by looking it up in a database of designs, as there are just too many possible combinations of initial requirements. Simple choices do not imply simple designs or a simple design process. Many engineers share our view that a significant portion of design activity is routine.

In our work, we use the architecture of a hierarchically organized community of design agents called *specialists*. This hierarchy reflects the hierarchical structure of the artifact under design. Our view of routine design is that it is a largely top-down activity. We hypothesise that the specific problem-solving behavior corresponding to it can be captured as follows – each specialist has a repertoire of design plans to accomplish certain design tasks at its level of abstraction, it chooses from among the plans, makes some commitments, and directs specialists at lower levels of abstraction to "refine" the design. Failures cause different kinds of actions, such as choice of alternative plans, transfer of control to a parent specialist, etc.

The upper levels of the hierarchy are specialists in the more general aspects of the component, while the lower levels deal with more specific subsystems or components. A hierarchy is used not because we are arguing that design is intrinsically hierarchical, but rather that people use hierarchies to manage complexity. The specialists chosen, their responsibilities, and their hierarchical organization will reflect the mechanical designer's underlying conceptual structure of the problem domain.

7.3. AN APPROACH TO ROUTINE DESIGN

7.3.1. Introduction

We will first describe the design agents, and then their interaction. By the term "Agent" we mean any active module of the problem-solver, such as a specialist. An agent represents a collection of knowledge about how to design a portion of the object.

7.3.2. Design Agents

7.3.2.1. Specialists

A *Specialist* is a design agent that will attempt to design a section of the component. The top-most specialist is responsible for the whole design. A specialist lower down in the hierarchy will be making detailed decisions. Each specialist has the ability to make design decisions about the part, parts or function in which it specializes. Those decisions are made in the context of previous design decisions made by other specialists. A specialist can do its piece of design by itself, or can utilize the services of other specialists below it in the hierarchy. We refer to this cooperative design activity of the specialists as *Design Refinement*.

7.3.2.2. Plans

Each specialist has a collection of plans. A *Plan* consists of sequence of calls to Specialists or Tasks (see below), possibly with interspersed Constraints. It represents one method for designing the section of the component represented by the specialist. The specialists below will refine the design independently, tasks produce further values themselves, constraints will check on the integrity of the decisions made, while the whole plan gives the specific sequence in which the agents can be invoked.

7.3.2.3. Steps, Tasks, and Constraints

A *Step* is a design agent that can make one design decision given the current state of the design, taking into account any constraints. For example, one step would decide on the material for some subcomponent, while another would decide on its length.

A *Task* is a design agent expressed as a sequence of steps, possibly with interspersed constraints. It is responsible for handling the design of one logically, structurally, or functionally coherent section of the component; for example a seat for a seal, or a hole for a bolt.

Every specialist has some local design knowledge, some of which is expressed in the form of constraints. The constraints capture those major things that must be true of the specialist's design before it can be considered to be successfully completed. Other constraints, embedded in the specialist's plans, are used to check the correctness of intermediate design decisions, and do subproblem solution compatibility checking.

A *Constraint* is an agent that will test for a particular relationship between two or more attributes at some particular stage of the design. Constraints can occur at almost any place in the hierarchy. For example, a constraint might check that a hole for a bolt is not too small to be machinable given the material being used. See [6] for more on constraints in routine design.

7.3.3. The Four Phases

The design activity falls into four phases. Initially, the requirements are collected from the user and are verified both individually and collectively. For example, the MTBF required might be quite unacceptable. Alternatively, it might appear acceptable when considered by itself, but can be seen to be unreasonable when considered in the context of the required materials. This is a knowledge-based activity. Acceptable requirements do not necessarily mean that the design is achievable. Once it has been established that the requirements are acceptable, a rough-design is attempted.

Rough-design is poorly understood at present, but it serves at least two purposes. First, those values on which much of the rest of the design depends will be decided and checked. The actual attributes decided depends on the component and the domain, but, for example, it is likely that a value for the attribute "Material" will be chosen in this phase.

If these attributes can't be achieved then there is little point going on with the rest of the design. This also has the effect of pruning the design search space, as once the overall characteristics of the design are established it reduces the number of choices of how to proceed with the rest of the design. Second, as any mutually dependent attributes can prevent a design from progressing (i.e., A depends on B, and B depends on A), rough-design can, as human designers do, pick a value for one of the attributes and use that as if the dependencies didn't exist.

Specialists have both design and rough-design plans to select from depending on the current phase. Not all specialists will need both. It is entirely feasible that phases could be intermixed during problem-solving, but we have chosen to restrict the rough phase to be first, followed by the design phase.

Once rough-design is complete the *Design* phase can proceed. Design starts with the topmost specialist and works down to the lowest levels of the hierarchy. A specialist begins by receiving a design request from its parent specialist. It refers to the specification data-base for relevant specifications. A plan is selected using these data and the current state of the design. For more on plan selection see [3]. Our current form for plans is described in [4].

The specialist can fill in some of the design, and can call its successors in a given order with requests for refinement of the design of a substructure. The knowledge in the specialist prioritizes the plans, and invokes alternative plans in case of failure by one of the successors. When all of a specialist's plans fail the specialist communicates that to its parent.

If any failures occur during design, then a *Redesign* phase is entered. If that succeeds then the design phase can be re-entered. The system attempts to handle all failures at the point-of-failure before admitting defeat and passing failure information up the hierarchy. A step, for example, may be able to examine the failure and then produce another value, in order to satisfy a failing constraint, while still retaining local integrity. This local attention to failure is an essential element of failure handling behavior. Section 7.5 discusses failures during design in more detail.

7.3.4. Communication

The main means of communication in the system is by passing information and control messages between specialists across the connections forming the hierarchy. In this way the flow of control is restrained and the system exhibits clear, well-focused problem-solving activity.

Messages can request action, report failure, ask for assistance, and make suggestions. This rich variety of messages is the key to handling subsystem interactions. One part of the emerging theory of design problem-solving is the form and content of these design oriented messages. The design trace in Appendix C gives some indication of the types of messages used.

7.3.5. Other Agents

In general, in addition to the specialists in the hierarchy, other specialists outside the hierarchy may be needed. These are specialists in somewhat more general activities commonly needed by a number of the specialists in the hierarchy. For example, they may be certain kinds of stress calculation modules or data-base functions.

In a more general design system, requests could be made to other types of problem-solvers [10]. A human user could act as a problem-solver, as requests for assistance will occur at well defined points in the design. The expert system can subsequently check the acceptability of the results provided.

7.4. AN EXAMPLE OF ROUTINE DESIGN

7.4.1. The Air Cylinder

In the company that cooperated with us, an air cylinder (intended for accurate and reliable backward and forward movement of some component) had to be redesigned for every new customer. This was done in order to take into account the particular space into which it had to fit or the intended operating temperatures and pressures. We selected this air cylinder (AC) as a suitable object for our studies of design problem-solving. The AC has about 15 parts (See Figure 7-1).

The AIR-CYL design problem-solving system was developed using DSPL, which was in turn developed using Rutgers ELISP on a DEC system-20. AIR-CYL was used to investigate the viability of our theory of routine design. We are now working on extending the theory and examining the issues that arose while using the AC as our test case.

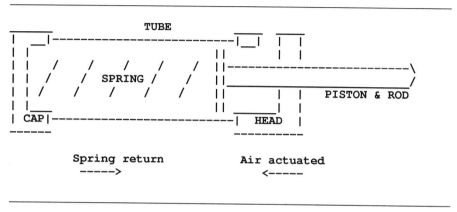

Figure 7-1: Air cylinder

7.4.2. The Conceptual Structure

An air cylinder designer was interviewed. The protocols were analyzed and the "trace" of the design process was obtained. This was analyzed to establish the underlying conceptual structure. For example, the head was clearly treated as a separate conceptual entity. Spring design was an essentially parallel activity, while the rest of the design was treated by the designer as the third major activity. The fact that the specialists can be fairly easily identified, and that the plans for each specialist are also identifiable and small in number strongly confirms that this is a routine design activity.

7.4.3. Design Agents

In the examples that follow we have used a simplified form of the DSPL language.

A *plan* consists of a set of actions, possibly with some in parallel. For example, in Figure 7-3 we show a Plan, where "Validate and Process Require-

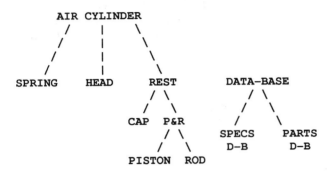

Figure 7-2: Partial AIR-CYL Structure

```
PLAN
  NAME                  Air Cylinder Design Plan
  TYPE                  Design
  USED BY               Air Cylinder  SPECIALIST
  USES                  Spring Head Rest SPECIALISTS
  QUALITY               Reliable BUT Expensive
  FINAL CONSTRAINTS     Design details OK?
  TO DO
      Validate and Process Requirements
      ROUGH DESIGN  Air Cylinder
      PARALLEL DESIGN   Spring AND Head
      TEST   Head and Spring Compatible?
      DESIGN   Rest
```

Figure 7-3: A Plan

ments" is the name of a Task, "Head and Spring Compatible?" is the name of a constraint, and "Rest" is the name of a Specialist. Note that this is a design plan. Some specialists will also have rough-design plans.

A *task* consists of the sequential use of a number of steps, and a *step* consists of obtaining required information followed by calculations and a decision about the value of a single attribute.

Figure 7-4 shows a step to decide on the width of the seat for the piston seal, where "Piston Seal" is the name of a task, "Seal Seat Width" is what is being

```
STEP
   NAME                    Piston Seal Seat Width
   USED BY                 Piston Seal
   COMMENT                 Written by DCB
   ATTRIBUTE NAME          Seal Seat Width
   FAILURE SUGGESTION      INCREASE Piston Thickness
   REDESIGN                NOT POSSIBLE
   TO DO
      KNOWNS     FETCH Piston Thickness
                 FETCH Piston Material
                 FETCH Minimum Thickness
                    OF Piston Material
                 FETCH Spring Seat Depth
      DECISION   Available IS
                 (Piston Thickness
                    MINUS DOUBLE Minimum Thickness)
                 Seal Seat Width IS 0.156
                 COMMENT Using one size only
                 TEST Available > Seal Seat Width?
                 STORE Seal Seat Width
```

Figure 7-4: A Step

decided, "INCREASE Piston Thickness" is what the step will suggest if it's not possible to make a decision, "Redesign not possible" means redesign is not possible for this step, "Piston Thickness" is an attribute that should already have been decided, and "Available > Seal Seat Width" is the name of a constraint.

7.5. HANDLING FAILURES

One view of failure handling considers all relevant knowledge to be immediately available at failure time. Our view is that data and control knowledge in human problem-solving is structured and probably incomplete, thus restricting the kinds of information available for handling failures. The structure of the design problem-solving system (i.e., specialists, plans, tasks and steps) provides the context in which to structure failure handling.

In our theory, all design agents detect their own failure, attempt to determine what went wrong, attempt to fix it locally, do so if they can, and report failure only if all attempts fail. Agents which have some control over other agents can use those agents when attempting to correct the detected problem. By using these ideas, our goal is to establish what is essential for failure handling in this kind of design activity. We believe that DSPL, and as a consequence AIR-CYL, is distinguished by its context-sensitive and knowledge-based treatment of failure. See Chapter 11 for a discussion of this claim. A detailed discussion of failure handling can be found in [5].

7.5.1. Redesign

Each kind of agent can have different kinds of reasons for failing. For example, a step finds that a decision violates some constraint, a task discovers that a step's failure can't be handled locally, a plan can fail if it is discovered that it's not applicable for the situation, while a specialist can fail if all of its plans fail.

For every kind of failure a message giving details is generated and passed back to the calling agent. The message includes, wherever possible, suggestions about what might be done to alleviate the problem. As there are usually many kinds of problems that can occur, an agent will first look at the message to decide what went on below. This is done by the *Failure Handler* associated with the agent. For some conditions immediate failure can be specified, for others an attempt to redesign might be attempted. A *Redesigner* is associated with an agent. It contains knowledge of how to change a design according to suggestions.

Appendix C presents an edited trace of the AIR-CYL system in operation. It shows recovery from constraint failures. It also shows a plan failing and a new and successful plan being selected.

7.6. THEORETICAL AND PRACTICAL RESEARCH ISSUES

7.6.1. Improvements to AIR-CYL

We feel that while the idea of design refinement captures the essence of design problem solving, at least in its relatively routine aspects, there are several important aspects of problem solving and the use of plans that need more research. DSPL is being studied and refined in order to make it more powerful, flexible, and easy to use. In addition we hope to improve the interface with the system to allow others to use it. Eventually we expect to provide a graphical interface to show the development of the design as it progresses.

7.6.2. Relaxation of Requirements

One possible way to deal with failures is to attempt to relax one or more of the constraints or requirements. Clearly some can be "softer" than others, and asking the user for some relaxation may clear the way to a successful design. If a lot of effort has been expended on a design by machine and human this makes a lot of sense. It may be possible for the system to choose what to relax, but a lot of special knowledge would be necessary to implement that. Even knowing when to ask for a relaxation will be difficult. This is a matter for future research.

7.6.3. Limitations of Approach

We are quite aware that there are bound to be other examples of routine design tasks that cannot be brought under the plan refinement paradigm in a natural way. Even if it is true that design is a process of choosing plans and refining designs, our ability to construct expert systems for design is very much a function of the types of design knowledge that we are able to capture and manipulate. We would like, as a result of our research, to be able to characterize the kinds of design problems for which our approach will lead to effective expert systems.

7.7. CONCLUDING REMARKS

We have presented an approach to building expert systems for routine design activity in the domain of mechanical components. Much work remains to be done in this area before we can understand what design is and how best to build systems to do it. We feel that there is great need for tools that express knowledge at the task level. DSPL is an example of such a tool. We feel that our approach of using a hierarchically structured system with plan selection captures the essential qualities of routine design.

7.8. ACKNOWLEDGMENTS

Much of this work was supported at Ohio State by AFOSR grant #82-0255. Some of this work was supported by NSF grant DDM-8719960. We would also like to acknowledge the cooperation during the AIR-CYL research of the AccuRay Corporation, Dave Herman and Pete Schmitz. Dave Herman was responsible for Appendix A. This research owes much to our colleagues in the Lab for AI Research at OSU, and in the AI Research Group at WPI.

This paper is essentially the same as that in IEEE Computer, Vol.19, No.7, July 1986, but it contains some additional material.

7.9. APPENDIX A: DSPL RESEARCH AT OHIO STATE UNIVERSITY

7.9.1. Introduction

In this appendix we will present DSPL-related activity taking place at the Lab for AI Research at Ohio State University. Since the development of AIR-CYL, the DSPL system has progressed in several dimensions. First, DSPL has been reimplemented in a more interactive Lisp environment. Second, DSPL has been used as a testbed for exploring certain facets of the generic task theory, such as explanation of problem solving behavior and the integration of multiple generic tasks in a single environment. Finally, DSPL has been successfully applied to several new design and planning domains.

7.9.2. Implementation

Initially, the DSPL system was implemented on a DEC system-20 in ELISP, with a version of FRL used for the design data-base. The syntax of the original version was very Lisp-like, and addition and modification of design knowledge was somewhat awkward. A new version of DSPL has been implemented in Interlisp-D. Although the architecture and language syntax of the new version are essentially identical to the ELISP version, the user interface to the system is much improved.

Considerable effort was spent creating a more friendly interface which takes full advantage of the Interlisp-D mouse/window environment. In particular, all design knowledge in a DSPL problem solver may be browsed via a single, top-level window which displays the specialist hierarchy of the problem solver. Design knowledge may be inserted or deleted through simple mouse actions, and a syntax checking editor ensures correct input to the system. Also, the flow of control of the design system may be graphically traced during execution.

In addition to the Interlisp-D version, DSPL is also being ported to Intellicorp's KEE, as part of an integrated toolbox which will incorporate several of the generic task tools in a single, unified environment. In as effort to further simplify the use of DSPL, this implementation will dispense with the Lisp-like syntax in favor of a form-based input.

7.9.3. Extensions and Applications of DSPL

As mentioned above, our laboratory is developing a toolbox based on the Generic Task architecture for knowledge based systems. The toolbox will be a collection of expert system shells, such as DSPL, each of which captures a different generic task. The toolbox can be used to create complex expert systems that utilize several different generic tasks to solve a single problem. A portion of our ongoing research is concerned with investigating the issues raised when multiple problem solving strategies are used within a single expert system. Other research is concerned with developing explanation facilities which can best take advantage of the knowledge and control strategies associated with each generic task.

The development of the Mission Planning Assistant (MPA) [16] has aided our understanding of the generic task toolbox, as well as the DSPL system itself. MPA is an expert system in the domain of tactical mission planning which was written in DSPL. It was developed with two goals in mind. First, we wished to examine the use of DSPL in the domain of routine planning. Second, we were interested both in exploring the particular explanation facilities necessary for planning systems and expanding our general theory of explanation within the generic task framework.

The first goal, that of applying DSPL to a routine planning domain, was achieved without any modification to the DSPL architecture. The basic MPA problem solving was directly implemented in the vocabulary of the DSPL shell. We discovered that certain types of routine planning can be conceived of as being analogous to routine design: certain types of plans can be decomposed into sub-problems just as certain mechanical design problems can be decomposed into the design of sub-components. Further, details of the plan were selected in a fashion similar to the selection of attributes in a particular component. The MPA system successfully demonstrated the applicability of the DSPL strategy to a simple planning domain.

The second goal of the MPA system, that of exploring necessary explanation facilities, required some extension to the DSPL shell. The basic DSPL architecture was unchanged, but facilities were added to allow simple queries to be directed at the system's output. Explanation of the system's output was generated by combining a trace of the system's behavior with the knowledge in the MPA system coded in DSPL. Since the use of knowledge in the DSPL system is closely associated with the particular control strategy embedded in DSPL, a more cogent explanation of the system's behavior is generated. In the Interlisp-D version of DSPL, the explanations are derived directly from the DSPL source code by re-parsing the source code using a translator which generates English text, rather than executable code.

Other applications of DSPL have not involved breaking new theoretical ground. One application in the domain of chemical engineering designs distillation columns from specifications of the components of the feed to the column and certain parameter's describing the column's environment. In this case the system takes advantage of the results of mathematical models of the column's behavior at various points during the design of the column. Notice that DSPL does not embrace a model of the column's behavior to focus problem solving, but rather uses the results of various models to produce a behavior similar to that of a human expert in the domain.

7.9.4. Summary

The DSPL shell for building routine planning and design expert systems is the focus of several important research issues at the OSU LAIR. We believe that it can play an important role in the creation of many practical and useful expert systems. We are taking several steps to expand its usefulness and theoretical interest.

7.10. APPENDIX B: DSPL RESEARCH AT WORCESTER POLYTECHNIC INSTITUTE

7.10.1. Introduction

In this appendix we will present DSPL-related activity taking place in the AI Research Group at Worcester Polytechnic Institute. Since the development of AIR-CYL, the DSPL research has been proceeding more or less independently at WPI and OSU. At WPI, research is progressing on two main fronts. The first is an extended study of the ways in which routine design knowledge becomes routine. That is, how it becomes organized for the efficient solution of a small class of design problems. The second is to improve the interaction with the system by providing acquisition and explanation systems.

7.10.2. Compilation

By *knowledge compilation* we mean the process by which knowledge gradually becomes efficiently organized so that problem-solving based on that knowledge becomes routine. This can logically be divided into formation and adjustment phases. We are currently concentrating on the adjustment of the design knowledge and strategies that occurs once they have been collected together by significant use. We are concentrating on small improvements only, leaving larger changes for later study.

We hypothesize that there are several mechanisms for making small changes. One mechanism is the replacement of simulations by constraints, either of which may be used to verify design decisions. One type of constraint can replace the sort of simulation that occurs when a person reasons about whether two sub-problem solutions will fit together. Another type of mechanism is the adjustment of constraints in the design knowledge. In particular we are looking at the ways in which constraints might migrate to a position earlier in the design knowledge.

7.10.2.1. Reasoning about fit

To study the formation of constraints about subproblem compatibility we are investigating the process of qualitatively reasoning about whether two components might fit together [14]. The stages are the *grouping* of features on the objects to characterize their potential for match, *orientation* of the objects into a position of potential match, *matching* of clusters of features, and *confirmation* on a feature-by-feature basis within clusters. A prototype implementation has been written in VAXLISP.

All reasoning is done without using any numbers. The result of the process is a decision about qualitative fit, which can be interpreted as a statement about the potential for actual fit. It also results in a description of the fit that isolates the key dimensions of key features. This could then be used to control a test for fit using actual lengths, which can then be turned into one or more constraints.

7.10.2.2. Adjustment of constraints

In the adjustment phase of compilation, constraints can appear, disappear and move. Movement of constraints to earlier points in the design process has the aim of catching design problems earlier. This movement will occur in response to repeated constraint failure and subsequent analysis. As constraints move they need to be changed. We are studying the nature of this movement and change [7].

7.10.2.3. Analogy

Another way that routine design knowledge gets formed is by analogy with existing design knowledge. We are investigating the process of getting "new DSPL from old" by analogy, given slightly different design requirements.

7.10.3. Interfaces

In order to improve the interface to the DSPL interpreter we are working on a collection of tools with which the user can interact. The two main ones are the DSPL Acquirer and the Explanation facility.

7.10.3.1. Acquisition

The Acquirer uses the structure of DSPL, as well as an explicit acquisition strategy, to control a question and answer session with the user [12]. In response to questions the user gives fragments of design knowledge which the Acquirer converts to DSPL and assembles. The result is a file of DSPL that can act as the knowledge-base of a design expert system.

7.10.3.2. Explanation

We assaume that the user of a DSPL-based design expert system can interrupt the action of the system at any major break in the design activity and ask one of a set of standard low-level questions. The Explainer has explanation routines for every DSPL agent [17]. A focusing mechanism, initially set to the interrupt point, determines which agent will be used to answer the question. If that agent is unable to provide the answer, the focus is moved up the agent hierarchy. This explanation research has concentrated on producing explanation using the minimum of trace information.

7.10.4. Conclusion

Other new work in progress is a study of failure handling, constraint relaxation and the use of dependency knowledge. A more detailed survey of recent research can be found in [9].

In summary, research into the use of DSPL for the representation of routine design knowledge is providing the focus for many investigations into design problem-solving. Our work has concentrated on the compilation of routine design knowledge and on interfaces for the DSPL system.

7.11. APPENDIX C: AN ANNOTATED TRACE OF AIR-CYL

This is a trace generated by the AIR-CYL system. It has been highly edited for brevity, and for presentation in this format. The trace is of a successful design with step redesign and selection of alternative plans. We have omitted the reporting of the final design.

```
***** AIR-CYL Air-cylinder Design System *****

*** Requirements input
    From file DCB:AC-Requirements-Test
```

There are about 20 values given as requirements, including the maximum operating temperature and pressure, and the size of the envelope in which the air-cylinder must fit.

```
* Do you wish to alter the requirements?  >>>?????>yes

EnvelopeLength         ---- 7.83
EnvelopeHeight         ---- 1.5
EnvelopeWidth          ---- 1.75
MaxTemperature         ---- 250
OperatingMedium        ---- Air
OperatingPressureMax   ---- 60
OperatingPressureMin   ---- 30
RodLoad                ---- 1.4
Stroke                 ---- 1.75
RodThreadType          ---- UNF24
RodThreadLength        ---- 1.031
RodDiameter            ---- (LNGTH 0.312 0.0 2.e-3)
Environment            ---- Corrosive
Quality                ---- Reliable
MTBF                   ---- 100000
AirInletDiameter       ---- 0.374
MountingScrewSize      ---- (LNGTH 0.19 5.e-3 5.e-3)
MountingHoleToHole     ---- (LNGTH 0.625 5.e-3 5.e-3)
MaxFaceToMountingHoles --  (LNGTH 0.31 5.e-3 5.e-3)

* Alterations from user

System name for requirement is >>>?????>EnvelopeWidth
        Current value is 1.75
        New value is >>>?????>1.35
```

We have cut down the width of the envelope without altering any other requirement in order to make the design harder.

```
System name for requirement is >>>?????>quit
```

```
* End of alterations from user
*** Requirements Input Complete

--- Entering Specialist
    ...AirCylinder... Mode = Design

----- Entering Plan
    ...AirCylinderDP1... Type = Design

------- Entering Task
    ...CheckRequirements

--------- Entering Step
    ...CheckEnvelope

--------- Leaving Step
    ....CheckEnvelope...Result= Success Msg
```

Here the system continues to check requirements. Next the design plan being followed specifies the use of the AirCylinder specialist in Rough Design mode. A rough design plan is selected and followed, leading to a successful rough design. The AirCylinder specialist then leaves rough design mode and continues in design mode. After quite a lot of decision making involving sub-specialists we get to this point.

```
------- Entering Specialist
    ...Rest... Mode = Design

--------- Entering Plan
    ...RestDP1... Type = Design

----------- Entering Specialist
    ...PistonAndRod... Mode = Design
```

At this point the system is working on the design of the piston and rod assembly. This is where the trouble starts.

```
------------- Entering Plan
    ...PistonAndRodDP1... Type = Design

    !!! etc !!!

--------------- Entering Task
    ...PistonSeal

----------------- Entering Step
    ...PistonSealType

----------------- Leaving Step
    ....PistonSealType
    ...Result= Success Msg

----------------- Entering Step
    ...PistonSealSeatWidth
```

The constraint test that follows will discover that there isn't enough

space in the piston for the seat for the seal that will go around the
piston. Its failure produces a message which shows in detail how the
failure occurred. Here we show only part of the message. It suggests
two alternative ways to attempt to fix the problem.

```
------------------- Entering TEST-CONSTRAINTS
                ...(Available>Width)

------------------- Leaving TEST-CONSTRAINTS
                ....(Available>Width)...Result=
                Failure "Constraint failure"
                Explanation "Seal width is greater than
                             available space in piston"
                Suggest (INCREASE PistonThickness
                         BY 1.517e-2)
                    Suggest (DECREASE PistonSealSeatWidth
                             BY 1.517e-2)
```

The failure handlers for a step which are built into the system determine
that a domain specific failure handler will be able to decide what to do.
Domain specific failure handlers are written in DSPL by the expert or
knowledge engineer.

```
--------------------------- Entering FailureHandler
                        ...PistonSealSeatWidthFH
```

The failure handler says to try redesign.

```
--------------------------- Entering Redesigner
                        ...PistonSSWRedesigner
         Step = PistonSealSeatWidth
         Suggest = (DECREASE PistonSealSeatWidth
                    BY 1.517e-2)

--------------------------- Leaving Redesigner
                        ....PistonSSWRedesigner
                        ...Result= Success Msg
```

The piston seat width redesigner was able to decrease the width as
suggested.

```
--------------------------- Leaving FailureHandler
                        ....PistonSealSeatWidthFH
                        ...Result= Success Msg
```

We leave the failure handler and return to the step. The redesign was
successful, so the step is successful and acts as if no problems were
encountered.

```
------------------ Leaving Step
                ....PistonSealSeatWidth
                ...Result= Success Msg

      !!! etc !!!

------------- Leaving Plan
```

```
        ....PistonAndRodDP1
        ...Result= Success Msg

------------ Leaving Specialist
        ....PistonAndRod...Result= Success Msg

------------ Entering Specialist
        ...Cap... Mode = Design
```

Now we attempt design of the cap, and discover another problem.

```
-------------- Entering Plan
        ...CapDP1... Type = Design

   !!! etc !!!

---------------- Entering Task
        ...CapInternal

------------------- Entering Step
        ...CapInternalDiameter
```

The constraint tests to see if the internal diameter of the cap is larger than the outside diameter of the spring, as one must fit in the other. It fails. Two alternative suggestions are provided.

```
-------------------- Entering TEST-CONSTRAINTS
        ...(CapID>SpringOD)

-------------------- Leaving TEST-CONSTRAINTS
        ....(CapID>SpringOD)...Result=
        Failure "Constraint failure"
        Explanation "Cap internal diameter
                     too small for spring"
        Suggest (DECREASE SpringOD
                  BY 9.9e-2)
            Suggest (INCREASE CapInternalDiameter
                      BY 9.9e-2)

-------------------------- Entering FailureHandler
        ...CapIDFH
```

The domain specific failure handler says to try redesign.

```
---------------------------- Entering Redesigner
                ...CapIDRedesigner
        Step = CapInternalDiameter
        Suggest = (INCREASE CapInternalDiameter
                    BY 9.9e-2)

------------------------------ Entering TEST-CONSTRAINT
                ...(CapID>SpringOD)

------------------------------ Leaving TEST-CONSTRAINT
                ....(CapID>SpringOD)
                ...Result= Success Msg

------------------------------ Leaving Redesigner
                ....CapIDRedesigner
```

```
                    ...Result= Success Msg
```

The redesign is successful. The suggested increase could be made, and the constraint was satisfied.

```
---------------------------- Leaving FailureHandler
                    ....CapIDFH
                    ...Result= Success Msg
```

The step is successful, as the failure was handled.

```
------------------ Leaving Step
                    ....CapInternalDiameter
                    ...Result= Success Msg

    !!! etc !!!
------------- Leaving Plan
                ....CapDP1...Result= Success Msg

----------- Leaving Specialist
                ....Cap...Result= Success Msg

    !!! etc !!!
----------- Entering Specialist
                ...Bumper... Mode = Design
```

The bumper is being designed here. More problems are encountered.

```
------------- Entering Plan
                ...BumperDP1... Type = Design

---------------- Entering Task
                ...BumperFlange

------------------ Entering Step
                ...BumperFlangeDiameter
```

The bumper flange diameter must be large enough to support the spring. The constraint tests that, but fails.

```
-------------------- Entering TEST-CONSTRAINTS
                    ... (BFD>SpringOD)

-------------------- Leaving TEST-CONSTRAINTS
                    ....(BFD>SpringOD)
                    ...Result=
                    Failure "Constraint failure"
                    Explanation "Bumper flange is too
                                    small for spring"
                    Suggest (DECREASE SpringOD
                            BY 2.995e-2)
                    Suggest (INCREASE BumperFlangeDiameter
                            BY 2.995e-2)

-------------------------- Entering FailureHandler
                    ...BumperFDFH
```

The domain specific failure handler says to try redesign.

```
------------------------------ Entering Redesigner
                     ...BumperFDRedesigner
      Step = BumperFlangeDiameter
      Suggest = (INCREASE BumperFlangeDiameter
                 BY 2.995e-2)
```

The redesigner fails as there is no knowledge
about increasing the value of that attribute.

```
------------------------------ Leaving Redesigner
                     ....BumperFDRedesigner
                     ...Result=
                     Failure "Redesigner action
                             section fails"
```

The failure handler reports failure and
eventually the step gets told of the bad news.

```
--------------------------- Leaving FailureHandler
                     ....BumperFDFH...Result=
                     Failure "Redesigner action
                             section fails"
```

            !!! etc !!!

```
----------------- Leaving Step
                ....BumperFlangeDiameter
                ...Result=
                Failure "Step failure"
```

The task passes the failure message from the step to
its failure handler. It will determine if
the task can do anything about the step failure.

```
------------------ Entering FailureHandler
                ...BumperFlangeFH
```

The failure handler for the task discovers that no suggestions have been
passed up from below. This means that no redesign can be considered. The
failure handler fails as it couldn't handle the problem.

```
------------------ Leaving FailureHandler
                ....BumperFlangeFH
                ...Result=
                Failure "No relevant suggestions
                        for task redesigner"
```

The step failure and subsequent failing redesign attempt leads to a failure
in the task.

```
--------------- Leaving Task
                ....BumperFlange
                ...Result=
                Failure "Task failure"
```

And the plan fails due to the failing task.

```
------------- Leaving Plan
             ....BumperDP1
             ...Result=
             Failure "Plan failure"
```

The next plan is selected, as the last one failed.

```
------------- Entering Plan
             ...BumperDP2... Type = Design

---------------- Entering Task
             ...BumperFlange2

------------------ Entering Step
             ...BumperFlangeDiameter2

-------------------- Entering TEST-CONSTRAINTS
             ...(BFD<CapID)
```

*This is the same constraint that failed in the last plan. This time it is
OK. The step succeeds.*

```
-------------------- Leaving TEST-CONSTRAINTS
             ....(BFD<CapID)
             ...Result= Success Msg

------------------ Leaving Step
             ....BumperFlangeDiameter2
             ...Result= Success Msg

        !!! etc !!!

------------- Leaving Plan
             ....BumperDP2
             ...Result= Success Msg

----------- Leaving Specialist
             ....Bumper...Result= Success Msg

--------- Leaving Plan
             ....RestDP1...Result= Success Msg

------- Leaving Specialist
             ....Rest...Result= Success Msg

----- Leaving Plan
             ....AirCylinderDP1...Result= Success Msg

--- Leaving Specialist
             ....AirCylinder...Result= Success Msg

*** Design attempt succeeds
***** AIR-CYL Air Cylinder Design System *****
```

7.12. BIBLIOGRAPHY

[1]   Birmingham, W. and Siewiorek, D., "MICON: A Knowledge Based Single Board Computer Designer," *Proceedings of the 21st Design Automation Conference (IEEE)*, pp. 565-571, 1984.

[2]   Brown, D. C. and Chandrasekaran, B., "An Approach to Expert Systems for Mechanical Design," *IEEE Computer Society, Trends and Applications '83*, pp. 173-180, May 1983.

[3]   Brown, D. C. and Chandrasekaran, B., "Plan Selection in Design Problem-Solving," *Proceedings of the AISB85 Conference*, April 1985.

[4]   Brown, D. C., "Capturing Mechanical Design Knowledge," *Proceedings of the 1985 ASME International Computers in Engineering Conference*, ASME, August 1985.

[5]   Brown, D. C., "Failure Handling in a Design Expert System," *Computer-Aided Design*, November 1985.

[6]   Brown, D. C. and Breau, R., "Types of Constraints in Routine Design Problem-Solving," *Proc. of the First Int. Conf. on Applications of AI to Engineering Problems*, CM Publications, Southampton, UK, April 1986.

[7]   Brown, D. C., and Sloan, W. N., "Compilation of Design Knowledge for Routine Design Expert Systems: an Initial View," *Proceedings of the 1987 ASME Conference on Computers in Engineering*, August 1987.

[8]   Brown, D. C. and Chandrasekaran, B., *Design Problem Solving: Knowledge Structures and Control Strategies*, Morgan Kaufmann Publishers, Inc., 1989.

[9]   Brown, D. C., "Research into Knowledge-based Design at WPI," *Fifth International Conference on Applications of AI in Engineering*, Gero, J., Ed., Springer- Verlag, July 1990.

[10]   Chandrasekaran, B., "Towards a Taxonomy of Problem-solving Types," *AI Magasine*, Vol. 4, No. 1, pp. 9-17, 1983.

[11]   Chandrasekaran, B. , "Generic Tasks in Knowledge-Based Reasoning: Characterizing and Designing Expert Systems at the Right Level of Abstraction," *Proceedings IEEE Computer Society International Conference on Artificial Intelligence Applications*, December 1985, [Key Note Presentation].

[12]   Chiang, T. T-L., "A System for the Acquisition of Routine Design Knowledge," M.S. Thesis, Computer Science Department, WPI, Worcester, MA 01609, March, 1987.

[13]   Dixon, J. R., Simmons, M. K., and Cohen, P. R., "An Architecture for Application of Artificial Intelligence to Design," *Proceedings of the IEEE 21st Design Automation Conference*, pp. 634-640, 1984.

[14]   Green, D. S., and Brown, D. C., "Qualitative Reasoning during Design about Shape and Fit: A Preliminary Report," in *Experts Systems in Computer Aided Design* , Gero, J., Ed., North-Holland Publishing Company, 1987.

[15]   Grinberg, M. R., "A Knowledge-based Design System for Digital Electronics," *Proceedings 1st Annual National Conference on AI*, Morgan Kaufman Publishers, pp. 283, 1980.

[16]   Herman, D., Josephson, J. and Hartung, R., "Use of DSPL for the Design of a Mission Planning Assistant," *Proceedings of the IEEE Expert Systems in Government Symposium*, October 1986.

[17]   Kassatly, A., "Explanation for Routine Design Problem Solving," M.S. Thesis, Computer Science Department, WPI, Worcester, MA 01609, March, 1987.

[18]   Kowalski, T. and Thomas, D., "The VLSI Design Automation Assistant: Prototype System," *Proceedings of the IEEE 20th Design Automation Conference*, pp. 479-483, 1983.

[19]   McDermott, D. V. , "Circuit Design as Problem Solving," in *AI and Pattern Recognition in CAD*, Latombe, J-C., Ed., North-Holland, pp. 227-245 , 1978.

[20]   McDermott, J., "R1: A Rule-Based Configurer of Computer Systems," *Artificial Intelligence*, Vol. 19, pp. 39-88, 1982.

[21]   Mitchell, T. M., Steinberg, L. I., and Shulman, J. S., "A Knowledge-Based Approach to Design," *IEEE Trans. on Pattern Analysis and Machine Intelligence*, Vol. PAMI-7, pp. 502-510, September 1985.

[22]   Stefik, M., "Planning with Constraints (MOLGEN: Part 1)," *Artificial Intelligence 16:2*, pp. 111-140, May 1981.

[23]   Sussman, G. J., "Electrical Design: A Problem for Artificial Intelligence Research," *Proceedings Fifth IJCAI*, pp. 894-900, 1977.

Chapter 8
DESIGN AS TOP-DOWN REFINEMENT PLUS CONSTRAINT PROPAGATION

Louis I. Steinberg

Abstract

Underlying any system that does design is a model of the design process and a division of labor between the system and the user. One appealing model views design as the result of top-down decomposition plus constraint propagation. We have studied this model by embodying it in VEXED, a design aid for NMOS digital circuits, and by experimenting with this system. In this chapter, we describe the VEXED circuit design system. We also discuss EVEXED, a domain-independent shell extracted from the VEXED system, and MEET, a mechanical design system built using EVEXED. A number of conclusions can be drawn from our experience with these systems, including the need for certain extensions to this model of design and some limits on its applicability.

8.1. INTRODUCTION

There is a large and growing interest in the use of knowledge-based approaches to building computer systems that aid in the process of design. Some of this work, including [1, 2, 5, 6] as well as the work described in Chapter 8 (Volume II) and Chapter 12 (Volume I) of this book, is aimed at specific design tasks in specific domains (e.g., the physical placement task in the domain of VLSI digital circuits). In contrast to this, our primary aim in the AI/Design group at Rutgers is to develop an understanding of principles and techniques that are domain-independent, that is, that apply to as broad as possible a range of design tasks and domains.

The ideal would be to find principles that apply to *all* tasks and domains.

Artificial Intelligence in Engineering Design
Volume I
Design Representation and Models of Routine Design

However, it quickly became clear to us that, designing, say, a spoon is quite different from designing a circuit. Only a small fraction of design knowledge will apply to *all* domains, and that knowledge will be at a very abstract level and thus hard to apply to any given specific task.

On the other hand, it has also become clear that some domains are not so different from each other, e.g., circuit design and programming. Even if a piece of knowledge does not apply to all possible domains, it may still apply to a *range* of similar domains.

Thus, our broad goals are to:

- develop a set of design principles and techniques that apply to a range of related domains;

- understand what that range of domains is;

- learn what it is about domains that lead them to be similar (or different) in terms of which principles apply.

One way to capture a group of ideas about design in some domain is in terms of a *model of the design process*. Such a model is intended to capture the sequence of states a design goes through from initial specifications to final product, the operations that move it from state to state, and the decision process that selects which operation to apply when.

Since all existing systems require some human participation in the process, at least to provide the initial specifications, it is also useful to think about the *division of labor (between system and human(s))*, that is, how the task is to be divided between the user and the system.

Having described our broad goals, we now turn to the specific research that will be described in this chapter. Our strategy, like that of the researchers whose work is described in Chapter 7 (Volume I) and Chapter 9 (Volume II), has been to focus on a specific model of the design process and a specific division of labor. The model we have chosen can be summarized by the equation,

```
DESIGN = TOP-DOWN REFINEMENT
         + CONSTRAINT PROPAGATION
```

In designing a complex structure, one attractive design method is to use top-down refinement: first decompose the structure into a few main pieces and completely define the interfaces between the pieces, so that the design of each piece becomes a totally independent sub-problem. Each can be designed separately, and the pieces simply plugged together to solve the original problem. Unfortunately, until we explore the space of possible designs for the pieces, it is often impossible to know exactly what the interfaces should be.

One solution to this is common practice among human designers, and has also been used by Stefik in the MOLGEN system [10]: leave the interfaces only partially specified. As you proceed with the design, decisions you make while working on one piece will further constrain what the interfaces of that piece must be, and thus constrain the alternatives for designing other pieces. We refer to this process of inferring how decisions at one place put constraints on options elsewhere as "constraint propagation."

Within this model of the design process, the division of labor we chose to study can be summarized as having the system decide what is possible and the user decide what is wise. That is, the system keeps track of which modules need refining and what the alternative refinements are for a given module. It carries out the refinement chosen by the user and also does constraint propagation. The user chooses which piece to refine next, out of all those still needing further refinement, and also chooses which way to refine it, out of all the alternatives that the system knows about that are consistent with the current constraints.

We first tested the model by using it as the basis for a specific design aid, VEXED,[2] in a specific domain, digital MOS circuit design. More recently, we have extended the test by using the same model (and indeed almost entirely the same code, but with different knowledge bases) to build MEET, a design aid in another domain - mechanical design [7, 11]. This chapter will focus on results from the circuit design domain, but will also briefly describe the MEET system.

In short, the results are that this model is appealing, but too simple. In the following two sections we will first describe our experience with VEXED, and then discuss the conclusions that can be drawn from this experience about this model of design.

8.2. THE VEXED CIRCUIT DESIGN SYSTEM

This section will discuss our experience with VEXED. First we will describe the way VEXED embodies this model of design: how it represents the circuit being designed, how it does refinement and how it does constraint propagation. Then we will show an example of VEXED's use and then discuss the implementation status of VEXED and describe the experiments we have done. Finally we will briefly discuss EVEXED, a domain-independent version of VEXED, and MEET, a system for mechanical design built using EVEXED.

---

[2]VEXED stands for Vlsi EXpert EDitor.

8.2.1. How VEXED Embodies the Model of Design

To embody our model of design, VEXED must represent both the structure and operation of the partially-designed circuit, and must be able carry out refinement and constraint propagation. We will deal with these issues in that order.

VEXED represents the structure of a circuit in a fairly standard way. A *module* represents either a single component or a group of components being viewed as a functional block. A *data-path* similarly represents either a single wire or a group of wires. The operation of a circuit is represented in a somewhat less standard way. The signal on a given data-path is called a "data-stream", and is thought of as a sequence of "data elements", e.g., a sequence of bits or characters. An individual data element is referred to by its "subscript", i.e. its position in the sequence. Elements have a number of "features", including Type (e.g. Boolean), Data-Value (e.g. FALSE), Encoding (how the abstract data-type is encoded as voltages), and various timing-related features. For a further discussion of these representations, see [4].

VEXED's knowledge of refinement methods is embodied in a set of "refinement rules", e.g., INCLUDE-MEMORY:

> IF the output at time t2 depends on an input at time t1, THEN one way to refine the module is into a memory, which holds the value from t1 to t2, and another module, which uses this stored value at time t2 to compute the output.[3]

The IF part of the rule describes the class of modules that this refinement method applies to. The THEN part describes how to do the refinement: the submodules, their initial specifications,[4] and how they are connected. It is important to note that these refinement rules describe *legal, correct* implementations, but not necessarily optimal or even preferred implementations. They define the "legal moves" in the search for possible circuit implementations, but not a strategy for choosing among alternatives.

It is also worth noting that in VEXED, refinement involves structural decomposition, breaking a module into its pieces, while in MOLGEN [10] refinement involves going from a more abstract operation to a more specific one.

Constraint propagation in VEXED is done by the CRITTER system [4]. Critter does two kinds of propagation.

- Firstly, CRITTER does a form of goal regression [13]. Given a specification on the data-stream output by a module, and given the

---

[3]This is, of course, an English paraphrase of the formal notation.

[4]To be augmented later by constraint propagation.

behavior of this module, CRITTER can determine what must be true of the inputs to the module to ensure that the output specification will be met.

- Secondly, CRITTER does a form of symbolic evaluation. Given a (possibly partial) description of the behavior of a module's inputs, and given the module's behavior, CRITTER can infer a description of the module's outputs.

Because of our representations, constraint propagation is simply a matter of symbol substitution (see [3]). However, this process results in very large, complex expressions. Therefore, CRITTER also has an expression simplifierthat uses a set of rewrite rules to simplify the resulting expressions as much as it can.

Finally, CRITTER is capable of verifying that the specifications on a data-stream are satisfied by that data-stream's behavior. Again, this is done by a process of symbol substitution and simplification.

8.2.2. Example

Figure 8-1 shows the user interface for VEXED, at the beginning of a typical design session; VEXED is implemented for Xerox Interlisp-D machines using the Strobe object-oriented programming system from Schulmberger-Doll Research. The circuit being designed is named TEST1. The screen is divided into several regions, or windows. The largest window is the region in which the circuit will be designed, and initially contains a large rectangle representing the circuit TEST1 to be designed. The user has already entered the specifications for this circuit. These specifications include a description of the inputs and outputs of TEST1, as well as a description of the function to be implemented. Figure 8-2 gives part of these specifications: the value of the output OUT at each clock cycle must equal two times the sum of the values of the inputs at that cycle, and for this output the numbers are represented by 4 parallel bits, with high voltage representing 1 and low representing 0; VEXED can also handle sequential circuits. Various features of the signal timing could also have been specified.

Attached to the main window is a list of commands and a list of pending tasks. As shown in the figure, the only pending task at this point is to refine TEST1. This list of pending tasks will be updated as the design proceeds, and new circuit submodules are introduced. In general, the user controls which portion of the design to focus on next by selecting one of the pending tasks from this list.

In the current example, the user selects the (REFINE TEST1) task, and the

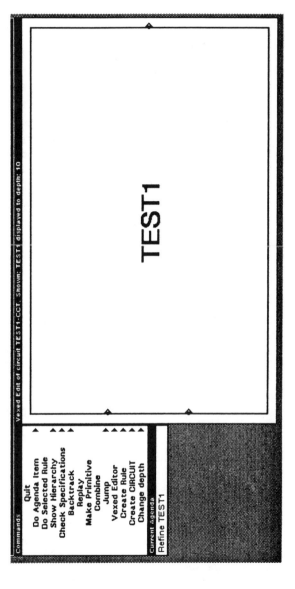

Figure 8-1: The VEXED Interface

```
((I (ALL I))
 (EQUAL
  (DATA-VALUE OUT I)
  (TIMES (PLUS   (DATA-VALUE MATCH I)
                 (DATA-VALUE DATA-IN I))
         2)))

 (EQUAL
  (ENCODING OUT I)
  (INTEGER (BITS 4) (WIRES 4)
   (BIT-ENCODING (NMOS-BOOLEAN (FALSE LOW)
                               (TRUE HIGH))))))
```

Figure 8-2: Part of the Specifications for TEST1

system then considers its collection of rules to determine which ones apply to this module. In this case, the advice offered by the system is that there are four rules, each suggesting an alternative method for refining TEST1. The user may select one of these rules to be executed or, alternatively, may elect to ignore the system's advice, and manually edit the circuit.

Figure 8-3 shows the result of the user selecting the rule TIMES-AS-SHIFT for the system to carry out. This rule implements multiplication by two as a shift. Execution of this rule has lead to a refinement of TEST1 into three modules. F:A1167 computes the argument to be shifted, in this case the sum of the inputs. TX1:A1152 and TX2:A1161 implement the shift. They "convert" the four-wire bus coming out of F:A1167 into four separate wires and then back into a bus; they do not represent any real components, but rather are "pseudo-modules" representing a change in the way we view the signals.

TX1:A1152 and TX2:A1161 are modules instantiated from primitives defined in VEXED's library. F:A1167 is a non-primitive, still requiring further refinement. The rule has given it some specifications and other specifications may be derived from constraint propagation. E.g., TX1:A1152 requires parallel input, so F:A1167 must produce parallel output. The list of pending tasks has also been updated.

Refinement of the circuit continues in this fashion. The user directs the focus of attention by selecting which module is to be refined next. The system examines its rule base to determine applicable rules, and presents these to the user. The user may then select one of these, or may ignore this advice and elect instead to refine the module by editing it manually.

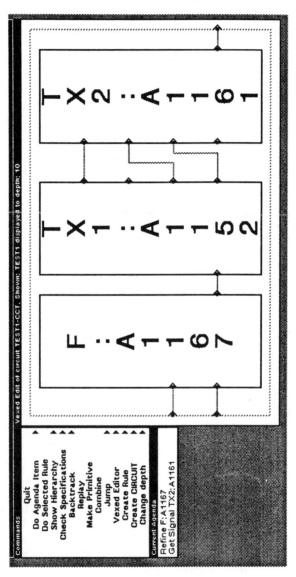

Figure 8-3: Result of Executing Rule TIMES-AS-SHIFT

8.2.3. Status

VEXED has been implemented and documented. It has 50 to 100 refinement rules covering most of the standard NMOS design techniques for boolean functions, and also for a few latches and a few arithmetic functions.

Furthermore, VEXED has been used by students in our VLSI design class to do a homework assignment. The assignment was done by about ten teams of students, mostly two students per team. Each team designed one of three small circuits; one circuit was a full adder, and the others were of about the same size. The students were given no more documentation and other help (lecture, hands on help, etc.) than they are typically given for any other design aid used in the course. Nevertheless, they did succeed in specifying and designing their circuits. The few who did not finish were those who were halted by one or another of the minor[5] bugs left in VEXED.

Thirdly, VEXED has had a number of capabilities added to it beyond refinement and constraint propagation.

- One facility any real system needs is a backtrack or "undo" facility that allows the user to retract decisions that turn out not to have the desired effect. VEXED has a chronological backtracking facility that allows the user to return the circuit to the state it was in at any previous time.

- It turns out that when a module is refined into sub-modules, a sub-module may occasionally need a signal as input that was not originally among the inputs of the parent module. Typically this happens with signals like clocks, ground, etc. To handle this situation, VEXED has "Get Signal" tasks, which are automatically entered on the task agenda when needed, and are handled by the user manually specifying where the needed signal should come from.

- A facility has been added for "Module Combining Rules." These specify how two modules can be combined into one simpler one, and provide for a kind of peephole optimization. For instance, two inverters in series can be combined into just a simple wire (as long as this change does not violate some timing constraint). Since it is always appropriate to try to combine modules, and since the circuit can be considered complete even if no combinations are done, these tasks do not go on the agenda. Rather, the user can point to a module and request that an attempt be made to combine it with each of its neighbors. There are currently only a few such rules, and this facility was not used by the VLSI students.

---

[5]"Minor" in the sense that we were able to quickly fix them.

• Finally, there is now a "replay" facility for VEXED. This takes the
sequence of refinements applied previously to some other circuit, or
even to other parts of the current circuit, and applies them to the
current module. To the extent that the refinement operations used
previously are general, and apply in somewhat new circumstances,
this is a way to reuse the *ideas* of a previous design even when the
specific circuit is not applicable. See Chapter 2 (Volume II) for a
further discussion of this facility.

8.2.4. Testing Generality: EVEXED and MEET

In order to test the degree to which our model of design is in fact domain-
independent, we took the development of VEXED one step further: we
modified VEXED to produce EVEXED,[6] a domain-independent shell for implementing VEXED-like systems, and used this shell to implement MEET, a
system for the design of rotation transmitters, in particular, gear chains.

The process of producing EVEXED from VEXED turned out to be almost
trivial. VEXED already allowed the user to load a different set of rules and
primitive modules, and the representations used in VEXED were tuned much
more to the model of design than to the specific circuit design domain.

We chose rotation transmission as the next problem domain specifically because of its similarity to digital circuit design. We viewed a "rotation" as being
quite similar to a "signal" - instead of having features like *start-time*, *value*, and
encoding, a rotation has features like *speed*, *direction* (e.g. "clockwise"), and
power. A module such as a gear pair takes a rotation as input and produces
another as output.

A small number of rules were implemented for MEET, enough to test the
general feasibility of the idea and to come to some conclusions about the
generality of our model of design. These are discussed below and, at greater
length, in [11].

---

[6]The name was chosen by analogy with EMYCIN [12], an expert system shell based on
MYCIN without its domain-specific (medical) knowledge.

8.3. CONCLUSIONS

As mentioned above, we began with a model of the design process and of the division of labor between the user and the system, and we implemented VEXED to test these models. Our conclusions can be seen as dealing with four broad questions:

1. Can a design aid embodying these models be implemented? Is it possible for a system to have a sufficient body of refinement methods to find those applicable to a given module, to carry out the one selected by the user, and to do the constraint propagation?

2. If such a system were implemented, could designers, especially those with no AI or even computer science background, use it to produce designs? The concern here was both whether the users could understand and use this design process, and also whether they could learn our specification language, which is quite different from standard hardware specification languages in its LISP-like syntax, in its data-flow style semantics, and in its representation of a data-stream as a sequence of values.

3. What, if anything, is missing from the model? Are there operations we need to do besides decomposition and constraint propagation?

4. How general are these models of the design process and of the division of labor? What must be true of a design task for them to be useful?

We will discuss each of these issues in turn.

8.3.1. Can VEXED be Implemented?

The fact that VEXED has been brought to the point where students in our regular VLSI class could successfully use it is evidence that it has indeed been implemented, at least on a small scale. Two issues need to be considered in regard to scaling up to larger problems, however. One is the size and coverage of the set of refinement rules, and the other is the cost of constraint propagation.

As noted above, the current refinement rules cover most boolean combinational circuits for the NMOS circuit technology, and some latches. A truly useful system would require more complete coverage of combinational circuits and latches, as well as rules for a number of other kinds of circuits, e.g. multiplexors, and rules for higher level data-types such as integers and characters. However, in principle there seems no reason why these rules could not be added to VEXED. Based on the number of current rules and the coverage they give, we estimate that a version of VEXED that would be useful for real designers would need less than 1000 rules, and so would be within the scope of current technology for building and maintaining rule-based systems.

Remember also that user can step in and do a refinement manually whenever the system does not have a rule for the desired refinement method. This helps in two ways. First of all, it means that there need not be as many rules before the system is useful; it probably takes far fewer rules to cover 90% of the refinement steps in each of a range of designs that it would take to cover 100% of the steps. Secondly, since the rules do not have to contain any control information, i.e. any information on which of the locally plausible refinements to actually do in a given design, it turns out that it is relatively easy to observe the user doing such manual refinements, and infer general rules. We have built a system called LEAP [8, 9] that will do just this.

Finally, VEXED uses an indexing structure to find relevant rules for refining a given module without testing the left hand sides of every rule, so the time to find relevant rules should grow less than linearly with the number of rules, and the time to find relevant rules is currently fairly short. Thus we do not expect the time to find relevant rules to be a major problem even with many more rules.

While the size of the rule set does not seem to be a problem, the cost, both in terms of memory space and in terms of time, to do constraint propagation does seem to be a major issue. In a circuit such as a full adder described at the transistor level, with about 20 modules, it takes five to ten minutes on a Xerox 1109 (DandeTiger) to do the constraint propagation after each refinement. Based on some initial studies (see [14]), the cost of propagation in the current VEXED grows quadratically with circuit size in most cases and, for certain kinds of circuits, exponentially. So, to design anything much larger it will be necessary to reduce this cost.

One simple answer, of course, is to optimize our code, which is currently not very optimal, or to get a faster machine. In particular, the task of constraint propagation seems inherently parallel, since each constraint can be propagated along each path more or less independently; thus it would seem a natural application for a parallel machine. Another answer is to find a way to do less propagation. At the moment, VEXED propagates every constraint everywhere it can as soon as it can. Perhaps limiting or delaying some of this propagation can reduce the cost.

8.3.2. Can VEXED be Used?

Given that VEXED can be implemented, can it be used? Can non-AI people learn our specification language, and can they successfully do design with such a design aid as VEXED? Again, the answer is, "Yes, but."

About half of the class were students from the Electrical Engineering Department with no AI background and indeed relatively little Computer Science background, and even the Computer Science students included some who had not had any AI courses. The students were given no more documentation and other help (lecture, hands on help, etc.) than they are typically given for any other design aid used in the course. Nevertheless, they did succeed in specifying and designing their circuits. As mentioned before, the few who did not finish were those who were halted by one or another of the minor bugs left in VEXED.

On the other hand, the circuits some students designed were wildly suboptimal. They took many more transistors than were necessary. That is, when they chose which refinement rule to use, they did not choose wisely. Partly this may be due to their inexperience as VLSI designers in general. Partly it may be due to their difficulty in understanding what each rule did. Each rule had a canned English description that said what its effect was, and another that tried to give advice on when to use it, but a major complaint from the students was that it was hard to understand this documentation and to figure out what the rules did.

Finally, the difficulty in choosing rules may be inherent in the structure of a system like VEXED. I am a better designer than the students, and I understand the rules quite well, and thus I can get much better designs out of VEXED. However, I have to think very hard to do so. The problem is that VEXED's constraint propagation tells you the effects of *previous* refinement decisions in limiting the choices for the current decision, but it does not show you how each current alternative will limit the choices you will have on later decisions. To get a good circuit out of VEXED, the user has to have a clear global strategy in mind, and has to weigh each decision in the light of how it will contribute to that strategy.

Perhaps VEXED could try the constraint propagation that would result from each alternative, and inform the user what the effects of each would be on the remaining alternatives elsewhere. However, given the cost of constraint propagation, this may not be practical, and anyway it would show the effect on tasks already on the agenda, but not the effect on tasks that will be put there in the future. The basic problem seems to be that since VEXED leaves the control issues entirely up to the user, it has no internal representation of the goals and plans that go into a strategy for designing the circuit, and thus cannot offer the user any support in deciding which module to work on next or which refinement to make. The DONTE system developed in our research group by Chris Tong, and described in Chapter 9 (Volume II), is an attempt to study some of the issues of how a system based on top-down refinement and constraint propagation might also make these control decisions.

In addition to the problems with choosing the right rule that the students actually had, there are two problems that did not come up but might have had they been designing larger circuits. One is that certain kinds of circuit are quite difficult to specify in our language. These are the circuits whose output at a given time depend on the entire past history of their inputs, or at least on an unbounded set of past inputs. These are not easy to express in a data flow oriented form. The solution here is either to find a more algorithmic specification language that can be translated into the data flow form, or to find a way to do constraint propagation directly with the more algorithmic language.

The second potential problem with larger circuits is that design really does involve more kinds of operations than just decomposition and constraint propagation. This is discussed next.

8.3.3. Extensions to the Model

It turns out that with just decomposition and constraint propagation, there are certain kinds of designs that cannot be produced, or at least that do not seem reachable without contorting the process in ways that seem unnatural. Several additional kinds of operations are needed. It is useful to be able to undo and redo decomposition steps. It is useful to be able to rearrange the functionality in various ways. And it is useful if different parts of the circuit can share either designs or actual hardware. We discuss each of these kinds of operations in turn. Finally we discuss problems that arise because VEXED equates design goals with modules to be refined.

It should be noted that the following list is probably not complete; it simply contains the things that have become apparent to us so far from the work on VEXED.

8.3.3.1. Undoing and redoing

Even if all you are really doing to the circuit is decomposition, there are two useful facilities to have.

Firstly, one facility any interactive system needs is a backtrack or "undo" facility that allows the user to retract decisions that turn out not to have the desired effect. VEXED has a chronological backtracking facility that allows the user to return the circuit to the state it was in at any previous time. It would be nicer to allow the user to "undecompose" any module, that is, to retract the decompositions applied to it and to all its submodules and return it to being simply a black box, but to leave untouched other decompositions that may have been done since the ones you are undoing. To do this requires being careful about which constraints get retracted - not only constraint originating from the retracted decisions, but also constraints *propagated through* the retracted submodules must be deleted. However, this seems to be a straightforward matter of bookkeeping.

Secondly, a "replay" facility is useful. This takes the set of decompositions applied previously to some other module[7] and its descendants, and applies these decompositions to the current module. To the extent that the refinement operations used previously are general, and apply in somewhat new circumstances, this is a way to reuse the *ideas* of a previous design even when the specific circuit is not applicable. The BOGART system provides just such a facility for VEXED. See Chapter 2 (Volume II) for a further discussion.

8.3.3.2. Rearranging

A number of useful operations can best be seen not as decompositions but as rearrangements of various kinds. First, there are several kinds of rearrangements that VEXED can do, at least somewhat.

- It turns out that when a module is refined into sub-modules, a submodule may occasionally need a signal as input that was not originally among the inputs of the parent module. Typically this happens with signals like clocks, ground, etc. One way this arises is when a function is implemented as a more general function with a constant for some input, e.g. an incrementer implemented as an adder with a constant 1 as one addend. Another way it arises involves encodings. To compute, say, a boolean function of input signals it is really necessary to interpret the input voltage waveform as a stream of bits, and then compute the boolean function on these bits. Usually the interpretation of a waveform as bits can be done implicitly, but occasionally explicit circuitry is required and sometimes this circuitry needs an input such as a clock.

  To handle such situations, VEXED has "Get Signal" tasks in addition to "Decompose" tasks. Get Signal tasks are entered on the task agenda by the rules that create the need for them, and are

---

[7]Either in the current circuit or in another one.

handled by the user manually specifying where the needed signal should come from.

• Sometimes an operation can best be seen not as a decomposition but rather as a transformation or recasting. For instance, a complex boolean expression may be converted to sum-of-products form so that a particular standard circuit structure may be used to implement it. VEXED currently can only handle these via "decompositions" that decompose a module into a single sub-module.

• Often it is possible to optimize a circuit by combining modules that arise from quite different parts of the decomposition tree but happen to be connected. E.g., the last primitive in one main module and the first primitive on the next may both be inverters. If these inverters are not needed for timing or current driving purposes, then the two inverters in series amount to a no-op, and may both be removed. This kind of operation is similar to peephole optimization in a compiler.

VEXED has a facility for such "Module Combining Rules." Since it is always appropriate to try to combine modules, and since the circuit can be considered complete even if no combinations are done, these tasks do not go on the agenda. Rather, the user can point to a module and request that an attempt be made to combine it with each of its neighbors. There are currently only a few such rules, and this facility was not used by the VLSI students.

There are also two kinds of rearrangements for which VEXED does not yet have any facilities at all, largely because of the way such facilities would interact with constraint propagation.

• First of all, there is the operation we call "exporting functionality." For example, we might have an AND gate fed by two other modules, and we might decide to implement the AND as a NOR, and require the two other modules to output the NOT of what they were originally supposed to output. VEXED does have a rule which can decompose (AND expression-1 expression-2) into modules computing (NOT exp-1), (NOT exp-2), and NOR, but what it cannot do is change the value computed by submodules that already exist and already have the value of their outputs specified. To do so would require the ability to retract or modify constraints. There appears to be no basic reason this could not be done, but it will take care in handling interactions between such a facility and the constraint propagator.

• Secondly, it is sometimes useful to knowingly build a circuit in which certain constraints are violated, and then patch it by inserting a "subgoal" module to resolve the conflict. E.g., it may be desirable to build part of the circuit to work on parallel signals and part on serial, and to resolve the conflict by inserting a parallel-serial converter between the modules. The problem for VEXED is that once the decision was made to do, say, the second module in serial, constraints would be propagated which would require the output of the first module to also be serial. In order to do this style of design, VEXED will have to be able to hold off on propagating some constraints some of the time, or else to temporarily retract some constraints. The question is, which constraints and when?

8.3.3.3. Sharing

Finally, there are rearrangements that involve separate modules sharing either hardware or designs.

The greatest degree of sharing is where the same signal needs to be produced at two different places in the circuit, and instead is produced once and wired to both places that need it. VEXED has a simple rule that allows this: to produce any output, ask the user to find an existing signal that meets the specifications of the output and wire it to that output.

More complex is timesharing, where a component, say an adder, acts as part of two different modules at two different times. VEXED has no facilities for such sharing.

Finally, rather than modules sharing signals or components they can share designs. It is quite common to notice that a given functionality, say a latch, is needed several places in a circuit, to make one design of a module that will work correctly in any of the places, and to simply copy this design each place it is needed. With VEXED, the user can manually create a set of specifications, design a module to meet them, and then later copy that module in wherever needed. However, it would be better if the user could simply indicate a number of places in the circuit and let the constraint propagator compute a sufficient set of specifications to satisfy the needs of all the uses.

8.3.3.4. Goals are not modules

All the operations we have mentioned so far apply to either a single module or to modules that are (or become) directly connected to each other. The hidden assumption has been that modules interact by passing signals back and forth, and thus the design problems for two modules only interact if the modules are directly connected. In other words, every subgoal of the design process can be associated with some specific connected group of modules.

This breaks down in two ways. First of all, it is possible for two modules to be connected only indirectly through other modules, but for their designs to strongly interact, in such a way that most ways of implementing either one rule out all ways of implementing the other. In such a case, it is best to think of there being a single design goal, "find a consistent pair of implementations," rather than two separate goals.

Secondly, the equation of goals and modules breaks down when we consider constraints on global resources. Suppose there is a maximum power consumption for the circuit as a whole. Then any decision to consume some amount of power in one module reduces the amount left, and thus interacts with the design of all other modules. We could imagine a "pseudo-wire" connecting all modules representing this interaction, but because this wire does connect all modules rather than just a local group it turns out not to give us very useful constraints. For instance, the fact that the half of the circuit remaining to be designed may consume 10 milliwatts does not give much help in deciding how much power we may consume in a sub-sub-submodule of that half. See Chapter 9 (Volume II) for some ideas on how to approach this problem.

8.3.4. Generality of the Model

The final set of issues we will discuss involve the generality of the model of the design process. Our experience has shown us that the model makes at least three assumptions about the design task, and if any of these are violated the model is not applicable.

The first assumption is that little is known *a priori* about the *structure* of the artifact to be designed. Consider the spectrum that classifies design tasks according to how much is known apriori about this structure, and thus about what decisions will come up in the process of design. At one end of the spectrum, systems like AIR-CYL (Chapter 7, Volume I) assume the structure of the artifact is totally known, and all that is needed is to choose appropriate values for a predetermined set of parameters (resistances, lengths, materials, etc.). At an intermediate point in the spectrum we have tasks such as micro-processor design, where the major building blocks are known (registers, ALU, controller, etc.), but some are optional (e.g., caches), and there also exist a set of "glue" components (e.g., multiplexors) that are used as needed. VEXED addresses tasks that lie still farther along this spectrum; nothing is assumed *a priori* about the structure of the artifact, and thus we know nothing about what values there will be to be constrained. Therefore, in VEXED, as the design proceeds and we learn what the parts will be, both the set of constraints and the set of choices being made grow.

It would be possible to apply VEXED to problems like those AIR-CYL tackles, where the structure is known *a priori*. However, to do so would be to give up the power that AIR-CYL gains from organizing its specialized knowledge according to the artifact's structure. For instance, while VEXED has to propagate constraints to all parts of the circuit where they might have any impact, in AIR-CYL there is specialized knowledge about what constraint to propagate when to exactly which parameter of which part of the structure.

Another assumption our model of design makes is what we term the *meson model* of the artifact. In this model, pieces of the artifact interact by passing some kind of entity, e.g. signals or rotations, from one piece to the next. We term these entities *mesons*, by analogy with the sub-atomic particles which other particles (such as protons and neutrons) exchange as they interact with each other. Our model of design assumes that the specifications of a module can be expressed as constraints on the mesons it inputs and outputs, and that it is easy to determine which modules those inputs come from and those outputs go to. Our attempts to transfer VEXED to a mechanical design domain have shown us that these assumptions are not always true. For instance, some constraints are constraints not on the input or output of a module, but rather on how it is to be constructed, e.g. constraints on what metal a gear is to made of. More importantly, in some tasks it is not at all easy to determine which modules interact, e.g., through physical interference (i.e. bumping into each other). There often is nothing analogous to the principle that modules can only interact along wires.[8]

Finally, our model of the division of labor assumes that there will be relatively little backtracking or other search involved in the process of design. Control is left to the user, and people are both too slow to execute massive searches, and not good at carrying them out in an organized and complete manner. However, even with constraint propagation, some design tasks will require such search. This often occurs where there are global constraints, for which constraint propagation does not help (see Section 8.3.3.4 above).

---

[8]Even in circuit design, there really are other kinds of interaction, e.g. by one chip heating an adjacent one.

8.4. SUMMARY

In summary then, design can be seen as a process of top down decomposition, constraint propagation, and a number of other kinds of operations. We have illustrated some of these other operations. Preliminary results indicate that it is possible and useful to base a knowledge based design aid on this model, but there are a number of remaining questions. It remains to be seen if ways can be found to help the user choose the right rules, if the cost of constraint propagation can be controlled, and if the specification language can be improved. It also remains to be seen if the additional operations which appear to be feasible to add to EVEXED can indeed be added. The most difficult problem to address appears to be the implicit identification of design goals with the modules in the structural decomposition.

8.5. ACKNOWLEDGMENTS

This work is being supported by NSF under Grant Number DMC-8610507, and by the Rutgers Center for Computer Aids to Industrial Productivity as well as by DARPA under Contract Numbers N00014-81-K-0394 and N00014-85-K-0116. The opinions expressed in this chapter are those of the author, and do not reflect any policies, either expressed or implied, of any granting agency.

Both the programs and the ideas presented here are the work of many people in the Rutgers AI/Design group. I particularly want to thank Tom Mitchell, Jack Mostow, Noshir Langrana, Chris Tong, Jeff Shulman, Tim Weinrich, Mike Barley, Kevin Kelly, Van Kelly, and Atul Agarwal.

8.6. BIBLIOGRAPHY

[1]   Bushnell, M. and Director, S., "VLSI CAD Tool Integration Using the Ulysses Environment," *Proceedings of 23rd Design Automation Conference*, ACM/IEEE, pp. 55-61, 1986.

[2]   Joobani, R. and Siewioriek, D., "WEAVER: A Knowledge Based Routing Expert," *Proceedings of the 22rd Annual Design Automation Conference*, June 1985.

[3]   Kelly, Van E., "The CRITTER System Automated Critiquing Of Digital Circuit Designs," *Proceedings of the 21st Design Automation Conference*, IEEE, Albuquerque, New Mexico, pp. 419-425, June 1984, [AI/VLSI Project Working Paper No. 13].

[4]   Kelly, V., *The CRITTER System - An Artificial Intelligence Approach To Digital Circuit Design Critiquing*, unpublished Ph.D. Dissertation, Rutgers University, New Brunswick, New Jersey, January 1985.

[5]   Kim, J. and McDermott, J., "TALIB: An IC Layout Design Assistant," *Proceedings of AAAI-83*, pp. 197-201, 1983.

[6]   Kowalski, T, *An artificial intelligence approach to VLSI design*, Kluwer Academic Publishers, Boston, 1985.

[7]   Langrana, N. and Mitchell, T. and Ramachandran, N., *Progress Toward A Knowledge-Based Aid for Mechanical Design*, Technical Memo CAIP-TM-002, Center for Computer Aids for Industrial Productivity, Rutgers University, jan 1986.

[8]   S. Mahadevan, *An apprentice-based approach to learning problem-solving knowledge*, unpublished Ph.D. Dissertation, Rutgers University Computer Science Department, 1989, [Rutgers Computer Science Technical Report Number ML-TR-30].

[9]   Mitchell, T. M. and Mahadevan, S. and Steinberg, L., "LEAP: A Learning Apprentice for VLSI Design," *Proceedings of IJCAI-85*, Los Angeles, CA., August 1985.

[10]   Stefik, M., "Planning with constraints (MOLGEN: Part 1)," *Artificial Intelligence 16:2*, pp. 111-140, May 1981.

[11]   Steinberg, L., Langrana, N., and Fisher, G., "MEET: Decomposition and Constraint Propagation in Mechanical Design," *Proceedings of the NSF Engineering Design Research Conference*, Amherst, MA, pp. 363-375, June 1989, [Available as Rutgers AI/Design Project Working Paper Number 121.].

[12]   Van Melle, W., Scott, A.C., Bennett, J.S., Peairs, M., "The EMYCIN Manual," Report No. STAN-CS-81-885, also Heuristic Programming Project report HPP-81-16, 1981.

[13]   Waldinger, R., "Achieving Several Goals Simultaneously," in *Readings in artificial intelligence*, Webber, B. and Nilsson, N., Eds., Morgan Kaufmann, pp. 250-271, 1981.

[14]   Kelly, K., Steinberg, L., and Weinrich, T., *Constraint Propagation in Design: Reducing the Cost*, unpublished Working paper, March 1988, [Rutgers University Department of Computer Science AI/VLSI Project Working Paper No. 82].

Chapter 9
A KNOWLEDGE-BASED FRAMEWORK
FOR DESIGN

Sanjay Mittal and Agustin Araya

Abstract

Many design problems can be formulated as a process of searching a "well-defined" space of artifacts with similar functionality. The dimensions of such spaces are largely known and are constrained by relations obtained from the implicit functionality of the designed artifact. After identifying the kinds of knowledge that mediate the search for acceptable designs, a computational framework is presented that organizes the required knowledge as design plans. A problem solver is described that executes these plans. The problem solver extends the notion of dependency-directed backtracking with an advice mechanism. This mechanism allows information from a constraint failure to be used as advice in modifying a partial design. An expert system called PRIDE, for designing paper transports inside copiers, has been successfully built based on this framework.

9.1. INTRODUCTION

Increasing attention is being paid to the development of knowledge-based systems for design, especially of mechanical systems [4, 5]. The expectation is that these computer systems can improve the quality of designs and shorten the time required to find satisfactory designs.

Some of the major stages in designing a complex system are: i) a definition stage where precise functional specifications are developed from the requirements; ii) a generation stage where many satisfactory designs may be created; and iii) an evaluation stage where these different designs are compared or op-

Reprinted from 'A Knowledge-Based Framework for
Design,' *Proceedings of the AAAI Fifth National
Conference on Artificial Intelligence,* Volume II,
pp. 856–865. Copyright © 1986 American Association
for Artificial Intelligence.

timized by some criteria. These stages are not necessarily sequential because the latter stages can provide feedback to earlier ones. In this paper we shall be primarily concerned with the middle stage, i.e., the generation of designs that satisfy some functional specification.

The general problem of designing artifacts that satisfy some arbitrary functionality is not well understood [9]. However, there seem to be many design problems where the search space has been largely defined by the expert designers (or can be obtained from them). This means that the kinds of dimensions of the design space are by and large known, i.e., the kinds of design parameters are known. Furthermore, the design parameters of the search space are constrained to produce artifacts which have the "same" functionality. We shall call problems with these two properties as *well-defined*.

In this paper we present a framework for building computer programs that can assist in the design of systems that have well-defined search spaces. The framework rests on the key observation that given such spaces, the process of generating alternative designs is largely a process of searching these spaces. This is not to suggest that the space is small, or that it does not vary in details, or that substantial reasoning may not be needed for finding satisfactory designs. On the contrary, the search process is guided by knowledge about how to define partial designs in this space and knowledge about how to modify a partial design when the constraints are violated. Furthermore, the search may be ordered by heuristic knowledge obtained from experience.

The proposed framework organizes these different kinds of knowledge into design plans. These plans are carried out by a problem solver that can engage in exhaustive search if the knowledge is insufficient. The problem solver extends the notions of dependency-directed backtracking with an advice mechanism. This mechanism allows advice based on a failed constraint to reorder the generators at a prior decision point, allowing rapid convergence in many cases.

Based on this framework we have successfully built an expert system called PRIDE [8] of paper transports inside copiers. In this paper we shall focus on the ideas behind the design framework and not the expert system itself. We start by describing an example of an artifact with a well-defined design space. The next section makes our notion of design-as-search more precise. The subsequent three sections describe the framework itself. We conclude with a discussion of some of the questions raised by our work.

9.2. KNOWLEDGE ABOUT THE ARTIFACT BEING DESIGNED

We begin with a simplified example taken from the domain of paper handling systems inside copiers and duplicators.

9.2.1. An Example of an Artifact

A paper handling system in a copier is used to transport paper from an input to an output location, avoiding certain obstructions. One kind of paper transports are built from the pinch-roll technology. In this technology, a "baffle" is used to guide the paper along a certain path and "roll stations" are placed along this path to move the paper (see Figure 9-1). Roll stations consist of one or more pairs of rolls mounted in corresponding shafts. Each pair, in turn, consists of a driver roll, which is powered, and an idle roll, which spins freely.

A typical design problem specifies the velocity and angle of the paper at the input and output locations of the transport, maximum acceptable skew of the paper while being transported, characteristics of the papers that will be transported (e.g., length, weight, etc), and so on. The problem is to determine the shape of the baffle, the number, position and kinds of roll stations, the properties of drivers and idlers, and many other properties of these and other components.

9.2.2. Different Kinds of Knowledge

There might be several kinds of artifacts, based on different technologies, that can exhibit the "same" functionality. For instance, paper transports can also be built from belt-transport technology.

For each technology, it is necessary to know the kinds, and numbers, of parts (or components) and how those parts compose or interact to form the artifact. Parts might be further decomposed into other parts. Certain parts might have alternative decompositions into subparts, and it is necessary to know the conditions under which each alternative is more suitable.

Parts have "relevant" properties, i.e., properties that can affect the functionality of the artifact. (e.g. width and diameter of a driver roll, which may affect the velocity with which the paper moves while passing through the station). When parts interact with other parts of an artifact, they can exhibit certain relevant behaviors (e.g., velocity of a driver, skew of the paper), which depend on properties and behaviors of these or other parts.

Corresponding to each property, one needs to know what the plausible values are for that property, e.g., the different known diameters of a drive roll may be 10, 20, 40 mm; the width of a driver can be between 5mm and 50mm in increments of 1mm; the baffle gap can be between 2 and 10mm in increments of 0.5 mm; etc. Certain properties of parts can only take values from a pre-existing set of values. This is the case when it is desirable to select parts from existing ones. For other properties it might be known how to design them taking into account the given specifications and the properties and behaviors of other parts.

9.3. DESIGN AS KNOWLEDGE-GUIDED SEARCH

The process of designing such an artifact can be usefully viewed as a search of a multi-dimensional space of possible designs. The dimensions of such a space are the parameters of the artifact such as the properties of the individual parts and the structural relationships between the parts. For example, in the case of a paper transport, some of the parameters would be "input velocity of the paper coming into the transport", "lengths and widths of the different kinds of paper", "length of the paper path", physical characteristics of each of the driver and idler roll at each station such as diameter, width, material, and velocity, etc. The actual number of parameters varies from case to case, depending on the number and kinds of parts that are needed.

Typically such design spaces are very large and searching for suitable designs can be very time consuming. Two major factors contribute to this. First, significant computation may be involved in defining a point in the space, i.e., assigning values to the different parameters. Because the space is quite sparse, in that there are far fewer acceptable designs than the ones ultimately rejected, most of the search effort may be expended in finding solutions that will be rejected later on. One approach to mitigate this problem is to analyze partial designs as early as possible, instead of waiting for the complete design.

This brings us to the second cost, i.e., the computation in evaluating a design for suitability. Many of the analysis techniques are time-consuming and a design may pass one analysis only to be rejected later by another one. By appropriately ordering the generation of the design and its evaluation for suitability, some of the wasteful computation may be avoided.

Given this complexity, experienced designers use knowledge of various kinds to direct their search. As discussed in the previous section, one obviously needs to have a great deal of knowledge about the artifact itself. Here we will discuss some of the knowledge used in exploring the space and directing the search.

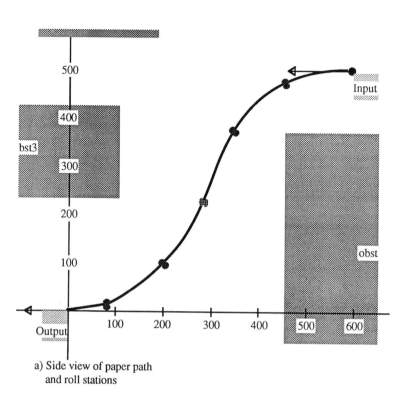

a) Side view of paper path
and roll stations

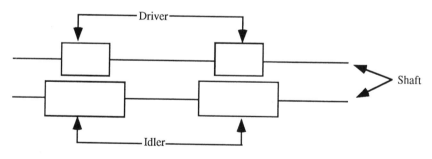

b) Front view of roll station

Figure 9-1: Paper Path in PRIDE

9.3.1. Ordering Knowledge

A simple, yet powerful piece of knowledge is information that creates an order in which decisions get made. Use of such ordering information is quite
prevalent [9]. However, the characteristics of the search space which create
such order are not well understood. The ordering knowledge may be simply
based on the dependencies between decisions. For example, in our sample
problem, decisions about roll station placement depend so intrinsically on the
length of the paper path that they have to be made later.

A different kind of order is created by structuring the space hierarchically. By
this we mean that instead of having the complete space explicitly defined, decisions along some dimension open up sub-spaces. Thus, different choices at some
level could lead to very different sub-spaces being opened up for design. A
simple example from paper transport domain involves choice of technology.
Depending on the technology chosen such as rolls or belts, very different design
spaces are opened up for further exploration.

9.3.2. Constraints between Parameters.

The parameters of the design artifact are not independent. Often, they are constrained by relations. Some of these constraints may be derived from the explicit
specifications of the particular design problem. For example, the locations and
angles of the input and output of the paper transport constrain the shape of the
paper path.

A different set of constraints is derived from the intrinsic properties of the
structure and behavior of the artifact being designed. All paper transports must
satisfy some basic constraints on velocities, frictions, and forces acting on a
moving paper, otherwise they will fail in their essential functionality. For example, the distance between two consecutive roll stations must be less than the
smallest paper that will be transported by the paper handling system, otherwise
for certain sections of the path the paper will no longer be under the control of
any station. Both kinds of constraints determine the suitability of a design in
terms of providing the desired functionality.

The way these constraints are used is crucial in determining how efficiently
the design process operates. It is well known that a generate-and-test model in
which the constraints are primarily used to test the generated solutions will be
quite inefficient. More powerful problem solvers such as dependency-directed
backtracking [2] also have some well-known deficiencies. Some of these
deficiencies can be compensated by using appropriate knowledge, in terms of
"ordering" information based on how the variables are constrained.

We have found it useful to make a distinction between tight and loose coupling between a set of variables. In the case of tightly coupled variables, a search procedure that tries to assign a value to one of these variables and then propagate it over the constraints may have to back up many times before finding a consistent solution. However, in the case of loosely coupled variables, it is often possible to find a partial order in which the variables are decided which will work with relatively small amounts of backtracking.

9.3.3. Advice for Modification

A major piece of knowledge that expert designers seem to use when the design fails some acceptability condition (constraint) is how to modify the design. Consider a dependency-directed backtracking problem solver in constrast. It knows enough to back up to a relevant decision point but does not have any way of deciding how to modify its decision. Good designers, on the other hand, not only know where the relevant prior decision points are but also analyse the failure to decide how to modify their past decisions. Being able to advise a prior decision point (and a problem solver in general) is crucial in reducing the search. In the best case, the advice would enable a previous decision to be modified in exactly the way needed to fix the current constraint failure. In general, the advice may only help partially. In the framework we have developed, and described in the rest of the paper, this ability to advise plays a central role in problem solving and is an important advance over most of the earlier approaches.

9.4. STRUCTURING DESIGN KNOWLEDGE AS PLANS

In the previous section we identified four major kinds of knowledge that are needed during the design process: defining the dimensions of the design space; choices along each dimension; constraints on these choices; and advice for modifying some design choice. In addition, there were heuristics on ordering the decisions, structuring the space, and ordering the choices for some dimension that aid in making the design process be more effective. These different pieces of knowledge can be effectively integrated into knowledge structures that we shall call design plans. In this section we introduce the different plan elements and describe their structure. The next section discusses how they are used in problem solving.

9.4.1. Goals

Plans are organized around goals for making design decisions about a set of design parameters. Each goal is responsible for a few of these parameters, i.e., it represents one or more decision points from a problem solving viewpoint. A goal also defines some of the dimensions of the design space. By this we mean that only by scheduling a goal does the design sub-space defined by that goal become ready for exploration.

In our paper transport domain, some typical goals would be "Design Paper Transport", "Design Paper Path", "Design Driver Roll", and "Design Driver Width". The first of these is a top-level goal, which can recursively expand into a tree of sub-goals (Figure 9-2).

Each of these goals defines a space of partial designs. As we move down the goal tree fewer dimensions are considered. Thus, the goal "Design Driver Width" is concerned with only one design parameter, whereas the goal "Design Driver Roll" is concerned with all parameters of a driver roll. The former is a sub-goal of the latter. Each goal explicitly specifies the design parameters it is responsible for. Goals also specify the design parameters on which they depend. For example, the goal "Decide number and location of roll stations" specifies that it depends on knowing the paper path length. The dependency information may be either statically described or dynamically determined from the particular design method that is being tried or both.

9.4.2. Design Methods

Design goals have different design methods associated with them, which specify alternate ways to make decisions about the design parameters of the goal. These methods capture the knowledge about the possible values of properties of components, as well as knowledge about the behavior of components. The role of the design methods is then to generate partial designs.

The knowledge about carrying out a goal may be available in many different forms. This diversity is reflected by the different kinds of methods that exist in our representation. One kind of methods are generators which specify a set, or range of values to be generated. They can also encode heuristics about ordering the values, initial guesses, etc. For example, a generator method for driver width is shown in Figure 9-3. It shows both the range of values as well as the initial choice heuristic.

Another kind of methods are calculations which apply some mathematical function over a set of previously decided parameters. A calculation may be viewed as a combination of a generator and an equality constraint. This method always produces the same value for the same set of its input parameter values. Some of the other kinds of methods are procedures (which embed arbitrary computations) and constrained generators (which can look ahead to the constraints on the goal to generate values).

There is another set of method types which primarily provide control knowledge on the use of other methods. A simple example are conditional methods (also called rules) which allow some conditions to be specified on the suitability of applying a method. The action part of a rule must be a method. Other examples of such control methods are rule groups and conjunctive methods. An important property of control methods is that they make explicit the separation between two kinds of knowledge: one for making design choices and the other for selecting a suitable set of choices or ordering the different sets of choices.

9.4.2.1. Subplans

Another kind of control method is called a subplan. These methods specify a set of goals that must be carried out in order to satisfy the higher level goal. The actual order in which the goals are carried out is specified by the input and output dependency descriptions attached to a goal. The subplan method is the only mechanism for creating goal trees. This has some important consequences. First, alternate plans for decomposing a goal into sub-goals can be easily represented. For example, very different sub-plans exist for a goal if different technologies are available for the implementation of the goal's specifications. Second, given that a subplan method is like any other method, it can be embedded inside control methods. This allows, for example, plan selection knowledge to be represented inside control methods.

Finally, subplan methods and other more direct methods can be simultaneously specified for the same goal. In other words, a goal may be achieved in different ways. One way may be to decompose it into smaller sub-problems. Another way might be to use previously designed pre-packaged solutions. For example, the goal for "Design driver roll" may have one method which decomposes the goal into sub-goals: "design diameter", "design width", "decide tolerances", "decide material", etc. A driver designed in this way may need to be manufactured from raw stock. Another method may be a generator which selects from some standard off-the-shelf driver rolls. Typically, this latter method would be tried before the more general subplan and be so specified.

Statically no distinction can be made between goals which have sub-goals and those which have direct methods. During the execution of the plan, however, some differences arise. The primary difference arises from the fact that a sub-goal is responsible for a subset of the specifications of its super-goal. In such cases, the most specific goal is held responsible for the shared design parameter during problem-solving, which is described in the next section.

In addition to the method types described above, we also specify an abstract problem solving protocol that must be followed by a method. Thus, new method types can be created. In fact, the current set has evolved over the course of representing the knowledge about paper transports.

9.4.3. Design Constraints

The third major element of a plan are constraints on the design parameters. These constraints are attached to some goal. Typically, they would be associated with the goal for the less constrained variable, as heuristically determined by experts. However, they can be as well attached on separate goals which then depend on the goals for the constrained parameters. Notice, that much of the ordering in the plan arises from where the constraints are attached. This is because the parameters in a constraint are also used to order the goal during run-time scheduling. As we discussed in the previous section, this is very appropriate because much of the ordering seems to come from the constraints on a parameter.

We view a constraint as an object which basically specifies a relation between a set of design parameters. These relationships may reflect the conditions on the underlying structure or behavior of the artifact or they may be derived from the specifications of an individual problem. In the next section we elaborate on how constraints are used.

9.4.4. Advice for Modification

The last major element of a design plan is advice to the problem solver. We have identified the need for many different kinds of advice. In this paper we will focus on only one kind of advice, namely, modify parameter advice. This is the advice attached to constraints and activated when constraints fail. These advice descriptions can be obtained in two ways. For certain kinds of constraints one can analyze the expression and determine which parameters must be modified and how to satisfy the constraint. In many other cases, the experts know from experience which parameter may be more easily modifiable and the system can determine how much to change the parameters in order to satisfy the constraint.

In our framework we can represent both kinds of advice. This implies that part of the constraint protocol is being able to automatically analyze the failure. Once a piece of advice is created, no difference is made between the heuristic (produced by the expert) and direct (produced by the system) advice.

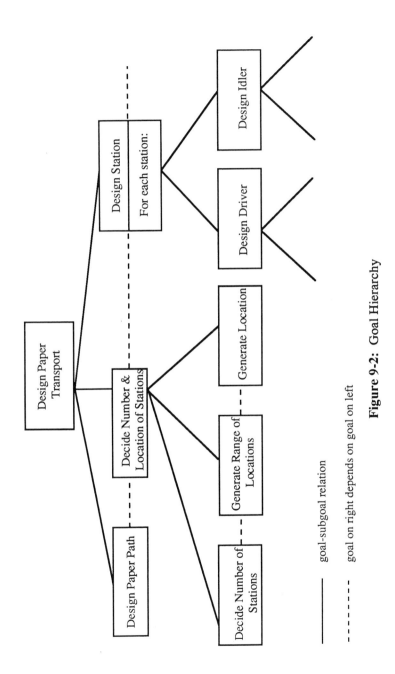

Figure 9-2: Goal Hierarchy

```
Idler width generator

    parameter    : Idler width
    min value    : 10mm
    max value    : 100mm
    step         : 1mm
    initial value : if driver width known
                    then 2 * driver width
                    else 40mm
```

Figure 9-3: Generator Method

Some of the other kinds of advice we have found useful are processing advice which advises the problem solver itself to give up or suspend a particular exploration path; selection advice which causes a particular plan to be aborted in favor of another; and modify specification advice which advises the user (or another system) to change some problem specification.

9.5. PROBLEM SOLVING USING THE PLANS

We start by describing the basic problem solver that tries to carry out these design plans. Later we will briefly describe the more extended version which supports a more comprehensive design process. The basic problem solver comprises three major parts: i) a goal scheduler which uses an agenda to post goals, try them out, suspend them if needed, and revise them; ii) a dependency net which is created dynamically (this data structure associates a designed parameter with the goal which designed it and the goals which directly depend on it); and iii) a set of protocols which each of the plan elements is expected to follow. The protocols can be viewed as falling in two groups: *initial design* and *revision*.

9.5.1. Initial Design Protocol

Before a goal is run, its preconditions are checked. These are computed both from the input parameter dependencies as well as direct dependency on other goals. The latter is a heuristic way of ordering goals which reflects processing considerations.

The activated goal tries methods from its list of design methods to find the first that runs successfully. A method could cause a goal to suspend by surfacing some new dependencies. Most methods fail or succeed right away. Subplan methods, on the other hand, post new goals and suspend the higher goal. If all methods fail, then the goal fails. Notice, that if the goal was embedded in a subplan method, and all but the top goal are, this failure propagates to the method and up.

Once a method succeeds, the constraints are tried. If all constraints are satisfied, the goal succeeds. If a constraint fails, however, the problem solver (often working with the user) will either relax the constraint or try to satisfy it by revising the partial design.

9.5.2. Revise Design Protocol

In order to revise the design the problem solver has to: i) determine what design parameter(s) to modify, ii) determine which goal to backtrack to, and iii) try to effect the change. The first piece of information comes from the advice attached to constraints. Given the advice, the dependency net is examined to determine the goal which can handle the advice. This goal is then activated in a "revise" state.

The revised goal adds the advice as a new constraint. It then asks the previously executed method to revise itself if it can. Different methods handle advice differently. A generator tries to generate a different value which conforms to the advice. A calculation, on the other hand, can revise itself only by creating a new piece of advice which may cause the problem solver to backup further. If the original method fails, then the goal searches among its other methods for the first method that succeeds. If none of the methods succeed then the advice has failed and control returns to the original point of failure. Often there are other pieces of advice that can be tried. If a method does succeed in producing a value then the constraints are checked again. If the constraints are satisfied then the advice has succeeded and design will proceed, eventually reaching the goal which originally failed and continuing beyond if the advice was appropriate.

Notice that at the revised goal, some constraints which originally succeeded may now fail. This can create new advice causing the problem solver to back up further. Also, some new constraints may have been added which can fail. In fact the calculation methods effectively propagate the advice backwards by this mechanism.

9.5.3. Illustration of the Advice Mechanism

We shall illustrate how the advice mechanism works with the help of a simple example. Consider the following two constraints on three variables x, y, and z.

```
x + y + z >10          (C1)
x + y + z < 20         (C2)
```

Furthermore, let us assume that independent of these constraints, we also know the sets from which each of the three variables can take values.

```
x: {1, 3, 5}            (4)
y: {2, 4, 6, 8}         (5)
z: {1 .. 100}           (6)
```

One way to represent this problem in our framework is to have separate goals for x, y, and z. Let us call them Gx, Gy, and Gz, respectively. Each of these goals will have a single method, which is a generator incorporating the choice sets in (4) - (6) respectively. Let us name the methods Mx, My, and Mz. Also assume that there is no knowledge about initial guesses for these variables in the generators. Constraints C1 and C2 can be either attached to one of these goals or a fourth one. Let us say we adopt the latter representation and call the goal with the constraints Gc [A discussion of the differences between the two choices are beyond the scope of this paper].

In the initial design phase, the goals Gx, Gy, and Gz will be trivially satisfied (because no constraints are attached to them) by making the following choices.

```
x=1; y=2; and z=1
```

However, goal Gc will fail because while C2 is satisfied, C1 is not.

Constraint C1 can generate many different types of advice for modification:

```
x^, > 7          (A1)
y^, > 8          (A2)
z^, > 7          (A3)
x^ & y^          (A4), etc.
```

The advice A1 means "increase x such that it is greater than 7". In this example, we will only consider advice that tries to change one variable at a time. The advice A1 when sent to the problem solver will cause goal Gx to try to revise itself. However, the method Mx at Gx cannot find a value for x that is greater than 7, so this advice will fail. Goal Gc will then send advice A2, which also fails. Next A3 is tried which succeeds in modifying z to 8 and now the constraints are satisfied.

Notice that the revision of z will cause all goals dependent on z to be "undone" and retried. Also, even though we started with arbitrary values for the three variables, we were able to quickly find a solution. The generators keep track of the choices they have made, so the same value will not be generated again in the same context (see section 6 for more on the context mechanism).

Suppose we were to impose a new constraint on z at this point:

```
z > 10          (C3)
```

This constraint will fail creating an advice:

```
z^, > 10                    (A5)
```

This advice will cause the value of z to change to 11. The change in z will undo goal Gc which will recheck its constraints. The constraints C1 and C2 are still satisfied, so this new solution will be accepted. Notice, that if wanted to preserve the previous solution, this new constraint would be imposed in a subcontext, allowing both solutions to be explored further.

9.5.4. Example of Design Revision from Pride

Let us consider another example which is drawn from the paper transport domain. After the shape of the path to be followed by the paper has been defined, it is necessary to determine the number of roll stations and their locations. The placement of the stations has to satisfy various kinds of constraints [6].

In the design phase, a heuristic is used to propose the number of stations. Using this information, a method is applied which determines ranges of placements of stations such that the relevant constraints are satisfied. If it turns out that no such placement exist because for any placements there are constraints that are not satisfied, then a redesign episode takes place. A piece of advice is generated indicating, for instance, that the number of roll stations should be increased. This requires undoing the previous decision (and all the decisions that depended on it) and making a new decision using the advice. This is illustrated in Figure 9-4.

9.5.5. Discussion

Some important properties of our problem solver are novel and crucial to its success. Our problem solver augments a weak-method, i.e., dependency-directed backtracking, with an advice mechanism. In other words, the dependencies between design parameters are used in determining a relevant decision point to back up to. Furthermore, the failed constraint(s) is analyzed to determine a piece of advice for the revised decision. Thus the problem solver is not only capable of searching its entire design space but still does so intelligently and directed by advice from failures. Moreover, this general search method is integrated in a framework which is knowledge-rich. This means that if knowledge exists about ordering goals or making plausible choices, it can be profitably used. Recourse is made to the general method only where sufficient knowledge does not exist or is incomplete.

Finally, notice that our approach avoids another typical shortcoming of purely knowledge-based approaches which rely on heuristically determined order between goals. In our scheme even if two goals were ordered the wrong way, the advice mechanism would produce the correct result in one round of revision. This is because the advice mechanism allows constraints imposed later in design to be propagated back as advice. The same mechanism can also be used to do a rough design followed by a more precise design.

9.5.6. Limitation

Even though the problem solver we have described can perform arbitrary search, it will clearly be too inefficient in some cases. One such situation arises

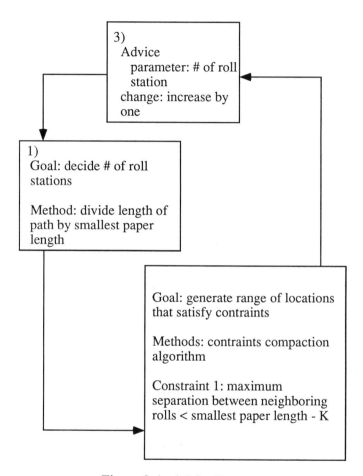

Figure 9-4: Advice Example

in cases of tightly coupled variables. That is, if there is a set of variables which are so inter-constrained that no local propagation of values or advice will suffice to efficiently find a consistent solution, then one might want to look for other problem solving methods for that subproblem. For example, in the paper transport design, the roll placement problem has this property. It is important to emphasize that these special problem solvers can still be embedded in our overall framework by embedding them inside design methods. The example discussed earlier illustrated this point. *This implies that the overall problem solving may still proceed as a process of solving loosely-coupled sub-problems with some backtracking, with the tightly-coupled decisions localized as a single decision-point, but still capable of being revised from the outside.*

9.6. EXTENDED PROBLEM SOLVER

We briefly describe two other components of the problem solver that play a major role in supporting the overall design process but are not essential in understanding how the problem solver works.

9.6.1. Multiple Design Contexts

We provide a facility for maintaining multiple design contexts [7]. A design context contains a complete description of the artifact being designed, a complete description of the state of the design plan corresponding to that design, and the state of the problem solver.

The advising mechanism makes use of the multiple contexts mechanism. Specifically, when the design problem solver processes an advice, it can do so in a separate context. This ensures that if a specific advice fails to revise the design satisfactorily, the system can back up to the context in which the advice was originated and continue with a different advice.

The ability to create multiple partial designs and keep them distinct is crucial in exploring different choices simultaneously. For example, at certain choice points, one can explore the different choices simultaneously by creating a sub-context for each choice. We have chosen not to do so because of the size of the design space, i.e., the number of choice points and choices at each point are far too many. Ultimately, some incorporation of ATMS [3] ideas may be worthwhile.

9.6.2. User Control of the Search

Pragmatically, the user and the automated problem solver have to work together. This is because of the complementary nature of their strengths. Most automated problem solvers can tirelessly search a design space, manage the dependencies, selectively undo parts of the design, and consistently check the constraints. However, they rarely have enough knowledge to avoid unnecessary work. Human problem solvers, including experts, are rarely systematic in the above activities, but often have knowledge that lets them avoid or minimize the search. It seems natural, therefore, that there be a way for the human user to steer the problem solver in more suitable regions of the search space.

We provide many entry points for a user to interact with the problem solver. The advice mechanism turns out be quite suitable for many such interactions. Thus, a user can easily enter a piece of advice. This means that the user can choose to advise arbitrary goals and thereby affect the course of design.

Another natural place is in the selection of advice. A failed constraint typically has alternative advices on how to satisfy it. However, it is often hard for the system to decide which advice is more likely to succeed. We allow the user to not only change the order of the advice but also change its content in some cases.

There are many situations where the design methods are incomplete in their description of the design space. In such situations, it is natural for the user to be able to make a design decision and let the system do the rest. In fact it is possible for the user to not only make the decision but also handle the ensuing advice from a constraint failure at some subsequent goal. On a very pragmatic basis, these 'hooks', along with the multiple context facility, allow a user to work with the system in exploring a design space and looking at alternatives quite rapidly.

9.7. DISCUSSION AND CONCLUSIONS

The framework described in this paper has been successfully used to build a knowledge-based system, called Pride, for designing paper transports inside copiers and duplicators [8]. A prototype version of Pride has been ready and in field test for over a year now. It has been tested on real design problems from previous and ongoing copier projects. It has been successful in not only producing acceptable designs but also in analyzing designs produced by engineers and identifying shortcomings in their designs.

The notion of plans for representing design knowledge was independently developed by Brown and Chandrasekaran [1] (see also Chapter 7). Our framework, however, is more general in many ways. First, we impose fewer restrictions on the kinds of artifacts we can handle. Second, we provide a problem solver that can search the design space more thoroughly. Finally, our multiple contexts mechanism allows different design alternatives to be simultaneously explored.

Many interesting research issues are still unresolved in the work we have presented. For example, we have not explored the limitations of the advice mechanism. In particular, we have not looked at the general case where many constraints can simultaneously fail and the problem caused by conflicting advice. Another area of investigation is a categorization of constraint types and the constraint satisfaction methods that may be most suitable for each type.

Another interesting issue we are investigating is the relationship between the structure and function of the artifact on one hand and the design plans on the other. This seems to be important both from the point of view of acquiring additional knowledge as well as generating the design plans more automatically. As was indicated in the introduction, the proposed framework supports the "generation of alternative designs" stage of the overall design process. We are trying to extend the framework to cover the other stages also. In particular, we want to study the processes involved in the comparison of designs according to a set of criteria. Also, we want to extend the advice mechanism to support the feedback processes between the different stages.

9.8. ACKNOWLEDGEMENTS

The Pride project is a joint effort between Xerox PARC and Xerox RBG (Reprographics Business Group); the work was done when the authors were at Xerox PARC. Mahesh Morjaria (who is currently with General Electric), George Roller and many other engineers at RBG have collaborated on this project from the start. Felix Frayman (who is currently with Hewlett-Packard) has contributed many ideas and programming effort to the project. Mark Stefik has supported the work both as the manager of Knowledge Systems Area at PARC and as a research colleague. Daniel Bobrow, Felix Frayman, Ken Kahn, Mark Stefik, and the referees provided invaluable feedback on earlier drafts of the paper.

9.9. BIBLIOGRAPHY

[1]   Brown, D. and Chandrasekaran, B., "Expert Systems for a Class of Mechanical Design Activity," in *Knowledge Engineering in Computer-Aided Design*, Gero, J., Ed., North Holland, pp. 259-290, 1985.

[2]   de Kleer, J., J. Doyle, G. L. Steele, and G. J. Sussman, "Explicit Control of Reasoning," in *Artificial Intelligence: An MIT Perspective* , Winston, P. and Brown, R., Ed., M.I.T. Press , 1979.

[3]   de Kleer, J., "An Assumption-based TMS," *Artificial Intelligence*, Vol. 28, No. 2, pp. 127-162, 1986.

[4]   Dym, C. L., Ed., *Applications of Knowledge-Based Systems to Engineering Analysis and Design*, ASME, , 1985.

[5]   Gero, J., Ed., *Knowledge Engineering in Computer-Aided Design*, North Holland, Amsterdam, 1985.

[6]   Mittal, S., and Stefik, M. J., *Constraint Compaction: Managing Computational Resources for Efficient Search*, Memo, Xerox Palo Alto Research Center, Palo Alto, April 1986.

[7]   Mittal, S., Bobrow, D. G. and Kahn, K. , "Virtual Copies: At the Boundary Between Classes and Instances," *Object-Oriented Programming Languages, Systems and Applications (OOPSLA)*, ACM, 1986.

[8]   Mittal, S., Dym, C. L., and Morjaria, M., "PRIDE: An Expert System for the Design of Paper Handling Systems," *IEEE Computer*, pp. 102-114, July 1986.

[9]   Mostow, J., "Towards Better Models of the Design Process," *AI Magazine*, Spring 1985.

Chapter 10
BIOSEP DESIGNER: A PROCESS SYNTHESIZER FOR BIOSEPARATIONS

Charles A. Siletti and George Stephanopoulos

Abstract

Designing a commercial scale protein purification process is a knowledge intensive and nonroutine engineering design task which can be facilitated by computer aids. BioSep Designer is a prototype design program that uses a hierarchical design procedure with search to automatically generate alternatives for purification processes.

10.1. INTRODUCTION

10.1.1. The Nature of the Problem

In developing a software system for any engineering application, but especially for an expert system, one must establish who would use the system and whether it will be beneficial. The best applications are tasks which are performed frequently, are tedious, time consuming, or require much information [4]. Many problems in engineering design fit these guidelines, and the design of purification processes for protein products is no exception. New purification processes will have to be designed frequently for new products and because there is a large body of data to consider in developing a design it is difficult for a human designer to consider all the possibilities for a given purification problem. Moreover, the current designers of such processes are often protein biochemists who are very familiar with protein biochemistry but who may not be familiar with the design of large scale chemical processes. There are no established methods for designing protein purification processes, but the basic physical and chemical principles behind such processes are understood, and there is a large body of information about available processing equipment as well as a number of heuristic guidelines.

In this article, we describe protein purification processes and compare their design to other engineering design tasks for which automated systems have been developed. We then explain our design methodology and its computer implementation, BioSep Designer. Finally, we describe how BioSep Designer generates design alternatives for the large scale recovery and purification of the recombinant pharmaceutical, urokinase type plasminogen activator.

10.1.2. Protein Recovery

The protein products with which we will be concerned are biochemically active compounds like the enzymes found in laundry detergent and food processes as well as pharmaceuticals such as insulin. Originally found in plant or animal tissue, the industrial versions of these compounds are produced by microorganisms or cultured cells. Although this method yields the product in a more concentrated form then a natural source, the result of microbial fermentation can only be described as a dilute solution including the product and a variety of other substances, such as nucleic acids, salts, sugars, possible toxins, and other proteins. Most protein products, and especially pharmaceuticals, must meet stringent purity requirements, so a series of separation steps, as shown in Figure 10-1, is used to purify and concentrate the product. The traditional approach to designing the processes to achieve this purification has been to scale up the laboratory procedure for purifying the protein. Using this approach, however, a designer may overlook alternative processes that would have proven more efficient on the large scale. BioSep Designer uses knowledge about the properties of the product, its contaminants, and the operations and equipment used for purification. The ultimate objective is defined by the user but generally is to design the most economical process that achieves a required degree of purification.

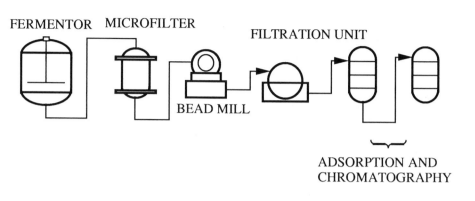

FERMENTOR MICROFILTER

FILTRATION UNIT

BEAD MILL

ADSORPTION AND
CHROMATOGRAPHY

Figure 10-1: A Typical Protein Purification Process

10.1.3. Engineering Design and Process Design

A design is a description of a physical artifact that must achieve some specified functionality within specified constraints, and the process of design is the way one derives a description of the artifact from some initial set of constraints and specifications [9], and design problems may be classified in a variety of ways. Many types of designs, including chemical process designs, consist of a series of descriptions of parts or steps. An example might be the design of an entire chemical process consisting of chemical reactors, distillation columns, pumps, and compressors [5], the design of a building consisting of beams, floors, and other building components [12], or a series of procedures [13]. Often in mechanical engineering problems of this sort, and perhaps most notably in the elevator design system, VT [8] (See Chapter 11), the various parts must fit together so closely that they can not be designed independently; trial and error must be used to find a design that meets all the constraints. Interactions among components in process design are generally much weaker because the interactions are introduced by the process streams between processing units, and a given processing unit is good for a range of stream conditions.

For routine design problems of this nature, the components are known, and there are well established methods for assembling them to form a satisfactory design. For example, the design of a distillation column is considered to be a routine design problem [10]. The design of entire chemical plant (of which a distillation column may be part) is not, because the designer must first establish what the processing steps will be before doing the design. This definition, of course, is more a matter of practice than a true characterization of the problem. It is certainly possible that someone could develop a new and innovative distillation column, and plant design could be handled in a routine manner, although in practice the benefits of possible innovations in a plant design far outweigh those of innovations in a single column.

There is often a multiplicity of designs that meet the initial specifications, and for some design problems, a design that satisfies the specifications and constraints is enough. AIR-CYL, a program that designs pneumatic diaphragms, succeeds when it finds one solution to the problem [2]. In process design, one would like to find those solutions that are in some sense optimal, or at least retain a set of promising solutions. A search for optimal designs, however, is thwarted by the combinatorial nature of the problem. For example, if we were to try assembling and analyzing all the combinations of protein recovery processes, the number of designs could be estimated by the relation,

$$S = M^N$$

where S is the number of possible designs, M is the number of separation steps, and N is the number of different types of processes. For a typical protein purification, there may be 10 separation steps and 30 different separation methods, giving about 10^{30} designs. Thus for real problems, the design space is too large for a simple search. Furthermore, not even the number of steps required for a design can be determined a priori.

10.2. DESIGN METHODOLOGY

10.2.1. General Considerations

Neither a biochemical engineer nor a computer program can evaluate, or even consider, all the possible equipment configurations for all protein recovery problems. We therefore resort to a design methodology that uses weaker methods, such as heuristic search, to generate plausible and explainable, if not optimal, designs. While there is no general theory describing how a design is constructed, Mostow, in a recent review [9], provides a vocabulary for describing the issues faced both by designers and automatic design systems. All design systems either explicitly or implicitly address 1) the state of the design, 2) the ultimate and intermediate goals in design, 3) decision making, 4) the rationale behind the decisions, 5) control of the design process, and 6) knowledge acquisition.

10.2.2. Components of the BioSep Designer Methodology

In an automated design system, the state of design is simply the representation of descriptions of a partially completed design. This representation is directly related to the nature of the design problem and to the design methodology to be used. Some designs, like the elevator designer, VT, must proceed through a series of approximations of the complete design that are refined until a consistent solution is reached. In BioSep Designer, as in a number of design systems [10, 12, 13], the states of the design are increasingly detailed descriptions of the object being designed. BioSep Designer's descriptions of protein recovery processes are shown in Figure 10-2. The design begins as a hypothetical process consisting only of the inflowing feed stream and final product streams. As more detail is added, the state of the design proceeds from the initial specifications, to a description of the basic unit operations needed to purify the product, to the equipment selection and finally a fully specified design.

The goal structure is related to the order in which procedures are performed; some operations must be carried out before others. BioSep Designer must, for example, determine the cellular location and conformation of the desired product before it can decide whether cell harvesting or disruption operations are needed. The goal structure in BioSep Designer is fairly rigid; the ultimate goal is, of course, to specify equipment for the given recovery problem. The subgoals are to develop the basic unit operations, and to select the equipment to carry them out. These may involve still further subgoals dependent upon the goals already established. There may be interactions among the subgoals. For example, selections of equipment for carrying out the basic unit operations can not be made independently. If one were to include an ammonium sulfate precipitation in a protein recovery process, the operation immediately following the precipitation must either be insensitive to ammonium sulfate or include a step to remove it, and the operations preceding the precipitations should have removed all particulates such as cell debris. BioSep Designer handles such interactions by applying domain knowledge to determine the best order in which to make decisions such as equipment selections.

There is always a rationale behind the making of a decision, and this rationale should be accessible to the user. BioSep Designer employs sets of if-then rules the antecedents of which are matched against the current state of the design and with static information from the database, e.g. protein properties. Rules will be further described in Section 10.4. The reasoning behind decisions made by BioSep Designer is a combination of physical "common sense" reasoning, heuristics that have been published in the open literature, and suggestions from experts in the field. The wording of the rules and documentation associated with the rules provides the user with the rationale used. A justification system keeps track of the reasoning for every change made in the state of the design by recording which rules brought about each change in the state of the design and the facts which supported which rules. The explanation system uses this justification to provide the user with explanations for the presence or absence of specific features in a given design.

The control mechanism in BioSep Designer is described in Section 10.2.3. Finally, because a widely recognised value of knowledge based systems is their ability to capture the specialized knowledge of experts, BioSep Designer must have facilities for acquiring knowledge from the user. BioSep Designer is equipped with facilities for editing rules and creating new types of equipment. Because all the design heuristics and guidelines are represented as rules, the user may modify and add design knowledge to the system by using the rule editing facilities, which allow the user to modify existing rules, add new rules, or create entirely new rule bases. Equipment items are defined in terms of their design attributes, modeling equations and graphical images; the user may modify any of these for existing equipment. New equipment types may be defined as needed to introduce new types of technology into the system, and these may be created as specializations of existing equipment types or as completely new types.

The process of gathering biochemical knowledge and entering it into BioSep Designer remains a laborious one, however, because to add useful knowledge one must be intimately familiar with the representation and nomenclature in BioSep Designer. These difficulties could be reduced, at least in part, by implementing rule and object editors that compare newly entered information to that already in the system to ensure that the new rules or objects are consistent with the existing information and are catalogued properly.

10.2.3. The Design Procedure

There must be an orderly mechanism for establishing the goals and making design decisions, i.e. a control mechanism. Design actions manipulate the state of the design, activate the evaluation of rules, or perform input/output operations. These actions are executed in the order in which they appear on the agenda. Actions may be part of the starting agenda, or they may be added as the result of other actions or by rules. The overall design procedure, as shown in Figure 10-2, is established by the starting agenda and consists of the following steps.

Step 1, Input: The state of the design at this point is merely the problem specifications. The information specified includes the protein product and its physical characteristics, the biological source of the product, the contaminants which may be present, and a statement of the purity and condition required of the final product. Additional information, such as the physical and chemical properties of the protein, is either looked up in the system's database or else estimated. The user is questioned only when the information is absolutely necessary.

Step 2, Basic operations: In the second step, a purification scheme consisting of the general operations required, but without specific equipment, is developed based on the statement of the problem.

Step 3, Ordering: In this procedure, the order in which to specify equipment for each of the abstract unit operations is decided upon. Specifying a particular type of equipment for one of the abstract steps may put constraints on the other steps. For example, ion exchange chromatography for protein fractionation is not practical until nucleic acids have been removed from the solution. A reasonable way to handle this problem is to specify equipment for the most constrained and most critical processes first allowing any constraints to fall on the remaining operations.

Step 4, Make selections: Fourth, in the order determined in the third step, equipment is specified for each of the basic operations. For a given operation in the abstract process, all the equipment pertinent to that step is screened, and equipment that would destroy the product or introduce incompatibilities with already selected equipment are omitted from further consideration. For example, heat treatment would be omitted from consideration as a means of lysing cells containing a thermolabile product.

The equipment to perform an abstract operation is selected on the basis of a preliminary estimate of the performance of the flowsheet. Unless, as in some situations, there are very strong heuristics to recommend the particular type of an equipment.

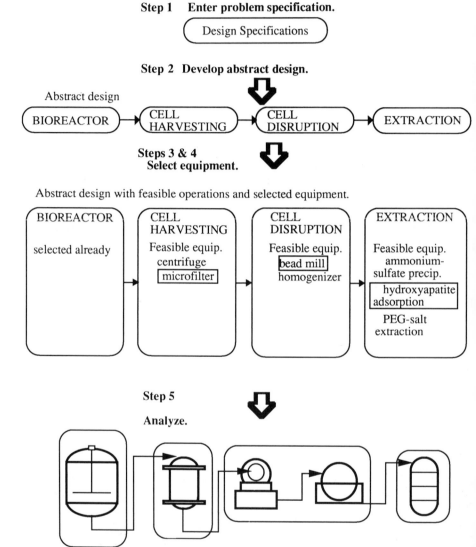

Step 1   Enter problem specification.

(Design Specifications)

Step 2 Develop abstract design.

Abstract design

(BIOREACTOR) → (CELL HARVESTING) → (CELL DISRUPTION) → (EXTRACTION)

Steps 3 & 4
Select equipment.

Abstract design with feasible operations and selected equipment.

BIOREACTOR	CELL HARVESTING	CELL DISRUPTION	EXTRACTION
selected already	Feasible equip. centrifuge microfilter	Feasible equip. bead mill homogenizer	Feasible equip. ammonium-sulfate precip. hydroxyapatite adsorption PEG-salt extraction

Step 5

Analyze.

Step 6 Generate alternate designs.

Figure 10-2: Schematic of the Design Procedure

Step 5, Analysis: The sizes and specifications of the equipment are selected to satisfy the original problem specification, and, if sufficient information is available, the flowsheet is quantitatively analyzed in terms of performance and cost.

Step 6, Generating Alternatives: Although the equipment selections are the best that can be made with the available information and heuristics, they are not guaranteed to be optimal; a user guided search is therefore introduced.

The user may direct the system to generate and test alternative processes by the following procedures:

1. Backtrack to a specified decision point, e.g., an equipment choice, make a different choice, and making all subsequent modifications necessary.

2. Generate all the processes that can be formed, by selecting all the possible choices for the most important abstract step.

3. Do the above, beginning with the least important abstract step.

4. Execute a bounded search of the feasible processes, using cost as an objective function.

The first choice allows the user to ask questions like "What would the best process be if high pressure homogenization was used for cell disruption instead of bead milling?" The second and third methods are simply automatic ways of enumerating and evaluating the feasible designs. The analysis of the processes is done quantitatively if the available information is sufficient; otherwise, alternative processes must be evaluated by the user. The fourth procedure guarantees an optimal solution, but the user must specify an objective function, such as cost, for which to optimize, and there must be a method for optimistically estimating this objective function for any state of the design. As the states of alternative designs are developed, those for which the estimated objective proves worse than that of the initial design may safely be discarded. This, of course, is simply a version of the A* search algorithm [15].

10.3. AN EXAMPLE

We illustrate the abilities of the current implementation of BioSep Designer by designing a recovery process for urokinase a blood clot dissolving enzyme with a selling price of approximately $400/mg [6]. Human urokinase has been successfully cloned and produced in the bacteria, E. coli [14], allowing the drug to be produced by a relatively simple bacterial fermentation.

To design a purification process with BioSep Designer, a biochemical engineer provides the specifications shown in Figure 10-3. This information is entered in a series of successive menus, which can help the user in deciding what choices to make by offering multiple choices for symbolic information, such as the product location, and by checking the units and magnitude range of numerical values. Additional necessary information, such as the physical properties of the product and information about the micro-organism is read from the database.

If the product is a new protein, the important physical properties are estimated from the chemical composition of the protein as shown in Figure 10-4. The distribution of isoelectric points and molecular weights of proteins are estimated from an O'Farrell gel mapping of cell lysate [11]. This laboratory technique, which provides a two-dimensional chart of protein isoelectric point versus molecular weight, has been used to map the proteins in many types of cells including E. coli and blood proteins [1, 7].

After selecting the necessary abstract steps, the system displays the abstract design as shown in Figure 10-5 and stops to allow the user to query the system about the current state of the design. In the urokinase design, the user would find that cell harvesting and cell disruption steps were necessary because the product is intracellular. The precipitation step was chosen because the product was also located in cellular inclusion bodies (partially precipitated masses of protein). The system inferred that because the product was precipitated in an inclusion body, it would likely be misfolded, and by examining the amino acid sequence of the product, the system further concluded that improper disulfide bridges were likely. The system therefore added reduction, oxidation, unfolding, and refolding steps. Finally, because inclusion body proteins are never completely pure, a resolution step was added to ensure a pharmaceutical grade product would be produced.

Continuing, the system generates an initial design, which appears automatically as shown in Figure 10-6. At this point, the user could ask for explanations for each of the equipment choices. For example, the system would reveal that ion exchange and controlled pore glass (CPG) adsorption were selected because the product has a high isoelectric point, as compared with E. coli proteins and because CPG is known to be selective for relatively hydrophobic proteins like urokinase. Furthermore, neither operation will dilute the product.

This is however only an initial flowsheet, and if the user were to examine the abstract steps shown in Figure 10-7, most of the steps would be found to have a number of feasible equipment types from which to choose. For example, the user could ask the system to use centrifugation, as opposed to membrane filtration, for the cell harvesting step. Whereupon the system would check the decisions made subsequently to cell harvester selection and propagate the effects of the change. Alternatively, the user might use the interactive design facilities to add or delete equipment items directly or have the system generate alternative designs. In either case, alternative designs are simulated and compared on the bases of purification, yield, and cost.

10.4. REPRESENTATION AND IMPLEMENTATION

The design procedure in BioSep Designer requires the ability to represent physical entities like proteins or micro-organisms, less tangible entities such as heuristics or states of the design, and procedures, like equation solving. Physical entities need to be organized according to their function in the design, and it is convenient to separate process design information, such as operating temperature from system information like graphical image position.

10.4.1. Objects

Object-oriented programming provides the above features in BioSep Designer; everything from a protein to a problem specification is represented as an object having attributes with values and methods with procedural abilities. The knowledge needed to design protein recovery processes is represented in three basic forms; physical entities are represented as objects; design guidelines and heuristics are represented as production rules (actually specialized objects); and the execution of the design procedure is achieved through the application of procedures taken from a library of design actions. Finally, a set of special objects is used to record the user's specifications and to manage the design strategy. Good examples of objects in BioSep Designer are the processing unit shown in Figure 10-8, and the classification of equipment data in Figure 10-9.

| Product : | urokinase |

Source:	E. coli
Product location:	inclusion bodies
% Product in total protein:	10 %

Fermentor	
Mode of operation	batch
Volume	500 l
Turnaround time	24 h
Medium	yeast extract/sugar
cell concentration	15 g/l

General Specifications	
Selection emphasis:	purity
product use	pharmaceutical

Figure 10-3: Specifications for Urokinase Purification

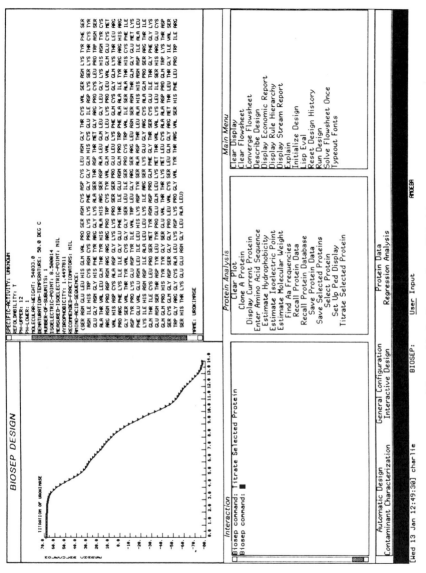

Figure 10-4: Properties of Urokinase

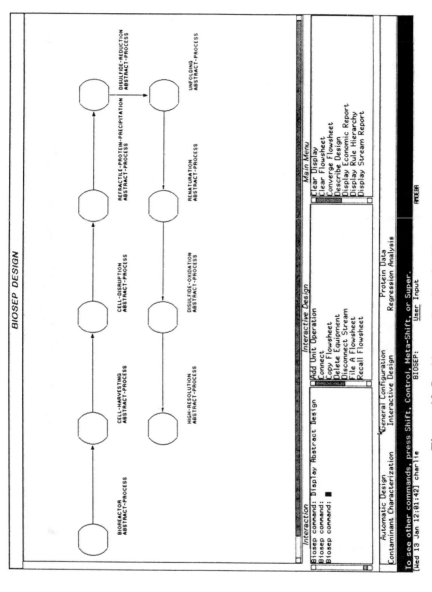

Figure 10-5: Abstract Design for Urokinase Recovery

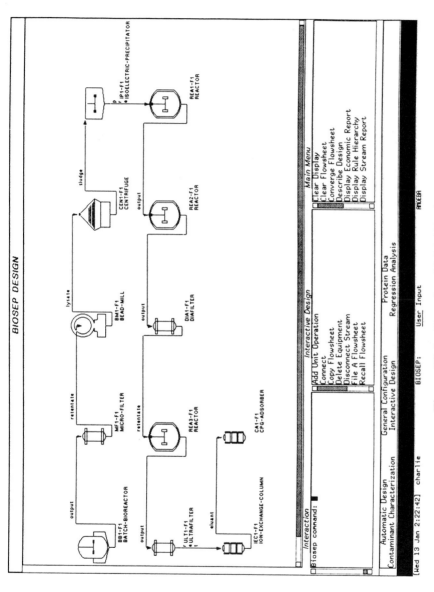

Figure 10-6: Completed Initial Design

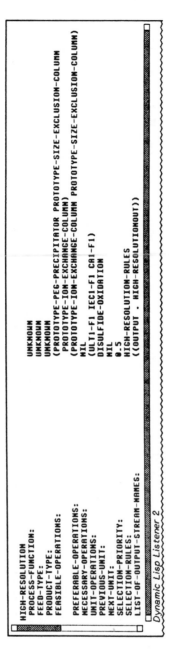

Figure 10-7: Description of an Abstract Unit

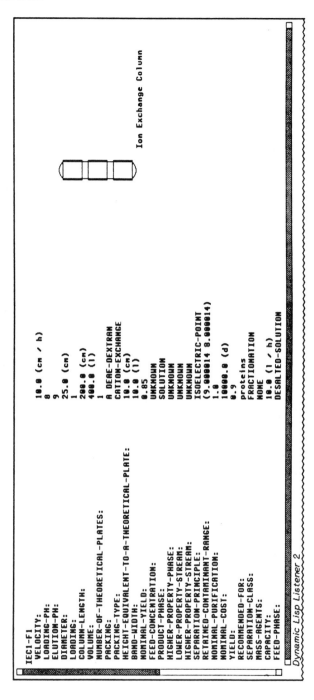

Figure 10-8: A Processing Unit

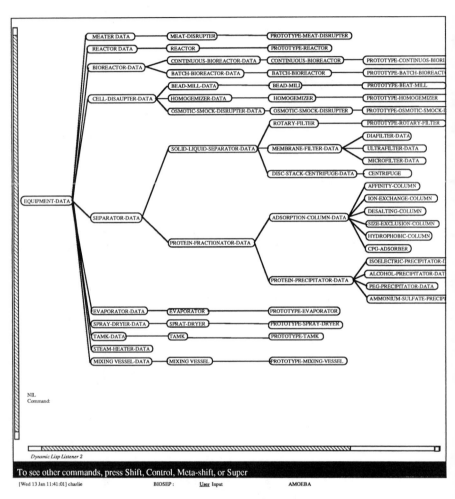

Figure 10-9: Organization of Equipment Objects

10.4.2. Rules

In addition to physical objects, a computer design system must have a representation for the less tangible knowledge of how to design, that is, a set of criteria for how and when to select the equipment for a given recovery problem. This includes quantitative criteria such as the material balances, sizing, and costing for the overall process that are represented by sets of equations, which can be solved as needed for unspecified variables. Much of the design knowledge, however, is heuristic or qualitative in nature. Production rules [3] are an appropriate way of handling this sort of knowledge. Production rules are simply if-then statements which can be used to evaluate and act on the current state of the knowledge in the system. They allow a modular representation of knowledge that is easy to comprehend and explain. Rules generally have two possible outcomes; they may make inferences which change what we know about the problem, or they may make design decisions which change the state of the design. Shown below are some example rules.

1. **A rule for making a design decision: Denaturing Processes Rule of Abstract Design Rules.** For any equipment in the class EQUIPMENT-DATA such that the operating-temperature of the equipment is greater than the denaturation temperature of the product or the operating-pH of the equipment is outside the stable pH range of the product, Then add the equipment to the denaturing processes of the current design.

2. **An inference about the nature of the product: Denatured Product Rule of Abstract Design Rules.** If the product-location of the current-organism is inclusion-bodies, Then assert that the conformation of the product is denatured.

Rules are grouped into sets or rule bases, such as the Abstract Design rule base shown above, that are associated with each of the steps in the design methodology. This precludes any necessity for a "current context" clause in each rule or for manipulation of the conflict resolution system to impose order in rule evaluation. Only rules from a single rule base are evaluated at a given time, though rules may invoke the evaluation of other rule bases. For example, if it is determined that a cell harvesting step is needed in the process, a specialized rule base will be called to select an appropriate separator.

The inference engine in BioSep Designer evaluates rule in a forward chaining breadth first manner during the initial design ensuring that all possibilities are checked. It uses a depth first, data-driven strategy for evaluating the effect of changing an existing design, in this case all the inferences must be either a direct or an indirect result of the initial changes made.

10.4.3. Design Actions

The assembly of equipment, process streams and the like into a design is finally accomplished through high level functions termed design actions. Design actions may appear directly on the agenda or in the antecedents or conclusions of rules. Some example design actions are shown below.

Design Actions

assert-that	`the attribute of an object is some value.`
run-rule-base	`execute the rules in a given rule base.`
estimate-purification	`for a given design.`
estimate-purification-contribution	`for an equipment item.`
simulate-flowsheet	`do sequential modular simulation.`

10.5. SOFTWARE/HARDWARE NOTE

BioSep Designer has been implemented on a Symbolics 3650. The inference engine, analysis facilities, and graphical interface have all been developed using Symbolics CommonLisp. The object-oriented programming system is built on Symbolics Flavors.

10.6. CONCLUSIONS

The design of commercial scale protein recovery processes is an engineering design task that requires assembling a large variety of interacting pieces to meet a number of requirements and constraints. BioSep Designer represents the elements of a complete computer facility tailored to solving this problem. The system synthesizes processes by using an abstract refinement procedure to generate the feasible processes, from which the "best" design is selected based on a number of heuristics. Then the system searches the remaining feasible processes for improved designs. The user may intervene in the design process by guiding the search step, by interactively modifying a synthesized design, or by assembling a completely new one. If all the necessary quantitative values and relations are known, the system can find an optimal process, but if, as is often the case in bioprocess engineering, exact values are not known, BioSep Designer makes use of heuristics as well as the expertise of the user to generate reasonable processes.

10.7. BIBLIOGRAPHY

[1]   Bloch, P.L., T.A. Phillips and G. C. Neidhardt, "Protein Identifications on O'Farrell Two Dimensional Gels: Locations of 81 E. coli Proteins," *J Bacteriol*, Vol. 141, pp. 1407-1420, 1980.

[2]   Brown, D. C., *Expert Systems for Design Problem-Solving using Design Refinement with Plan Selection and Redesign*, unpublished Ph.D. Dissertation, CIS Dept., OSU, Columbus, OH 43210, 1984, [Also Published as a Book Co-authored with B. Chandrasekaran].

[3]   Davis, R., B. Brachaman, and E. Shortliffe, "Production Rules as a Representation Language for a Knowledge-Based Consultation Program," *Artificial Intelligence*, Vol. 8, pp. 15-45, 1977.

[4]   Davis, R., *Expert Systems: Where Are We? And Where Do We Go From Here*, Technical Report Memo No. 665, AI Laboratory, M.I.T., 1982, [See also AI Magazine].

[5]   Douglas, J., M. Malone, and M. Doherty, "The Interaction Between Separation System Synthesis and Process Synthesis," *Computers and Chemical Engineering*, Vol. 9, No. 5, pp. 447-462, 1985.

[6]   Dwyer, J. L., "Scaling Up Bio-Product Separation With High Performance Liquid Chromatography," *Bio/Tech*, Vol. 8, pp. 957, 1984.

[7]   Garrels, J. A., "Two-Dimensional Gel Electrophoresis and Computer Analysis of Proteins Synthesized by Clonal Cell Lines," *Journal of Biological Chemistry*, Vol. 254, 1979.

[8]   Marcus, S., Stout, J., and McDermott, J., "VT: An Expert Elevator Designer," *AI Magazine*, Vol. 8, No. 4, pp. 39-58, 1987.

[9]   Mostow, J., "Towards Better Models of the Design Process," *AI Magazine*, Spring 1985.

[10]   Myers, D., J. Davis, D. Herman, and B. Chandrasekaran, "Use of DSPL for Distillation Column Design," *Proceedings Columbia Workshop on AI in Process Engineering*, Venkatasubramanian, V. et al., Eds., Dept. Chemical Engineering, Columbia University, March 1987.

[11]   O'Farrell, P. Z. et al., "High Resolution Two Dimensional Electrophoresis of Basic as Well as Acidic Proteins," *Cell*, Vol. 12, pp. 1133-1142, 1980.

[12]   Sriram, D., *Knowledge-Based Approaches for Structural Design*, CM Publications, UK, 1987.

[13]   Stefik, M., "Planning with Constraints (MOLGEN 1)," *Artificial Intelligence*, Vol. 16, pp. 111-140, 1981.

[14]   Winkler, M. E. and Blaber, M., "The Purification and Characterization of Recombinant Single- Chain Urokinase Produced in Escherichia coli," *Biochemistry*, Vol. 25, pp. 4041, 1986.

[15]   Winston, P., *Artificial Intelligence*, Addison-Wesley Publishing Company, Massachusetts, 1984.

Chapter 11
VT:
AN EXPERT ELEVATOR DESIGNER THAT USES KNOWLEDGE-BASED BACKTRACKING

Sandra Marcus, Jeffrey Stout, and John McDermott

Abstract

VT (vertical transportation) is an expert system for handling the design of elevator systems that is currently in use at Westinghouse Elevator Company. Although VT tries to postpone each decision in creating a design until all information that constrains the decision is known, for many decisions this postponement is not possible. In these cases, VT uses the strategy of constructing a plausible approximation and successively refining it. VT uses domain-specific knowledge to guide its backtracking search for successful refinements. The VT architecture provides the basis for a knowledge representation that is used by SALT, an automated knowledge-acquisition tool. SALT was used to build VT and provides an analysis of VT's knowledge base to assess its potential for convergence on a solution.

11.1. INTRODUCTION

In some cases, plausible guessing combined with the ability to backtrack to undo a bad guess can be the most efficient way to solve a problem [17]. Even least commitment systems such as MOLGEN [15, 16] are sometimes forced to guess. In the course of designing genetics experiments, MOLGEN tries to avoid making a decision until all constraints that might affect the decision are known. In some cases, this postponement is not possible, and the system becomes stuck; none of the pending decisions can be made with complete confidence. In such a

Artificial Intelligence in Engineering Design
Volume I
Design Representation and Models of Routine Design

case, a decision based on partial information is needed, and such a decision might be wrong. In this case, a problem solver needs the ability either to back-track to correct bad decisions or to maintain parallel solutions corresponding to the alternatives at the stuck decision point. However, if alternative guesses exist at each point, and there are many such decision points on each solution path, a commitment to examine every possible combination of alternatives proves un-wieldy. Such complexity exists in the VT task domain.

VT performs the engineering task of designing elevator systems. It must use the customer's functional specifications to select equipment and produce a parts configuration that meets these specifications as well as safety, installation and maintenance requirements. Because of the large number of potential part com-binations and the need for customizing the layout to the space available in in-dividual buildings, VT must construct a solution. Like MOLGEN, VT tries to order its decisions so that they are made only when all relevant constraints are known; it guesses only when stuck. Unlike MOLGEN, VT's decisions about part selection and placement are so interdependent that plausible reasoning (guessing) is a major feature of its search for a solution. Thus, VT's problem-solving strategy is predominantly one of constructing an approximation and suc-cessively refining it.

Systems that use plausible reasoning must be able to identify bad guesses and improve on these decisions in a way which helps converge on a solution. VT is similar to AIR-CYL [1] (See Chapter 7) and PRIDE [12] (See Chapter 9) in that it uses a knowledge-based approach to direct this search; that is, it uses domain-specific knowledge to decide what past decisions to alter and how to alter them. This approach contrasts with EL [14, 19], an expert system which shares many architectural features with VT but which uses domain-independent strategies to limit the search during the backtracking phase. As with EL, the VT architecture makes clear the role that domain-specific knowledge plays in the system and the interconnections among decisions used to construct and refine a solution. This architecture provides the basis for VT's explanation facility, which is similar to that of EL and the related CONSTRAINTS language [20], with some exten-sions. We have exploited the structure provided by this architecture even further by using it to manage VT's knowledge acquisition.

VT's architecture provides structure for a representation of its domain-specific knowledge that reflects the function of the knowledge in problem solv-ing. This representation serves as the basis for an automated knowledge-acquisition tool, SALT [8, 9, 18], which has been used to build VT. SALT elicits from experts all the knowledge VT needs in order to design elevators and represents that knowledge in a way which enables VT's problem-solving method to use it. SALT's knowledge representation can also be used to assess the adequacy of the knowledge base for convergence on a solution.

The next section presents VT mainly from a user's point of view. Section 11.3 describes the VT architecture in detail, with respect to problem solving, explanation, and knowledge acquisition. Section 11.4 describes how SALT's knowledge base analysis supports VT's domain-dependent backtracking. Section 11.5 compares VT to other expert systems that perform design, planning, or scheduling tasks. Section 11.6 reports some of VT's performance characteristics.

11.2. WHAT VT DOES

VT is used by Westinghouse Elevator engineers to design elevator systems to customer's specifications. VT has enough domain knowledge to perform the design task unaided. VT also has an interactive capability that allows a user to directly influence its decisions.

11.2.1. The Engineer's Task

Westinghouse Elevator design experts receive data collected from several contract documents. These data are transmitted to the engineering operation by the regional sales and installation offices. There are three main sources of information: (1) customer requirement forms describing the general performance specifications, such as carrying capacity and speed of travel, and some product selections, such as the style of light fixture in the cab; (2) the architectural and structural drawings of the building, indicating such elements as wall-to-wall dimensions in the elevator shaft (hoistway) and locations of rail supports; and (3) the architectural design drawings of the elevator cabs, entrances, and fixtures. Because all this information is not necessarily available at the start of a contract, the engineer must sometimes produce reasonable guesses for incomplete, inconsistent or uncertain data to enable order processing to proceed tentatively until customer verification is received. (These guesses are in addition to whatever guesses might be required during a problem-solving episode based on these data.)

Given this information, experts attempt to optimally select the equipment necessary and design its layout in the hoistway to meet engineering, safety code, and system performance requirements. This task is a highly constrained one. A completed elevator system must satisfy constraints such as the following: (1) there must be at least an 8-inch clearance between the side of the platform and a hoistway wall, and at least 7 inches between the platform side and a rail separating two cars; (2) a model 18 machine can only be used with a 15, 20 or 25 horsepower motor; and (3) the counterweight must be close enough to the platform to provide adequate traction but far enough away to prevent collision with either the platform or the rear hoistway wall (by an amount dependent on the distance of travel).

The design task also encompasses the calculation of the building load data required by the building's structural engineers, the reporting of the engineering and ordering data required for the field installation department and regional safety code authorities, and the reporting of the mechanical manufacturing order information.

11.2.2. A Quick Look at VT in Action

VT is comprised of several distinct parts, described briefly in the following sample interactions. VT prompts appear in boldface. User replies appear in italics.

Welcome to VT --- The Elevator Design Expert System

1. INPUT   Enter contract information
2. RUN   Process the input data
3. SHOW   Display output information
4. EXPLAIN   Explain the results of a run
5. SAVE   Save data for the current contract
6. EXIT   End this session with VT

Enter your command [INPUT]: *<cr>*

The previous display illustrates the top menu, where the user indicates what VT is to do. The INPUT command allows the user either to enter data on a new job or to modify data from an existing job. The other modes use previously input data. VT displays a default command in brackets at the bottom of the screen that the user can issue by hitting a carriage return (<cr>). Users can also issue single or multiple commands by typing only a portion of a command word or the number in front of it.

VT's input is menu driven, allowing entire screens of questions to be answered at once by providing defaults wherever possible. The input mode also provides consistency checking of data and a general question-asking mechanism that is used throughout VT. A completed sample input screen follows. Prompts for data appear on the left, defaults and input on the right.

```
INPUT GD DUTY      GR 24364     ADMINISTRATION & SERVICE CENTER

Car:1
 1. Type of loading             PASSENGER
 2. Machine                     GEARED
 3. Machine location            OVERHEAD
 4. Power supply                208-3-60
 5. Capacity                    3000
 6. Speed                       250
 7. Travel                      729
 8. Platform width              70
 9. Platform depth              84
10.Counterweight location       REAR
11.Counterweight safety         NO
12.Compensation specified       NO

Action [ EXIT ]:
```

Using a simple command language, the user can confirm some or all values shown, enter or modify values, or register uncertainty about values. Fourteen of these data menus currently exist in the INPUT portion of VT. Once all the data have been entered, the user returns to the top menu, at which point the data can be saved for future use (SAVE) or used immediately in the design task (RUN).

As VT runs, it tentatively constructs an elevator system by proposing component selections and relationships. At the same time, VT specifies constraints with which to test the acceptability of the resulting design and tests each constraint whenever enough is known about the design to evaluate it. Whenever constraints are violated, VT attempts to alter the design (for example, by selecting more expensive equipment) in order to resolve the problem. We refer to these alterations as fixes. VT reports any such constraint violation and the fix that is made, as in the following example:

```
The CAR-RUNBY (estimated to be 6) has been changed to 6.125.

The MACHINE-SHEAVE-HEIGHT (estimated to be 30) has been changed to 26.

The CWT-STACK-WEIGHT (estimated to be 4316.25) has been changed to 4287.
36.

The MAXIMUM-TRACTION-RATIO constraint was violated.
The TRACTION-RATIO was 1.806591, but had to be <= 1.783873.
The gap of 0.2272000E-01 was eliminated by the following action(s):
   Decreasing CWT-TO-PLATFORM-FRONT from 4.75 to 2.25
   Upgrading COMP-CABLE-UNIT-WEIGHT from 0 to 0.5000000E-01

The MINIMUM-MAX-CAR-RAIL-LOAD constraint was violated.
The MAX-CAR-RAIL-LOAD was 6000, but had to be >= 6722.295.
The gap of 722.3 was eliminated by the following action(s):
   Upgrading CAR-RAIL-UNIT-WEIGHT from 11 to 16
```

```
The MINIMUM-PLATFORM-TO-CLEAR-HOISTWAY-RIGHT constraint was violated.
The PLATFORM-TO-CLEAR-HOISTWAY-RIGHT was 7.5, but had to be >= 8.
The gap of 0.5 was eliminated by the following action(s):
   Decreasing CAR-RETURN-RIGHT from 3 to 2.5


The MINIMUM-PLATFORM-TO-CLEAR-HOISTWAY-LEFT constraint was violated.
The PLATFORM-TO-CLEAR-HOISTWAY-LEFT was 7.5, but had to be >= 8.
The gap of 0.5 was eliminated by the following action(s):
   Decreasing CAR-RETURN-LEFT from 25.5 to 25


The MAXIMUM-MACHINE-GROOVE-PRESSURE constraint was violated.
The MACHINE-GROOVE-PRESSURE was 149.5444, but had to be <= 119.
The gap of 30.544 was eliminated by the following action(s):
   Increasing HOIST-CABLE-QUANTITY from 3 to 4


The MINIMUM-HOIST-CABLE-SAFETY-FACTOR constraint was violated.
The HOIST-CABLE-SAFETY-FACTOR was 8.395078, but had to be >= 10.
The gap of 1.60492 was eliminated by the following action(s):
   Upgrading HOIST-CABLE-DIAMETER from 0.5 to 0.625


The MINIMUM-MACHINE-BEAM-SECTION-MODULUS constraint was violated.
The MACHINE-BEAM-SECTION-MODULUS was 24.7, but had to be >= 24.87352.
The gap of 0.1735 was eliminated by the following action(s):
   Upgrading MACHINE-BEAM-MODEL from S10X25.4 to S10X35.0


The CHOICE-SET-HOIST-CABLE-DIAMETER constraint was violated.
The HOIST-CABLE-DIAMETER was 0.625, but was constrained to be 0.5.
The HOIST-CABLE-DIAMETER became a member of the set by the following
action(s):
   Upgrading MACHINE-MODEL from 28 to 38.
```

There are two types of fix reports. The report shown for MAXIMUM-TRACTION-RATIO is the more common version. It mentions the constraint that was violated, describes the degree of the violation and lists the corrective action taken. The fix report describing the change to CAR-RUNBY is a special case. This version is used when VT makes an initial estimate for a value in order to calculate a precise value for it. The value of the constraint is the precise value; the estimate is simply changed to this value.

During a noninteractive run, VT uses its own knowledge base to decide how to remedy constraint violations. This knowledge base represents engineering practices that Westinghouse plans to make standard. The RUN can also be done interactively, in which case VT asks for confirmation of each fix before it is actually implemented. If a particular fix is rejected by the user, VT can either find another fix or provide a list of all possible fixes and ask the user to suggest a particular one. Records are kept of user overrides. These overrides are taken into consideration by the system maintainers when modifying the knowledge base. The overriding of a VT-proposed fix by the user might indicate that a standard does not yet exist on a decision VT makes. It might also be the result of outside factors that were too transitory to make it into the VT knowledge or data base, such as a temporary surplus or shortage of a particular equipment model.

On completion of the run, control returns to the top menu, at which point the user normally goes into SHOW mode. SHOW allows users to view data a screenful at a time. Some of the screens are intended for just such a review, and others are intended as input data for other Westinghouse systems (such as manufacturing-oriented programs, cost estimators, and a CAD system). The following two SHOW screens are representative of the sixteen that currently exist; the user accesses these screens by a tree of menus similar to the input menu, as depicted in Figure 11-1.

If the user sees something unusual while in SHOW (for example, an unexpected value), the EXPLAIN mode can be used to determine the cause. EXPLAIN can also be used by relative novices to understand how VT performs the design task.

The user interacts with VT's explanation facility by asking questions. The type of information given in the explanation depends on the type of question asked. VT's explanation facility currently provides several types of queries that can be asked about individual system values. These query types are discussed in detail in the next section. The following sample interaction demonstrates some of the tools the explanation facility provides, including the use of VT's lexicon of synonyms for system value names:

```
EXPLAIN        GR 24364          ADMINISTRATION & SERVICE CENTER

Explain:  how car runby

The CAR-RUNBY was determined by a fix.

The CHOICE-SET-CAR-RUNBY constraint was violated.
The CAR-RUNBY was 6, but was constrained to be 6.125.
The CAR-RUNBY was changed from 6 to 6.125.

HOW [ CHOICE-SET-CAR-RUNBY ]: <cr>

The CHOICE-SET-CAR-RUNBY (6.125) = PIT-DEPTH (72) - [ PLATFORM-HEIGHT (
6.625) + SAFETY-HEIGHT (9) + CAR-BUFFER-HEIGHT (28.75) + CAR-FOOTING-
CHANNEL-HEIGHT (3.5) + CAR-BUFFER-BLOCKING-HEIGHT (18)]

HOW [ PIT-DEPTH ]: <cr>

The PIT-DEPTH (72) was input by Bob Roche on 25-MAR-1985.

HOW [ PLATFORM-WEIGHT ]: safety height

The SAFETY-HEIGHT (9) was determined by a database lookup.
It was found in the HEIGHT column of the SAFETY table.
It met the following constraints:
     MODEL = SAFETY-MODEL (B1)

HOW [ SAFETY MODEL ]: <cr>

The SAFETY-MODEL (B1) was determined by a database lookup.
It was found in the MODEL column of the SAFETY table.
It had the SMALLEST HEIGHT that met the following constraints:
```

```
SHOW LAYOUT SPECS    GR 24364    ADMINISTRATION & SERVICE CENTER

Loading: PASSENGER                  Governor: B5B   Support: STEEL
Capacity: 3000                      Governor Cable: 0.375
                                        Length: 2130
Speed: 250                          Hoist Cables: (3)-0.5
                                        Length: 1089
Operation: 1C-2BC-ERL               Compensation: 3/16-CHAIN
                                        Length:  993
Travel: 729                         Car sling: 2.5B-18
Stops: 6        Openings: 6         Crosshead Beam: W8X18
Machine: 28     Sheave: 30          Platform Thickness:  6.625
Deflector Sheave: 20                Sling Weight.......... 292
Groove: K3269  Pressure: 90.03      Platform Weight....... 738
Angle of Contact: 159.09            Safety Weight......... 465
Traction Ratio: 1.79                Cab Weight............1668
Machine Load: 11691                 Misc. Weight.......... 434
Motor H.P.: 20                      Total Car Weight......3609
Power Source: ---                   Counterweight Weight: 4824
Power Supply: 208-3-60              Subweight Weight:     4287
Rails........Car: 16   Cwt: 11      Buffer Reaction Car: 26437
                                                   Cwt: 19296
Guide Shoes..Car: 6-R  Cwt: 3-R     Machine Weight: 1700
Buffer.......Car: OH-1 Cwt: OH-1    Heat Emission in M.R.: ---
Stroke.......Car: 8.25 Cwt: 8.25    Cable Hanger ---
Safety.......Car: B1   Cwt: ---     Safety to Pit:  42

Press RETURN to continue [ MENU ]: show layout cwt

SHOW LAYOUT CWT    GR 24364    ADMINISTRATION & SERVICE CENTER

!-----------------------85.5------------------------!
!                     Hoistway                      !
!                                                   !
!--------------!---------28-------------!-----------!
!              !      Cwt BG            !           !

------------------------------------------------     ------------
!                     9                 !  !    !        !
!              -----------------------     !  12.5    !
!     !- !       7           !  -!       !  --!--     18.25
!     !  !-----------------------!  !     !  ! Cwt Space
!              2.25                       !  5.75     !
!     --------------------------------    !  --!-------!-
!  !                                      !  !
!  !                 Platform            !  !
~~~~~~~~~~~~~~~~~~~~~~~~~~~~~~~~~~~~~~~~~~~~~~~~~~~~~~
Cwt Assembly Weight      537    Overall Cwt Height          138
Cwt Subweight Weight     4287   Maximum Subweight Weight    5273
Total CWT Weight         4824   Cwt Stack Height             87
                                Maximum Stack Height        107
Maximum Building Tolerance: 1   Stack Percent                81

Press RETURN to continue [ MENU ]:
```

Figure 11-1: Examples of VT's SHOW screens

```
    MAX-SPEED > SPEED (250)
    MAX-PLATFORM-WIDTH <= PLATFORM-WIDTH (70)
    MIN-PLATFORM-WIDTH <= PLATFORM-WIDTH (70)
```

HOW [SPEED]: *what if safety model B4*

```
The SAFETY-MODEL is currently B1.
If it were B4, the following major changes would occur:
```

NAME:	ACTUAL:	PROPOSED:
MACHINE-GROOVE-PRESSURE	114.118	155.563.
TRACTION-RATIO	1.80679	1.76682.
CWT-OVERTRAVEL	49.835	52.835.
CAR-BUFFER-REACTION	26709.4	27652.4.
CWT-STACK-PERCENT	84.1122	88.148.
CWT-BUFFER-REACTION	19684	20627.0.
CWT-PLATE-QUANTITY	90	94.3184.
CWT-WEIGHT	4921.0	5156.76.
CAR-BUFFER-LOAD	6677.35	6913.11.
CAR-WEIGHT	3677.35	3913.11.
DEFLECTOR-SHEAVE-DIAMETER	25	20.
CAR-BUFFER-BLOCKING-HEIGHT	18	17.125.
HOIST-CABLE-MODEL	(4)-0.5	(3)-0.5.
CAR-RUNBY	6.125	6.
SAFETY-MODEL	B1	B4.

```
Would you like to see ALL values which would change [ NO ]: <cr>

Would you like to implement this [ NO ]: <cr>
```

How [MACHINE-GROOVE-PRESSURE]: *safety load*

```
There is more than one SAFETY-LOAD:

1. SAFETY-LOAD-CAR-SIDE-CAR-TOP
2. SAFETY-LOAD-CAR-SIDE-CAR-BOTTOM
3. SAFETY-LOAD-CWT-SIDE-CAR-TOP
4. SAFETY-LOAD-CWT-SIDE-CAR-BOTTOM

Which would you like to know about? [ SAFETY-LOAD-CAR-SIDE-CAR-
    TOP ]: 2
```

The only major part of VT that is not visible in the previous examples is VT's database. The database is read-only and primarily contains data about pieces of equipment and machinery that VT must configure. Each piece of equipment has its own table; the rows of each of these tables represent different models of the equipment from which to choose, and the columns represent attributes relevant to the type of equipment. These attributes can be restrictions on each model's use (for example, maximum elevator speed or maximum load supported by the equipment), values of equipment attributes (for example, height and weight), or lists of model numbers of compatible pieces of equipment.

Calls to the database indicate which table is to be used and what value is to be returned. This value can be either the name of the particular model or the value of one of its attributes. A call might also include an arbitrary number of constraints on the values of each column.

In the event that multiple entries in the database satisfy all the constraints in a call, each table is ordered along an equipment attribute (for example, size) to indicate a preference or priority. The entries in a table are examined from best to worst, and the first entry satisfying all the constraints is the one from which the return value is obtained.

11.3. THE VT ARCHITECTURE

VT solves its problem by constructing an approximate elevator design and successively refining it. The process of constructing an approximate design is forward-chaining. Each step in this phase extends the design by procedures that use input data or results of prior decisions to determine a value for a design parameter. Some of these steps embody heuristic knowledge about how to propose an approximate design extension. These steps are needed when the decision is underconstrained or when it must be based on partial information. As VT builds a proposed design, constraints on the elevator system are specified whenever enough information is available to determine their values. The control in this constructive phase is data driven; any step can be taken as soon as the information called for by the procedure associated with the step is available. As it extends the design, VT also builds a dependency network that records for each value which other values were used to derive it.

The dependency network developed during the forward-chaining constructive phase is enough to identify all contributors to a violated constraint and the value it constrains. These contributors represent potential points to backtrack to in order to revise the proposed design. However, domain expertise is needed to indicate what changes in the proposed design are least costly in real-world terms. While it is not possible to assign a dollar cost to each revision, domain knowledge determines which of the potential alterations are legal as well as the order of preference among the legal ones.

Demons are used to check for constraint violations; whenever enough is known about the proposed design to supply values for both a constraint and the value it constrains, they are compared. Whenever VT detects a constraint violation, it tests the effectiveness of suggested changes in order of decreasing preference rating until it finds one that is successful. As VT moves through the list of potential fixes for a constraint violation, it first tries every individual fix at a given preference level. Next it tries combining each fix at the current preference level with those of greater or equal preference. (Constraints can be numeric or symbolic, and procedures for determining values often involve non-linear functions such as selections from the database.)

Once VT identifies a change to explore, it first verifies that no constraints on the changed value itself are violated by the change. It then makes the proposed change and works through the implications according to its knowledge about constructing a proposed design. It continues this procedure until it has enough knowledge to evaluate the originally violated constraint. If a proposed change violates the constraints, it is rejected and another selection is made. This lookahead is limited because it only considers constraints on the changed value and the originally violated constraint. The purpose of this lookahead is to limit the work done in exploring the implications of a proposed guess until VT has reason to believe it is a good guess. Once a good guess has been identified, VT applies a truth maintenance system; that is, it uses the dependency network constructed during the forward-chaining phase to identify and remove any values that might be inconsistent with the changed value. VT then reenters the data-driven constructive phase for extending the design with the new data.

11.3.1. A Detailed Look at Problem Solving

In order to better illustrate how VT arrives at a solution, we describe the forward-chaining and backtracking done in a small portion of the sample run. The detail focuses on steps leading to the specification of MACHINE-GROOVE-PRESSURE and its constraint MAXIMUM-MACHINE-GROOVE-PRESSURE and follows the backtracking initiated by a violation of this constraint.

A step to extend the proposed design specifies a value for a design parameter, often using results of decisions already made. For example, the step to select the model of the machine that moves the elevator car can be given the following English translation:

```
(1) MACHINE-MODEL step:

IF      a value has been generated for SUSPENDED-LOAD, and

        there is no value for MACHINE-MODEL,

THEN    Look in the database in the MACHINE table for the entry with the
        SMALLEST WEIGHT whose listing for MAX-LOAD is greater than the
        SUSPENDED-LOAD.

        Retrieve the value under MODEL for that entry and assign
        that value to  MACHINE-MODEL.

        Leave a trace that SUSPENDED-LOAD contributed to MACHINE-MODEL.
```

```
Leave a declarative representation of the details of the
database call.
```

The first line of this step specification sets up the forward-chaining control. This rule is eligible to fire as soon as a value for SUSPENDED-LOAD is made available and uses this value to supply MACHINE- MODEL. Leaving a trace of the contribution adds to the dependency network used by the truth maintenance system in backtracking. Leaving a declarative representation of the action taken by this rule is used by the explanation facility.

To see how this step might interact with others, consider the following two steps:

```
(2) MACHINE-SHEAVE-DIAMETER step:

IF      a value has been generated for MACHINE-MODEL, and

        there is no value for MACHINE-SHEAVE-DIAMETER,

THEN    Look in the database in the MACHINE table for the entry whose
        listing for MODEL is the same as MACHINE-MODEL.

        Retrieve the value under SHEAVE-DIAMETER for that entry and
        assign that value to MACHINE-SHEAVE-DIAMETER.

        Leave a trace that MACHINE-MODEL contributed to MACHINE-SHEAVE-
        DIAMETER.

        Leave a declarative representation of the details of the
        database call.

(3) MACHINE-GROOVE-PRESSURE-FACTOR step:

IF      a value has been generated for HOIST-CABLE-DIAMETER, and

        there is no value for MACHINE-GROOVE-PRESSURE-FACTOR,

THEN    Compute 2 * HOIST-CABLE-DIAMETER.

        Assign the result to MACHINE-GROOVE-PRESSURE-FACTOR.

        Leave a trace that HOIST-CABLE-DIAMETER contributed to
        MACHINE-GROOVE-PRESSURE-FACTOR.

        Leave a declarative representation of the details of the
        calculation.
```

According to the control shown here, step 1 must be applied before step 2 since step 1 creates the conditions under which step 2 will be satisfied. If step 3 is satisfied at the same time as either of the other steps, it does not matter which procedure is applied first.

The machine moves the elevator by turning the machine sheave. The machine sheave contains grooves that grip the hoist cables which support the elevator car. Some pressure is required, but if the pressure on each individual cable is too great, there is excessive wear on the cables. Steps 1 and 2 are on the inference chain that produces a value for MACHINE-GROOVE-PRESSURE. This value is the result of a calculation using MAX-TOTAL-LOAD-CAR-SIDE, MACHINE-SHEAVE-DIAMETER, and HOIST-CABLE-QUANTITY. Step 3 is on the inference chain that produces a value for MAXIMUM-MACHINE-GROOVE-PRESSURE. This value is a function of the MACHINE-GROOVE-MODEL, the SPEED the elevator will travel, and MACHINE-GROOVE-PRESSURE-FACTOR. Once values for both MACHINE-GROOVE-PRESSURE and MAXIMUM-MACHINE-GROOVE-PRESSURE are available, they are compared. Because the constraint is a maximum, the constraint is flagged as violated if the value of MACHINE-GROOVE-PRESSURE is greater than the value of MAXIMUM-MACHINE-GROOVE-PRESSURE. Flagging the constraint as violated causes VT to shift control into fix exploration.

As a first step in exploring remedies for the constraint violation, VT proposes potential remedies. For this particular violation, a propose-fix step for the VT knowledge base looks as follows. This is an abbreviated listing of fixes for MAXIMUM-MACHINE-GROOVE-PRESSURE. We return to a complete treatment of this example in section 11.4.

IF   there has been a violation of MAXIMUM-MACHINE-GROOVE-PRESSURE,

THEN   Try a DOWNGRADE for MACHINE-GROOVE-MODEL which has a preference
          rating of 1 because it CAUSES NO PROBLEM.

          Try an INCREASE BY-STEP of 1 of HOIST-CABLE-QUANTITY which has a
          preference rating of 4 because it CHANGES MINOR EQUIPMENT SIZING.

Downgrading the MACHINE-GROOVE-MODEL to one that grips the cable less increases the allowable MAXIMUM-MACHINE-GROOVE-PRESSURE. Increasing the HOIST-CABLE-QUANTITY distributes the load and decreases the actual MACHINE-GROOVE-PRESSURE on each groove. VT's domain expert felt these two potential fixes would be practical to attempt. Of the two fixes, the first is preferable.

VT first considers a downgrade of MACHINE-GROOVE-MODEL by trying to select the next higher groove according to the preference ordering.[2] If there is such a preferred groove, VT determines what the MAXIMUM-MACHINE-GROOVE-PRESSURE for this groove is. If this value is not less than the value of MACHINE-GROOVE-PRESSURE, VT tries to downgrade the groove model

---

[2]The "down" in downgrade usually pertains to a decrease in size and/ or cost. In the VT domain, size tends to vary inversely with preference.

further. When there are no longer any models to try (there are only two groove models), VT considers an increase of HOIST-CABLE-QUANTITY by adding 1 to its current value. It first checks to see whether this quantity is larger than the MAXIMUM-HOIST-CABLE-QUANTITY (which in any application is never more than six cables). If not, VT then recomputes the MACHINE-GROOVE-PRESSURE using the new HOIST-CABLE-QUANTITY to see if this quantity brings the pressure under the maximum. If it does not, VT tries adding another hoist cable and repeats the procedure. If VT exceeds the MAXIMUM-HOIST-CABLE-QUANTITY before bringing MACHINE-GROOVE-PRESSURE under its maximum, it then attempts a combination of the two fixes. If none of the specified fixes resolve the violation, VT has reached a dead end (that is, the constraint violation cannot be corrected). In the sample run shown previously, the proposed design already employed the preferred groove at the time of the constraint violation; adding a single hoist cable was the selected remedy.

Once VT finds the fix it wants to implement, it uses the dependency network built during the forward-chaining to remove any values that depended on the one it changed. It then returns to the forward-chaining phase with the new HOIST-CABLE-QUANTITY and continues.

11.3.2. A Detailed Look at the Explanation Facility

Every decision VT makes must be justifiable to the user. This condition is provided for by making a record of each decision as it is made. The dependency network built for VT's truth maintenance system can provide the foundation for a very useful explanation facility [5, 20]. This network is augmented by the details of the contribution relation, for example, a description of an algebraic formula or the relation between values required by a precondition. In addition, VT records adjustments to the proposed design that it makes, such as fixes of constraint violations. The explanation facility pieces these individual actions together to describe VT's line of reasoning.

VT's explanation facility does more than just examine past decisions; it also performs some hypothetical reasoning to demonstrate the effect of alternative decisions the user suggests. Hypothetical explanations are relatively simple to construct given the VT knowledge representation. What the system must do in order to answer hypothetical queries is closely related to how it resolves constraint violations.

Explaining Past Decisions

The *how* query is probably the most fundamental and can be thought of as asking the question "How did you determine the value of <x>?" First, the explanation facility looks for the appropriate node in the dependency network that recorded the decision which VT made regarding the value assigned to <x>. This decision record would include, for example, not only a formula but also any conditions in the system that made the formula appropriate. The dependency network provides pointers to the actual values that were used in determining the value in question.

If the user were to ask how the machine groove pressure was determined, VT would respond with something like the following:

```
The MACHINE-GROOVE-PRESSURE (90.0307) = MAX-TOTAL-LOAD-CAR-SIDE
(6752.3042) / [[ MACHINE-SHEAVE-DIAMETER (30) * 0.5 ]
                          * HOIST-CABLE-QUANTITY (5)]
```

The machine groove pressure was determined by a calculation, which is displayed both in terms of the names of the system values and their values.

If the value being explained was obtained via a database lookup, the explanation facility responds with something like the following:

```
The MOTOR-MODEL (20HP) was determined by a database lookup. It was
found in the MODEL column of the MOTOR table. It had the LARGEST
HORSEPOWER that met the following constraints:
    HORSEPOWER > REQUIRED-MOTOR-HP (18.705574)
```

The facility reports the name of the table and the column within the table from which the value was obtained as well as what criterion was used in ordering the table. It then lists the constraints that were applied to the attributes in the table which narrowed the choice.

If the method used to calculate the value in question was selected according to a precondition, the description of the method is followed by a description of the precondition, as follows:

```
The CAR-RETURN-LEFT (25) = PLATFORM-WIDTH (70) -
                    [ OPENING-WIDTH-FRONT(42) + CAR-RETURN-RIGHT (3) ]

This particular method was used because:
[ DOOR-SPEED-FRONT = TWO ] AND [ OPENING-STRIKE-SIDE-FRONT = RIGHT ]
```

In addition, the *how* query finds possible reasons why a quantity in the system might have a value that the expert believes to be out of the ordinary, unexpected, or just plain incorrect. In VT, several kinds of "unusual" values can occur, as the following paragraphs illustrate.

- *Conflicting input values.* Some inputs to VT can come from multiple sources. If these sources specify different values, one is chosen (by applying a specified strategy), and a record is made of the event. Obviously, the choice can be incorrect, which can cause unusual values to propagate throughout the system.

- *Inconsistent input values.* This situation occurs when two input values violate an expected relationship between them. For example, inputs exist for the number of front openings, number of rear openings, and the total number of openings in an elevator shaft. Obviously, "front" plus "rear" should equal "total," but if such is not the case, a decision is made about how to make the values consistent, and a record is made of the event.

- *Unusual input values.* Some inputs have a reasonable range of values specified. A value outside the reasonable range is allowed (as long as it does not violate the absolute range) but is an indication that VT is receiving an input which is out of the ordinary. As stated earlier, this unusual value can propagate other unusual values throughout the system.

- *Default input values.* If the user chooses not to answer a particular question in the input, a default value is assigned. The chances that the default chosen is actually the correct value depends on the particular question.

- *Fixed values.* A value changed by the fix mechanism can look unusual to a user, particularly if the value changed is an input or if a low-preference fix was required.

When the user makes a *how* query about a value, unusual occurrences are reported as well:

Explain: *how hoist cable quantity*

The HOIST-CABLE-QUANTITY (4) was determined by a fix:

The MAXIMUM-MACHINE-GROOVE-PRESSURE constraint was violated. The
MACHINE-GROOVE-PRESSURE was 149.5444, but had to be <= 119. The gap of
30.544 was eliminated by the following action(s):
    Increasing HOIST-CABLE-QUANTITY from 3 to 4

Of course, it is simplifying the process of extending a design to say that a value is determined by its direct contributors or unusual decisions which directly change its value. Everything upstream in the dependency network contributes to the proposed value. The explanation facility allows the user to step back through the network by repeated questioning and provides default queries after each answer to aid in this process, as shown earlier in section 11.2. The facility also searches the upstream network on its own and in answering any *how* query reports any unusual decisions made about upstream contributors. In searching for reasons why <x> might be unusual, the explanation facility examines all the items that directly contributed to <x> as well as the items used in evaluating any preconditions on <x>'s method. This examination is recursive in that each of these contributors is also examined similarly and so on until the explanation facility grounds out on either inputs or constants.

The following example illustrates an unusual explanation; the user asks how TRACTION-RATIO was determined:

```
Explain: how traction ratio

The TRACTION-RATIO (1.796574) =
     MAX [ TRACTION-RATIO-CAR-TOP-FULL (1.759741)
           TRACTION-RATIO-CAR-BOTTOM-FULL (1.796574)
           TRACTION-RATIO-CAR-TOP-EMPTY (1.742178)
           TRACTION-RATIO-CAR-BOTTOM-EMPTY (1.696701) ]

The value for TRACTION-RATIO may be unusual because:
     (1)   The MACHINE-MODEL was changed due to a constraint on
           the HOIST-CABLE-DIAMETER.  (Depth = 3)
     (2)   The CAPACITY was an inconsistent input value.  (Depth
           = 3)
```

The depth indicates how far upstream the contributor is.

Hypothetical Reasoning

The data-driven control for the forward-chaining construction of the proposed design assumes that the dependency network built while the design was extended is a directed acyclic graph. Because of this assumption, hypothetical queries can proceed in two directions -- upstream and downstream. The two hypothetical query types -- *why not and what if* -- differ in their emphasis on what direction is of interest to the user. Thus, the answer to the query is reported differently depending on the query type. However, fixes for constraint violations can form loops in VT's line of reasoning. Downstream constraint violations can cause upstream design adjustments that can affect the node from which the query originated. Thus, when hypothesizing about a change to a node in the dependency network, the system must be run to quiescence to ensure that the reported causes or effects are taken from a consistent, acceptable design.

The *why not* query can be thought of as asking the question *"Why wasn't the value of <x> a particular value?"* This question is appropriate if the user expected (or desired) a certain value, and VT did not produce it. The explanation facility then suggests what has to be done in order to obtain the desired result. The *how* query does a search for reasons why a value might be unexpected, and the *why not* query looks for a way to bridge the gap between the system's model and that of the user.

If the user expected VT to choose a larger safety, the question "Why not safety model B4?" could be posed, which results in the following:

Explain: *why not safety model B4*

The SAFETY-MODEL (currently B1) could be B4, but that is less desirable because it has a larger HEIGHT. A SAFETY-MODEL of B1 was selected because it met the following constraints:

    Its MAX-SPEED (500) was at least as much as the SPEED (250).
    Its MAX-PLATFORM-WIDTH (93) was not less than the PLATFORM-WIDTH (70).
    Its MIN-PLATFORM-WIDTH (54) was not more than the PLATFORM-WIDTH (70).

Thus, in this case, the user's expectation is possible but not preferred. Here, the explanation facility locates all constraints in the system that constrained the safety model (including implicit constraints in database calls) and reports them.

The following case is the opposite. The suggested value is preferred but is not possible, except perhaps by changing values upstream (for example, introducing nonpreferred values elsewhere).

Explain: *why not safety model B1*

A SAFETY-MODEL of B1 would have been used (instead of B4) if:
    The PLATFORM-WIDTH were 84 instead of 86.

In order to handle this second case, VT uses knowledge that was acquired solely for the purpose of handling hypothetical queries about the value of SAFETY-MODEL. The form of the knowledge required is the same as that required for fixing designs that violate constraints. VT must have knowledge of what contributors to SAFETY-MODEL are changeable, the relative preference for possible changes, and the nature of the change in a contributor that would produce the desired difference in SAFETY-MODEL. As mentioned earlier, the system continues to completion to verify that changes made to produce the desired SAFETY- MODEL can stay in place regardless of any fixes for subsequent constraint violations. If the proposed changes cannot be incorporated into an acceptable design -- that is, some constraint violation is impossible to fix

-- this condition is reported. Otherwise, the explanation facility is poised to describe the effects of these changes in the same way it does for *what if* queries, and VT offers to display this information to the user.

The *what if* query can be thought of as asking the question *"What would happen if I changed <x> to be a particular value?"* The user then sees the impact this change would make on the system when VT lists which important system values would change. (The term "important" is predefined and is part of VT's knowledge base.) Sixty system values are currently considered to be important in this context, but usually only a relatively small subset of these 60 change in a given scenario; thus, the user is not overwhelmed by information.

Here is the *what if* explanation of the scenario that was shown for the first *why not* example:

Explain: *what if safety model B4*

The SAFETY-MODEL is currently B1.
If it were B4, the following major changes would occur:

NAME:	ACTUAL:	PROPOSED:
MACHINE-GROOVE-PRESSURE	114.118	155.563
TRACTION-RATIO	1.80679	1.76682
CWT-OVERTRAVEL	49.835	52.835
CAR-BUFFER-REACTION	26709.4	27652.4
CWT-STACK-PERCENT	84.1122	88.148
CWT-BUFFER-REACTION	19684	20627.0
CWT-PLATE-QUANTITY	90	94.3184
CWT-WEIGHT	4921.0	5156.76
CAR-BUFFER-LOAD	6677.35	6913.11
CAR-WEIGHT	3677.35	3913.11
DEFLECTOR-SHEAVE-DIAMETER	25	20
CAR-BUFFER-BLOCKING-HEIGHT	18	17.125
HOIST-CABLE-MODEL	(4).5	(3).5
CAR-RUNBY	6.125	6
SAFETY-MODEL	B1	B4

Would you like to see ALL values which would change [NO]: *<cr>*

Would you like to implement this [NO]:

If the user does wish to examine detailed information, the option is provided to see all the values that would change. The ability to implement a suggested change is provided. As was the case with the fix mechanism when run interactively, this option is provided as a way to force VT to produce nonstandard results (perhaps in response to inventory fluctuations or other transient situations).

Internally, the *why not* and *what if* queries are virtually identical. Because they both propose a value for a particular quantity, they must be able to go upstream and modify values in order to make the system consistent with the new value and then propagate the value downstream. This process is exactly what the fix mechanism follows, and in fact, these two queries effectively add a dynamic constraint to the system. As mentioned earlier, VT must have fix knowledge to go with these constraints, something which is impractical for all values that VT derives while it constructs a design. When the user asks a *why not* or *what if* query about a value that VT has no fix knowledge for, the user is so warned. The *what if* report might still be of interest, but it is then up to the user to verify upstream consistency.

11.3.3. SALT: A Look at Knowledge Acquisition

VT's problem-solving strategy imposes an organization on the system's knowledge that can be exploited for knowledge acquisition. Given the assumed propose-and-revise strategy, domain-specific knowledge must perform one of three roles with respect to the problem solver: (1) PROPOSE-A-DESIGN-EXTENSION, (2) IDENTIFY-A-CONSTRAINT on a design extension, or (3) PROPOSE-A-FIX for a constraint violation. A representation scheme for a domain-specific knowledge base such as VT's should recognize these roles and the interdependencies among them. Understanding knowledge roles and relationships is crucial to acquisition and maintenance of the knowledge base and provides the key to how and when the knowledge should be used by the problem solver.

SALT is an automated knowledge-acquisition tool that assumes the systems it generates will use a propose-and-revise problem-solving strategy. SALT acquires knowledge from an expert and generates a domain-specific knowledge base compiled into rules. This compiled knowledge base is then combined with a problem-solving shell to create an expert system. SALT maintains a permanent, declarative store of the knowledge base which is updated during interviews with the domain expert and which is the input to the compiler, or rule-generator. This intermediate representation language seeks to make the function of domain knowledge explicit.

As with CONSTRAINTS, SALT's representation scheme is built around the framework of a dependency network. For SALT, each node in the network is the name of a value; this name can be that of an input, a design parameter, or a constraint. Three kinds of directed links represent relations between nodes: (1) "contributes-to" links A to B if the value of A is used in a procedure to specify a value for B; (2) "constrains" links A to B if A is the name of a constraint and B is the name of a design parameter, and the value of A places some restriction on the value of B; (3) "suggests-revision-of" links A to B if A is the name of a constraint, and a violation of A suggests a change to the currently proposed value of

B. Each of these links is supported by additional information in the knowledge base: (1) contributes-to links are supported by details of how contributors are combined to specify the value of the node pointed to; (2) constrains links are supported by a specification of the nature of the restriction; and (3) suggests-revision-of links are supported by a declaration of the nature of the proposed revision (for example, direction and amount of change) and its relative preference.

For SALT, the knowledge-acquisition task becomes one of fleshing out the knowledge base using these representational primitives. SALT allows users to enter knowledge piecemeal starting at any point. The grain size of the pieces corresponds roughly to the three knowledge roles for the propose-and-revise strategy: Users can supply a procedure for specifying a parameter value, identify a constraint on a parameter value, or suggest a remedy for a constraint violation. SALT keeps track of how the pieces are fitting together and warns the user of places where pieces might be missing or creating inconsistencies.

SALT users must first specify which of the three roles each piece of entered knowledge plays. Once this choice is made, SALT presents a set of prompts for the detailed knowledge required by this role. For example, a filled-in schema for PROPOSE-A-DESIGN-EXTENSION for CAR-RETURN-LEFT follows; SALT prompts appear on the left and user responses on the right:

```
Name:                CAR-RETURN-LEFT
Precondition:        [ DOOR-SPEED-FRONT = TWO ] AND
                     [ OPENING-STRIKE-SIDE-FRONT =   RIGHT ]
Procedure Type:      CALCULATION
Formula:             PLATFORM-WIDTH - OPENING-WIDTH-FRONT +
                     CAR-RETURN-RIGHT
```

The IDENTIFY-A-CONSTRAINT schema prompts for similar information to acquire a procedure for determining a value (or values in the case of a set constraint) for the constraint. In addition, the schema requires the user to specify what parameter is constrained and what kind of constraint it is (for example, a maximum).

Collection of information to direct backtracking is also highly structured. Each piece of PROPOSE-A-FIX knowledge is a proposal for remedying the violation of a particular constraint by changing one of the decisions made while extending a design. Procedures used in the forward-chaining portion of extending a design produce values the expert would prefer in an underconstrained case. Associated with the potential fixes is some reason why they are less preferred than the originally proposed value. The reasons are drawn from the following list:

```
 1.  Causes no problem
 2.  Increases maintenance requirements
 3.  Makes installation difficult
 4.  Changes minor equipment sizing
 5.  Violates minor equipment constraint
 6.  Changes minor contract specifications
 7.  Requires special part design
 8.  Changes major equipment sizing
 9.  Changes the building dimensions
10.  Changes major contract specifications
11.  Increases maintenance costs
12.  Compromises system performance
```

These effects are ordered from most to least preferred. The reasons mainly reflect concerns for safety and customer satisfaction as well as dollar cost to the company. Relative position on this scale is significant, but absolute position is not. When more than one fix is suggested to remedy a particular constraint violation, the most preferred fix of those suggested is attempted first.

In addition, the domain expert must indicate the kind of change that should be made. This indication can be a perturbation of whatever the current value is, or it can entail a change that doesn't reference the current value, such as the substitution of some other system value. An example of a filled-in schema for a fix for MAXIMUM-MACHINE-GROOVE- PRESSURE is shown as follows:

```
Constraint Name:      MAXIMUM-MACHINE-GROOVE-PRESSURE
Value to Change:      HOIST-CABLE-QUANTITY
Change Type:          INCREASE
Step Type:            BY-STEP
Step Size:            1
Preference Rating:    4
Preference Reason:    CHANGES MINOR EQUIPMENT SIZING
```

In addition to providing a language for representing domain-specific knowledge, SALT analyzes the knowledge base and guides the user's input to ensure that the knowledge base is complete and consistent. SALT's overall design and operation are described in more detail elsewhere [8, 9]. The next section describes an analysis SALT provides to test any knowledge base it collects for adequacy with respect to the problem-solving method it assumes.

11.4. MANAGEMENT OF KNOWLEDGE-BASED BACKTRACKING

The kind of domain-specific information that SALT initially collects to direct backtracking is relatively easy to supply because the expert can focus on one constraint violation at a time. However, a search that relies solely on this local information and ignores potential interactions among fixes for different constraint violations can run into trouble. One naive way to ensure that a system that uses backtracking converges on a solution, if one exists, is to open the search completely and try every possible combination of values for every potential fix before announcing failure. This solution is not practical for domains that have any significant amount of complexity, such as VT's domain. VT can currently encounter 52 different constraint violations. Most constraint violations (37 of 52) have only one fix -- one parameter that might be revised. However, typically there are several or many alternative values a parameter might assume. This case also exists for the remaining constraints with multiple fixes; 10 have two fixes each, 3 have three fixes, and 2 have four potential fixes, with multiple possible instantiations for each fix. A blind search that considered all possible combinations of these fixes would have a potentially large search space. In fact, it might be unnecessarily large because it might not be the case that every fix interacts with every other.

SALT helps manage knowledge-based backtracking by mapping out potential interactions among fixes for different constraint violations. A developer can then examine cases of interacting fixes for their potential to cause trouble for convergence on a solution. Nonproblematic fixes can be handled using local information only. This treatment ignores potential interactions among fixes for different constraints. Trouble spots are treated as special cases that take into account global information.

11.4.1. VT's Local Treatment and Its Trouble Spots

In the local treatment, deciding which upstream value is to be modified is conditioned on individual constraint violations. Potential fixes considered are only those which the domain expert identified as relevant to the current violation, and these are selected in order of the expert's preference. Until a remedy is found for this violation, all possible combinations of these constraint-specific remedies are tried. If the system reaches a dead end -- that is, none of these combinations remedy the local constraint violation, the system announces that there is no possible solution. If fixes for one constraint violation have no effect on other constraint violations, this strategy guarantees that the first solution found is the most preferred and that the system correctly reports failure if no successful fix is found for an individual constraint.

However, it is possible that remedies selected for one constraint violation might aggravate constraint violations that occur further downstream. In some instances, this situation can result in failure to find a solution when one does exist.[3] In these cases, a fix that appears optimal based on local information would not be preferred if more were known about the search space.

For example, the most preferred fix for one constraint violation might aggravate a downstream constraint violation to such a degree that it reaches a dead end when exploring its own fixes. If less preferred fixes for the first constraint do not have the same negative effect downstream, then a solution might be possible. The undesired behavior of the system in this case would be a premature announcement of failure.

Another potential problem is that unproductive looping can occur between fixes for two constraint violations if each has a preferred fix with a counteracting effect on the other. This situation occurs, for example, if fixing one constraint violation increases a certain value that leads to the violation of another constraint whose fix results in decreasing the same value, and so on. Repeated violations of the same constraint are not necessarily pernicious, but such a case of antagonistic constraints might result in an infinite loop.

SALT provides a mapping of the interactions among fixes in a knowledge base. It does this mapping using its understanding of dependencies among procedures for extending a design plus identification of constraints and fixes. We used this map to analyze VT's knowledge base for its potential to get into trouble with a local, constraint-specific search. We then hand coded a special case treatment for the problem spots we found. We plan to automate this entire process in SALT.

11.4.2. VT's Fix Interactions and Their Special Handling

The VT knowledge base contains 37 chains of interacting fixes. Eleven of these chains are short and nonproblematic. The rest represent different entry points for loops on 8 constraints. Two of these looping constraints represent no danger for the local treatment. Three pairs of constraints might cause thrashing under the local treatment and are treated as special cases in VT.

---

[3]A related but less serious problem is that a remedy not chosen might have an ameliorating effect on a downstream constraint violation. In such a case, the system might miss a solution in which the total cost of fixing the two violations might be less if a more costly fix were chosen for the first.

The 11 short chains each involve at most three constraints and the effects of only one fix per constraint. The most common scenario for these chains is that when a constraint violation causes one piece of equipment to be upgraded (or increased in size), the values of constraints on related equipment are affected and might require that the related equipment be upgraded as well. For example, if the number of hoist cables needed for a job exceeds the maximum allowable for the machine model selected, the fix is to choose a larger machine that can accommodate more cables. The machine model's specifications limit what machine sheave heights it can be used with; larger machines require larger machine sheaves. If the current machine sheave is too small for the newly upgraded machine model, a larger machine sheave (the smallest one that meets constraints) is substituted.

The situation involving the two nonproblematic looping constraints, CHOICE-SET-HOIST-CABLE-QUANTITY and CHOICE-SET-HOIST-CABLE-DIAMETER, also involves a rippling effect of upgrading equipment. Most of the equipment selection in VT depends on the weight of other components selected. The hoist cable quantity and diameter depend on hoist cable quantity and diameter (that is, they must be able to support their own weight) as well as properties of other parts that require knowledge of hoist cable quantity and diameter in their selection. The VT strategy estimates the lowest acceptable value for hoist cable quantity and diameter using rough criteria, selects other parts using these estimates, and derives from these estimates a constraint on the quantity and diameter that must be used. If the value of the constraint does not match the initial estimate, quantity and diameter are increased. Violations of other constraints on the system derived from this major equipment selection, such as the MAXIMUM-MACHINE-GROOVE-PRESSURE shown earlier, also call for changing hoist cable quantity or diameter but always in the direction of increasing the values. Furthermore, the VT knowledge base also contains knowledge of MAXIMUM-HOIST-CABLE-QUANTITY and MAXIMUM-HOIST-CABLE-DIAMETER. (SALT asked for this information when fixes were entered that called for increasing the quantity and diameter.) Thus, this loop does not present the danger of infinitely looping. Because the values start at the lowest possible point and always increase until the maximums are reached, the system does not thrash.

Three cases, however, might result in infinite loops under the local treatment. These cases contain a pair of antagonistic constraints that might cause thrashing. A local treatment of one of these constraints, MAXIMUM-MACHINE-GROOVE-PRESSURE, was described earlier. Its antagonistic constraint is MAXIMUM-TRACTION-RATIO. The complete set of potential fixes for each of these follows:

IF   there has been a violation of MAXIMUM-TRACTION-RATIO,

THEN   Try a DECREASE BY-STEP of 1 inch of CWT-TO-PLATFORM-DISTANCE
          which has a preference rating of 1 because it CAUSES NO
          PROBLEM.

          Try an UPGRADE of COMP-CABLE-UNIT-WEIGHT which has a preference
          rating of 4 because it CHANGES MINOR EQUIPMENT SIZING.

          Try an INCREASE BY-STEP of 100 lbs. of CAR-SUPPLEMENT-WEIGHT
          which has a preference rating of 4 because it
          CHANGES MINOR EQUIPMENT SIZING.

          Try an UPGRADE for MACHINE-GROOVE-MODEL which has a preference
          rating of 11 because it INCREASES MAINTENANCE COSTS.

IF   there has been a violation of MAXIMUM-MACHINE-GROOVE-PRESSURE,

THEN   Try a DOWNGRADE for MACHINE-GROOVE-MODEL which has a preference
          rating of 1 because it CAUSES NO PROBLEM.

          Try an INCREASE BY-STEP of 1 of HOIST-CABLE-QUANTITY which has a
          preference rating of 4 because it CHANGES MINOR
          EQUIPMENT SIZING.

          Try a DOWNGRADE of COMP-CABLE-UNIT-WEIGHT which has a preference
          rating of 4 because it CHANGES MINOR EQUIPMENT SIZING.

          Try a DECREASE BY-STEP of 10 lbs. of CAR-SUPPLEMENT-WEIGHT
          which has a preference rating of 4 because it CHANGES MINOR
          EQUIPMENT SIZING.

Figure 11-2 shows the relevant segment of the VT knowledge base as SALT represents it. Constraints are connected to the values they constrain by the dotted arrows at the bottom. Above these arrows is the portion of the dependency network that links the constraint-constrained pairs to their potential fix values. Contributors are linked to the values they contribute to by a solid arrow. In order to make the figure readable, not all contributors are shown. In addition, suggests-revision-of links are not shown as arrows. Instead, suggested revisions in response to a violation of MAXIMUM-MACHINE-GROOVE-PRESSURE are surrounded by rectangles, and suggested revisions for violations of MAXIMUM-TRACTION-RATIO are enclosed in ovals.

One scenario can illustrate the potential for thrashing in this part of the network. This scenario uses the knowledge shown in Figure 11-2 plus information supporting the links, including formulas for combining contributors, the nature of constraints, and the suggested direction of revisions. Suppose MAXIMUM-TRACTION-RATIO is violated, and VT responds by increasing CAR-SUPPLEMENT-WEIGHT. This situation increases CAR- WEIGHT, which, in

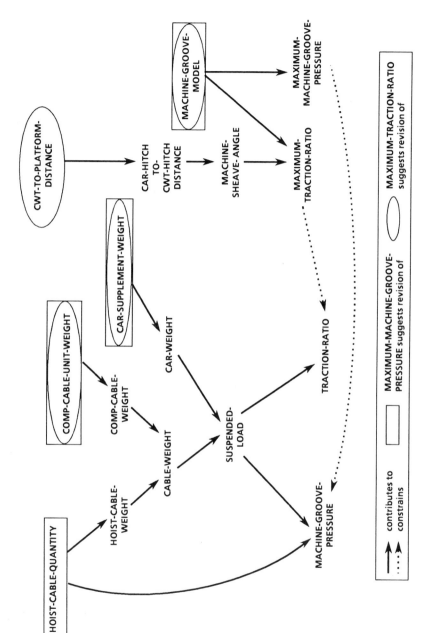

Figure 11-2: Segment of VT Knowledge Base Containing Antagonistic Constraints

turn, increases SUPPORTED-LOADS. This condition decreases TRACTION-RATIO but increases MACHINE-GROOVE-PRESSURE. An increase in MACHINE-GROOVE-PRESSURE makes it likely for it to exceed its maximum. A violation of MAXIMUM-MACHINE-GROOVE-PRESSURE could call for a decrease of COMP-CABLE-UNIT-WEIGHT, which, in turn, would decrease COMP-CABLE-WEIGHT, CABLE-WEIGHT and SUPPORTED-LOADS. Decreasing SUPPORTED-LOADS increases TRACTION-RATIO making it more likely to violate MAXIMUM-TRACTION-RATIO. At this point, the scenario could repeat itself.

SALT analyzes the knowledge base for scenarios such as this one and produces messages such as the following:

```
*
MAXIMUM TRACTION RATIO ------------------------------------------------|
*                                                                      |
        (CWT TO PLATFORM DISTANCE, Down)                               |
                                                                       |
        (COMP CABLE UNIT WEIGHT, Up)                                   |
                MAXIMUM MACHINE GROOVE PRESSURE                        |
                        (MACHINE GROOVE MODEL, Down)----** LOOP **-----|
                        (HOIST CABLE QUANTITY, Up)                     |
                        (COMP CABLE UNIT WEIGHT, Down)--** LOOP **-----|
                        (CAR SUPPLEMENT WEIGHT, Down)---** LOOP **-----|
                                                                       |
        (CAR SUPPLEMENT WEIGHT, Up)                                    |
                MAXIMUM MACHINE GROOVE PRESSURE                        |
                        (MACHINE GROOVE MODEL, Down)----** LOOP **-----|
                        (HOIST CABLE QUANTITY, Up)                     |
                        (COMP CABLE UNIT WEIGHT, Down)--** LOOP **-----|
                        (CAR SUPPLEMENT WEIGHT, Down)---** LOOP **-----|
                                                                       |
        (MACHINE GROOVE MODEL, Up)                                     |
                MAXIMUM MACHINE GROOVE PRESSURE                        |
                        (MACHINE GROOVE MODEL, Down)----** LOOP **-----|
                        (HOIST CABLE QUANTITY, Up)                     |
                        (COMP CABLE UNIT WEIGHT, Down)--** LOOP **-----|
                        (CAR SUPPLEMENT WEIGHT, Down)---** LOOP **-----|
```

The top leftmost constraint, MAXIMUM-TRACTION-RATIO, is an arbitrary starting point. Potential fixes for its violation appear in parentheses and indented one level. The suggested changes to three of these values -- MACHINE-GROOVE-MODEL, COMP-CABLE-UNIT-WEIGHT, and CAR-SUPPLEMENT-WEIGHT -- would make violation of MAXIMUM-MACHINE-GROOVE-PRESSURE more likely, as indicated by its appearance indented below these fixes. Violation of MAXIMUM-MACHINE-GROOVE-PRESSURE, in turn, could call for changes to these same three fix values. The LOOP flags indicate that these changes might make a violation of MAXIMUM-TRACTION-RATIO more likely. As shown by a lack of nesting, decreasing the CWT-TO-PLATFORM-DISTANCE to fix MAXIMUM-TRACTION-RATIO does not affect MACHINE-GROOVE-PRESSURE or its maximum. Adding hoist cables to fix MAXIMUM-MACHINE-GROOVE-PRESSURE tends to relieve a problem with MAXIMUM-TRACTION-RATIO, although the effect is not substantial enough to warrant its inclusion as a fix for this constraint. As long as only one of the two constraints is violated, the local search for a solution based on isolated constraint violations is satisfactory. However, if both constraints are violated, the system might thrash. We added to the VT shell the ability to treat this latter situation as a special case and investigate fixes for the two in tandem. To do this investigation, VT required one additional piece of information. If both constraints cannot be remedied at the same time, our domain expert relaxes MAXIMUM-MACHINE-GROOVE-PRESSURE before violating MAXIMUM-TRACTION-RATIO. If both cannot be fixed, VT tries to minimize the violation of MAXIMUM-MACHINE-GROOVE-PRESSURE without violating MAXIMUM-TRACTION-RATIO.

Whenever a demon detects a violation of one of these constraints, VT checks to see if the other has been violated. If it has, it resets the values of all potential fix values to the last value they had before the first violation of either constraint. It then tries out potential fixes, making sure that it does not repeat a combination of them, in the following order according to whether the fix: (1) helps both, (2) helps one and doesn't hurt the other, or (3) helps one but does hurt the other. In the third case, the system applies the fix in the direction intended to remedy the constraint most important to fix. If there is asymmetry in the amount of change in a bidirectional fix, as there was for CAR-SUPPLEMENT-WEIGHT discussed earlier, after fixing the most desired constraint, VT changes the value in the other direction by the largest amount that still leaves the first constraint unviolated.

Nowhere in the VT knowledge base did we observe a problem that might cause the declaration of a premature dead end. In most cases, a failure report cannot be premature because the fixes that cause downstream violations are the only possible fix at their point of origin. Thus, any dead end observed at the aggravated downstream point is unavoidable. This situation is true for hoist cable quantity and diameter. For the other cases, the aggravating fix is the most expensive alternative for its constraint violation and won't be implemented unless nothing else works at this point. Again, this situation means that any dead end downstream would be unavoidable.

If we had identified a chain of interacting fixes that might result in premature dead end, it would have been relatively simple to provide a customized treatment for the potential site of the dead end. The VT shell could be modified so that whenever a dead end were found for such a constraint violation, VT would go back and try more expensive fixes at the relevant prior constraint violation(s). SALT's map of interacting fixes could be used to identify the relevant prior fixes.

For VT then, SALT's analysis located cases in which fixes for different constraints interacted. Our examination showed in most cases the propagation of changes was such that a search based on fixing one constraint at a time would either converge on a solution or correctly announce that no solution was possible. In three cases involving pairs of constraints, the system might thrash if constraint violations were fixed independently; so, additional knowledge was used to deal with the interacting constraint violations in combination.

Domain knowledge is needed to specify what revisions are possible in the real world and what their relative desirability is for fixing particular constraints. As a first step, SALT asks the domain expert to address each constraint violation individually. The form of the query relieves the expert from having to anticipate the ramifications for the rest of the design -- something that is difficult for a person to do in a complex domain. SALT can help decide whether this approach is adequate for a problem solver because it has access to the entire knowledge base and because its representation of the knowledge base makes clear how the knowledge is to be used. In the case of VT, a search space with hidden mine fields for a locally based search was much more manageable when supplemented with analysis-based special case treatment. The particular solutions to knowledge base inadequacies used in VT might not be sufficient for all constraint-satisfaction tasks. However, SALT's representation scheme and analyses still help in addressing inadequacies because they make obvious the ramifications of problem-solving decisions with a given knowledge base. Thus, they can identify the need for additional knowledge and identify considerations that should go into deciding how and when knowledge should be used [cf. [10, 18]].

11.5. COMPARISON TO OTHER CONSTRUCTIVE SYSTEMS

The ordering of decisions in VT is in the spirit of the Expert Executive for aerospace vehicle design described in [2]. The Expert Executive knows the inputs required and outputs produced by each of the procedures, or programs, it must configure. A program is run only when all other programs have been run whose outputs serve as its inputs. Unlike VT, the Expert Executive and the programs it configures are intended to be a design aid rather than a design expert. The Expert Executive and program configurations leave to the human expert the task of suggesting plausible starting values for free parameters, checking constraints, and directing revisions. VT performs these functions as well.

VT's architecture is probably most similar to that of EL, an expert system which performs analysis of electric circuits. EL makes a guess for, say, the current at a particular node and uses principles such as Ohm's Law and Kirchoff's

Law to propose values at other points in the circuit. It is similar to VT in that it builds up a dependency network representing this propagation, backtracks whenever constraints are violated (when some point is assigned two different values), and uses a truth maintenance system. The main difference between EL and VT is that EL uses a domain-independent strategy of dependency-directed backtracking as opposed to VT's domain-specific knowledge-based approach. EL's decision of where to backtrack to is based solely on the dependency network's record of what guesses contributed to the conflicting constraints. Furthermore, EL is committed to a search that tries all possible combinations of all guesses, although it prevents thrashing by keeping track of combinations already tried and never repeating a combination. The related CONSTRAINTS language allows the user to direct backtracking and is similar to VT when running in interactive mode or performing what-if explanation.

Domain-independent dependency-directed backtracking is not satisfactory for VT's domain. VT is not simply searching for a single solution that meets constraints, where any solution is equally good. Generally, many possible solutions exist, and these solutions differ in domain-specific disadvantages. These differences are expressed in VT by using the expert's most preferred procedure to determine an initial value and using explicit preferences supplied by the expert on potential fixes for constraint violations.

GARI [4] does incorporate a notion of domain-specific preference in its plausible reasoning but in an indirect and difficult to maintain manner. GARI's task is to devise a plan for machining parts that meets constraints on the order in which operations should be performed and the orientation of parts with respect to the machining tools. It employs backtracking whenever constraints conflict, and the decision about what point to backtrack to is determined by weights taken from domain experts. GARI backtracks to its most recent, lowest- weight decision. GARI does not use a dependency network or any relation of contribution in this decision. The result is that the decision it changes might be irrelevant to the constraint conflict which has arisen. In addition, although the weights are taken from domain experts, the designers note that the experts find the weights difficult to assign and that afterwards, knowledge engineers must adjust these weights by experimentation. This process must be particularly difficult because these weights might have evolved to express both a combination of expense in terms of material, equipment cost, and so on, and of their likelihood to converge on a solution.

Two other design systems, AIR-CYL (Chapter 7) and PRIDE (Chapter 9), use a knowledge-based approach to revising designs in response to constraint violations but differ somewhat from VT in the knowledge used. AIR-CYL has failure handlers that respond to constraint violations by calling for redesign of particular parts, or values, of the design. If more than one value might be revised, AIR-CYL uses a least backup strategy; it attempts revision at the most recently established relevant value. AIR-CYL moves back to the next most recently established only if it fails to remedy the violation at the current point, and so on. Brown wants to restrict the range of backtracking on the grounds that this is what human design experts do. PRIDE also uses domain expertise to suggest how to revise parts of the design in response to constraint violations. For PRIDE, the presence of more than one suggestion about how to respond to a particular constraint violation causes the system to set up multiple contexts for exploring each suggestion. The PRIDE user can then select among alternatives. VT explores design revisions sequentially. In interactive mode, users can determine the order in which revisions are explored and can suggest revisions of their own. In the absence of user input, VT has domain expertise regarding the preference of alternative fixes that it uses to decide the order in which it explores them.

R1 [11] is a system that constructs a solution but uses a strategy for plausible reasoning which might be described as lookaround. Whenever a decision based on partial information is required, R1 tries to collect as much information as it can to ensure that the decision is acceptable. The kind of information it collects might be the same kind of information that could be used to augment fix knowledge, that is, information about how close the current solution is to violating related constraints. Without the kind of dependency network representation that VT/SALT uses, it is difficult to identify the role of this information. R1 is currently being revised to more clearly represent the roles that knowledge plays with respect to its own problem-solving method [21]. This revision should make it easier to compare the two systems.

As mentioned at the outset, VT does postpone decisions where possible, but most of its effort goes into plausible guessing combined with backtracking. This system contrasts with MOLGEN whose main effort is put into managing its least commitment planning. Although MOLGEN has the ability to backtrack, its guessing and backtracking capability is underdeveloped, and MOLGEN often does not recover from bad guesses [16].

ISIS [7, 13] is another constraint-satisfaction planner that uses least commitment in job shop scheduling. ISIS expresses preferences as constraints. When forced to guess, that is, to choose among constraints it will meet when it can't meet all of them, ISIS conducts a beam search by maintaining in parallel the most preferred solutions. If a solution is not found by scheduling in the forward direction, that is, from first operation in time to last, then a second attempt is made starting from the last operation. The efficiency and probability of the search's success depends on the weights assigned to the constraints and the width of the beam. As with GARI, this architecture can lead to a difficult problem in credit assignment.

MOLGEN, ISIS, AIR-CYL, and PRIDE share the property of being hierarchical in that they select a meta-level plan or design and then refine it. In Friedland's version of MOLGEN especially, selecting which metalevel plan to refine involves a great deal of search [3]. Although solution paths for extending a design for an elevator can differ depending on input parameters, these path differences are represented in VT as preconditions on individual steps. Nowhere are the path differences represented as separate metalevel designs. In the hierarchical planners, an abstract, metalevel design also serves to split the task into nearly independent subproblems. Interactions take the form of constraints that propagate from one subproblem to others. VT does not have a subtask level of organization to group procedures for extending a design and specifying constraints. One benefit of a subdivided architecture might be that it helps the system builders keep track of interactions among decisions. SALT's knowledge representation and the analysis it does based on the anticipated problem-solving strategy serves this function for VT (See also [10]).

11.6. VT'S PERFORMANCE

VT is an expert system slated to do real work in industry. It must function with a large knowledge base and converge on an acceptable solution within a reasonable amount of time. This section provides a description of its size and some indication of its performance characteristics.

11.6.1. Rule Characteristics

Because VT is implemented in OPS5 [6], it is appropriate to describe its size and complexity in terms of rules. VT currently has 3123 total rules. Of these, 2191 are domain-specific rules generated by SALT (70.2 percent). The remainder belong to the general shell for I/O, explanation, and problem solving control. There are several types of SALT-generated rules. Some are not directly used in problem- solving. These 698 rules (31.9percent of all SALT-generated rules) contain domain-specific information required for I/O and the explanation facility. The remaining 1393 SALT-generated rules break down into the following categories:

- 521 (23.8 percent) are forward-chaining rules for proposing a part of the elevator design.

- 120 (5.5 percent) are forward-chaining rules for specifying constraints on the design.

- 58 (2.7 percent) are rules for proposing potential fixes conditioned on the violation of particular constraints.

- 44 (2.0 percent) are rules for directing exploration of the implications of a fix (lookahead).

- 530 (24.2 percent) are lookahead rules for extending a design.

- 120 (5.5 percent) are lookahead rules for specifying constraints.

These rules represent procedures derived from the knowledge SALT collects in its three knowledge roles. The first three rule types make use of the knowledge in the roles of PROPOSE-A-DESIGN-EXTENSION, IDENTIFY-A-CONSTRAINT, and PROPOSE-A-FIX, respectively. The next group, rules for directing lookahead, define which procedures for proposing design extensions and identifying constraints are relevant to deciding whether proposed fixes actually remedy the constraint violation they are intended to fix. The last two categories employ the same knowledge encoded in the first two groups, PROPOSE-A-DESIGN-EXTENSION and IDENTIFY-A-CONSTRAINT. They differ from the first two in that the conditions under which they fire are set up by the rules that direct the lookahead. They are used to selectively explore implications of proposed fixes before choosing one to implement. Table 11-1 gives an impression of rule complexity in each of these categories.

Table 11-1: Rule Complexity

Rule Type	Condition Elements	Attributes per CE	Action Elements
Extend a design	3.74	2.06	3.48
Identify a constraint	3.42	2.03	3.74
Propose a fix	2.24	3.31	1.07
Direct to lookahead	1.00	1.00	5.36
Extend an exploratory design	5.31	1.99	3.23
Identify an exploratory constraint	5.39	1.94	3.29

11.6.2. Run Characteristics

Statistics reported here are based on a sample of six test cases that Westinghouse engineers feel are representative of the range of complexity which VT must handle. A breakdown of these cases on measures that reflect search complexity is given in Table 11-2. All constraint violations are fixed on these runs; that is, there are no dead ends.

Table 11-2: Complexity Measures On Test Case Runs

	Case 1	Case 2	Case 3	Case 4	Case 5	Case 6
Distinct constraints violated	7	8	8	12	9	12
Total constraint violations	9	9	12	16	17	23
Fixes explored per constraint violation	1.0	1.3	1.0	1.4	1.2	1.3
Nonconstraint values "undone" per implemented fix	18.9	25.7	26.0	33.7	29.6	40.4
Constraints "undone" per implemented fix	3.4	3.9	4.2	12.6	11.2	11.0

The breakdown of rule firings shown in Table 11-3 helps to give an idea of where the activity is focused during a run. The breakdown for these jobs in CPU time, as measured on a VAX 11/780 with 20MB of memory, is shown in Table 11-4.

11.7. CONCLUSION

VT is an expert system whose domain requires plausible guessing. Its problem-solving strategy incrementally constructs an approximate elevator design by proposing values for design parameters. At the same time, it identifies constraints on design parameters. If a constraint is violated, VT uses domain expertise to figure out how to revise the proposed design. In doing so, it uses an architecture that makes clear the role that each piece of domain-specific knowledge plays in proposing, constraining, and revising solutions. This

Table 11-3: Rule Firings Per Run

	Case 1	Case 2	Case 3	Case 4	Case 5	Case 6
SALT-Generated Rules						
Extend a design	821	868	1050	1777	1358	2545
Identify a constraint	239	227	268	360	405	627
Propose a fix	9	9	12	16	17	23
Direct to lookahead	9	11	9	28	27	25
Extend an exploratory design	57	93	52	378	237	356
Identify an exploratory constraint	5	9	5	6	19	18
Subtotal	1140	1217	1396	2565	2063	3594
General Control Rules						
Test a constraint	147	147	189	232	250	422
Control a fix	472	592	594	1393	1251	1664
Maintain consistency	831	1074	1422	2886	2570	4732
Other	222	372	308	806	726	862
Subtotal:	1672	2185	2513	5317	4797	7680
Total	2812	3402	3909	7882	6860	11274

knowledge representation serves as the basis for VT's explanation facility that can both explain past decisions and hypothesize about alternative solutions. It is also the foundation of an automated knowledge-acquisition tool, SALT, that can be used to generate expert systems that use this problem-solving strategy and explanation facility. SALT was used to acquire the knowledge for and to generate the system described here as well as to map out potential interactions among fixes. This analysis helps a developer assess the potential for the system to converge on a solution if one exists. Trouble spots located by this analysis can be given special treatment in the backtracking search. In the future we plan to continue our exploration of the use of knowledge-based backtracking through the use of SALT as a tool to acquire the knowledge for other types of constructive tasks.

Table 11-4: CPU Time Per Run

	Case 1	Case 2	Case 3	Case 4	Case 5	Case 6
Time in forward-chaining mode	4:52	4:17	6:23	7:10	7:19	10:40
Time in fix-exploration mode	2:16	2:53	3:32	8:39	7:26	11:09
Total time per run	7:08	7:10	9:55	15:49	14:45	21:49

11.8. ACKNOWLEDGMENTS

This paper was first published in the Winter 1987 issue of AI Magazine, a publication of the American Association for Artificial Intelligence. It is reprinted here by the permission of the publisher.

This research was sponsored by Westinghouse Elevator Company, Randolph, New Jersey. The views and conclusions contained in this document are those of the authors and should not be interpreted as representing the official policies, either expressed or implied, of Westinghouse Elevator Company. Many people have helped with VT's development. We would especially like to thank John Gabrick, Michael Gillinov, Robert Roche, Timothy Thompson, Tianran Wang, and George Wood.

11.9. BIBLIOGRAPHY

[1]   Brown, D., "Failure Handling in a Design Expert System," *Computer-Aided Design*, Vol. 17, pp. 436-441, 1985.

[2]   Chalfan, K. M., "A Knowledge System that Integrates Heterogeneous Software for a Design Application," *AI Magazine,* Vol. 7, pp. 80-84, 1986.

[3]   Cohen, P. and Feigenbaum, E., *The Handbook of Artificial Intelligence*, Vol. 3, William Kaufmann Inc., Los Altos, California, 1982.

[4]   Descotte, Y. and Latombe, J.C., "Making Compromises among Antogonist Constraints in a Planner," *Artificial Intelligence*, pp. 183-217, 1985.

[5]   Doyle, J., "A Truth Maintenance System," *Artificial Intelligence*, Vol. 12, pp. 231-272, 1979.

[6]   Forgy, C. L., *OPS5 User's Manual*, Technical Report CMU-CS-81-135, Carnegie-Mellon University, July 1981.

[7]   Fox, M., *Constraint-directed Search: A Case Study of Job-shop Scheduling*, CMU-CS-83-161, Carnegie Mellon University, Department of Computer Science, 1983.

[8]   Marcus, S., McDermott, J., and Wang, T., "Knowledge Acquisition for Constructive Systems," *Proceedings of the Ninth IJCAI*, Morgan Kaufmann Publishers, Inc., pp. 637-639, 1985.

[9]   Marcus, S. and McDermott, J., *SALT: A Knowledge Acquisition Tool for Propose-And-Revise Systems*, Technical Report, Carnegie Mellon University, Department of Computer Science, 1986.

[10]   Marcus, S., "Understanding Subtasks from a Piecemeal Collection of Knowledge," *Proceedings of the 1988 AAAI Workshop on Knowledge Acquisition for Knowledge-Based Systems*, Kluwer Publishers, 1988.

[11]   McDermott, J., "R1: A Rule-Based Configurer of Computer Systems," *Artificial Intelligence*, Vol. 19, pp. 39-88, 1982.

[12]   Mittal, S., and Araya, A., "A Knowledge-based Framework for Design," *Proceedings of the Fifth National Conference on Artificial Intelligence*, Morgan Kaufman Publishers, Inc., pp. 856-865, 1986.

[13]   Smith, S., Fox, M., and Ow, P., "Constructing and Maintaining Detailed Production Plans: Investigations into the Development of Knowledge-based Factory Scheduling Systems," *AI Magazine*, Vol. 7, pp. 45-60, 1986.

[14]   Stallman, R., and Sussman, G. J., "Forward Reasoning and Dependency-directed Backtracking in a System for Computer-Aided Circuit Analysis," *Artificial Intelligence*, Vol. 9, pp. 135-196, 1977.

[15]   Stefik, M., "Planning with Constraints (MOLGEN 1)," *Artificial Intelligence*, Vol. 16, pp. 111-140, 1981.

[16]   Stefik, M., "Planning with Constraints (MOLGEN 2)," *Artificial Intelligence*, Vol. 16, pp. 141-170, 1981.

[17]   Stefik, M. et al., "The Architecture of Expert Systems," in *Building Expert Systems*, Hayes-Roth, F., Waterman, D. A., and Lenat, D. B., Ed., Addison-Wesley Publishing Company, Inc., pp. 89-126, 1983.

[18]   Stout, J., Caplain, G., Marcus, S., and McDermott, J., "Toward Automating Recognition of Differing Problem-Solving Demands," *International Journal of Man-Machine Studies,* Vol. 29, pp. 599-611, 1988.

[19]   Sussman, G. J., "Electrical Design: A Problem for Artificial Intelligence Research," *Proceedings Fifth IJCAI*, pp. 894-900, 1977.

[20]   Sussman, G. J. and Steel Jr., G. L., "CONSTRAINTS - A Language for Expressing Almost-Hierarchical Descriptions," *Artificial Intelligence,* Vol. 14, pp. 1-39, 1980.

[21]   van de Brug, A., Bachant, J. and McDermott, J., "The Taming of R1," *IEEE Expert,* Vol. 1, pp. 1986, 33-38.

Chapter 12
A DESIGN PROCESS MODEL

Forrest D. Brewer and Daniel D. Gajski

Abstract

This paper describes an expert-system paradigm for design of complex VLSI systems. The paradigm allows iterative refinement of behavioral specifications to completed designs. The methodology describes how closed-loop execution and evaluation of the design is achieved using a simple 'Knob' and 'Gauge' approach. In particular the paradigm can be used for design of expert systems which control procedural layout generators and silicon compilers.

12.1. INTRODUCTION

In the past, the design process was carried out completely manually. As each level of the design was completed, it became a specification for the lower levels of the design. These lower levels were designed to fit the downwardly imposed design constraints and the upward physical constraints from their own design components. Failure in one or another level of design resulted in either redesign of that level or relaxation of the imposed constraints by redesign of a higher level of the design. The advent of VLSI technology put severe strain on this manual system by allowing tremendous growth in the design complexity. Thus the manual cycle time for design went from days to months to years, necessitating computer aided design systems.

Artificial Intelligence in Engineering Design
Volume I
Design Representation and Models of Routine Design

Sections 12.1 through 12.4 are based on 'Towards Intelligent Silicon Compilation' by Brewer and Gajski, pp. 365–383 of *Design Systems for VLSI Circuits, Proceedings of NATO Advanced Study Institute on Logic Synthesis and Silicon Compilation for VLSI Design.* Copyright © 1987 by Martinus Nijhoff Publishers, Dordrecht, reprinted by permission of Kluwer Academic Publishers, and also 'An Expert System Paradigm for Design,' by Brewer and Gajski, which appeared in the *Proceedings of the 23rd Design Automation Conference,* Las Vegas; 1986, pp. 62–68, © 1986 IEEE. Sections 12.5 through 12.12 are adapted by permission from 'Knowledge-Based Control in Microarchitecture Synthesis,' by Brewer and Gajski, in *Proceedings of the 24th Design Automation Conference,* Miami 1987; pp. 203–209, © 1987 Association for Computing Machinery.

Present day design systems use silicon compilers [2, 4, 6, 7] to generate layout for device fabrication, as well as timing, power, and simulation models for frequently used components (e.g., PLA's, RAM's, ROM's, Data-Path's, ALU's, Multiplexers, Counters). In addition, such design systems provide simulation and time verification functions to evaluate the generated design's performance. In these systems, transformations between levels of the design hierarchy are performed by fixed algorithms which optimize the design at each level. Failure analysis and design evaluation must still be done manually, and corrections to the design specification must be iterated through the entire process for evaluation.

Rule-based design systems have begun to appear on the CAD horizon [8, 10]. These 'expert designers' replace the fixed procedural algorithms of earlier CAD systems with rule-based expert systems. These systems have great potential in CAD as they can encapsulate expert design knowledge as well as the rapidly changing domain knowledge. Since they can be easily extended and modified, rule-based systems allow limited automated design before general algorithmic models and techniques appear. At present the rule-based systems are limited to a single design strategy and must conform to the design methodology of the algorithm they replace. These systems, however, fall short of the goal of completely automated design since they still require manual performance evaluation and redesign.

We therefore propose a new design model that simplifies implementation of a design system as a set of communicating expert systems and associated algorithmic tools. This model describes both upward and downward constraint propagation, and provides for iterative refinement of designs. The iterative refinement procedure requires a goal directed design strategy and closed-loop evaluation of the design performance. To close the loop we choose a simple 'Knob and Gauge' approach with 'Knobs' being downward propagated design constraints, and 'Gauges' being performance evaluations of the proposed design.

12.2. A NEW MODEL OF DESIGN

The design of any complex system is necessarily split into a hierarchy of design abstractions, with more abstract representations at the higher levels and less abstract ones at the lower levels. To accommodate the changing rules and design granularity, each level of abstraction requires its own dedicated designer or design expert system. The purpose of the expert on a given level is to control synthesis of a structure out of the design components predefined for that level and to partition the global design constraints into component constraints. This structure implements the behavioral specification produced by the previous higher level (more abstract) designer.

Conventional models of silicon compilation pursue a straight top-to-bottom transit of the design hierarchy. Thus, each level of the design is completed, optimized and (sometimes) evaluated before the subsequent design proceeds. In this case, evaluation is performed by a human designer who first determines the relative priority of the design goals, and selects appropriate performance measures. He then analyzes the design to produce corrections in the design specification. Sometimes these changes are made directly to the present level of design. This results in the possibility that the high-level specification does not match the final design. In this case the designer is 'on his own' to ensure that the design change does not violate any other constraints. Usually, however, the designer must change the high level specification to effect changes in the final design. Apart from the relatively long turnaround of design changes, the designer has little direct control of the design process at lower levels. Worse, if he does change the specification at a lower level, there is no automatic way for the system to correct the higher-level design.

Design in the proposed model proceeds from top to bottom as each level is completed, with the provision that each level may fail in its attempt to achieve its goals. When this occurs, control passes back to the parent in the form of a failure report. The higher level task may decide to re-allocate constraints, or change styles, or indeed fail itself. This procedure allows backtracking of earlier design decisions between levels of the design hierarchy, forcing iterative refinement of the design. In addition, this model supports a constraint handling procedure which manages both upward and downward propagation of design styles and parameters. Constraint propagation and failure reporting augment the completed design specification to provide communication between the different design levels. This additional information is used by the expert designer to formulate strategies for the completion of the design. In this way a decision made by the expert is based on much the same design context as that implicitly used by a human designer.

Closed-loop iteration of the design requires that the refinement of the design structure be guided by a functional specification at *each level*. By explicitly saving the desired function along with the detailed implementation, the process of evaluating how well a design performs is simplified. Also, this allows the lower level design procedures greater freedom to select the particular functional equivalent implied by the specification. As an example one can partition any digital design into a set of communicating finite state machines (FSM). The functional decomposition allows the FSM designers to use knowledge about the intended use and required performance of the sub-systems to drive the selection of the implementation strategy. In this way the structural design produced by a more abstract level designer becomes the detailed functional specification needed by a lower level.

Within a level of design abstraction there are usually several possible alternative structures for a particular desired behavior. Each of these may exhibit differing cost and performance characteristics and require different refinement and optimization techniques. These structures can be grouped into sets of similar characteristics called *design styles*. Styles reflect various design approaches forced by different design constraints to achieve the same behavior. A simple example is the choice of ripple-carry addition versus carry-look-ahead. The ripple-carry adder is appropriate if space is at a higher premium than delay.

As each level is designed, constraints are produced which must be propagated to the designers at the lower levels. These constraints reflect design style decisions, or structural partitions of higher-level design constraints. Style decisions constrain the design styles and strategies of sub-section designers. An example is the decision to use pre-charged carry addition, forcing the use of appropriate implementation components. Structural partitioning refers to the dividing of global constraints such as time, power, or area into local constraints on these values. A requirement of 175nS as maximum cycle time makes demands on the critical path of operations in each cycle. As the design is implemented, this puts a partitioning constraint on the design of each functional component.

Iterative refinement of a design requires continuous performance monitoring relative to the design goals. This model assumes a simple approach similar to 'Knobs' and 'Gauges'. A human operator monitoring a process closes the loop manually by reading the appropriate gauges and making adjustments to the knobs (parameters) controlling the process execution. We apply this same simple approach to controlling the design process. Each iteration of the design process results in subtle changes in the design. These changes are keyed to the desired performance of the structure and to the process constraints. An evaluation of the partial design is performed periodically to determine if the present style and refinement techniques are driving the performance closer to that desired. The action taken on an evaluation depends on the options available to the system. It may try to isolate a problem area and optimize, or change styles, or fail and try a reallocation of the constraints. In this analogy, the knobs correspond to refinement modifications or style decisions while the gauges correspond to performance evaluations.

Figure 12-1 details the flow of the design paradigm. The proposed paradigm organizes the design experts at each level into several smaller tasks. These tasks are: *Planning, Refinement, Optimization, Constraint Propagation*, and *Evaluation.*

Planning refers to the section of the expert system which performs the control function for the designer. It uses the functional specification and the design constraints to 'envision' possible design strategies and then selects the most promising of these and begins the design process. As the process continues, the planner evaluates the progress of the design to ensure that the plan is feasible. Problems are handled by first determining the cause and then envisioning

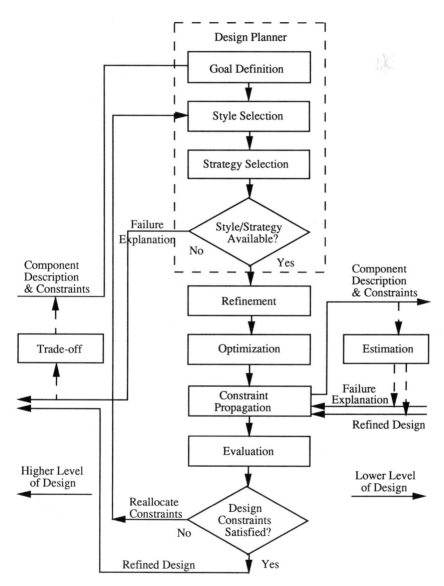

Figure 12-1: Design Process

Adapted by permission from 'An Expert System Paradigm for Design,'
by Brewer and Gajski, which appeared in *Proceedings of the 23rd Design
Automation Conference*; Las Vegas 1986; pp. 62–68. © 1986 IEEE.

modifications in either the constraints or the partitioning or, if necessary, the style. The planning section defines the present goals, selects the design styles, and chooses an appropriate design strategy for the refinement and optimization tasks. It is important to note that the expert design planner is responsible only for the quality of the synthesized design, not the correctness. In other expert approaches this distinction is not made and consequently the expert is far more complex as it includes rules to implement design refinement and optimization tasks as well as design planning. The proposed design process model separates these tasks to allow implementation of efficient design systems.

The 'Envisioning' process estimates performance regimes for the design styles and uses the constraints to decide on those design styles most likely to provide workable solutions. Figure 12-2 shows a set of possible design styles to implement a multiplier. Each style has particular advantages and problems in addition to the particular trade-off shown. Downward constraints partition the space of possible designs into regions of acceptability. Goals act to drive the design in particular directions within these regions subject to the design strategy. In the figure, a cell array or iterative multiply style is chosen, depending on the inherited style, constraints and goals. Thus, the envisioning process in the simplest case is simply forward tree pruning of obviously unacceptable branches. It seeks to apply simple rules to determine feasibility of different design styles. More complex envisioners could build a tree of possible design routes, which is then pruned by estimation techniques. The purpose of these complex routes is to let the design expert consider designs which may seem unacceptable in a cursory evaluation, but which may lead to a better overall design. In this way the envisioner can use expert knowledge to avoid the pitfalls of locally minimal designs. This is the same problem addressed by simulated annealing [9]. An example of this problem would be choice of the cell-array multiplier to appease a speed goal when the design requires a wide ALU which might enhance the iterative multiply approach. Determining which of these designs to implement and exactly how the refinement will proceed is purpose of the design strategy.

A strategy is an ordered set of Refinement, Optimization, and Evaluation steps carried out for a particular design style. The order and character of steps in the strategy may be quite complex when good strategies are known, or very simple when they are not. The strategy may also define explicit backtracking procedures when the design constraints or strategy measures are not met. Strategic measures refer to special evaluations which don't correspond to design constraints but give clues of possible design improvements. A possible example is Function Unit usage statistics over several micro-instructions. These statistics could be used to determine seldom-used or redundant Function Units. A refinement step may impose constraints that cannot be satisfied. The strategy can use this information to perform pruning of the possible designs. This increases the efficiency of the designer by eliminating poor branches early in the design process.

The design strategy for each style may be quite different since the style imposes an order on the possible design performance measures. If, for example a carry-save multiplier style was chosen, one may assume that speed is of particular importance and complexity is only of secondary importance. This ordering and the constraints imposed by the decision of a particular design style aid the system in developing a strategy for this level of design. Thus for each design style decision there is a goal-directed reason which can be propagated upwards to higher level designers in the event of a design failure. This information can be used by the higher-level designer to reallocate design constraints and allow the design to continue.

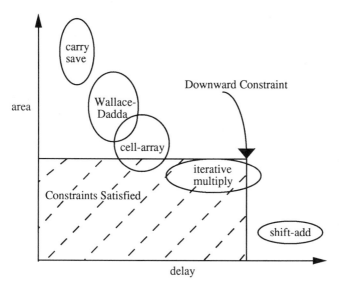

Figure 12-2: Multiplier Styles

Adapted by permission from 'An Expert System Paradigm for Design,' by Brewer and Gajski, which appeared in *Proceedings of the 23rd Design Automation Conference*; Las Vegas 1986; pp. 62–68. © 1986 IEEE.

Refinement is the task of translating the desired behavioral function into a structure of predefined components from the next lower level of the design abstraction. Thus, for a selected style, the refinement consists of building a structure within the constraints of the style which performs the given function. An example would be a logic implementation of boolean equations, subject to a style requirement of 2-level implementation. This implementation would not necessarily be minimal but would always be functionally correct. Refinement is separated from Optimization in that refinement builds a structure out of the design components that corresponds to the behavioral specification, while Optimization modifies the structural design without changing the function and tries to improve the quality. There are four reasons for this separation. The first is that it is very inefficient to carefully craft and optimize a design which has no possibility of success. The second is that by analyzing the performance of the partial design, the expert designer can concentrate its time optimizing the critical parts of the system. Third, we wish to ensure that the design refinement runs to completion. If the task includes complex optimizations (e.g., layout compaction) there is no guarantee that the refinement will succeed. Instead, we refine to an unoptimized (but functionally complete) design and then try possible optimizations. Lastly, the planner may not be extensive enough to provide strategies which match an arbitrary set of constraints. In this case we can use the refiner to explore possible designs by building functionally correct structures which can be evaluated, optimized and iteratively modified until the constraints are met. This iterative approach allows the design paradigm to produce viable designs in cases where one-pass (non-iterative) systems lack strategic knowledge and hence produce poor quality designs. In summary, to provide a time efficient structure generator we simplify the refinement task by:

1. structuring the design rules around a given style;

2. removing time-consuming optimization rules from this task.

Optimizations are those rules which search for methods to improve the implementation without making performance/cost tradeoffs. That is, the task seeks to improve performance or reduce cost by intelligent modifications of the design. Optimization routines perform local modifications of the structure which do not change its function. An example is term minimization or cover reduction in logic design. The necessary generality of the refinement functions may lead to implementations with inefficiencies which can often be removed by pattern matching to known efficient structures. The optimization task may also include well-known algorithms which simply search the design space for better implementations. Commonly these algorithms are quite time consuming so strategically this task allows a design time vs. design quality trade-off. The optimization task is style specific in that different patterns and algorithms are needed for different styles. Sample optimizations include PLA folding, register merging, and geometric compaction.

Constraint Propagation is the task which manages passing constraint information both up and down the design level hierarchy. The major task of the propagator is to partition the high-level constraints onto the components of the structural design. The information used by the propagator are estimates of component performance updated by actual design performance figures from the component design level. As the design is iteratively refined, these figures become more accurate allowing better partitioning of constraints.

Non-partitionable design style decisions are another kind of constraint. Examples are: Process Technology (i.e. CMOS, ECL, BiMOS, GaAs etc.), Layout Technology (i.e. Std. Cell, Gate-Array, Custom), Packaging Technology (i.e. Dip, Flat, SOT) and Clocking schemes. These decisions limit the style choices at lower levels of the design by forcing compatible component selection. Such decisions are passed by inheritance to the lower levels. This means that all of the physical partitions of a structure inherit the style decisions made for that structure.

Evaluation is the task of determining how well the design strategy has worked so far. The evaluation task consists of rules for evaluating various performance measures such as power consumption, area, delay time, critical path delay, etc. These rules provide the 'Gauges' used by the strategy to determine how the design will proceed, or whether to back-track and change a style decision, or finally to admit defeat and produce a failure analysis for the next higher level of design. Because of the simple control approach, the evaluator must be able to interpret the operation of the structure relative to the desired functional behavior. This interpretation problem is simplified by requiring that the evaluations be simple numeric parameters, usually related to a performance measure.

There are certain structural evaluations (strategic measures) which are not related to performance figures but which are used by the planner to determine possible design improvements. These are usage statistics, layout density, redundancy and testability figures and other parameters relating various local efficiency measures of designs. These measures are used to determine areas where favorable design trade-offs may be made by locating infrequently used or redundant components, or unused space.

The evaluations commonly depend on accurate estimations of the performance of the components at this level of design. The iterative approach of this paradigm insures that as the lower levels of the design are completed, these better performance figures are propagated to the higher level evaluators. Thus the evaluation at a particular point in the design reflects the best knowledge of the design performance available to the system.

Trade-off and Estimation provide facilities at the highest and lowest levels of the design. The estimation task provides design and constraint estimation for some (arbitrary) low-level of the design. In the simplest case the estimator merely queries a data-base for component information of already designed components. Examples would be Standard Cells or Gate Array modules. A more complex case could be calls to silicon compiler layout generators. The trade-off task performs a similar service at the highest level of the design. Its purpose is to determine what to do when the design task fails; possibilities are to simply query the user, or to provide a method for constraint relaxation.

In summary, the paradigm divides the expert system into 5 smaller tasks: Planning, Refinement, Optimization, Constraint Propagation, and Evaluation. The planner uses the imposed constraints and goals to select appropriate design styles and strategies for the other tasks. Refinement creates a structural design out of the indicated components which corresponds to the behavioral specification. This structure is conditionally optimized and evaluated to determine if the constraints have been met. The planning strategy then takes appropriate action depending on the outcome of the evaluation. The Knob and Gauges approach reduces the complexity of the planning to that of the global design parameters and constraints. Thus the local design decisions are made with respect to their effect on the global design parameters. The style-directed refinement ensures a functionally correct structure that corresponds to the selected style. The evaluation provides the expert system with a means of determining focus to the relevant design problem(s). Finally constraint propagation ensures upward and downward compliance with the imposed constraints and style selections.

12.3. ADVANTAGES OF THE DESIGN MODEL

The proposed model has several advantages over present implementations of silicon compilers. Most notably it specifically encourages iterative refinement of the design, and removes the need for a human to close the design loop. This allows the computer to complete the entire design process quickly without tedious and error prone intervention of the human operator. If the operator does decide to modify the design, his controls are the same 'knobs' that are used by the design experts. He therefore has control local to each level of the design and assurance that the internal constraint propagation will enforce a correct final design.

Since the design model is completely closed-loop, a proposed design can be implemented in several different styles and the best chosen. In present systems, long optimizations are required to perform the same refinement. For these optimizations, unless the design space is very well explored, most of the time spent optimizing is spent optimizing bad designs. Worse, if the final design is simply not good enough the optimization time is wasted. In contrast the proposed design model gets an approximate design quickly by refinement and then seeks to improve on it. Since the design behavior is kept throughout the system, localized evaluations can point out areas where special design effort is needed. In these areas, the optimizations performed enhance the entire design. A pictorial example of this is shown in Figure 12-3. Although a global optimizing algorithm will in general produce a slightly better design, the space it has to explore may be very large. The design model makes use of local evaluations to determine design choices and by comparison searches a smaller space.

Since the design system at each level is an organized expert, the system is amenable to changes in strategy or to changes in technology without massive changes in the structure. In fact, the partitioning of design knowledge into separate styles reduces the required generality of the rules, and should make system design and update easier. Finally, the control structure of the expert system is quite clear, allowing rule evaluations to become algorithmic when good algorithms are known. This allows the expert designer to make use of rapidly executing programs for certain optimization and evaluation tasks where rule execution would be either inefficient or unnecessarily complicated.

12.4. APPLICATION OF THE DESIGN PARADIGM TO MICRO-ARCHITECTURE

Walker and Thomas define a standard set of design levels of abstraction for silicon compilation [19]. In this section we will describe how the design paradigm can be used to implement a rule-based design system for the Micro-Architecture, Layout, and Logic-Design levels. For another approach to the micro-architecture level see Chapter 8, Volume II.

Design at the micro-architecture level entails creating a register-transfer level design from an algorithmic behavioral specification. The components at this level of design are registers, memories, PLA's, and functional units such as ALU's. Usually a direct correspondence exists between the operators of the algorithm and the component functional specifications. Thus, the design task amounts to creating a network of components interconnected by busses or muxes that conforms to the behavioral specification. Furthermore, the design must satisfy all of the imposed constraints such as speed, power consumption, and area. Common design practice decomposes this problem into the coupled designs of a Control Unit, and a Data Path.

Style Selection and Strategies. At the micro-architecture level the mapping of the register-transfer level design to quality and performance measures is highly complex because performance estimation is strongly dependent on the initial behavioral specification. Because of this difficulty, we propose a strategy of local

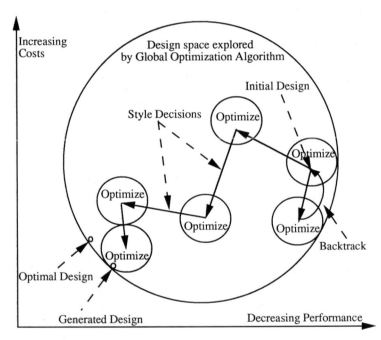

Figure 12-3: Design Process Comparison

Adapted by permission from 'An Expert System Paradigm for Design,'
by Brewer and Gajski, which appeared in *Proceedings of the 23rd Design
Automation Conference*; Las Vegas 1986; pp. 62–68. © 1986 IEEE.

exploration of the design space by iterative refinement of the design. Specifically, we can simply carry out a design given some style and component constraints and then evaluate that design to determine the performance and cost. The resultant figures (the gauges) are compared to the constraints to determine a better selection of styles and component limits. This process is shown pictorially in Figure 12-4. An initial design is carried out using a simple parallel style, assuming infinite resources in chip area for the data path. The control is assumed to be simple and relatively fast. This design is evaluated by using component delays and areas to determine the time/area/power of the design (*point 1*). It is noted that this design satisfies the time and power constraints but exceeds the area limit. A new design is allocated more limited resources in area, but since power is already satisfied, these resources could be faster. The evaluation of this design is shown as *point 2*. As more designs are evaluated, the resource allocations can be interpolated from those of previous designs. If none of the designs come close to the desired trade-off, a design style change is in order. Finally, if there are no available styles, the planner should generate a failure report to try to relax the constraints at the previous higher-level design. In the example the second design violates the time constraint but does satisfy the area. This design is further modified to increase its performance with only small increases in the area. The resulting design evaluation is plotted at *point 3*.

To achieve the iterative refinement described above, there must be a mapping of design refinement knowledge into the desired performance changes. For this purpose we introduce *Style Networks*, and *Strategy Networks*. A style network is an acyclic directed graph with style decisions at the nodes and desired performance trade-offs labeling the edges. Similarly, a strategy graph is a directed tree with refinements at the nodes and trade-offs marking the edges. A simplified control style network and data path strategy graph are shown in Figure 12-5. In use the style network indicates the possible styles available from a particular design state. The styles are selected by evaluating the trade-offs which label the arcs. Each decision is inherited in the design so that the design state is the entire path through the graph, not just the last node. Terminal nodes indicate that no further refinement is possible within the imposed constraints of earlier decisions (i.e. the design style selection is complete.) If the resulting design cannot be made to fit the constraints, some of the design decisions will have to be retracted. As each decision is backtracked, the style network will indicate the new possible styles and will flag the paths which have already been tried.

After the style selections for a design are complete, the structural design is generated by the refiner and optimized according to the planning strategy. The strategic knowledge required by the planner is organized into *strategy networks*. The strategy network shown in Figure 12-5 gives the strategies associated with the distributed data-path style. In general the refinement expert is driven either by a specific style or by a strategy network selection for a more general style.

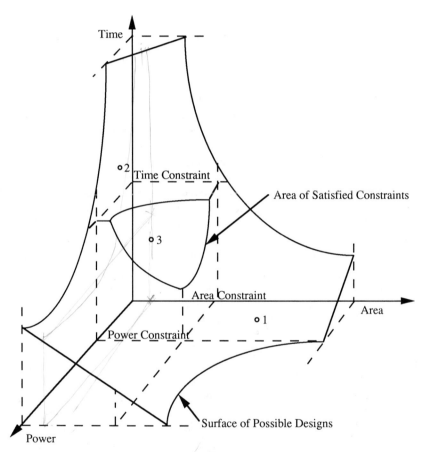

Figure 12-4: Iterative Refinement of Performance

Reprinted by permission of Kluwer Academic Publishers, from 'Towards Intelligent
Silicon Compilation,' by Brewer and Gajski, pp. 365–383 of *Design Systems for
VLSI Circuits, Proceedings of NATO Advanced Study Institute on Logic Synthesis
and Silicon Compilation for VLSI Design,* © 1987 Kluwer.

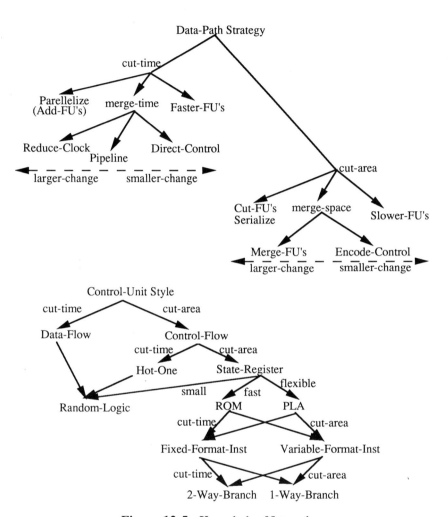

Figure 12-5: Knowledge Networks

Adapted by permission from 'An Expert System Paradigm for Design,'
by Brewer and Gajski, which appeared in *Proceedings of the 23rd Design
Automation Conference*; Las Vegas 1986; pp. 62–68. © 1986 IEEE.

This is necessary since the design models for data-path design are far more general than those for design of the control unit. To deal with this increased generality the strategy network provides a selection of modifications to the refiner which drive the design in a particular direction.

Strategy Networks are used much like style networks but the nodes are not exclusive, at each planning step the graph is consulted from the root and the appropriate refinement action is selected. Once selected, the refinement is run directly on the potential design and new performance figures are calculated. Thus at each step the trade-off evaluations are based on genuine design quality measures. This differs from the method proposed by Knapp (see Chapter 8, Volume II) who chooses instead to evaluate the plan in a separate planning space and iterate the design constraints only after the entire plan has been generated.

Refinement. The tasks for the micro-architecture refiner are: control step partitioning, register, bus and function unit allocation, and functional design of the control module(s). This is commonly done in two steps. The first step is to build a control/data flow graph for the algorithm [14] and partition the graph into 'states' for the control synthesizer [17]. This is a simple means of ensuring that the data and control dependency requirements are met. The next step is to allocate functional units to the 'operation' graph nodes, busses to the arcs between units, and registers to those variables in arcs crossing state boundaries. Finally, the symbolic microcode derived from the last step must be encoded into the control unit.

Optimization. Optimizations of the register-transfer level structure re-arrange operations subject to their dependencies to minimize either the hardware (by making a particular unit unnecessary) or the cycle time (by moving an operation to an available unit in a previous cycle). This optimization is especially important if a pipeline style is chosen to prevent many cycles wasted because of branching. The optimization may also involve recognizing conditions under which registers and function units can be shared. These conditions arise when the registers, busses, or function units are used exclusively on each time step. In the function unit case the sharing requires that the shared unit is capable of performing both functions. Sharing of registers requires that the variables stored in them are not simultaneously alive. This can be determined by keeping a table of register bindings active at each time step. Busses can also be shared. As an example several registers used exclusively on a bus can be incorporated into a register file, saving significant area. In the control unit design, the optimization usually tries to minimize the size of the ROM or PLA by state encoding [3], control encoding, PLA and Decoder merging.

Evaluation. The proposed design is evaluated to allow comparisons with the design constraints and to make measurements which aid the expert system in determining how to improve the design. The design evaluations can help to point out critical function units or paths which should be optimized, and put bounds on the possible performance available from a given structure. An example of this for PLA generation is given in [11]. In addition to the normal area, power, testability figures other useful evaluation measures exist as well. These measures include: usage statistics for various function units, and critical path delays keyed to worst-case control steps. The usage figures can detect operations which are rarely performed or busses which are rarely used. These items would then be prime candidates for sharing or deletion which would increase the design efficiency. The critical path delays can determine where control steps should be re-partitioned or which function units are critical in the design. Thus the evaluator supports the efforts of the planner to close the design refinement loop.

12.5. THE CHIPPE SYSTEM

Figure 12-6 shows an overview of the basic functions in Chippe [1]. The system input is a hardware description language reminiscent of PASCAL with modifications to allow specification of interface protocols and bit-fields. The language is translated by the compiler to a control-data-flow-graph CDFG[2] representation with data and operation dependencies inserted. This initial graph is stored as the starting point for all of the future refinements imposed on the design. This allows backtracking control-flow refinements to the graph.

12.6. REFINEMENT TOOLS

The Slicer [16] is the scheduler for Chippe, producing a valid set of micro-instructions for the CDFG. Slicer uses the control-delay and clock-cycle-time along with estimates of the operation times (from the expert) to partition the critical path. Operations not on the critical path are assigned to states based on the dependencies and available hardware. Thus the constraints to Slicer are the function-unit allocations, the control style, and the clock-time. Slicer correctly

---

[2]A representation similar to the Flow-Graph [14] and DACON or Value-Trace [10] with added control information.

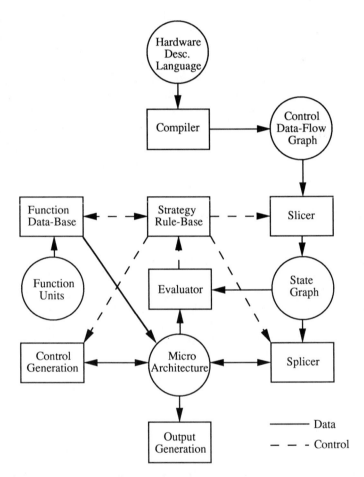

Figure 12-6: Chippe Block Diagram

Adapted by permission from 'Knowledge-Based Control in Microarchitecture,'
by Brewer and Gajski, in *Proceedings of the 24th Design Automation Conference*;
Miami 1987; pp. 203–209. © 1987 Association for Computing Machinery.

schedules units with delays longer than the clock and will attempt to chain units sequentially in a single state if the delays are short enough. In addition, Slicer can schedule pipelined units and keep track of the position of the scheduled operations and operands in successive clocks.

Slicer's timing model consists of a control state which is partitioned into one or more micro-instructions each of which can be partitioned into several chain slices. The micro-instructions correspond to cycles of the system clock and also correspond to the time granularity of the design's control unit. To prevent races in the data path, a register is assumed for each bus crossing a micro-instruction boundary. Chain slices allow execution of units from data that is not available in a register at the start of the cycle, but which will be available as output from a function unit. Figure 12-7 depicts a fragment of the state graph showing several micro-instructions. In the figure the chain slice allows binding of the subtract operator to the end of the multiply operation without the addition of a register. Note that the multiply function was allowed to run over several state boundaries. To insure the correct operation of the designed machine, such an operation requires either the input busses to be held active for the duration of the operation, or that the input of the function unit be latched. This input latch is available to the expert as an optional attribute to set for the function unit. Pipelined units are treated as operators which become available periodically (not necessarily on clock boundaries) and whose outputs are delayed by an appropriate number of clock-times.

Splicer [15] performs the connectivity binding and unit allocation (selection of which units to use for each operation) for Chippe. Splicer is designed around a depth-first search using both backtracking and branch bounding to bind operations to units and connections to busses. Its input will accept an arbitrarily connected partial design and use connections it can find or optionally introduce new ones if necessary. The use of depth first search allows an initial (greedy) solution to be found quickly so that Splicer can be used by the expert to explore the design space for potential design candidates. Splicer uses preset cost heuristics in calculating the quality of its designs. These costs are selected by the expert to guide the design search.

12.7. DESIGN STYLE SELECTIONS

There are two major style selection decisions supported by Chippe. These are selection of the global control unit style and selection of the function units which are used to implement the design. Other possible style decisions could be added, most notably connection and layout styles. These would require

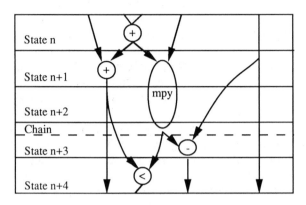

Figure 12-7: Fragment of State Graph

Adapted by permission from 'Knowledge-Based Control in Microarchitecture,'
by Brewer and Gajski, in *Proceedings of the 24th Design Automation Conference*;
Miami 1987; pp. 203–209. © 1987 Association for Computing Machinery.

floorplanning and layout refinement tools which have not been implemented yet. In the present version, Chippe allows connectivity constrained only by the allocated function units and area constraints.

Chippe's global control generation is performed by the Cogent [5] sub-system. Cogent allows the selection of several parameterized control unit styles and modifies the graph dependencies of the CDFG accordingly. It allows the specification of a control or data-path implementation for each control signal encountered in the graph. Data path implementations require merging of control macro-states to increase the available parallelism. Control path implementations require state assignments and transitions in the global control unit. In addition, Cogent combines all of the state data from Slicer and the allocation data from Splicer to produce the actual microcode for the control unit.

The function unit data base supports the expert by supplying possible units and estimates for the operation of those units. The data-base supports several selectable attributes for function units such as input latching, multi-level pipelining, and several implementations of each function with different area-time tradeoffs. It provides insulation between the technology dependent component data-base and the rule base of the expert system. This allows the function unit data-base to be easily replaced as required by the application specific design technology. When the system is interfaced to a structural compiler these estimates can be tuned to the lower level structural design.

12.8. DESIGN EVALUATION IN CHIPPE

The evaluator assembles the data from the state graph and the partial design to produce the quality measures used by the expert. It ensures that each subsystem has the current version of the data it requires and manages constraint handling for the system. For example, it insures that the Slicer has the correct estimate of the control-unit delay. When Chippe is interfaced to a structural silicon compiler, the evaluator will manage the data passed back from the actual design layout to correct these estimations. The last part of the evaluator is a set of functions called from the expert which produce local and global evaluations of the graph and connectivity. These are used by the expert to focus the design effort onto specific local trade-offs.

The expert is driven by relating imposed goals for the design to evaluations made by routines which measure various parameters of the potential design. The basic measures are estimates of the area, power dissipation and execution time. These estimates are compiled from the allocated function units, the connections, and the control unit. At present there is no method of including layout constraints in the design parameters as has been done in BUD [13]. All of the above quality measures point out problems with the design but do not indicate how to correct these problems. For this purpose several other quality measures are used. These include 'overlap', 'dead-time', 'bus-usage', and identification of components on the critical path.

The overlap function determines the number of scheduled states for which two units are active at the same time. This measure helps determine the relative effect of merging or eliminating units on the schedule. If the overlap is zero (i.e. the units are exclusive) then merging can be done without lengthening the schedule. Small numbers reflect relatively small changes in the execution time. Large numbers indicate that the merging will cost a great deal of time and should only be done if the area must be significantly reduced.

The dead-time and critical path functions are used to determine means of increasing the performance by alterations of the system clock-time and the critical components respectively. In a case where a small time improvement is needed it may be possible to substitute a faster (and larger) unit on the critical path. The dead-time measure collects information on how poorly the system clock fits the execution time of the function units in the design. That is, how much time expires for each unit after it has completed its task and is waiting for more inputs.

This measure quantifies the efficiency of the global control clock granularity to the present design schedule. Large values of dead-time indicate possible performance increase by modification of the system clock. It is important to note that modifications of the system parameters to modify a measure may change other measures in ways that are not desired. For example a change in the system clock to reduce the dead-time may modify the schedule enough so that the performance of a time critical macro-state is decreased. To help avoid these problems the expert is designed to perform certain simple strategies of design refinement.

12.9. THE EXPERT

The expert's view of the design process consists of three basic structures. These are the function unit bindings, the global parameters and goals, and an abstracted CDFG. The expert maintains a list of function units which are bound to the operations they can perform. In addition the function units have attributes such as pipelining, input latching, power dissipation, area, number of clocks to complete an operation, and flow delay time. The expert maintains its own version of the CDFG at the granularity of control-flow blocks. Each block corresponds to a straight-line section of the CDFG, with a control condition determining the next possible blocks. Thus the design's CDFG is modeled as a finite state machine whose 'states' correspond to (macro-)states of operations of the machine separated by explicit conditional transitions to other macro-states. These macro-states reflect the finest granularity of modifications to the graph by the expert system. Each macro-state has several attributes such as total execution time, function unit usage and type of control transition. Finally, the expert has a collection of parameters corresponding to the global state of the design. These include the system clock time, the systems total area, total power dissipation, control time delay, and other quality measures for the machine.

The organization of the macro-state graph is determined by the possible refinements selected by the expert. Modifications of the macro-state blocks, such as merging two states, results in the corresponding modifications of the CDFG and global control unit. For example, a state block with two successor blocks can be merged into a single larger block by the insertion of multiplexors controlled by the condition. This is shown in Figure 12-8. The actual merging of the blocks and updating of the state graph is performed by the Cogent subsystem along with local optimizations to increase the design efficiency. This change amounts to selecting a data-path implementation of the conditional rather than using the global control unit to select the next state. If the two conditional blocks use exclusive parts of the machine then the parallelism of execution can be increased without the addition of significant hardware. Macro-states can often be merged vertically if the conditions are not dependent; This allows multi-way selection of next states if the control unit can perform multi-way branches. Other possible macro-state refinements include the familiar compiler control-flow changes such as constant folding and loop unwinding.

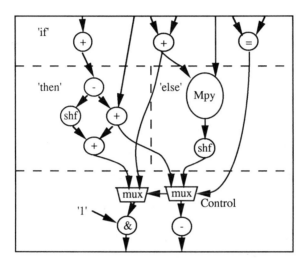

Figure 12-8: Merging State Blocks

Adapted by permission from 'Knowledge-Based Control in Microarchitecture,'
by Brewer and Gajski, in *Proceedings of the 24th Design Automation Conference*;
Miami 1987; pp. 203–209. © 1987 Association for Computing Machinery.

The purpose of these modifications is to change the control structure from one that is easily described by a programming language to one that is efficient for a potential design. The control of the machine is determined by a control unit which is selectable by the expert. This selection is based on the goals set for the final design and the evaluation of the desired behavior. In addition the expert can select the direct implementation of the control for unique state transitions. The reasons for this ability is that the changes to the total design from modifications of the control are not well understood. The coarse granularity of the data path representation indicates that much better knowledge about the optimization of this part of the design exists so that direct rule based control is deemed unnecessary. Instead, this part of the design is amenable to standard data-flow optimizations which are handled in Slicer and Splicer.

Refinements to the control flow are often irreversible after the optimizations and dependencies are resolved. Since the intended result of the modification cannot be assured at the outset the expert must have a method for backtracking its actions on the CDFG. For this purpose the expert maintains a stack of earlier states and potential operations. If the refinements to the design fail to achieve the goals the design can be backtracked to an earlier state with knowledge of the modifications which led to failure.

12.10. DESIGN STRATEGY

The expert maintains control of the system by modification of knobs. These knobs include modifications in the function unit allocations, the design global parameters (clock length, type of control, control delay etc.), selection of limits and heuristics for Slicer, Splicer, and Cogent subsystems. The primary control of the expert over the data-path is from the function-units which are selected to be the components of the design. These units are kept in a data base and are matched by desired functionality and area/time/power characteristics. The expert can select many parallel fast units for a time constrained design or a few highly merged units (those performing a large number of operations) for an area constrained design. Since the system design philosophy is design by iterative refinement there are rules in which the action part increases the merging of units as well as rules to split units, adding to the achievable parallelism. This merging also has a strong effect on the connections needed to complete the design. A smaller number of function units requires a correspondingly smaller number of busses for interconnection. Lastly, the selection of individual units performing identical functions offers additional design tradeoffs. A function unit can be pipelined or implemented with carry-lookahead or ripple logic. For example, an adder on the main data-path may be wide enough to require a lookahead function while a narrower incrementer could be fast enough (and save space) if implemented as ripple-carry.

The decision-making process of the expert is performed in two phases. First the goals are compared to the evaluations to select a strategy for change. Then selected rules use local measures to determine possible actions. The action with most promise is tried first, after which the design is re-evaluated to determine the changes. Finally, the design can be backtracked if the strategy proves useless. An example of a strategy for minimizing the area usage by merging is shown in Figure 12-9. These rules are arranged in order of increasing change to the schedule. The first rule which potentially solves the problem is fired and the schedule and graph are updated.

```
Rule: Remove-Redundant::
    If ( Never-used( FU1) )
    Then (
        Remove( FU1) )


Rule: Merge-Exclusive::
    If ( Compatible( FU1, FU2) &&Exclusive( FU1, FU2) &&
        Smaller-Area( Merge( FU1, FU2),  FU1+FU2) &&
        Largest-Gain( FU1, FU2) )
    Then (
        Add( Merge( FU1, FU2)) &&Remove( FU1, FU2) )


Rule: Merge-Trade::
    If ( Compatible( FU1, FU2) &&
        Smaller-Area( Merge( FU1, FU2), FU1+FU2) &&
        Overall-Cost( FU1, FU2)< Largest-Gain( FU1, FU2) )
    Then (
        Add( Merge( FU1, FU2)) &&Remove( FU1, FU2) )
```

Figure 12-9: Function Unit Merge Rules

Adapted by permission from 'Knowledge-Based Control in Microarchitecture,' by Brewer and Gajski, in *Proceedings of the 24th Design Automation Conference*; Miami 1987; pp. 203–209. © 1987 Association for Computing Machinery.

A possible strategy for the selection of function units is to first allocate a unique unit to each operation in the graph. After scheduling, the graph can be scanned for unused units and for potential merging candidates. The resulting machine is evaluated and compared to the goals. Since the machine is implemented with many parallel units, if the performance is not high enough then some of the units will need to be replaced with faster versions. If the area is too large then the merging candidates can be evaluated for potential gains and the allocation appropriately modified by pair-wise merging of the candidates. After a strategy has been selected (for example, cutting the number of instantiations of a unit), a set of rules for that strategy is activated. This has the effect of inducing a two level control on the rule-base: First the strategy is selected by evaluating the measures against the desired (global) goals, then the implementation of that strategy is activated. The rules that represent the action of a particular strategy determine the particular (local) change required. If no candidate meets the requirements of the activation of a given strategy, the activation fails and a new strategy is chosen. When all strategies for a given desired change fail the expert can optionally backtrack to earlier design decisions (such as selection of a control style).

The system clock length has a drastic effect on the final design. The flexibility of the scheduling algorithm allows clocks which may be either faster or slower than the execution delay of the units. The faster clocks reduce the granularity with which the control can be scheduled. This reduces the 'dead-time' when a unit is unused and awaiting new operands. However, it also increases the number of states which must be encoded in the control unit, thus increasing the unit's size and delay. Longer clock time allocations allow more units to execute in sequence within a single clock. This can lead to efficient operation at relatively slow clock speeds. It must be noted that the clock length should not exceed the execution time of an entire macros-state as no further operations can be chained in sequence. Thus, designs with many small macro-states (such as a controller with many ports to service) should use higher clock rates to reduce the response time.

The design of this system is based on simple tradeoffs controlling fast search of the design space. For the connections between the function units in the design several possible cost strategies with different tradeoffs are possible. The design can be interconnected using sufficient busses to run the schedule as fast as possible or the units can be merged, slowing the schedule and reducing the bussing requirements. In addition heuristics which give adequate results for very short iteration limits are different from those which produce high quality designs in longer searches [15]. The expert should not spend long searches to optimize designs which are far from satisfying the goals, so time can be traded against quality of the design produced. In the final stages of the design process (when the design is close to the imposed goals) the design can be connected with high quality minimal connections for the final designs.

12.11. WALK-THROUGH EXAMPLE

Figure 12-10 shows the hardware description for a small loop. This test case was used by the HAL system [18]. We will examine a run of Chippe on this fragment and indicate the trade-off decision points. All of the following examples were produced by Chippe from this one code fragment. The area and time bounds were set at the beginning and the examples were sampled as the design progressed.

```
program diffeq(input,output);
/*      Example from HAL: A Multi-Paradigm Approach to
        Automatic Data-Path Synthesis 23rd DAC      */
type    integer = {0..11};
reg     three : integer;
        five : integer;
var     a, dx, x, u, y, y1, u1, u2, u3, u4, u5, u6 : integer;
begin
   if (x < a) then
        repeat
           u1 := u * dx;
           u2 := five * x;
           u3 := three * y;
           y1 := u * dx;
           x  := x + dx;
           u4 := u1 * u2;
           u5 := dx * u3;
           y  := y + y1;
           u6 := u - u4;
           u  := u6 - u5;
         when x < a
   end.
```

Figure 12-10: Hardware Description Language for HAL Example

Adapted by permission from 'Knowledge-Based Control in Microarchitecture,'
by Brewer and Gajski, in *Proceedings of the 24th Design Automation Conference*;
Miami 1987; pp. 203–209. © 1987 Association for Computing Machinery.

Figure 12-11 traces the evolution of the small design test case. The goals for
the system were area < 3000 gates and delay < 1.0 uSec. These constraints are
shown as the vertical dashed box in the figure. The figure shows that the first
set of merges (two of the multipliers) reduced the area but did not change the
performance, since these units were not used simultaneously in the schedule.
The later merges required more states to complete the loop but in each case the
trade was in favor of the desired goal. In this case the area bound was first met
and then the time performance goal was attempted. This resulted from the large
difference between the initial area and that of the goal requirement, which led to
the selection of the simple strategy outlined above for area reduction. After the
area constraint was satisfied the controller tried to speed up the machine since
the time bound was now violated. In searching for modifications to speed up the
machine, the rule base used a usage measure to determine where the biggest gain

could be made by a unit modification. The unit returned was the multiplier which was used in nearly all states of the loop. A data-base query determined that this unit could be pipelined. The strategy here was that the system clock could be shortened, decreasing the loop delay. These changes led to the large drop in loop delay in the figure. Finally, the change in the clock led to a last potential merge, producing the final design.

These changes are shown pictorially in Figures 12-12, 12-13, and 12-14. The tables that appear under each figure are the output symbolic microcode for these three designs. The symbolic microcode and the micro-architecture contain sufficient data to build the control unit. Estimates of the control unit size based on implementation and the micro-code are thus quite accurate. Each numbered block corresponds to a state of the machine while the lines describe which units are accessed and where the results are placed. The FUxx, rxxx, and bxx are function units, registers, and busses respectively. Operands are supplied to the function-units on the indicated busses. In these examples (to conform to the original HAL paper) the initial values for the registers are assumed to be stored at the start of the code fragment. In a more realistic case these values could be loaded from a constant ROM or from external ports in the environment.

Figure 12-12 shows the design after one unit was merged, the adder-subtractor. In this very parallel version the six multiplies are carried out in just two states, leaving the other states relatively empty. The area requirement for this design was far greater than the goal so the expert chose to remove multipliers as they provide the largest gain in area. This design also made use of the chaining ability of Slicer/Splicer. Since the clock time set by the expert allows the multiplies to execute in one cycle, there is sufficient time to perform both and add and a subtract in a single state.

The design in Figure 12-13 shows the result after several more merges. The gate usage in this example is still about 5500. Fewer registers are used in this example since the decrease in parallelism allowed a schedule with one fewer temporary register. The plethora of muxes in this design are an artifact of the design strategy (which forbids optimization at this point in the design) and the Splicer heuristic (picked by the expert to minimize busses at the expense of muxes). If this design was close to the desired goal, much better optimization would be used. This design iteration took less than 1% of the total design time for the code fragment. Optimizations at this step would have simply wasted design time.

The final design shown in Figure 12-14 shows the design after the inclusion of a 2-stage piped multiply unit. This design modification occurred because the number of sequential multiplies became large enough for a pipe to be efficient. Notice that the two-level muxing structure has resulted in a design with four input busses and two output busses. The optimization of this design clearly splits the registers into two structural units, R0, R2, R4, and R1, R3, R5, R6. Additional rules could create register arrays for these partitions.

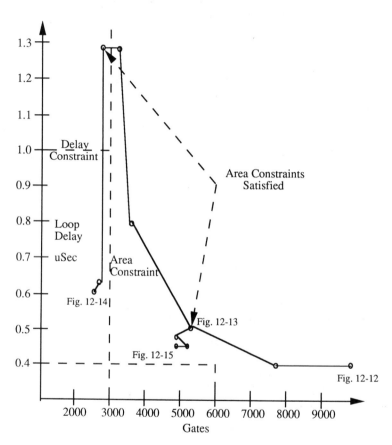

Figure 12-11: Design Evolution

Adapted by permission from 'Knowledge-Based Control in Microarchitecture,'
by Brewer and Gajski, in *Proceedings of the 24th Design Automation Conference*;
Miami 1987; pp. 203–209. © 1987 Association for Computing Machinery.

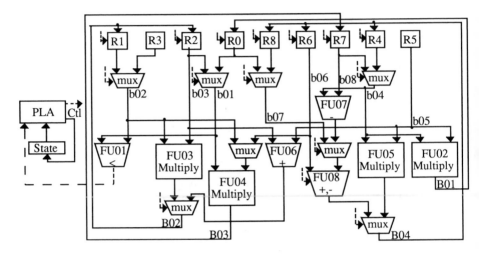

MI#	ACTIONS	Nxt	Conditions
1 a	FU01(< :r002,b01;r003,b02)	2 1	x < a : TRUE x < a : FALSE
2 a	r000,B01 = FU02(*:r004,b04;r005,b05) r001,B02 = FU03(*:r001,b02;r002,b03) r007,B03 = FU04(*:r000,b01;r006,b06) r008,B04 = FU05(*:r004,b04;r005,b05)	3	
3 a	r007,B03 = FU04(*:r000,b01;r001,b02) r002,B02 = FU06(+:r002,b03;r005,b05) r000,B01 = FU02(*:r007,b04;r005,b05) r006,B04 = FU08(+:r006,b06;r008,b07)	4	
4 a 4 b	B05 = FU07(-:r004,b04;r007,b08) FU01(< :r002,b01;r003,b02) r004,B04 = FU08(-:B05;r000,b07)	2 1	x < a : TRUE x < a : FALSE

Figure 12-12: The HAL Design After One Merge

Adapted by permission from 'Knowledge-Based Control in Microarchitecture,'
by Brewer and Gajski, in *Proceedings of the 24th Design Automation Conference*;
Miami 1987; pp. 203–209. © 1987 Association for Computing Machinery.

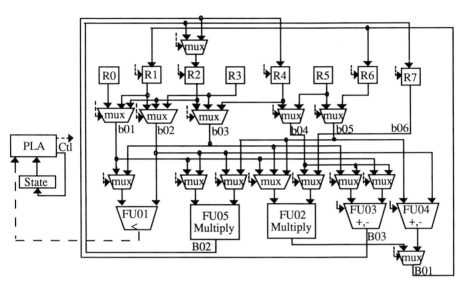

MI#	ACTIONS	Nxt	Conditions
1 a	FU01(< :r002,b01;r003,b02)	2 1	x < a : TRUE x < a : FALSE
2 a	r001,B01 = FU02(*:r004,b03;r005,b04) r007,B02 = FU05(*:r001,b01;r002,b02)	3	
3 a	r002,B02 = FU05(*:r000,b01;r006,b05) r001,B01 = FU02(*:r001,b02;r007,b06) r002,B03 = FU03(+:r002,b03;r005,b04)	4	
4 a	r001,B01 = FU02(*:r005,b05;r004,b04) r004,B03 = FU03(-:r004,b04;r001,b01) r002,B02 = FU05(*:r002,b02;r005,b05) FU01(< :r003,b03;r002,b02)	5	
5 a	r006,B01 = FU04(+:r006,b05;r001,b02) r004,B03 = FU03(-:r004,b03;r002,b01)	2 1	x < a : TRUE x < a : FALSE

Figure 12-13: Intermediate HAL Design

Adapted by permission from 'Knowledge-Based Control in Microarchitecture,'
by Brewer and Gajski, in *Proceedings of the 24th Design Automation Conference*;
Miami 1987; pp. 203–209. © 1987 Association for Computing Machinery.

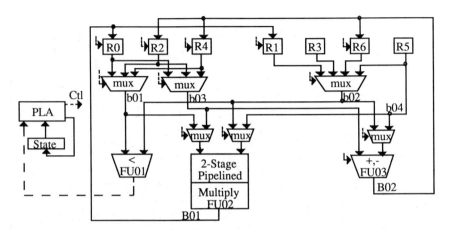

MI#	ACTIONS	Nxt	Conditions	
1 a	FU01(< :r002,b01;r003,b02)	2	x < a	: TRUE
		1	x < a	: FALSE
2 a	FU02(*:r004,b01;r005,b02)	3		
3 a	r001,B01 = FU02(*:) FU02(*:r002,b01;r001,b02)	4		
4 a	r000,B01 = FU02(*:) FU02(*:r000,b01;r006,b02)	5		
5 a	r000,B01 = FU02(*:) FU02(*:r000,b01;r001,b02) r002,B02 = FU03(+:r002,b03;r005,b04)	6		
6 a	r001,B01 = FU02(*:) FU02(*:r004,b03;r005,b04) FU01(< :r002,b01;r003,b02)	7		
7 a	r000,B01 = FU02(*:) FU02(*:r000,b01;r005,b04) r004,B02 = FU03(-:r004,b03;r001,b02)	8		
8 a	r001,B01 = FU02(*:) r006,B02 = FU03(+:r000,b03;r006,b02)	9		
9 a	r004,B02 = FU03(-:r004,b03;r001,b02)	2	x < a	: TRUE
		1	x < a	: FALSE

Figure 12-14: Final Design for HAL

Adapted by permission from 'Knowledge-Based Control in Microarchitecture,'
by Brewer and Gajski, in *Proceedings of the 24th Design Automation Conference*;
Miami 1987; pp. 203–209. © 1987 Association for Computing Machinery.

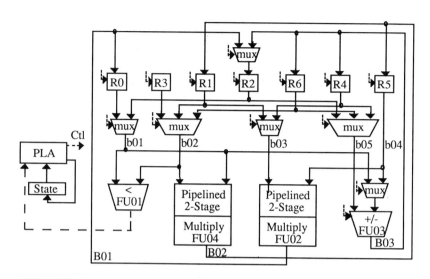

MI#	ACTIONS	Nxt	Conditions	
1 a	FU01(< :r002,b01;r003,b02)	2	x < a	: TRUE
		1	x < a	: FALSE
2 a	FU02(*:r004,b03;r005,b04) FU04(*:r001,b02;r002,b01)	3		
3 a	r001,B02 = FU04(*:) r000,B01 = FU02(*:) FU04(*:r006,b02;r000,b01) FU02(*:r004,b03;r005,b04)	4		
4 a	r002,B01 = FU02(*:) r001,B02 = FU04(*:) FU04(*:r001,b02;r000,b01) r002,B03 = FU03(+:r002,b05;r005,b04)	5		
5 a	r005,B02 = FU04(*:) FU02(*:r001,b03;r005,b04) r006,B03 = FU03(+:r006,b05;r002,b01) FU01(< :r002,b01;r003,b02)	6		
6 a	r000,B01 = FU02(*:) r002,B03 = FU03(-:r004,b05;r005,b04)	7		
7 a	r004,B03 = FU03(-:r002,b05;r000,b01)	2	x < a	: TRUE
		1	x < a	: FALSE

Figure 12-15: Faster Design

Adapted by permission from 'Knowledge-Based Control in Microarchitecture,'
by Brewer and Gajski, in *Proceedings of the 24th Design Automation Conference*;
Miami 1987; pp. 203–209. © 1987 Association for Computing Machinery.

This total sequence of designs took about 6 sec of CPU time on a Pyramid processor (roughly 2.5 times the speed of a VAX-11/780). About 95% of this time was spent optimizing the connections in the last design, the other exploratory designs were not optimized.

Changing the design goals to time < .4 uSec and area < 6000 gates resulted in the design in Figure 12-15. The evolution to this design started out the same as in the previous one but deviates as soon as the area goal is satisfied. Several attempts to achieve the required time were made, including pipelining the (two) multipliers and changing the clock. These changes are depicted in the design evolution chart as the dashed line moving to Ex4. In this case the design attempt failed and is the best design found by the expert.

The present version of the function unit data base was implemented around the LSI Logic: LSI7000 series gate array products [12] as several of the functions needed were already designed and characterized. All of the timings and gate counts given are estimates based on the units allocated, the control unit design, and an estimate of the area used by bussing and connections.

12.12. CONCLUSIONS

In this paper we have introduced an expert-system design paradigm. The paradigm advocates iterative refinement of the design as opposed to forward design generation. To support this refinement the paradigm describes how to perform closed-loop evaluation of the proposed design and how to propagate the changing constraints to ensure correct design. Closing the loop between evaluation and design modification uses a simple Knob and Gauge approach. The Knobs are design styles and refinement actions applied to the design. The Gauges are the area, delay time, power consumption, and other performance parameters which are conventionally determined by simulation. The paradigm details how the gauges and constraints are used to evaluate trade-offs which select design styles and strategies to produce the refined design.

The paradigm also emphasizes the distinction between tradeoffs, refinement and optimization. *Tradeoffs* are managed by the design strategy of the expert and are insulated from the processes of creating correct and optimized design. *Refinement* is the process of creating a structure to implement a desired behavior. *Optimization* is the process of modifying this structure to improve the efficiency without changing the function. The separation of refinement and optimization guarantees a design solution; first we build the functional structure and then we optimize it. This technique also makes more efficient use of the design time by optimizing only where necessary.

The expert control for the Chippe system is presently under development to add more capabilities in design analysis. Specifically, rules are needed to control optimization routines for the graph and to optimize the control selection vs. the system clock time. Lastly, future research is needed in the language used to initially represent the design behavior.

There are several limitations inherent in the design model; most of these are related to the knobs and gauges control strategy. The system cannot make direct changes in the potential design without losing the ability to iterate the refinements. It can only change the knobs which control the refinement process and run optimization routines on the output design. Limitations in Chippe include several possible optimizations which could be performed at different stages in the design, most notably the generation of the initial control data-flow graph, where variations on compiler optimizations would be very useful.

The present system does show that design refinement can be carried out using strategies based on simple design tradeoffs. The simplicity of the expert control stems greatly from the generality of the underlying design model and the associated design tools. Several designs have been tested using the system and with few exceptions have all been amenable to the same rules. This gives support to the idea of a generalized set of design strategies for a wide class of architecture design problems.

12.13. ACKNOWLEDGMENTS

This work was supported in part by a grant from AT&T Bell Laboratories.

12.14. BIBLIOGRAPHY

[1]   Brewer, F. D., *Constraint Driven Behaviorial Synthesis,* unpublished Ph.D. Dissertation, University of Illinois, Urbana-Champaign, June 1988.

[2]   Buric, M. R. and Matheson, T. G., "Silicon Compilation Environments," *Proceedings of the Custom Integrated Circuit Conference,* Portland, Oregon, May 20-22, 1985.

[3]   De Micheli, G., "Optimal Encoding of Control Logic," *Proceedings ICCD,* Port Chester, New York, 1984.

[4]   DeMan, H., Rabey, J. and Six, P., "CATHEDRAL II: A Synthesis and Module Generation System for Multiprocessor Systems on a Chip," *Proceedings of the Nato Study Institute of Logic Synthesis and Silicon Compilation for VLSI Design*, L'Aqulia, Italy, July 7-18, 1986.

[5]   Dutt, N., "COGENT: A Parameterizable Control Generator for Constraint Driven Microarchitecture Synthesis," *Ph.D. Preliminary Proposal, University of Illinois, Urbana Champaign*, December 1986.

[6]   Gajski, D. D., "Silicon Compilation," *VLSI Design*, November 1985.

[7]   Johnson, S. C. and Mayor, S., "Silicon Compiler Lets System Makers Design their own VLSI Chips," *Electronic Design*, October 1984.

[8]   Joobani, R. and Siewioriek, D., "WEAVER: A Knowledge Based Routing Expert," *Proceedings of the 22nd Annual Design Automation Conference*, June 1985.

[9]   Kirkpatrick, S., Gelatt Jr., C. D. and Vecchi, M. P., "Optimization by Simulated Annealing," *Science*, Vol. 220, No. 4598, May 13, 1983.

[10]   Kowalski, T., *An Artificial Intelligence Approach to VLSI Design*, Kluwer Academic Publishers, Boston, 1985.

[11]   Kurdahi, F. J. and Parker, A. C. , "PLEST: A Program for Area Estimation of VLSI Integrated Circuits," *Proceedings of the 23rd Design Automation Conference*, IEEE, Las Vegas, June 1986.

[12]   *CMOS Macrocell Manual*, LSI Logic Corp., 1985.

[13]   McFarland, M. C. and Kowalski, T. J., "Assisting DAA: The Use of Global Analysis in an Expert System," *Proceedings ICCD*, 1986.

[14]   Orailoglu, A. and Gajski, D. D., "Flow Graph Representation," *Proceedings of the 23rd Design Automation Conference*, IEEE, Las Vegas, June 1986.

[15]   Pangrle, B. M., *A Behaviorial Compiler for Intelligent Silicon Compilation*, unpublished Ph.D. Dissertation, University of Illinois, Urbana-Champaign, July 1987.

[16]   Pangrle, B. M. and Gajski, D. D., "State Synthesis and Connectivity Binding for Microarchitecture Compilation," *Proceedings ICCAD*, 1986.

[17]   Parker, A. C., "Automated Synthesis of Digital Systems," *IEEE Design and Test of Computers*, pp. 75-81, November 1984.

[18]   Paulin, P.G., Knight, J. P. and Girczyc, E. F., "HAL: A Multi-Paradigm Approach to Automatic Data Path Synthesis," *Proceedings of the 23rd Design Automation Conference*, IEEE, Las Vegas, June 1986.

[19]   Walker, R. A. and Thomas, D. E., "A Model of Design Representation and Synthesis," *Proceedings of the 22nd Design Automation Conference*, June 1985.

Chapter 13
WRIGHT:
A CONSTRAINT BASED
SPATIAL LAYOUT SYSTEM

Can A. Baykan and Mark S. Fox

Abstract

WRIGHT formulates the problem of generating two dimensional layouts consisting of rectangular design units as a Boolean constraint satisfaction problem. Each layout is represented as a constraint satisfaction problem defined by a set of numerical variables with interval domains and algebraic constraints on them. A layout problem is defined by Boolean combinations of the algebraic constraints. Constraints are used to represent arbitrary amounts of expertise in a uniform and principled manner, and a function of texture measures, which are heuristic measures of the topological and other features of the constraint graph, controls the focus of attention during search in order to implement a fail-first strategy.

13.1. INTRODUCTION

WRIGHT is a constraint based spatial layout design system. It formulates layout problems as *constrained optimization problems* (COP) , and solves them by *constrained heuristic search* (CHS) . CHS combines constraint satisfaction with heuristic search , and adds to the definition of problem space composed of states, operators and an evaluation function, *problem textures* which are measures of problem topology that allows search to be focused in a way that reduces backtracking [13].

Spatial layout deals with the design of two dimensional configurations, such as site plans, floor plans, manufacturing facility layouts, and arrangement of

Artificial Intelligence in Engineering Design
Volume I
Design Representation and Models of Routine Design

395

equipment in rooms. In spatial layout, topological relations such as adjacency, alignment, grouping, and properties such as shape, dimension, distance, and other functions of spatial arrangement are a principal concern [8]. Spatial layout is a design task. It is an important aspect of architectural design and other fields that deal with physical design.

Design is the process of constructing a description of an artifact that satisfies a functional specification, meets explicit or implicit performance criteria, is realizable and satisfies restrictions on the design process itself [20]. There are requirements on performance in terms of time, space, energy consumption, simplicity, reliability, maintainability, fabrication and cost. These may either be specified by the client or by design codes or be implicit in established practice of good design in the field. Realizability means that the artifact conforms to limitations of the target medium, i.e. is a building that can be built by some means. It is natural to define design problems in terms of constraints. WRIGHT uses constraints to represent arbitrary amounts of expertise in a uniform and principled manner, and derives an understanding of the problem (search) space that leads to more efficient search from constraints.

For each design task, the availability of an implicitly specified set of primitive components and a set of primitive relations between the components can be assumed. For example, in electronics the primitive components are transistor, capacitor; and the relations are serial and parallel connections. In spatial layout, the primitive components can be a set of rooms with different functions, and the relations are topological and geometrical relations such as adjacency, distance and alignment.

The primitive objects are called *design units*, and the relations are called *spatial relations* in WRIGHT. Design units are rectangular shapes with discrete orientations pointing in one of the four principal directions. Spatial relations are topological or geometrical, such as adjacency, distance and overlap. The set of possible spatial relations is very large. Therefore, instead of defining a complete and fixed set, we have defined the relations that are required most often, and supplied a template for defining new spatial relations. WRIGHT formulates spatial layout as the generation of configurations of design units satisfying given spatial relations and limits on dimensions. A spatial layout problem is defined by the following inputs.

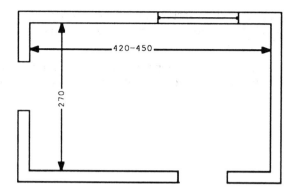

Figure 13-1: Plan Showing Initial Configuration of Kitchen

• An initial layout which may be an empty space,

• Design units to locate and/or dimension,

    1. Sink
    2. Refrigerator
    3. Range
    4. Sink center
    5. Mix center
    6. Range center
    7. Circulation area

• Constraints specifying spatial relations between design units and limits on their dimensions.

    1. Sink should be inside sink center
    2. Sink should be completely next to circulation area
    3. Sink should be facing circulation area
    4. Sink should be completely next to window
    5. Sink length $\geq$ 90 cm.

Spatial layout has the following characteristics:

• The variables under consideration such as length, width, area, and location of objects are continuous. Though dimensions and locations can be discretized using a grid, this arbitrarily eliminates some solutions.

- Spatial relations such as inside, non-overlap, next-to specify topology. Some of the relations, i.e. next-to, can be satisfied in multiple topologically distinct ways.

- A selection of "good" solutions are required for the designer to identify the possibilities and tradeoffs involved in a problem formulation.

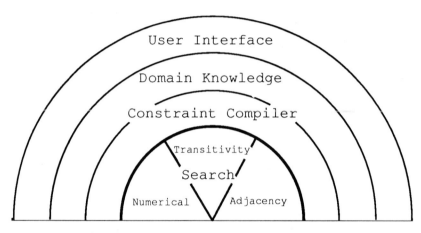

Figure 13-2: Components of WRIGHT

The components of WRIGHT are user interface, knowledge base, constraint Compiler, and search and reasoning module, as seen in Figure 13-2. The knowledge base contains prototype design units and constraints. The constraint compiler maps the constraints in the knowledge base into algebraic constraints on the lines and dimensions of the design unit instances in a particular problem, creating an and/or graph called the *constraint graph*. Search module uses the constraint graph to generate and test alternative configurations. Three modes of reasoning are used: numerical constraint propagation, path checking, and reasoning about adjacency graphs. The user interface enables the user to formulate layout problems, solve them interactively, and change the knowledge base.

13.2. BACKGROUND

Based on their underlying representations, previous approaches to spatial layout can be classified as *grid based, drawing based* and *relational*. Grid based representations partition objects to be located into subparts of equal area and divide the site into a grid of cells where each cell is equal in area to one subpart. Drawing based representations use polygons of fixed size and shape to represent objects. Relational representations use adjacency or incidence between points, between lines and regions, or between regions to model layouts.

In spatial layout, search operates by selecting a design unit(s) and an operator, and generates a new configuration by applying the operator to the design unit(s) in some state. There are two basic variations in search organization: *organize-by-design-unit* and *priority* solution methods [8]. In an organize-by-design-unit strategy, a design unit is selected to enter the layout, placed at alternative locations and tested. All relevant attributes of the design unit are determined at the time it enters the configuration, and all applicable tests are carried out to select satisfactory locations. Search continues with the next design unit. Priority strategy orders search operators as in hierarchical planning systems. Operators determining the important attributes are applied first, creating macro objects or configurations in unbounded space. A similar method that has been proposed is *projective location generation* [8]. The location of a design unit is found by intersecting the range of locations allowed by sequences of spatial relations. In projective location generation, the most efficient sequence for considering the spatial relations is in increasing order of *cost of executing test/probability of failure*. Some domain heuristics that have been proposed based on this would be to select spatial relations with smaller projected areas, spatial relations that can be executed quickly, and design units with large areas. This is similar in principle to WRIGHT's approach. An advantage of WRIGHT is that by representing the configuration as a constraint satisfaction problem, it is possible to consider relations between design units that do not have fixed locations or fixed dimensions. WRIGHT uses texture measures to order the spatial relations.

Instead of starting from an empty initial configuration and building-up, search can operate by changing a configuration in response to failing constraints, or in order to improve the score of an objective function. This is a hill-climbing approach.

Quadratic assignment formulation (QAP) [16, 17] is based on a grid representation. It is an optimization approach which tries to minimize total transportation costs of the layout. The representation makes it impossible to deal with variable sizes, and makes it very hard to deal with issues of shape and alignment. Both build-up and hill-climbing strategies are used with QAP.

The layout systems considered below use an organize-by-design-unit strategy.

DPS [21] and GSP [8] use drawing based representations. In GSP design units must be rectangles, and in DPS they can be arbitrary polygons. Dimensions of the design units must be fixed. In drawing based systems, locations tried for placing a design unit depends on the existing layout, as seen in Figure 13-3. As a result of this, configurations generated depend on the order in which design units enter the layout. Since GSP and DPS try only one ordering, they may miss possible solutions. Their correctness is not guaranteed.

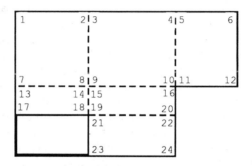

Figure 13-3: Locations Considered by GSP for Placing the Next Design Unit

Locations are defined by lines projected by the edges of the space and the objects that are in place. Placing an object at every location above, in four possible orientations, results in 96 new configurations.

Reprinted by permission of Elsevier Science Publishers B.V. from 'Automated Space Planning,' by C.M. Eastman, in *Artificial Intelligence* (Vol. 4; p. 57, 1973).

Relational representations use nodes to denote points, lines, design units or some combination of these and edges to denote adjacencies between them. One possible representation is an adjacency graph, where nodes denote design units and edges between them denote adjacency, as in GRAMPA [15]. Another possibility is to use adjacencies between design units and the maximal lines bordering them in an arrangement. This is called a wall-representation and is used in DIS [10] and LOOS [12].

The representation used in DIS and LOOS has two steps: determining the relational structure of an arrangement using north-of and east-of relations and

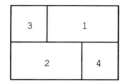 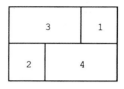

Figure 13-4: A DIS Structure and Possible Configurations Represented by it

Reprinted by permission of Pion, Ltd., London, from 'Wall Representations of
Rectangular Dissections and Their Use in Automated Space Allocation,' by
U. Flemming, in *Environment and Planning B* (Vol. 5; p. 225, 1978).

deriving the constraints on the dimensions of the design units based on the
topology defined by the wall-representation.

Figure 13-4 shows a configuration of four design units labeled 1 to 4. The
relational structure is seen at left, where north-of relation is indicated by solid
arrows and east-of relation is shown by dotted lines and arrows. Design units 1
and 3 are north-of 2 and 4, 1 is east-of 3, and 4 is east-of 2. The three configurations in the same Figure show possible layouts that are represented by this relational structure. This structure gives rise to constraints on the dimensions of the
design units called dependent constraints. Let x_i and y_i be the x and y-
dimensions of the ith design unit. The dependent constraints for the configuration seen in Figure 13-4 are $x_1 + x_3 = x_2 + x_4$, $y_1 = y_3$, $y_2 = y_4$. Required adjacencies between design units also result in dependent constraints. For example, the requirement design unit 3 must be adjacent to design unit 4 for at
least L units results in $x_3 - x_2 \geq L$.

Both WRIGHT and DIS/LOOS use constraints to define an equivalence class
of configurations, but WRIGHT uses constraints to define both topology and
dimensions whereas DIS and LOOS use a relational structure to define topology
and to derive dependent constraints. Relational systems have built in assumptions that permit only well-formed arrangements to be described. In the three
relational systems above, GRAMPA, DIS and LOOS, well-formedness means
that design units do not overlap. Relational systems use a restricted set of relations to describe configurations so it may not be possible to describe all aspects
of a configuration we are interested in. For example, adjacency graphs do not

describe alignment or relative location such as north-of or south-of. The wall-representation does not explicitly describe alignment or adjacencies between regions using the relations but uses the dependent constraints to represent them. WRIGHT expresses topology by algebraic relations between the lines of the design units, which is also how spatial relations *spatial relations* are defined. A configuration is represented by a CSP where the variables such as the locations and dimensions of the design units are interval variables, and the attributes of the layout such as adjacencies and distances are algebraic constraints on the variables. Alternative configurations are generated by solving a discrete CSP, where the variables are the spatial relations to be satisfied and their values are the distinct ways of satisfying them. WRIGHT employs a priority strategy, where search operators determine only the attributes specified by the selected constraint. The topology and dimensions of a configuration can be decided in any order due to the CSP formulation used.

GSP and DPS implement fail-first using domain heuristics for selecting a design unit, such as selecting the largest one or the one most strongly connected to those already located. Since DPS can deal with arbitrary polygons, it also uses a priority strategy by forming macro design units out of those that are strongly connected, and then treating it as one object. In DIS and LOOS, the order of entering the design units is given by the user.

Issues in CSP literature relevant to WRIGHT's method are balancing search and consistency methods, variable and value selection heuristics, and comparing dynamic versus fixed variable selection. REF-ARF [9] combines constraint manipulation with assigning values to variables by backtracking search. A variable is selected by first looking at the constraints which have the least number of free variables. Among that set, it attempts to use constraints which most severely restrict the values of the variables recurring in them. Constraints are mathematical equations, inequalities and disjunctions. The relations specified in constraints are ordered from most to least restrictive. Equations are assumed to be most restrictive and disjunctions least restrictive. Among those variables occurring in the most restrictive set of constraints, the one with the smallest range is selected for assigning a value at that search level. Other heuristics mentioned are selecting a variable with least number of constraints, selecting a variable with most number of constraints, and selecting a variable connected most strongly to previous variables [6]; partitioning constraint graphs into stable sets [14]. Purdom [22] determined that dynamic variable ordering during search is efficient only in problems with an exponentially small number of solutions but that require exponential search.

13.3. USER INTERFACE

Design is engaged in determining the specifications as much as in searching for solutions. In descriptive studies of design, it is observed that designers identify new constraints throughout the design process [1, 3, 7]. Thus there are two aspects to design [1, 3]:

1. creating an artifact that satisfies the constraints: *problem solving*,

2. defining or modifying a problem by identifying, refining, relaxing, and retracting constraints: *problem structuring*.

A model has been proposed by Simon [23] to account for both types of behavior. The model consists of a problem solver which operates in a well-structured problem space at any given point in time, and a noticing and evoking mechanism which modifies that problem space. The user interface is based on the premise that WRIGHT finds the solutions satisfying the set of constraints, and the designer is the problem structuring agent, even though s/he may also search for solutions.

Below is a list of possible tasks that may be carried out during design, using WRIGHT:

1. Defining new design units. It is possible to modify the hierarchy of design units in the domain, for example to define a new a type of room or appliance to be used as a primitive at some level of design.

2. Identifying new spatial relations. Some domains such as site layout or kitchen layout may require a new spatial relation in order to express desired configurations. Spatial relations are defined in terms of algebraic relations and the designer can introduce new ones.

3. Changing the set of design units in a configuration. After looking at some candidate solutions, the designer may determine that it is possible to place another bedroom in the house or a that hallway is needed.

4. Identifying new constraints. Looking at a particular configuration, the designer may identify additional constraints and need to include them in the knowledge base.

5. Relaxing constraints. When it is not possible to satisfy all the constraints, some have to be relaxed.

6. Maintaining multiple alternatives. These are pareto optimal partial solutions that are significantly different from each other.

7. Selecting a partial solution to expand.

8. Selecting an operator for generating new alternatives.

The first four operations are carried out only by the designer. Constraints, design units and spatial relations are defined declaratively and can easily be changed by the designer during the design process. The changes may become part of the knowledge base. The system carries out the last four operations, using the knowledge defined by design units, spatial relations and constraints.

Constraints specifying relations between design units at any level of the class hierarchy, including particular instances of design units, are posted, relaxed and retracted by selecting the elements from pop-up menus. The designer can interact with WRIGHT to make the layout decisions. There are commands to create, size, locate, and orient design units. The designer can define a rectangle by clicking at its top left and bottom right corners in the graphics window using the mouse. Rectangles are used to input minimum size, maximum size and bounding box of the location of objects. It is possible to think of a rectangle as a constraint, because it indicates bounds. During interactive sizing and locating operations, WRIGHT will not allow the user to violate existing bounds on a design unit. For relaxing bounds, one needs to move up in the search tree to a state where those values have not been determined yet or have looser bounds.

13.4. KNOWLEDGE-BASE

WRIGHT expresses domain knowledge using prototype design units, spatial relations and constraints. It has knowledge bases for designing kitchens, houses, manufacturing facilities and for solving bin-packing problems.

13.4.1. Design Unit Hierarchy

The taxonomy of design units in some layout domain are defined by prototype design units. These are organized hierarchically using *is-a* links. The design units used in the design of small home kitchens is seen in Figure 13-5.

Configuration knowledge is expressed as constraints on the prototypes. Constraints are inherited through the hierarchy, therefore its structure should facilitate organizing domain knowledge. A new prototype can be created and placed at the appropriate point in the hierarchy, so that it inherits constraints and

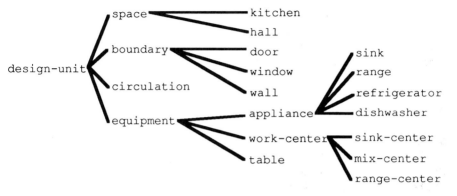

Figure 13-5: Taxonomy of Kitchen Design Units

values from above, and those below inherit from it. Inheritance of constraints eliminates duplication.

Abstraction by *aggregation* combines design units into larger design units, which are the primitive objects of configurations at another level of aggregation. A design problem may span more than one level. For example, in the design of a housing complex, the levels of aggregation are building, apartment, room, and furniture. The hierarchy in Figure 13-5 contains design units at three levels of aggregation: spaces, work centers and appliances. A kitchen contains the work centers and circulation. A sink-center may contain sink and dishwasher. WRIGHT can represent and solve spatial layout problems involving multiple levels. There is no difference in the way objects at different levels of aggregation are treated.

13.4.2. Spatial Relations and Limits on Dimensions

WRIGHT's constraints specify spatial relations between design units or limits on their dimensions. Spatial relations indicate the location of one design unit with respect to another. For example, adjacency is a spatial relation. Some spatial relations are purely topological, independent of any dimensions, such as adjacency. Others such as distance involve a dimension. Some spatial relations are dependent on the orientations of the design units.

There is a very large number of possible spatial relations. Therefore in WRIGHT, we have defined a set of spatial relations with the goal of expressing the characteristics of configurations that are of interest in spatial planning. If in some domain we need to express other relationships, it is possible to define new spatial relations using a grammar defined for this purpose.

The spatial relations currently defined in WRIGHT are seen in Figure 13-6. Spatial relations are grouped in two, based on whether the orientation of the design units is considered, or whether the relations are defined with respect to the global coordinates of the configuration. *Object-centered relations* are defined with respect to the orientation of one of the design units involved. *Global relations* are defined with respect to the global coordinates, which has the y-axis pointing down and the x-axis pointing towards the right.[2]

The types of global relations are position, spatial-overlap, alignment and adjacency. Position relations indicate the location of one object with respect to another. Spatial-overlap deals with combinations of overlapping or non-overlapping of the x and/or y components of rectangles. Alignment relations specify that the north, south, east or west lines of two rectangles are equal. Global relations are seen in Figure 13-7.

Note that the relations are not mutually exclusive. For example, non-overlap, west-of, completely-next-to, and align-one-side relations can hold at the same time between two design units. Also some relations are inverses, i.e. inside is the inverse of has-inside, and east-of is the inverse of west-of. Inverses are seen under the same picture.

There are object-centered relations corresponding to all global relations except spatial-overlap. These are similar to their global counterparts except they also depend on the orientation of the first design unit. Direction relations are on the orientations of both design units. Some object-centered relations are seen in Figure 13-8.

The set of spatial relations are not fixed in WRIGHT. It is possible to define new relations by specifying the semantics of the relation using a grammar defined for this purpose.

The second group of constraint types are limits on dimensions. Limits are *greater-than*, *greater-than-or-equal*, *less-than*, *less-than-or-equal*, and *equal-to*. They are for expressing constraints on dimensions. The use of spatial relations and limits in constraints are described below.

---

[2]This is based the convention used in most graphics systems today, and is defined for ease of displaying text by starting from the origin and going from left to right in positive x direction and top to bottom in positive y direction.

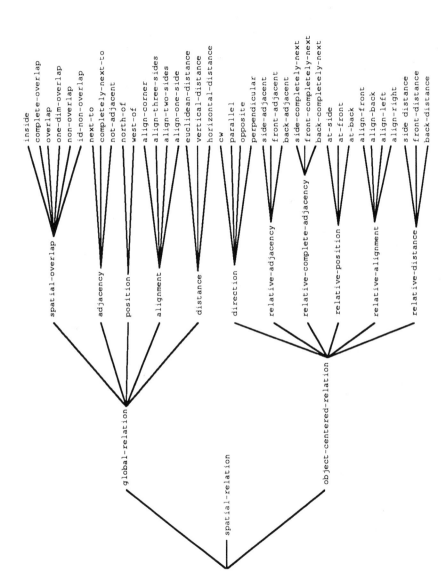

Figure 13-6: The Set of Spatial Relations in WRIGHT

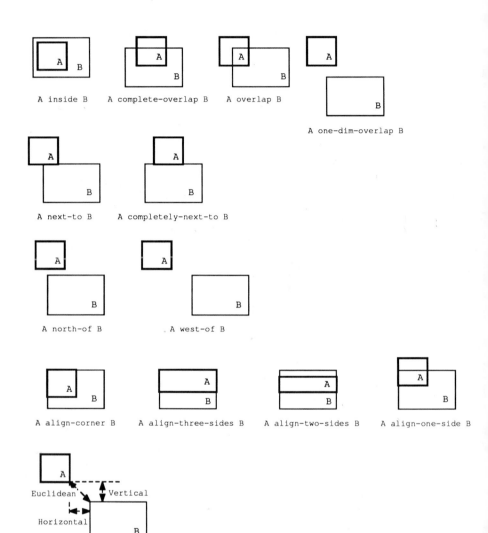

Figure 13-7: Global Relations

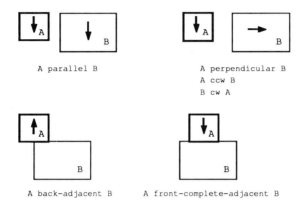

Figure 13-8: Object-centered Relations

13.4.3. Domain Constraints

Constraints express knowledge of the design domain in the form of desired relations between design units, *spatial constraints*, or limits on their dimensions, *dimensional constraints*.

Spatial constraints specify a relation between two design units. Since constraints expressing domain knowledge are posted to prototype design units, they must also contain quantifiers designating how they apply to instances. The quantifiers in WRIGHT are *all* and *some*. Some spatial relations, such as distance or next-to may require numerical values specifying a minimum or maximum. The following are spatial domain constraints:

```
All sink completely-next-to some window
All sink next-to some window ≥ 50 cm.
```

Dimensional constraints specify a design unit, a dimension of the design unit,[3] and an algebraic relation. Dimensional constraints also contain quantifiers.

Some sink length greater-eq 90 cm.

The constraint above requires that there must be at least one sink longer than 90 cm, while the constraint below requires that all sinks must be longer than 90 cm. in a layout.

All sink length greater-eq 90 cm.

The dimensional constraints above are *unary* dimensional constraints. *Binary* dimensional constraints specify a limit between two dimensions. There are no binary dimensional constraints in kitchens, so the following example is from the domain of house layout:

All masterbedroom area greater-than all bedroom area.

Every domain constraint is assigned an *importance* value between *0* and *1*, used for rating solutions. *Relaxations* are tried when a constraint can not be satisfied. Relaxation of a constraint is another constraint that specifies alternative relations, alternative design units, or looser bounds on numerical variables. Relaxations are specified explicitly, either by denoting one or more constraints as relaxations of some constraint, or by specifying that it is possible to omit the constraint, i.e., the empty relaxation. Constraints that may not be relaxed cause a configuration to be eliminated when they are violated. Relaxations have lower importance values than the constraint they relax, and an empty relaxation contributes an importance of *0*.

Design knowledge is expressed in terms of required spatial relations in WRIGHT. Consider the relationship of the sink to windows: "The average housekeeper spends nearly 1 and 1/4 hours at the sink each day so there is a good case for putting the sink at a window for good light and view." [2], p.72. One way of satisfying the requirements is placing the back of the sink completely next to the window, which is expressed by the following constraints:

• **All sink completely-next-to some window, importance=1**

• **All sink at-back some window, importance=1**

When it is not possible to put the sink completely next to the window, placing it in front of and perpendicular to the window will allow direct light and a view of

---

[3]Dimensional variables associated with design units are length, width and area. They are defined in the section on layout representation.

outside. The sink must also be close enough to the window. The following constraints express this case:

- All sink distance some window ≤ 120 cm., importance=0.8
- All sink one-dim-overlap some window ≥ 30 cm., importance=0.6
- `All sink perpendicular-to some window, importance=0.8`

The second set of constraints are a relaxation of the first two, and have lower importance values. Distance is measured between closest points, and one dimensional overlap means overlap in either the vertical direction or the horizontal direction.

13.5. REPRESENTATION OF CONFIGURATIONS

Configurations are made up of design unit instances and algebraic constraints which define their relative positions. A design unit instance is a structured variable which consists of 8 variables: north-line, south-line, east-line, west-line, length, width, area, and orientation. North-line, south-line, east-line and west-line are the *locations* of the four lines of the rectangle. Length and width are *dimensions*, indicating distances between pairs of lines. Area is another dimension, equal to length times width. Locations and dimensions are interval variables defined by a minimum and a maximum value. For locations, the domain initially is [−∞, ∞], and for dimensions [0, ∞]. Orientation indicates which way the front of the design unit is facing. The domain of orientation variables is {0, 90, 180, 270}. The algebraic constraints are: =, >, ≥, +, and ×.

A design unit defines constraints between its lines, dimensions and area, as seen in Figure 13-9.

Configurations are defined by algebraic relations between variables. In Figure 13-10, the sink is south of the window, and adjacent to it for 50 cm. or longer. The algebraic relations which define this configuration are seen in the same Figure. Variables *v1* and *v2* are created for expressing the adjacent distance between sink and window.

A configuration is formed by adding relations and sometimes new variables incrementally. After each change, local propagation using interval arithmetic maintains the consistency of the layout.

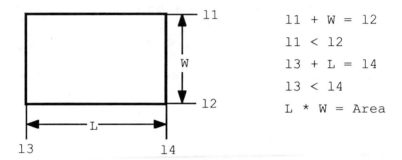

Figure 13-9: Constraining Relations Defined by a Design Unit

Reprinted by permission of Springer Verlag from 'Constraint Satisfaction
Techniques for Spatial Planning,' by Can Baykan and Mark Fox, in *Intelligent
CAD Systems III: Practical Experience and Evaluation* (p. 194, 1991).

13.6. CONSTRAINT COMPILER

The constraint compiler takes the prototype design units, domain constraints
and spatial relations in the knowledge base and the design unit instances in a
given problem, and creates a *constraint graph* which will be used for generating
and testing solutions.

The constraint graph is an and/or network that refines design knowledge
represented by constraints on prototype design units into a design specification
represented as combinations of algebraic constraints on the components of the
design unit instances.

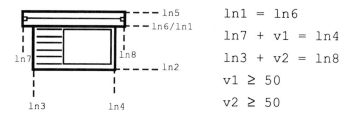

$$ln1 = ln6$$
$$ln7 + v1 = ln4$$
$$ln3 + v2 = ln8$$
$$v1 \geq 50$$
$$v2 \geq 50$$

Figure 13-10: A Configuration and the Algebraic Constraints Defining It

Reprinted by permission of Springer Verlag from 'Constraint Satisfaction Techniques for Spatial Planning,' by Can Baykan and Mark Fox, in *Intelligent CAD Systems III: Practical Experience and Evaluation* (p. 194, 1991).

13.6.1. Defining Spatial Relations

The prototype design unit hierarchy, spatial relations, domain constraints, and design unit instances have been defined above. Spatial relations are defined in terms of and/or combinations of algebraic constraints on the lines of two design units. The terms used in the grammar are: *and, or* or algebraic constraint such as *equal-to* or *less-eq* between two components. The first component is from the design unit listed first in the constraint, and the second component is from the design unit listed second.

The definition of completely-next-to relation is seen in Figure 13-11. There are four topologically distinct ways of satisfying the completely-next-to relation. These alternatives split the domains of location variables into discontinuous intervals, defining topologically different alternatives. The mapping of the spatial relations must be defined such that the alternatives are exhaustive and mutually exclusive, because they will be used for generating solutions.

```
(*OR*  (*AND*  (equal-to west-line east-line)
               (less-eq south-line south-line)
               (greater-eq north-line north-line))
       (*AND*  (equal-to east-line west-line)
               (less-eq south-line south-line)
               (greater-eq north-line north-line))
       (*AND*  (equal-to south-line north-line)
               (less-eq east-line east-line)
               (greater-eq west-line west-line))
       (*AND*  (equal-to north-line south-line)
               (less-eq east-line east-line)
               (greater-eq west-line west-line)))
```

Figure 13-11: Definition of *competely-next-to*
using WRIGHT's Mapping Grammar

13.6.2. Constraint Graph

The mapping of the domain constraint

All sink completely-next-to some window

into algebraic constraints on the component lines of sink1, window1 and
window2 using the definition of completely-next-to given above is seen in
Figure 13-12.

A constraint graph consists of nodes and links as seen in Figure 13-12. Internal nodes are of two types: and-nodes and or-nodes. And-nodes are expressed
by connecting the links leaving the node by an arc. The links in the constraint
graph indicate *reliance* between constraints. Leaf nodes are algebraic constraints. The leaf nodes are shown in abbreviated form, where an algebraic constraint and the variables it connects, such as *line1* = *line2*, are represented by a
single node.

The constraint graph specifies alternative ways of satisfying a constraint.
Prototype design units that have more than one instance and spatial relations that
can be satisfied in different ways introduce disjuncts to the constraint graph.
The top level of the graph is in *conjoint normal form*.

13.6.3. Abstract Constraints

When there are conditions which hold true in all the alternatives, they can be
used to bound solutions without committing to a specific alternative. These are
called abstract constraints. Abstract constraints exist for adjacency and distance
relations, and for dimensional constraints.

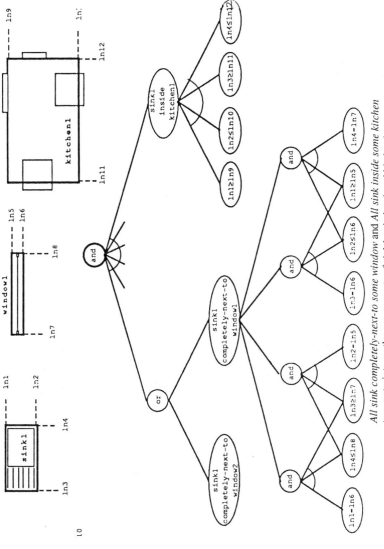

All sink completely-next-to some window and *All sink inside some kitchen* to constraints on the components of sink1, window1 and kitchen1.

Figure 13-12: Partial Constraint Graph Mapping the Constraints

Reprinted by permission of Springer Verlag from 'Constraint Satisfaction Techniques for Spatial Planning,' by Can Baykan and Mark Fox, in *Intelligent CAD Systems III: Practical Experience and Evaluation* (p. 196, 1991).

The abstract constraints for:

`sink1 completely-next-to window1`

where sink1 and window1 are as seen in Figure 13-12, are given below:

```
ln4 ≥ ln7
ln8 ≥ ln3
ln2 ≥ ln5
ln6 ≥ lnl
```

When it is determined that sink1 should be completely-next-to window1, these abstract constraints may be used to prune other alternatives without committing to a particular way of satisfying the sink1—window1 adjacency.

13.6.4. Formulating Spatial Layout as Constrained Optimization

A constraint satisfaction problem (CSP) [19] consists of a set of variables with predefined domains, and constraints between them. All variables and constraints are given at the start. The goal is to find one or all combinations of values that are consistent. The COP formulation of WRIGHT extends the CSP model by assigning importances to the values.

A spatial layout problem can be formulated as a CSP where the variables are the locations, dimensions and orientations. But location and dimension variables have continuous values, thus trying possible values using generate and test is infeasible. Though dimensions and locations can be discretized using a grid, this arbitrarily eliminates some solutions. Also, solutions found as a result of assigning values to interval variables will not be different from each other in significant ways.

In WRIGHT's formulation, the variables are the nodes connected to the root of the constraint graph. The values for the variables are the alternative ways of satisfying them, as given below them in the constraint graph. The consistency of the layout is ensured by keeping the interval values for locations and dimensions legal. For example, the variables in the constraint graph in Figure 13-12 are the two nodes connected to the root. The first variable has 8 alternative values. Four of them are the distinct ways of placing sink1 completely-next-to window1, and the other 4 are ways of placing sink1 completely next-to window2. The second variable has only one value as there is only one way of placing sink1 inside kitchen1.

The importance of each value is determined by the importance of the domain constraint it is derived form. When an alternative is due to a relaxation, it will have the importance of the relaxation. If a null relaxation has been specified for a constraint, it means that the variable can be removed from the COP, and not assigned a value. WRIGHT tries to find all pareto optimal solutions.

This is the dual of the problem where the variables are lines and dimensions, and the constraints are spatial relations and limits. The advantage of WRIGHT's formulation is that it becomes a discrete problem where the alternatives are structurally different.

13.7. SEARCH

WRIGHT formulates spatial layout as a COP and solves it by *constrained heuristic search*(CHS). CHS combines constraint satisfaction with heuristic search [13]. It retains heuristic search's synthetic capabilities, and adds to it the structural capabilities of constraint satisfaction. The CHS model adds *problem textures* to the definition of a problem space composed of states, operators and an evaluation function. Problem textures are based on the topology of the constraint graph and they allow search to be focused in a way that reduces backtracking.

The problem is solved by backtracking search combined with constraint propagation. Search operates by selecting a variable and assigning values to it. In this case, variables are the nodes that are connected to the root of the constraint graph, and possible values are the algebraic constraints it maps into. Satisfying the algebraic constraints removes values from the domains of numerical variables by constraint propagation. If the minimum of an interval variable becomes greater than its maximum, then the algebraic constraints are inconsistent. Reducing the domains of lines and dimensions may remove alternatives from search variables. If the range of a variable becomes empty, then that constraint is violated.

The cycle repeated in every state is

1. Select a dual variable with alternative values, using texture measures.

2. Create new states by assigning a different possible value to the variable in each state.

3. Propagate constraints, changing values of numerical variables. Test algebraic and orientation constraints, which will determine the status of nodes above them in the constraint graph. Satisfy dual variables with one remaining alternative.

The third step itself is a cycle that is repeated until quiescence. The whole cycle is seen in Figure 13-13.

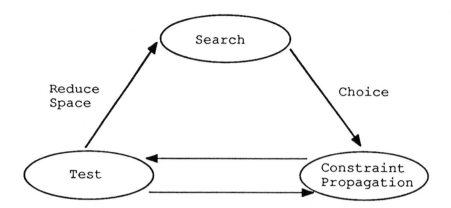

Figure 13-13: The Cycle of Operations in Every Search State

Given the constraint graph in Figure 13-12, the constraint

Sink1 inside kitchen1

will be satisfied first, because there is one way of satisfying it. The algebraic constraints at its leaves are satisfied by propagating values. Propagation will change the location of the sink so that when the active nodes in the constraint graph are checked, there remains two alternatives for the or-node, which are

1. placing sink1 south-of window1,
2. placing sink1 west-of window2.

Since it is the only active variable, search continues by trying its two values, resulting in two alternatives. At this point, all constraints are satisfied and the problem is solved. There are two equally good and significantly different solutions. When there is more than one active variable at some point in search, textures are used to select the next variable to assign values.

The search formulation described above constitutes a priority solution strategy, where operators can create macro objects or configurations in unbounded space. Textures select constraints that can be satisfied with high certainty or those most useful for simplifying search. Textures implement a fail-first and prune-early strategy.

Properties of the search architecture used in WRIGHT are

- Search is *monotonic*. States are generated by satisfying new algebraic constraints. Therefore a requirement that is satisfied can not be violated later.

- Disjuncts specified in the constraint graph are *mutually exclusive*. Therefore it is not possible to get duplicate solutions.

- Search efficiency depends on the order constraints are satisfied. Adding a set of constraints to the CSP in any order leads to the same solution.

13.7.1. Texture Measures

The philosophy behind this research is to use constraints to understand the structure of the problem space and make search efficient. The constraint graph and texture measures help in selecting an efficient ordering of variables. An efficient ordering reduces backtracking and requires assigning values to fewer variables before the values of all variables are determined.

Texture measures use two perspectives, a constraint perspective and a variable perspective. Textures using a constraint perspective look at the attributes of the constraint graph, such as the alternative ways of satisfying a constraint. Texture measures using a variable perspective evaluate constraints with respect to attributes of the variable they constrain, such as the number of active constraints on a design unit.

The heuristic implemented by textures is fail first. We try to pick a variable which will lead to fewer alternatives and which will eliminate more values from the domains of remaining variables. Since we are looking for all solutions, only variable selection heuristics are useful. Value selection heuristics do not come into play because all values of a selected variable must be tried.

The texture measures used in WRIGHT are reliance, contention and looseness. Contention uses a variable perspective, and reliance and looseness use a constraint perspective. The textures can be applied in any order and combination. They are applied lexicographically. The first texture assigns ratings to all the active variables, and eliminates those with lower values. If only one variable remains, there is no need to apply other textures. If there are more than one, the next texture is applied. If after applying all textures more than one variable remains, one is selected at random. How each texture assigns values to nodes in the constraint graph, and how these values are combined are described below.

Textures used in WRIGHT are

- *Reliance:* looks at the number of remaining values for each variable. The number of values is the number of states that will be generated at the next level if that variable is selected. This texture selects a variable with fewer values.

- *Contention:* looks at design units and as yet undetermined variables. The contention value for each design unit is the number of variables expressing a requirement for that design unit, that are not yet assigned values. The contention value for a variable is the sum of the contention values of the design units it is related to. This texture favors variables related to design units having a large number of requirements.

- *Looseness:* considers the location and dimension variables involved in each search variable and averages their domain size resulting from satisfying the relation. For example: let *l1*=[*100, 200*], *l2*=[*150, 180*], and *alt1* = *l1* ≥ *l2*. The resulting domains will be *l1*=[*150, 200*], *l2*=[*150, 180*]. The sizes of the domains are *50* and *30*, and the average is *40*. Looseness values are combined by averaging at and-nodes and taking the maximum at or-nodes. Looseness tends to favor larger design units and spatial relations which project tight locations.

The textures can be applied in any order and any combination. A variable is selected dynamically at each state, rather than fixing the order of variables before search starts.

13.7.2. Testing

Nodes in the constraint graph can have one of three values *satisfied, violated* or *undetermined.* Undetermined means that the bounds of the interval variables are so large that the constraint can be violated or satisfied depending on decisions that will be made later.

An and-node is satisfied when all of the nodes below it are satisfied. It is violated when one of the nodes below it are violated. An or-node is satisfied when one of the nodes below it is satisfied and violated when all of the nodes below it are violated. For example, if all nodes below an or-node are contradicted except one which is undetermined, the status of the or-node will be undetermined.

The structure of the constraint graph is such that every node connected to the root must be satisfied. Therefore when one of these nodes is violated, the rating of the state needs to be changed.

The result of checking an algebraic constraint is *satisfied, violated* or *undetermined* just as for other nodes in the constraint graph defined earlier. An algebraic constraint is satisfied when every combination of values in the domains of the variables satisfy the constraint. A constraint is violated if no combination of values in the domains of the variables satisfy the constraint. And when some combinations of values satisfy the constraint, and some don't, the constraint is undetermined. The conditions where a *greater-or-equal* constraint is satisfied, violated or undetermined is given below.

A *greater-or-equal* constraint: $[min_1, max_1] \geq [min_2, max_2]$, is satisfied when $min_1 \geq max_2$, and violated when $max_1 < min_2$. It is undetermined if $max_1 \geq min_2$ and $min_1 < max_2$.

An orientation constraint is violated if no combination of values in the domains satisfy the constraint, and satisfied when all combinations of values satisfy the constraint. For example, parallel requires two orientations to be equal. The constraint: *Orientation1 parallel orientation2* is satisfied when *Orientation1*={0} *and orientation2*={0}, undetermined when *Orientation1*={0, 90} and *orientation2*={0, 90}, and violated when *Orientation1*={0, 90} and *orientation2*={180, 270}.

Constraint propagation removes the values that can not be part of any solution from the domains of variables. Constraint propagation is a least-commitment formulation. Therefore sometimes a constraint that is satisfied transitively will not be detected as satisfied by checking values. Selecting it and propagating values will fail. Thus it is possible to also test constraints by propagation of markers and checking the existence of constraint paths. This is computationally expensive.

13.7.3. Constraint Propagation

Constraint propagation is started by selecting a new algebraic or orientation constraint to satisfy. The values of all variables in the constraint are made consistent. When the value of any variable changes, all of the constraints incident to it are used to propagate values to their variables. If during propagation, the range of an orientation becomes empty, or when the lower bound of an interval exceeds its upper bound, that means the constraint added last is inconsistent with the previous ones. How propagation is carried out for some orientation and algebraic constraints is given below.

The *v1 parallel v2* be an orientation constraint, and the domains of the variables be *v1*={0, 180} and *v2*={0, 90}. When the constraint is satisfied, {0, 180} is propagated to $v2$. The range of $v2$ becomes $\{0\}$. Then $\{0\}$ is propagated to $v1$, and the range of $v1$ becomes $\{0\}$.

The value of an interval variable $v1=[min_1, max_1]$ can change by increasing its lower bound, min_1, or by decreasing its upper bound, max_1, until $min_1=max_1$. Therefore, a new lower bound min_n, propagated to $v1$ is:

- *redundant* if $min_n \le min_1$,
- *contradicting* if $min_n > max_1$,
- *constraining* if $min_n > min_1$ and $min_n \le max_1$.

This is similar for upper bounds. A contradicting value stops propagation by detecting an inconsistency. A redundant value causes propagation not to spread from that variable, because its value is already consistent. A constraining value changes the variable and causes propagation to continue with the new value.

Let $v_1 = [min_1, max_1]$, $v_2 = [min_2, max_2]$, and $v_3 = [min_3, max_3]$. The following formulas are used for propagation due to the adder constraint: $v_1 + v_2 = v_3$:

1. $min_1 + min_2 \rightarrow min_3$

2. $min_3 - max_1 \rightarrow min_2$

3. $min_3 + max_2 \rightarrow min_1$

4. $max_1 + max_2 \rightarrow max_3$

5. $max_3 - min_1 \rightarrow max_2$

6. $max_3 + min_2 \rightarrow max_1$

When a value on the left side of the arrow changes, the result of the operation on the left is propagated to the variable on the right. Thus the first formula is used for propagating values when either min_1 or min_2 is changed. And when min_1 changes, formulas 1 and 5 are used.

Let A, B and C be three interval variables, $A=[1, 2]$, $B=[3, 4]$, $C=[4, 6]$, and $A+B=C$. Given values for two of the variables, the values propagated to the third are

- $A+B \rightarrow [4, 6]$,
- $C-B \rightarrow [0, 3]$,
- $C-A \rightarrow [2, 5]$.

The following formulas are used for propagation when $v_1 \le v_2$:

1. $min_1 \rightarrow min_2$

2. $max_2 \rightarrow max_1$

The relations that must be maintained by propagation are $min_1 \leq min_2 \wedge max_1 \leq max_2$, such that $v_1 \leq v_2$ is not violated.

Constraint propagation is carried out by a local propagation algorithm, also called the Waltz algorithm and arc consistency algorithm [18]. The algorithm keeps a list of changed variables. In WRIGHT, there are three lists: one for orientation variables, one for interval variables which had their lower bounds changed, and a list for interval variables which had their upper bounds changed. When an orientation constraint is satisfied, both of its variables are placed on the list of changed orientation variables. When an algebraic constraint is satisfied, all of its variables are placed on both the list for variables with changed upper bounds and the list for variables with changed lower bounds. Order of inserting and removing variables from the lists is FIFO, but a variable is not placed in a list again if it is already there. A variable is taken from a list, and all of its constraints are used to propagate values to the other variables in the constraint. If the range of a variable changes, it is inserted into the appropriate list. When the lists are empty, propagation stops.

The complexity of the Waltz algorithm used, when the domains of variables are finite sets, is found by [19] to be $O(ae)$ where a is the number of values in the domains of the variables and e is the number of constraints. This result applies to the propagation of orientations. In such a system of linear equations and inequalities with unit coefficients and interval domains, local propagation maintains node and arc consistency [5]. In the absence of loops, this is equal to path consistency. If there is a loop in the constraint graph, path consistency can not be maintained. Loops cause infinite looping during propagation when an inconsistent value is posted, unless the domains of the variables are bounded.

A configuration of two rooms and a corridor, where both rooms must be adjacent to the corridor for longer than 90 cm. is seen in Figure 13-14. The minimum width of the corridor is 120 cm.

This configuration results in a loop in the constraint graph, as seen in Figure 13-14. The inference that the minimum width of hall is 180 cm is not made unless one of the lines is fixed. When the lines are not fixed, it is possible to assign a value that is less than 180 cm. to hall width. This will cause an infinite loop if line locations are not bounded i.e. a minimum or maximum location is $\pm\infty$. If the lines have bounds that are slack, the contradiction will be eventually detected. In WRIGHT, bounds for the configuration space are always given as part of the problem definition to guard against infinite looping. Dimension variables are redundant in a fully specified configuration, because they can be derived from the locations. In a layout where locations have slack or missing bounds, no information about dimensions can be maintained during propagation unless they also are variables [5].

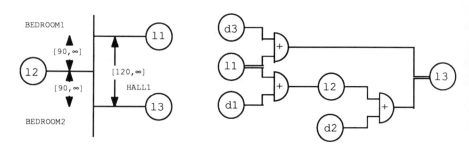

Figure 13-14: A Configuration and its Constraint Graph Containing a Loop

13.7.4. Adjacency Graph

Another reasoning mechanism is based on an adjacency graph representation. The nodes of the graph are the design unit instances and the edges denote adjacency. Edges are directed and of two types: horizontal and vertical edges. The graph representation is created at the time the constraint graph is compiled. When an adjacency constraint is created, its nodes are marked as vertical or horizontal edges. This representation is useful for two types of reasoning, as follows.

When a node corresponding to an edge is satisfied, other edges can be marked as violated and removed from consideration, based on rules about adjacency structures of rectangles. This is more efficient than checking constraints, and removes some alternatives that would not be detected by other tests but only detected during constraint propagation.

Edges have weights denoting the length of common border between the design units. The sum of weights going in to a design unit must be equal to its dimension, and must be equal to the sum of weights of the edges going out. This provides the additional constraints that maintain path consistency, when added to a configuration such as the one seen in Figure 13-14

13.8. PERFORMANCE

WRIGHT has been tested on kitchen layout, house layout and bin-packing/blocks problems. We have tried five kitchen layout problems that contain 7 design units to be located, have 2-6 solutions and approximately 80 conjunctive requirements. The house layout problem has 9 design units to locate, approximately 200 solutions and about 64 conjunctive requirements. The block problem has 6 design units, 24 and 72 solutions in its two variations, and 21 or 27 requirements.

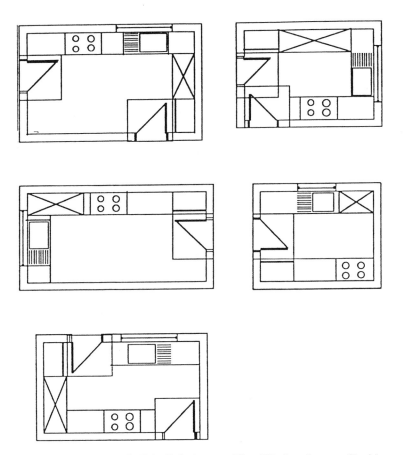

Figure 13-15: WRIGHT's Solutions to Five Kitchen Layout Problems

Adequacy of the knowledge representation and solution quality is evaluated by looking at the solutions WRIGHT generates. Five kitchens with different dimensions and door and window locations are selected from a kitchen design handbook [24]. These are configured by WRIGHT using the same domain knowledge. The solutions given by WRIGHT are compared against the solution given in [24]. WRIGHT finds the solution in the handbook in every case. One solution found by WRIGHT for each kitchen is seen in Figure 13-15. For the kitchens seen at top left and bottom, WRIGHT finds three equally good solutions, and for the kitchen seen at top right, it finds two. The design unit with the diagonals is the mix center. Sink center and range center are the rectangles containing the sink and range respectively.

Rather than applying all textures to all variables and combining the ratings, we apply textures sequentially, in order to minimize the processing time associated with dynamic selection. The first texture used assigns a rating to all active variables and removes from consideration all but the top rated ones. If more than one variable remains, the next texture is applied only to those, or if there is no other texture, one variable is selected at random.

The results of the experiments, as reported previously in [4, 13] are as follows:

1. A priority strategy is more efficient than an organize-by-design-unit strategy, leading to 50% fewer search states when solving the identical problem. Organizing by design unit forces determining all aspects at the same time, whereas priority strategy enables a least-commitment approach. Pursuing this strategy in WRIGHT is possible because of the CSP representation of configurations that enables incremental addition of constraints in any order.

2. Textures reduce search. Compared to random selection of variables, using all 3 textures reduces search states by 70% in kitchen problems and 84% in bin-packing problem.

3. The order textures are applied in has a significant effect on search efficiency. Since the first texture used eliminates most of the variables, it has the greatest effect. As a result, we have tried applying the textures in different orders and combinations. Domain size was the most useful texture in blocks problem, looseness in house layout, and contention in kitchen layout.

Figure 13-16 shows the number of search states required for finding all solutions to five kitchen layout problems, under different combinations of texture measures.

The combinations tested are

- *method 0:* select a constraint at random,
- *method 1:* contention
- *method 2:* reliance,
- *method 3:* contention and reliance,
- *method 4:* contention, reliance and looseness.

When a combination of measures is used, they are applied in the order: contention, reliance and looseness. Each measure eliminates some constraints from consideration. If more than one constraint remains after applying the texture measure(s), specified by the method, a constraint is selected at random. The number of states given for each problem-method combination is the average of three runs. In the second problem, method 4 reduces search by more than 80% compared to method 0, and in the third problem by 35%.

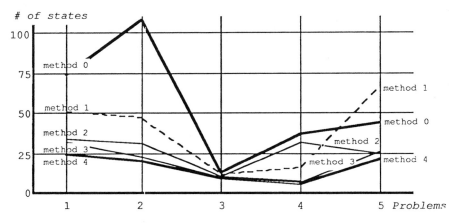

Figure 13-16: Effectiveness of Texture Measures in Reducing Search

In order to compare the CHS approach with generate and test, WRIGHT is compared with two space planning programs, DPS [21] which uses a drawing based representation, and LOOS [11] which uses a relational representation.[4]

---

[4]see Section 13.2 for a discussion of these programs

The problem used in the comparison is arranging six fixed size blocks in a box such that no blocks overlap. Due to the simplicity of the problem, exactly the same set of constraints can be used by all three programs. The programs are compared in terms of the number of states and search levels generated when finding the first solution and when finding all 24 solutions, seen in Figure 13-17; number of search levels is the number of intermediate states on a path from the initial state to a solution state.

	First Solution	All 24 Solutions
WRIGHT	5 levels 14 states	5-6 levels 111 states
LOOS	6 levels 68 states	6 levels 232 states
DPS	6 levels 72 states	*(not available)*

Figure 13-17: Comparison of WRIGHT, DPS and LOOS
in Terms of Search Efficiency

In DPS and LOOS, the number of search levels is always equal to the number of objects to be located, as a result of the organize-by-design-unit strategy. WRIGHT'S performance in terms of number of search levels and number of search states depends on number and strength of available constraints and their interactions. Although the constraints in this problem are not as varied as in kitchen layout, WRIGHT performs better than DPS and LOOS. WRIGHT looks at a smaller number of search states by selecting decisions with fewer alternatives, and by eliminating inferior alternatives earlier.

Performance of the system depends on available constraints. Having additional constraints improves performance as they reduce the number of solutions. Once the problem becomes overconstrained, performance degrades. In order to counteract this, explicit relaxations for some constraints are given in the knowledge base.

In an underconstrained problem, DPS and LOOS find the first solution faster, but there will be a large number of solutions. WRIGHT also finds the first solution faster, and will avoid generating a large number of solutions by having solutions at a higher level of abstraction. In an overconstrained problem, DPS will not be able find any solutions because it rejects a solution that fails any constraint. For LOOS, overconstrained problems pose the same difficulty as underconstrained ones: too many states with equivalent scores. Finding the first solution will take much longer too. Overconstrained problems will cause WRIGHT to search longer before finding the first solution. When all constraints can be satisfied, solutions are defined by alternative ways of satisfying all constraints. When all constraints can not be satisfied, combinations of constraints that result in equal ratings need to be tried. By defining explicit relaxations for some domain constraints in its knowledge base, WRIGHT avoids searching a large number of constraint combinations.

13.9. CONCLUSION

WRIGHT defines spatial planning as a constrained optimization problem and demonstrates the utility of textures and CHS. Advantages of its representation are as follows:

- Topology and dimensions are solved uniformly using algebraic constraints, and constraint propagation.

- Design units at different levels of aggregation can be handled uniformly by representing both inter-level and intra-level constraints explicitly and uniformly.

- Using constraints to guide the generation of significantly different alternatives permits solutions at a higher level of abstraction than in other layout systems, but enables determination of relevant aspects at a very detailed level.

This formulation takes a least-commitment approach by

- selecting constraints to satisfy rather than locations for design units, and

- removing from variable domains only those values which violate a constraint.

The abstraction mechanisms it makes possible are

- abstraction by aggregation, and
- abstract constraints.

The philosophy behind this approach is understanding the structure of the search space to make search efficient. Important points about WRIGHT's approach to search efficiency are

- Constraint propagation techniques dramatically narrow the space of alternative solutions prior to selection/search.
- Properties of the constraint network, known here as *textures*, can be used to focus attention of search (i.e., node and value selection), thereby reducing the amount of backtracking.

  - Contention selects a design unit which has a large number of conjunctive constraints remaining.
  - Reliance chooses to satisfy a constraint for which there are fewer alternative disjunctive decisions.
  - Looseness chooses to satisfy a constraint which reduces range of variables more.

- Both domain independent and dependent knowledge is represented uniformly as constraints thereby enabling the alteration of search behavior and the solutions generated by the search alteration or addition of constraints.

13.10. ACKNOWLEDGMENTS

Work on WRIGHT has been supported by a grant from Digital Equipment Corporation.

13.11. BIBLIOGRAPHY

[1]   Akin O., Dave B., and Pithavadian S., *A Paradigm for Problem Structur-ing in Design*, unpublished working paper, September 1987, [Department of Architecture, Carnegie Mellon University].

[2]   Architects Journal, "Domestic Kitchen Design: Conventional Plan-ning," *Architects Journal*, pp. 71-78, 3 October 1984.

[3]   Baykan, C.A., *Heuristic Methods for Structuring Architectural Design Problems*, unpublished working paper, 1984.

[4]   Baykan, C. and Fox, M.S., "Constraint Satisfaction Techniques for Spa-tial Planning," *Preliminary Proceedings of the Third Eurographics Workshop on Intelligent CAD Systems*, CWI, Amsterdam, pp. 211-227, 1989.

[5]   Davis, E., "Constraint Propagation with Interval Labels," *AI*, Vol. 32, No. 3, pp. 281-331, July 1987.

[6]   Dechter, R. and Pearl, J., "Tree Clustering for Constraint Networks," *AI*, Vol. 38, pp. 353-366, 1989.

[7]   Eastman, C.M., "On the Analysis of Intuitive Design Processes," in *Emerging Methods in Environmental Design and Planning*, Moore, Gary T., Ed., MIT Press, Cambridge,Mass., 1970.

[8]   Eastman, C.M., "Automated Space Planning," *AI*, Vol. 4, pp. 41-64, 1973.

[9]   Fikes, R.E., "REF-ARF: A System for Solving Problems Stated as Procedures," *AI*, Vol. 1, pp. 27-120, 1970.

[10]   Flemming, U., "Wall Representations of Rectangular Dissections and their Use in Automated Space Allocation," *Environment and Planning B*, Vol. 5, pp. 215-232, 1978.

[11]   Flemming, U., *On the Representation and Generation of Loosely Packed Arrangements of Rectangles*, Technical Report DRC-48-05-85, Carnegie-Mellon University Design Research Center, 1985.

[12]   Flemming, U., "On the Representation and Generation of Loosely Packed Arrangements of Rectangles," *Environment and Planning B*, Vol. 13, pp. 189-205, 1986.

[13]   Fox, M.S., Sadeh, N., and Baykan, C., "Constrained Heuristic Search," *Proceedings of IJCAI-11*, IJCAI, pp. 309-315, 1989.

[14]   Freuder, E.C. and Quinn, M.J., "Taking Advantage of Stable Sets of Variables in Constraint Satisfaction Problems," *Proc. IJCAI-9*, IJCAI, pp. 1076-1078, 1985.

[15]   Grason, J., *Methods for the Computer-implemented Solution of a Class of Floor Plan Design Problems*, unpublished Ph.D. Dissertation, Carnegie-Mellon University, May 1970.

[16]   Koopmans, J.C., Beckmann, M.J., "Assignment Problems and the Location of Economic Activities," *Econometrica*, Vol. 25, pp. 53-76, 1957.

[17]   Liggett, R.S., "The Quadratic Assignment Problem: An Analysis of Applications and Solution Strategies," *Environment and Planning B*, Vol. 7, pp. 141-162, 1980.

[18]   Mackworth, A.K., "Consistency in Networks of Relations," *AI*, Vol. 8, pp. 99-118, 1977.

[19]   Mackworth, A.K., and Freuder, E.C., "The Complexity of some Polynomial Network Consistency Algorithms for Constraint Satisfaction Problems," *AI*, Vol. 25, pp. 65-74, 1985.

[20]   Mostow, J., "Toward Better Models of the Design Process," *AI Magazine*, Vol. 6, No. 1, pp. 44-57, 1985.

[21]   Pfeffercorn, C., *Computer Design of Equipment Layouts Using the Design Problem Solver*, unpublished Ph.D. Dissertation, Carnegie-Mellon University, May 1971.

[22]   Purdom, P.W., "Search Rearrangement Backtracking and Polynomial Average Time," *AI*, Vol. 21, pp. 117-133, 1983.

[23]   Simon, H.A., "Structure of Ill-structured Problems," *AI*, Vol. 4, pp. 181-201, 1973.

[24]   Small Homes Council, *Handbook of Kitchen Design*, University of Illinois, Urbana, Illinois, 1950, [Circular C5.32R].

Chapter 14
DESIGNER: A KNOWLEDGE-BASED GRAPHIC DESIGN ASSISTANT

Louis Weitzman

Abstract

Designer is an interactive tool for assisting with the design of two-dimensional graphic interfaces for instructional systems. Graphic domain knowledge, stored in a frame-based representational facility, is coupled to a domain independent mechanism which analyzes and critiques the user's original design. The system then supports the synthesis of design alternatives. These alternative solutions are generated within a design context, or style, and are based upon graphic constraints. The underlying motivation is to improve the quality of the interfaces by making them more consistent and visually more effective.

14.1. INTRODUCTION

Applying technologies from artificial intelligence and cognitive science to the development of computer-based training and computer-aided design systems can provide support in areas where developers and users lack expertise. In addition, these technologies can substantially enhance the process of design. *Designer* is a tool to aid users of *Simulation Environment's Graphics Editor*. The Simulation Environment is a system to aid the construction of instructional environments for computer-based simulations [17]. Designer is just one tool, or activity, in the larger instructional simulation environment. Other activities in this environment include a model control facility, the Model Controller; a view construction facility, the Graphics Editor; a facility to create new icons with new behaviors, the Icon Editor; and a facility to create lessons for students based on particular views and simulation models, the Lesson Editor.

The original application, Steamer, was created to help students develop an understanding of the complex domain of steam propulsion [16]. The system consists of a color graphics interface to the underlying application or simulation. One can view and manipulate this application at a number of different hierarchical levels through the color interface. The Steamer system contains over one hundred color views which range from abstract, high-level representations of the plant (Figure 14-1) to detailed views of gauge panels quite like the actual gauge panels in a ship (Figure 14-2). It was apparent from the beginning that an editor for creating and maintaining this set of views was essential. The Graphics Editor allows nonprogrammers to graphically create these interactive, dynamic views of the simulation. Figure 14-3 depicts the black-and-white interface of the Graphics Editor. This tool has allowed propulsion engineering instructors to create substantial portions of the student interface to this advanced training system. Even though the Editor was originally built for the construction of Steamer views, the tool is domain independent and has been used to build interfaces in a wide variety of domains including monitoring the real-time performance of a computer operating system and controlling remote hardware devices such as a video switcher.

Views are constructed out of graphic components called *icons* which represent elements in the application domain. Icons perform two tasks. First, they graphically depict the state of the simulation. For example, pumps are red when stopped and green when operating, dials display their value by positioning an indicator, and pipes show their value by animating their fluid. Second, the user can affect the simulation via the icons. When the user positions a cursor over the icon and clicks the mouse, the state of the icon and its associated value in the simulation are modified. For example, a pump's state toggles from off to on and a dial's value is set by positioning the indicator. Figure 14-4 shows a sampling of the types of icons available to users of this Editor. In creating a view, the user selects the icons to be added to the view from a menu on the black-and-white screen. The user then positions and sizes the new icon on the color display. This icon has its parameters defaulted according to the type of icon chosen. Then, through a process of incremental refinement, the user modifies only those attributes that differ in this particular application.

It is unrealistic to assume that instructional designers are facile with graphic design. Facilities were built into the Graphics Editor to support the construction of *good* views. These facilities include various types of grid latching and the use of default graphic properties for icons. Because of the flexibility of the Editor, however, these constraints were often overridden by the designer. Even working within these constraints, users often violate important graphic design principles and have difficulty maintaining stylistic conventions across sets of views. Designer is a tool to enhance the Graphics Editor by supplementing the designer's domain knowledge with the necessary graphic expertise.

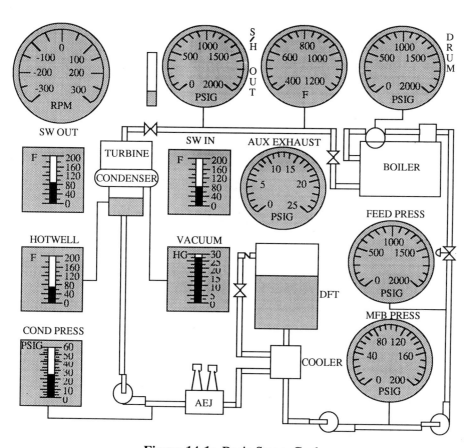

Figure 14-1: Basic Steam Cycle

The color interface can depict the simulation at many different levels of abstraction. This high-level, conceptual view illustrates the complete steam cycle.

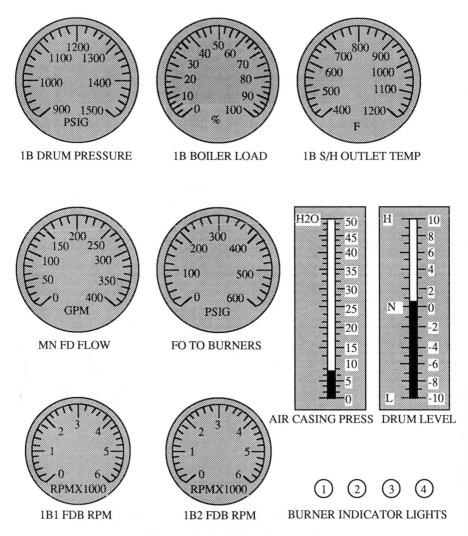

Figure 14-2: Boiler Console 1B

This view of the boiler console panel illustrates the color interface representing detailed views of actual engineering stations.

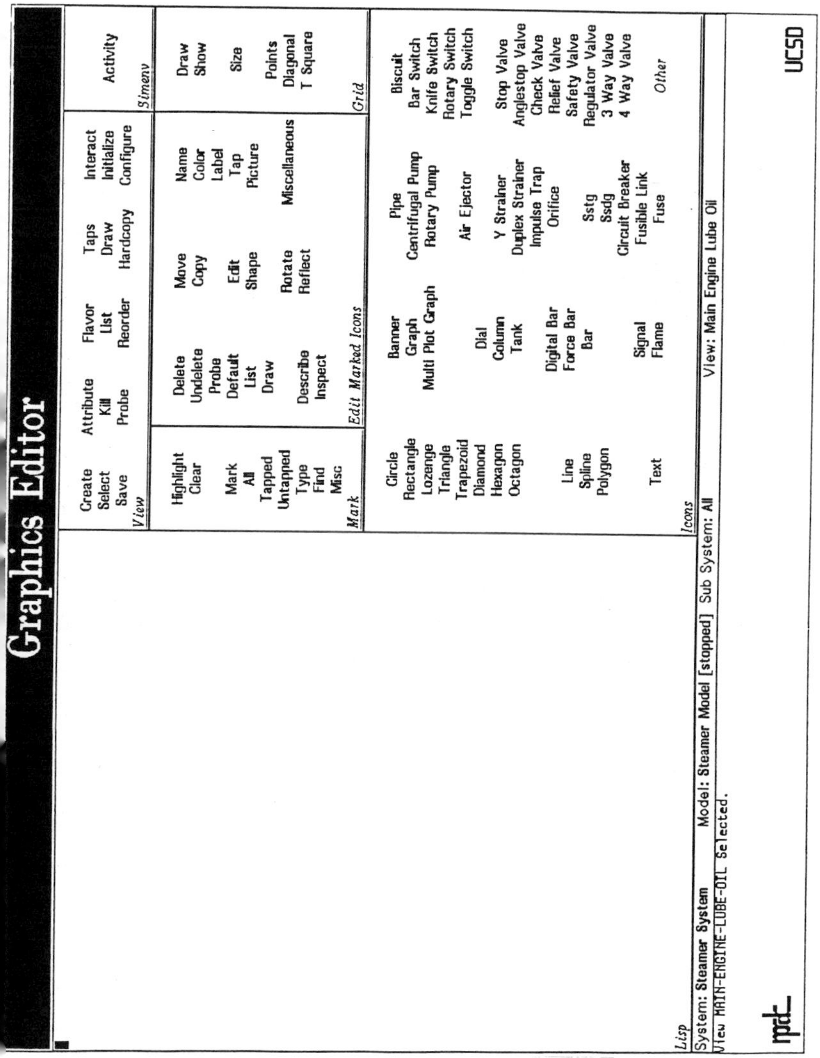

Graphics Editor

Create	Attribute	Flavor	Taps	Interact	Activity
Select	Kill	List	Draw	Initialize	
Save	Probe	Reorder	Hardcopy	Configure	

View · *Simenv*

Highlight	Delete	Default	Move	Edit	Name	Draw
Clear	Undelete	List	Copy	Shape	Color	Show
	Probe	Draw			Label	Size
Mark			Rotate		Tap	Points
All	Describe		Reflect		Picture	Diagonal
Tapped	Inspect				Miscellaneous	T Square
Untapped						
Type						
Find						
Misc						

Mark · *Edit Marked Icons* · *Grid*

Circle	Banner	Pipe	Biscuit
Rectangle	Graph	Centrifugal Pump	Bar Switch
Lozenge	Multi Plot Graph	Rotary Pump	Knife Switch
Triangle			Rotary Switch
Trapezoid		Air Ejector	Toggle Switch
Diamond	Dial		
Hexagon	Column	Y Strainer	Stop Valve
Octagon	Tank	Duplex Strainer	Anglestop Valve
		Impulse Trap	Check Valve
	Digital Bar	Orifice	Safety Valve
Line	Force Bar		Relief Valve
Spline	Bar	Sstg	Regulator Valve
Polygon		Ssdg	3 Way Valve
	Signal	Circuit Breaker	4 Way Valve
Text	Flame	Fusible Link	
		Fuse	*Other*

Icons

View: Main Engine Lube Oil

Lisp

System: Steamer System   Model: Steamer Model [stopped]   Sub System: All

View MAIN-ENGINE-LUBE-OIL Selected.

UCSD

Figure 14-3: Graphics Editor Interface

The Graphics Editor is a domain-independent tool allowing nonprogrammers to create graphic interfaces for monitoring and controlling underlying simulations or real-time processes.

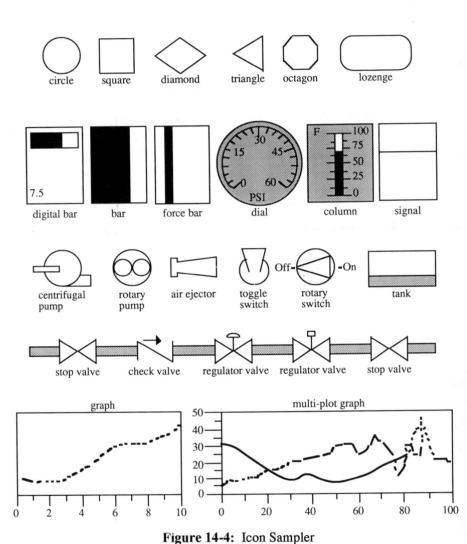

Figure 14-4: Icon Sampler

This view illustrates a sample of the graphic icons available to designers creating interactive interfaces.

14.2. OVERVIEW

Designer provides visual expertise to users of the Graphics Editor inter-actively constructing new Simulation Environment views or modifying existing ones. This visual expertise includes principles extracted from the fields of visual arts [13, 33] graphic design [3, 8, 19] and architecture [9, 30]. These prin-ciples are concerned with the graphic elements of the composition and how they interrelate. A typical example is the Principle of Significant Difference which states that when two elements are significantly different their graphic represen-tations should also be significantly different (and is discussed in more detail later). In addition, graphic standards may be enforced by the system. Since the Editor is flexible enough to create any type of view, Designer can assist by notifying the user about any design violations. For instance in the Steamer ap-plication, we desired graphic conventions to be maintained across a set of views. Typical standards here included color useage of the various icons and the exist-ence, size, and placement of view titles. These constraints are particular to the Steamer application and aren't included in the general category of graphic prin-ciples.

Designer relies on three interrelated processes: 1) parsing the design elements and relationships of the domain into a representation that it can then; 2) critiqu-ing based on the contraints of the principles and standards to indicate where the current design succeeds or fails; and finally 3) generation of design alternatives satisfying the constraint violations. These all occur within a design context, or style. These processes are called the *Analyzer*, the *Critiquer*, and the *Synthesizer*, respectively. Power is gained by the three processes communicat-ing through a central knowledge-base that maintains the domain-dependent in-formation of the design. This knowledge base consists of design elements, their attributes, and the design relationships between them. Techniques for the iden-tification of this knowledge is also stored in the knowledge-base. Constraints that establish style for critiquing a design and generative techniques for creating design alternatives are also maintained. The separation of the three processes from the knowledge-base provides independence and modularity to the system. It is the intention that the flexibility of this approach will create a technology that will be extensible to other design domains as well.

In order to support the internal mechanisms of Designer, a number of generic subsystems have been incorporated into the system architecture. These tools in-clude Steamer's frame-based knowledge representation facility (MSG) for stor-ing domain knowledge, and an Assumption-Based Truth Maintenance System (ATMS) for maintaining alternative design decisions which define the design space.

The system is being developed in the object-oriented programming environ-ment of Flavors on a Symbolics 3600 family processor. The use of object-oriented programming techniques of Flavors has greatly facilitated the implementation and is used throughout the system. A preliminary interface used in the development of the system is shown in Figure 5. The multi-paned interface provides access to existing Graphics Editor functions and new Designer functions through scrolling command panes (upper right collection of panes) while access to the domain knowledge is provided in a mouse sensitive graphing pane (upper left pane). A Lisp interaction pane is provided (lower left pane) along with a scrolling pane for Designer information (e.g., constraint violations; lower right pane). A status line, which is consistent throughout all Simulation Environment activities, displays information relevant to the current activity. In Designer, the status line (near the bottom of the screen) displays the current values for the system, subsystem, view, and design style. The labels and their values are all mouse sensitive, providing access to functions on the class of item (clicking on the label) or operations on the item itself (clicking on the specific value).

14.3. DOMAIN-DEPENDENT KNOWLEDGE REPRESENTATION

Much has been written about the knowledge required for graphic design. Unfortunately, the literature does not suggest a consistent representation for this knowledge. Designer attempts to incorporate this knowledge and maintain it in the frame-based representational system, MSG. Designer concentrates on the graphic knowledge describing the domain elements, their relationships, constraints imposed on both the elements and their relationships, and techniques for their modification. For general graphic design these domain elements refer to points, lines, planes, etc. [33]. In Designer, the domain elements are the icons contained within a Steamer view. These, along with their graphic properties, are stored in the knowledge-base.

MSG, a *flavor enhancer* developed as part of the original Steamer project, provides a class structure on top of the Flavors object-oriented programming facility. It provides the ability to define classes of objects and create instances of those classes. Each class provides a set of attributes, or slots, that define the characteristics of the class. Slots are grouped together in roles. Slots inherited from the class' abstractions, or parent classes, are included with the locally defined slots to completely describe the class. When a new class is defined, an instance of a meta-class is created that will maintain all pertinent information about the new class. This includes how to create new class instances, where to store the new instances, how to manipulate them, etc. In addition, when a new

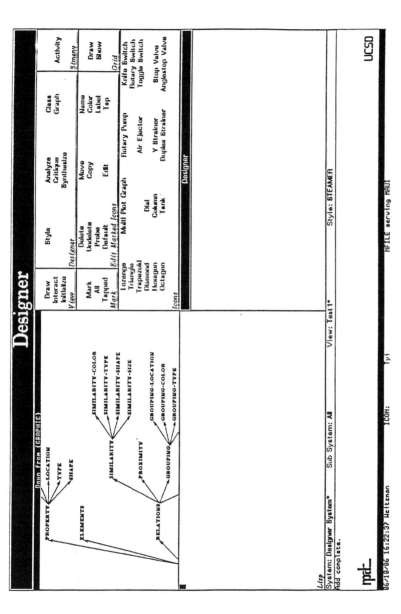

Figure 14-5: The Designer's Interface

The Designer interface provides access to all Graphics Editor commands while providing additional commands to control the design processes and related functions. Domain-dependent knowledge is displayed in a graphing window pane. State information (e.g., current values for system, subsystem, view, and style) is provided in the status line near the bottom of the screen.

class is defined, a new flavor of the same name is also defined. Instances of the class are actually instances of this new flavor with the instance variables corresponding to all slot attributes of the class. The new instances are stored on the class object. MSG can be used incrementally, so as new domain knowledge is defined and recorded in the knowledge base, this information will automatically be included in the analyses. Thus, as the system expands, new knowledge can be incorporated into the knowledge-base. This ability to incrementally build the domain knowledge is important in increasing the system's flexibility.

Designer includes a tool to create, maintain, and inspect the knowledge base as it grows and requires modification. It provides a flexible facility for graphing the domain-dependent knowledge base. The structure of the graphic class hierarchy is clearly visible in the window in Figure 14-6. The graph ranges from more abstract classes on the left to more specific classes on the right. The ability to edit and inspect classes and their instances can be accessed through mouse clicks and menu selections. The menu of commands to operate on the class, its instances, or its flavor is shown in Figure 14-6 for the class *elements*.

14.3.1. Elements

The MSG class of *elements* records all domain elements that will be used in subsequent design analyses. The following is the definition of this class which includes instance variables for a name, a description, all roles (subdivided into slots), all abstractions (parent classes), all used-as-abstractions (classes that use this class as an abstraction), and all of the instances of the class in the current design.

```
#<CLASS ELEMENTS 46622062>
An object of flavor CLASS, has instance variable values:

NAME:           ELEMENTS
DESCRIPTION: "a graphic element"
ROLES:      ((PROPERTIES ((COLOR (A COLOR) NIL NIL)
                          (SIZE NIL NIL NIL)
                          (LOCATION NIL NIL NIL)
                          (TYPE (A TYPE) NIL NIL)
                          (SHAPE (A SHAPE) NIL NIL)
                          (DOMAIN-ELEMENT NIL NIL NIL))))
ABSTRACTIONS: (GRAPHIC)
USED-AS-ABSTRACTION: NIL
INSTANCES:    (#<ELEMENTS DIAL-1 44645216>
              #<ELEMENTS DIAL-2 44644710>
              #<ELEMENTS DIAL-3 44644670>)
```

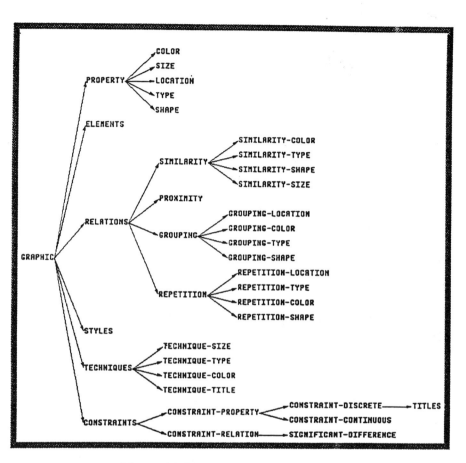

Figure 14-6: Domain Knowledge Base

A graphing tool aids the creation and maintenance of the domain knowledge represented in a frame-based system. Each node in this graph represents a class in the domain of graphic design. Class inheritance is immediately apparent with classes changing from abstract to more specific as one moves through the graph from left to right.

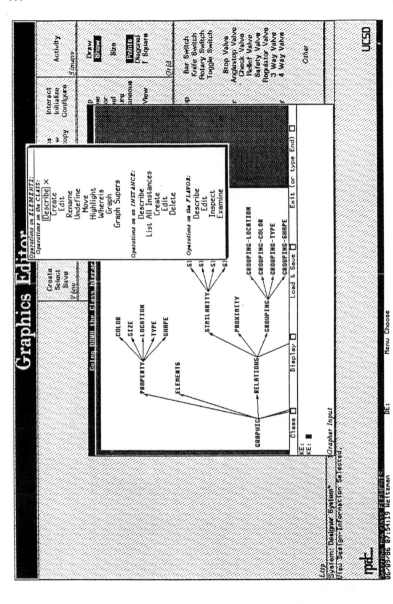

Figure 14-7: Operations on Domain Knowledge

The mouse sensitive graph nodes provide access to operations on the class, its instances, and its flavor definition through mouse clicks and menu selections. The menu is presenting operations for the selected class *elements*.

The slots of this class include graphic properties used to distinguish the elements. These are the graphic properties of color, size, location, type, and shape [13, 33]. The values of these properties on an instance are in fact instances of other MSG classes (see Figure 14-6) that represent valid values for the class. For example, the class of *color* includes instances for Steamer's basic colors. The class *size* includes instances describing a range of sizes from *very-small* to *very-large*, while the class *shape* includes instances of basic geometric shapes like linear, circular, rectangular, etc [13, 33]. Figure 14-8 illustrates the current set of instances for the classes *color, size, type,* and *shape*. In addition, there is a class slot to store the domain element an instance of this class will represent.

In the above example, three instances of the class *elements* are stored on the instance variable *instances*. All three of these objects represent dial icons in the current view. One of these three objects representing a small, blue dial is shown below.

```
#<ELEMENTS DIAL-1 44645216>
An object of flavor ELEMENTS, has instance variable
values:

IDENTIFICATION:      DIAL-1
STRING-FOR-PRINTING: NIL
COLOR:               #<COLOR BLUE 44644212>
SIZE:                ((:X #<SIZE SMALL 44644633>)
                     (:Y #<SIZE SMALL 44644633>))
LOCATION:            ((:X 0.846)
                     (:Y 0.521))
TYPE:                #<TYPE DIAL 44644216>
SHAPE:               #<SHAPE CIRCULAR 44644224>
DOMAIN-ELEMENT:      #<DIAL 44644230>
```

This example (of a class definition and description of one of its instances) illustrates that all class slots (i.e., color, size, location, type, shape, and domain-element) become instance variables on the flavor representing the class. These variables have been initialized on the actual instances to the appropriate class values (e.g., the *blue* instance of class *color* is stored on the *color* instance variable and the actual domain element, #<DIAL 44644230>, is stored on the *domain-element* instance variable).

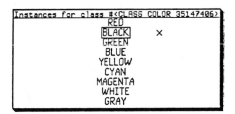

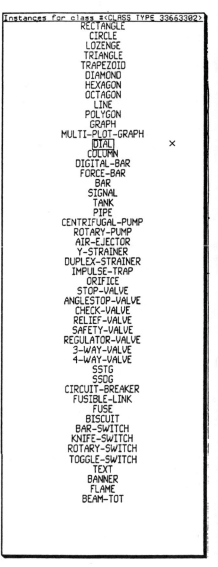

Figure 14-8: Instances of Graphic Property Classes

Menus list the instances of classes representing the four graphic properties *color, size, shape,* and *type.*

14.3.2. Relationships

Currently, the graphic relationships in the knowledge base are *similarity, proximity, grouping,* and *repetition.* As can be seen in Figure 14-6, the relationships of similarity, grouping, and repetition are further classified by the graphic properties of the elements (e.g., grouping by color, repetition by type, etc.). These relationships are often discussed in the literature [9, 13, 30, 33] and have been extracted as graphic relationships to be represented in the knowledge-base. An indication of the certainty of a relationship is also maintained. When parsing techniques are less exacting, the confidence in the relationship will be decreased. The following is the description of the MSG class of *similarity of color:*

```
#<CLASS SIMILARITY-COLOR 46622203>
An object of flavor CLASS, has instance variable values:

NAME:          SIMILARITY-COLOR
DESCRIPTION:   "the graphic
               relationship representing elements of the
               same color"
ROLES:         ((PROPERTIES ((DOMAIN-ELEMENTS NIL NIL NIL)
                             (CERTAINTY NIL NIL NIL))))
ABSTRACTIONS: (SIMILARITY)
USED-AS-ABSTRACTION: NIL
INSTANCES: (#<SIMILARITY-COLOR SIMILARITY-COLOR-BLACK 44645357>
            #<SIMILARITY-COLOR SIMILARITY-COLOR-BLUE 44645350>)
```

In the above example, there are two instances of the relation class *similarity-color,* one for black elements and one for blue elements. The instance representing the relation of similarity of color blue is illustrated below. Here, the previously described dials appear since they all have a blue face color. These elements are stored on the instance variable *domain-elements.*

```
#<SIMILARITY-COLOR SIMILARITY-COLOR-BLUE 44645350>,
An object of flavor SIMILARITY-COLOR,
has instance variable values:

IDENTIFICATION:       SIMILARITY-COLOR-BLUE
STRING-FOR-PRINTING: NIL
DOMAIN-ELEMENTS:      (#<ELEMENTS DIAL-1 44645216>
                       #<ELEMENTS DIAL-2 44644710>
                       #<ELEMENTS DIAL-3 44644670>)
CERTAINTY:            :HIGH
```

All relations know how to handle a generic message to identify occurrences in the design of the relation that they represent. When an occurrence is identified, a new instance of the class is created, stored on the class object, and initialized with all the elements participating in the relation. Relations can also build on one another. For example, elements in proximity to one another may form grouping relations, and groupings may form repetition relations (depending on the elements properties and their layout).

14.3.3. Constraints

Domain constraints consist of both basic graphic design *principles* important in the construction of two-dimensional views and view *standards* that are adopted for the current application. Principles are those constraints that transcend view sets and are generally accepted methods of making images consistent, unambiguous, and visually effective. The Principle of Significant Difference, as previously mentioned, states that when elements are different, they should be significantly different so as not to create a sense of ambiguity [30] (Figure 14-9). This principle can be applied to many of the elements graphic attributes such as size, location, and color. Its application to the size attribute would suggest that elements should be the same size as other, similar elements in the view. Graphic elements that are larger represent objects that are more important or physically larger in the real world. In Figure 14-1 of the Basic Steam Cycle, the dial indicating RPMs is significantly larger than the others, denoting the fact that it is the most important dial of the set. The principle when applied to the location attribute tends to align elements unless there is a reason (of importance or physical fidelity) to accentuate the differences in location. The knowledge base represents these principles as individual instances of the MSG class of significant difference.

Graphic design standards differ from principles because they are special constraints that tend to exist only for a given set of designs for a given application. The use of a title is a typical example of a standard used in Steamer. This standard employed three separate constraints on the graphic properties of *type, size,* and *color* which were restricted to the values of *text, large,* and *yellow,* respectively. Another example of a standard is the restriction of the width of all pipes to be within an acceptable range.

Constraints can be categorized as restrictions on properties of elements or restrictions on their relationships. Constraints on properties take the form of discrete constraints, restricting a property to be a specific value, or continuous constraints where the value can range between a minimum and a maximum value. An example of a set of discrete constraints is the title standard while the pipe width standard illustrates a continuous constraint.

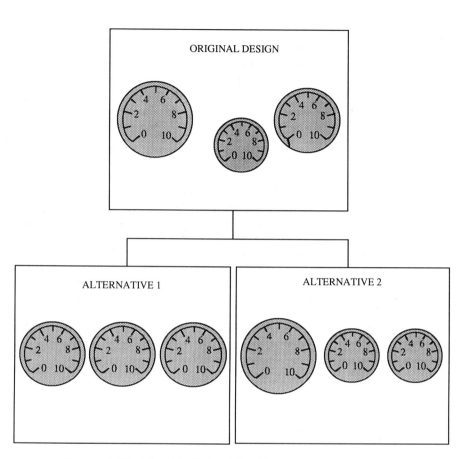

Figure 14-9: The Principle of Significant Difference of Size

This design principle states that when elements are a different size they should be significantly different so as not to create a sense of ambiguity. Given an original design consisting of three dials, two alternatives are presented from a larger solution space. The first alternative suggests no difference in importance and therefore no difference in size. Alternative 2 takes into account the fact that the right two dials are grouped together. The other dial, being physically separate and larger, may be perceived as more important and therefore should be *significantly* larger.

14.3.4. Design Context

A design should be sensitive to the context in which it is created. It is this context that defines the external constraints which shape and guide the final solution. In Designer, this context is referred to as a *style* and is constructed by selecting those constraints (principles and standards) that are to be enforced within this context. Good design in one style may not necessarily be good design in another. Modifying the style within which a critique is made ultimately affects the final form of the design.

A graphic style is also defined by the visual techniques employed in the communication of information. These visual techniques represent a vocabulary in which to describe the design and are used in conjunction with the constraints to suggest a variety of graphic procedures to modify an alternative. These procedures are similar to Mittal's [23] *design methods*. A style editor in Figure 14-10 illustrates several techniques adapted from [13]. For example, the visual technique of *Regularity* may take on a value of regular, neutral, or irregular, each suggesting alternatives consistent with its definition. Highly regular designs will accentuate similiarities of elements and relationships, while irregular designs accentuate the differences. It is the constraints that indicate a discrepancy in the design, while the interaction of the techniques suggest the graphic procedures (maybe more than one) that will modify the design. This editor allows the user to create and edit styles by selecting a name, graphic constraints to be active, and appropriate values for the visual techniques.

14.4. DESIGNER PROCESSES

Design involves a cycle of gathering information, making decisions based on that information, and reviewing the consequences of those decisions. New information gleaned from this process is incorporated back into the cycle for subsequent refinement of the design. This cycle is a general process used in all design whether it be for computer interfaces, industrial applications, or architecture. The process is domain independent.

Designer accomplishes the gathering of information in a process called *Analysis*. In this phase the system parses the partial design into domain elements and relationships. In order to make design decisions, the system must go through a *Critique* phase in which areas in need of improvement are located. After the first two steps have occurred, the system is ready to suggest alternative procedures for modifying the design. This is Designer's *Synthesis* phase.

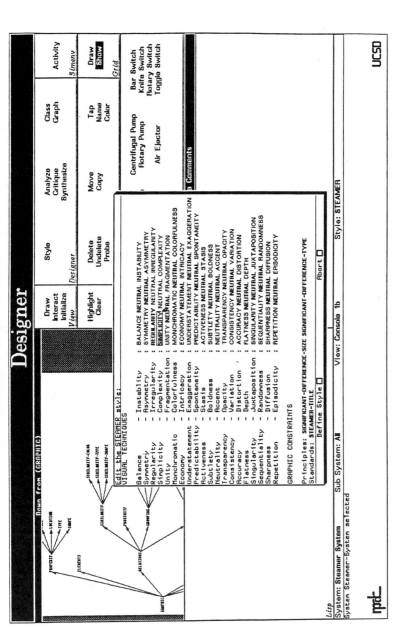

Figure 14-10: Style Editor

This menu edits the graphic style, or context, in which a design critique occurs. A style is defined by the graphic constraints (i.e., principles and standards) that are active and the values chosen for the visual techniques. These visual techniques in combination with the constraints generate the graphic procedures for modifying the design.

Since the overall goal is for the system to be an online assistant and not assume control, review occurs interactively with the user selecting and confirming decisions presented by the system. Information is incorporated back through the process as output from one cycle becomes the input for the next cycle of critique. Each of Designer's processes is described in more detail below.

14.4.1. Analysis

The analysis process parses the design and locates existing domain elements and relationships. Identifying the elements is straightforward because of the object-oriented implementation of the iconic interface. An instance of the MSG class *elements* is created for each icon and the slots are appropriately initialized. For example in the original design of Figure 14-9, the three dials would be represented by three separate elements. Their property values would be represented by the corresponding MSG object as shown in the earlier description.

Once the domain elements have been created, the system locates instances of domain relationships. This task is easy for people but very difficult for computers. Much work has been done in the area of image analysis, but seldom with the goal of *beautifying* drawings. Pavlidis and Van Wyk [25] created a system that inferred graphic constraints from simple drawings and then modified the drawings to satisfy the constraints. Similarly, Designer needs to infer when graphic relations exist between the elements of the view. To maintain the independent nature of the analysis, generic messages are sent to each relation class to identify instances of the class within the design. When an occurrence is found, an instance of the MSG relation class is created and initialized. This includes the recording of the elements that participate in the relation on the appropriate MSG slot.

14.4.2. Critique

As Christopher Alexander suggests, the notion of a *misfit* is more compelling than a *fit* and is a driving force behind the ultimate shape of a design [1]. In Designer, the misfits are identified as violations of the domain constraints and are the driving force in generating design alternatives. The Critiquer creates a *comment* for each unsatisfied design constraint within the current style. These critique comments are Flavor objects that store their underlying constraint and the elements involved in the violation. These comments, displayed in the lower right scrolling pane of the black-and-white interface (Figure 14-11), are mouse sensitive. When clicked on, they can be highlighted (graphically highlighting those elements involved) and/or described in the lower left pane in terms of their underlying constraint. Critiques themselves are implemented as flavor objects that store the object being critiqued (the view), the style in which the critique takes place, and a list of all the relevant comments for this object in this style. Figure 14-11 illustrates a critique based on the principle of the Significant Difference of Size of three dials shown in the original design of Figure 14-9. Two violations of this principle, one for similar typed elements and one for similar shaped elements are displayed in the scrolling pane. A description of the first violation is presented in the Lisp pane.

It thus becomes possible under this paradigm to request multiple critiques, each based on a different independent style. This is an especially powerful paradigm for views that may need to be presented in different media, each with different constraints. For example, a style appropriate for a high resolution color display may not be appropriate for a black-and-white hardcopy presentation. In the black-and-white style, text may be constrained to be solid (i.e., not dithered for different colors) to ensure readability, while a colored display style can support the distinction of the different colors.

14.4.3. Synthesis: Redesign

Design decisions are made in the synthesis phase in order to incrementally refine the elements and their relationships. The designs are not *synthesized* from high level functional specifications but rather are created as modifications of the user actions via constraint satisfaction. Knowledge of the elements and their relationships along with the comments from the critiquing phase forms the basis for these design modifications. Each comment communicates to the constraint on which it is based via generic messages in order to determine the graphic procedures for satisfying the existing violation. More than one procedure may be available to satisfy the constraint and all possiblities are presented to the user. These procedures are a result of the interaction of the various visual techniques and the design constraints which describe the style.

When the user decides to remedy a critique comment, various graphic procedures are presented when the comment is clicked on with the mouse (Figure 14-11). These procedures all modify the design in order to satisfy the constraint, but would do so differently. Since there is no *correct* solution there is no attempt to suggest that one alternative generating procedure may be better than another. The variation of alternatives are based on the definition of the style's visual techniques. A simple example illustrates how the interaction of

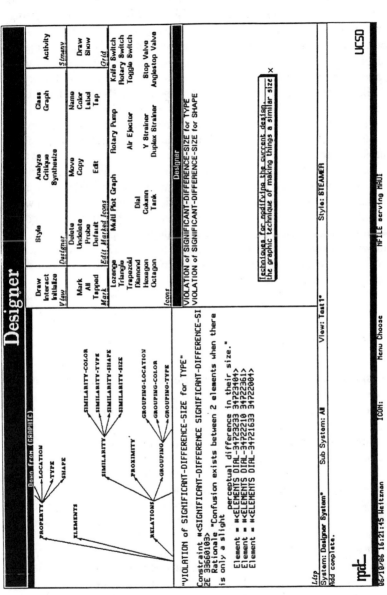

Figure 14-11: Critique of Three Dials

The Designer interface illustrates a critique in progress of the original design from Figure 9. This critique, being executed in the *Steamer Style*, has generated two critique comments based on the Principle of Significant Difference of Size. One comment refers to elements of a similar type while the other refers to elements similar in shape. A description of one violation is presented in the lisp pane and a menu of techniques for modifying the design based on this violation is presented in a pop-up menu.

the graphic constraints with the visual techniques will generate alternative solutions. If a style is defined to be *simple* and *regular*, the constraint of Significant Difference of Size will generate a very different solution than if the style is defined as *complex* and *irregular*. Figure 14-12 illustrates alternative solutions in three different styles all defined with the constraints of Significant Difference of Size and Location. The only difference between the styles is the articulation of the visual techniques ranging from simple and regular (Style 1, Figure 14-12a) to complex and irregular (Style 3, Figure 14-12c). With the same initial design, each style creates different solutions. These solutions satisfy the constraints but are based on varying procedures of generation from the defined visual techniques. In Style 1, the system looks for the simplest most regular solution possible. This results with all dials in each solution being the same size and aligned on an axis (similar location). Style 3, on the other hand, has chosen the opposite approach where no two dials in the final solution are the same size and no alignment occurs. Style 2 (Figure 14-12b) takes a more moderate approach with two distinct (and significantly different) dial sizes and some alignment.

These alternatives are maintained by a new form of truth maintenance system, an ATMS [10-deKleer86c]. With the ATMS multiple alternatives are maintained and can be explored simultaneously. Unlike previous truth maintenance systems which just manipulated justifications, this system additionally manipulates assumption sets. As a result, inconsistent information can exist and it is possible to work effectively and efficiently in the problem space. Context switching is free, and most backtracking and all retraction is avoided. In Designer, the assumptions that are manipulated are the alternatives created by incremental design decisions. Solutions at any stage in the design process are the consistent, noncontradictory environments maintained by the ATMS. Any contradictions that arise are handled by the ATMS and will not appear in the same environment.

This new form of truth maintenance system is well suited for tracking multiple alternatives in the design space where a reasonable number of the potential solutions must be examined. Designer interacts with this system by creating an ATMS class for each domain element. Whenever an element is modified, a new ATMS node is added to this class. These classes represent the different alternatives of the original domain element. Multiple nodes coexist in the solution space but only one will be present in any ATMS solution. The justifications of what style is current and what constraint generates the modified element are added to these nodes to restrict the space of valid solutions.

Because context switching is free, the user can explore the design space by interactively inspecting the individual ATMS environments. Each solution can be displayed on the color screen and explain itself in terms of the underlying assumptions and justifications. Based on these assumptions and justifications, an alternative can describe its derivation and individual decisions can be described

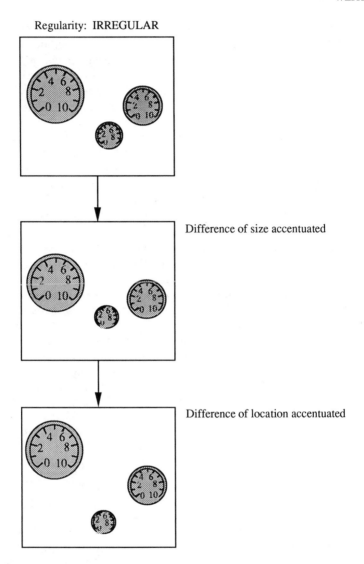

Regularity: IRREGULAR

Difference of size accentuated

Difference of location accentuated

Figure 14-12: Different Styles Generating Different Alternatives (a)

Given the same view as input, three different styles generate three completely different solutions. All three styles include the principles of Significant Difference of Size and of Location. They differ only in the articulation of the visual techniques defined, from simple and regular (a) to complex and irregular (c). The first level of design decisions is in response to element size while the second level is based on location considerations. These alternatives represent only a small portion of the solution space.

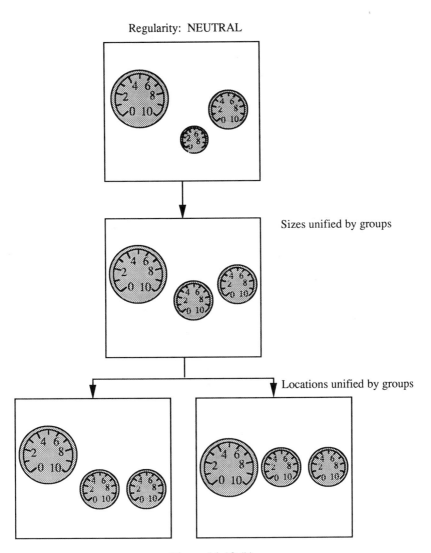

Regularity: NEUTRAL

Sizes unified by groups

Locations unified by groups

Figure 14-12 (b)

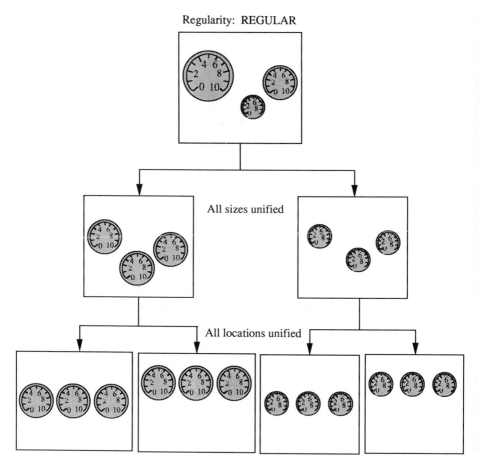

Figure 14-12 (c)

in terms of their potential contribution to a final solution. The system thus conveys design precepts while the user is viewing a specific instantiation of a design alternative. Hopefully this technique will enhance the user's knowledge of constructing visual presentations for future designs.

14.5. RELATED WORK

There exists a number of interesting research projects similar in nature to Designer. They are all knowledge-based systems providing an environment to aid the creation and verification of design alternatives. Some provide exploratory environments in well-defined domains (e.g., Palladio, for circuit design [6]) while others, like Designer, are systems in the ill-defined domain of graphic design (e.g., ACE: A Color Expert, an expert system for the selection of colors for synthetic scene imagery [22]; Descriptor, a generative system for graphic layout based on shape grammars [14]). Some of these systems, like Designer, try to encode the general process of design and then apply it to a prototypical domain (e.g., PRIDE, for the design of paper handling systems (Chapter 9).

Designer is much less rigid in its definition of the design process and future work may incorporate a more explicit representation of this process. An alternative approach would be to incorporate specific *plans* that would specify the order in which design steps are to be invoked by the various graphic techniques. This would be similar to the work done by Brown and Chandrasekaran (Chapter 7) in mechanical design. Redesign and design modification could work through the hierarchy of design decisions to find alternate solutions.

Designer differs from some systems in that it is a *reactive* system. It responds to the user's actions by analyzing and critiquing input. Then, incremental improvements are suggested interactively to the user. Some systems use a *top-down refinement* approach (e.g., Chapters 7 and 9) creating new designs based on high-level design goals or specifications. Designer's approach is less structured but it may support a more user directed exploratory process of design.

14.6. CONCLUSION

An initial implementation of Designer is underway. A functioning system has been used on existing Steamer diagrams and has provided useful feedback. The critique comments generated, based on only a handful of design constraints, were the result of poor size specification. It is very encouraging that even in views that were carefully crafted, the system was able to note inconsistencies and suggest improvements.

The perception of a problem and the shape of its solution are both affected by the depth and range of the design vocabulary [9]. It is therefore important that the domain knowledge base continue to grow. Only a few constraints currently exist and as more principles and standards are defined, more complete and robust alternatives will be presented. As more solutions become available, the need for better techniques to explore and understand their differences will be necessary.

It is not known how effective this approach will be representing more complex design problems. How will the system react to include larger sets of constraints, larger number of visual techniques, and a wider variety of alternatives? Even though preliminary use of the ATMS has shown its feasibility for representing multiple design solutions, how will the ATMS scale as the designs become more varied and the number of critique comments needing to be tracked greatly increases? In addition, the generality of this approach and how easily it will transfer to other domains has yet to be tested. These remain open questions.

14.7. ACKNOWLEDGMENTS

Earlier versions of this paper appeared in July 1986 as Technical report 8609 from the UCSD Institute for Cognitive Science, and in January 1988 as Technical Report ACA-HI-017-88 from MCC.

This project began as an Independent Exploratory Development Program (IED) with the Navy Personnel Research and Development Center in San Diego. Additional funding for this research was provided by the Personnel and Training Research Program of the Office of Naval Research (Contract N00014-85-C-0133, NR 667-541) and the Office of Naval Technology (522-801-018). I would like to thank all those involved with the UCSD/NPRDC joint program for making this research possible and those at MCC supporting its continuation. In particular I would like to thank members of both groups for their support *critiquing* early versions of this paper, including Jim Hollan, Mark Rosenstein, Dave Owen, Larry West, Barbara Morris, and Kathy Farrelly.

14.8. UPDATE

This chapter represents work on *Designer* that was originally done in 1985. Since then, work has continued on related tools at MCC. The *Icon Editor*, mentioned in the introduction, was redesigned and released to our shareholders in 1988 [28]. The research goals of the Icon Editor were to discover techniques for the graphical specification of behavior without coding and to develop a foundation for the connection of an application to an interface. It is part of an integrated set of knowledge-based tools for the construction of collaborative multimedia interfaces, the *Human Interface Tool Suite* [18]. The Graphics Editor and Icon Editor continue to support designers in the HITS environment. As tools of this nature become more powerful, it becomes more imperative to support designers with online design assistance. Hopefully, I will be able to return to the many open research questions in supporting interface designers to create graphically pleasing and effective solutions.

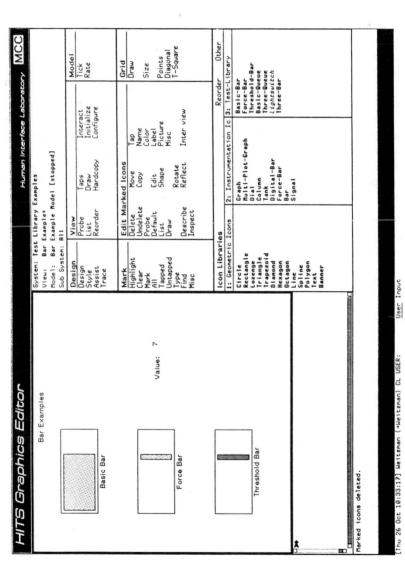

Figure 14-13: Graphics Editor Interface

This is an update of the interface of the Graphics Editor   for monitoring and controlling underlying or real-time
which allows non-programmers to create graphic interfaces   processes.

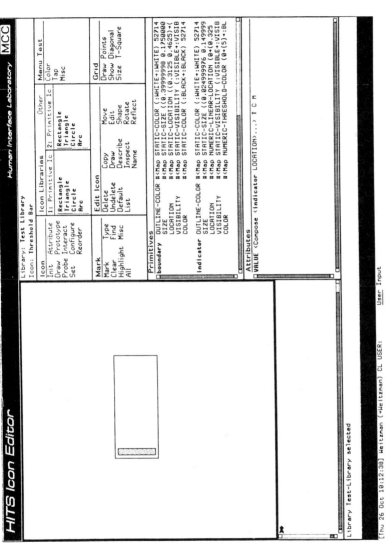

Figure 14-14: Icon Editor Interface

The Icon Editor is a tool allowing interface designers to create new dynamic icons to be used in the Graphics Editor. Users specify the icon's dynamic behavior interactively without coding.

14.9. BIBLIOGRAPHY

Additional sources not referenced in the paper are: [2], [4], [5], [15], [21], [20], [24], [26], [27], [29], [31], [32].

[1] Alexander, C., *Notes on Synthesis of Form,* Harvard University Press, Cambridge, Massachusetts, 1974.

[2] Beach, R. and Stone, M., "Graphical style towards high quality illustrations," *Computer Graphics,* Vol. 17, No. 3, pp. 127-135, August 1983.

[3] Bertin, J., *Seismology of Graphics,* University of Wisconsin Press, Madison, Wisconsin, 1983.

[4] Borning, A., "Defining constraints graphically," *In CHI'86 Proceedings,* Mantei, M. and Orbeton, P., Eds., Boston, April 13-17, pp. 137-143, 1986.

[5] Brown, D. C., *Expert Systems for Design Problem-Solving using Design Refinement with Plan Selection and Redesign,* unpublished Ph.D. Dissertation, CIS Dept., OSU, Columbus, OH 43210, 1984, [Also Published as a Book Co-authored with B. Chandrasekaran].

[6] Brown, H., Tong, C. and Foyster, G., "Palladio: An Exploratiry Environment for Circuit Design," *IEEE Computer,* Vol. 19, No. 7, pp. 92-100, December 1983.

[7] Brown, D. and Chandrasekaran, B., "Knowledge and control for a mechanical design expert system," *IEEE Computer,* July 1986.

[8] Cheatham, F. R., Cheatham, J. H. and Haler, S. A., *Design Concepts and Applications,* Prentice-Hall, Inc., Englewood Cliffs, New Jersey, 1983.

[9] Ching, F. D. K., *Architecture: Form Space & Order,* Van Nostrand Reinhold Company, New York, New York, 1979.

[10] de Kleer, J., "An assumption-based TMS," *Artificial Intelligence,* Vol. 28, No. 2, pp. 127-162, March 1986.

[11] de Kleer, J., "Extending the ATMS," *Artificial Intelligence,* Vol. 28, No. 2, pp. 163-196, March 1986.

[12] de Kleer, J., "Problem solving with the ATMS," *Artificial Intelligence,* Vol. 28, No. 2, pp. 197-224, March 1986.

[13] Dondis, D. A., *A Primer of Visual Literacy,* MIT Press, Cambridge, Massachusetts, 1973.

[14]   Glenn, B., *Descriptor: A model for describing shapes that infers relations for positioning them*, unpublished Ph.D. Dissertation, University of California, Los Angeles, 1986.

[15]   Gullichsen, E. and Chang, E., "Generative design in architecture using an expert system," *Graphics Interface '85 Proceedings*, Canadian Information Processing Society, 1985.

[16]   Hollan, J., Hutchins, E. and Weitzman, L., "Steamer: An interactive inspectable simulation-based training system," *AI Magazine*, Vol. 5, No. 2, pp. 15-28, 1984, [Also appeared in *Artificial Intelligence and Instruction: Application and Methods*, Greg Kearsley (Ed.)].

[17]   Hollan, J., Hutchins, E., McCandless, T., Rosenstein, M. and Weitzman, L., "Graphical interfaces for simulations," in *Advances in Man-Machine Systems Research*, Rouse, W., Ed., Jai Press, Greenwich, Connecticut, 1988.

[18]   Hollan, J. et al, *An Introduction to HITS: Human Interface Tool Suite*, Technical Report ACA-HI-406-88, Microelectronics and Computer Technology Corporation, December 1988.

[19]   Hurlburt, A., *Layout, The Design of the Printed Page*, Watson-Guptill Publications, New York, New York, 1977.

[20]   MacKinlay, J., *Automatic design of graphical presentations*, unpublished Ph.D. Dissertation, Stanford University, Stanford, California, 1986.

[21]   Marcus, A., "Graphic design of user interfaces," *NCGA 1986 Proceedings, Vol. 1, Tutorials*, 1986.

[22]   Meier, B., "ACE: A Color Expert," *NCGA 1986 Proceedings*, 1986.

[23]   Mittal, S., Dym, C. and Morjaria, M., "PRIDE: An expert system for the design of paper handling systems," *IEEE Computer*, Vol. 19, No. 7, pp. 102-114, July 1986.

[24]   Nelson, G. Juno, "A constraint-based graphics system," *Computer Graphics*, Vol. 19, No. 3, pp. 235-243, 1985.

[25]   Pavlidis, T. and Van Wyk, C. J., "An automatic beautifier for drawings and illustrations," *Computer Graphics*, Vol. 19, No. 3, pp. 225-234, 1985.

[26]   Reilly, S. S. and Roach, J. W., "Improved visual design for graphics display," *IEEE CG&A*, February 1984.

[27]   Roach, J., Pittman, S. S. and Savarse, J., "A visual design consultant," *International Conference on Cybernetics and Society*, Seattle, Washington, October 1982.

[28]   Rosenstein, M., Weitzman, L., *The HITS Icon Editor*, Technical Report ACT-HI-135-89, Microelectronics and Computer Technology Corporation, June 1989, [Reprinted in Proceedings of the 23rd Hawaii International Conference on System Sciences, January 2-5, 1990.].

[29]   Scholl, L., "Heuristic rules for visualization," *Graphics Interface '85 Proceedings*, 1985.

[30]   Sherwood, R., *Principles and Elements of Architecture*, University of Southern California Press, Los Angeles, California, 1981.

[31]   Stiny, G. and Gips, J., *Algorithmic Aesthetics, Computer Models for Criticism and Design in the Arts*, University of California Press, Los Angeles, California, 1978.

[32]   Taylor, I. A., "Perception and visual communication," *In Research Principles and Practices in Visual Communication*, Ball, J. and Pyres, F., Eds., Association for Education, Communication, and Technology, 1960.

[33]   Wong, W., *Principles of Two-Dimensional Design*, Van Nostrand Reinhold Co., New York, New York, 1972.

Index